ONIES in AMERICA;
WARE, PENSILVANIA,
ICUT, and RHODE ISLAND:
of the Confederate Indians;
and CHAMPLAIN,
FRANCE:
Explanation;
LAKE ONTARIO
Oswego
CAYUGAES
ONONDAGAES
SENECAS
Endless Mountains
NEW HAMPSHIRE
BOSTON
THE ATLANTIC OCEAN
DELAWARE BAY
Cape May
Albany
Will's Creek
Published according to Act of Parliament by Lewis Evans June 23 1755 and sold by R Dodsley in Pall Mall LONDON & by the Author in PHILADELPHIA
Longitude West of London

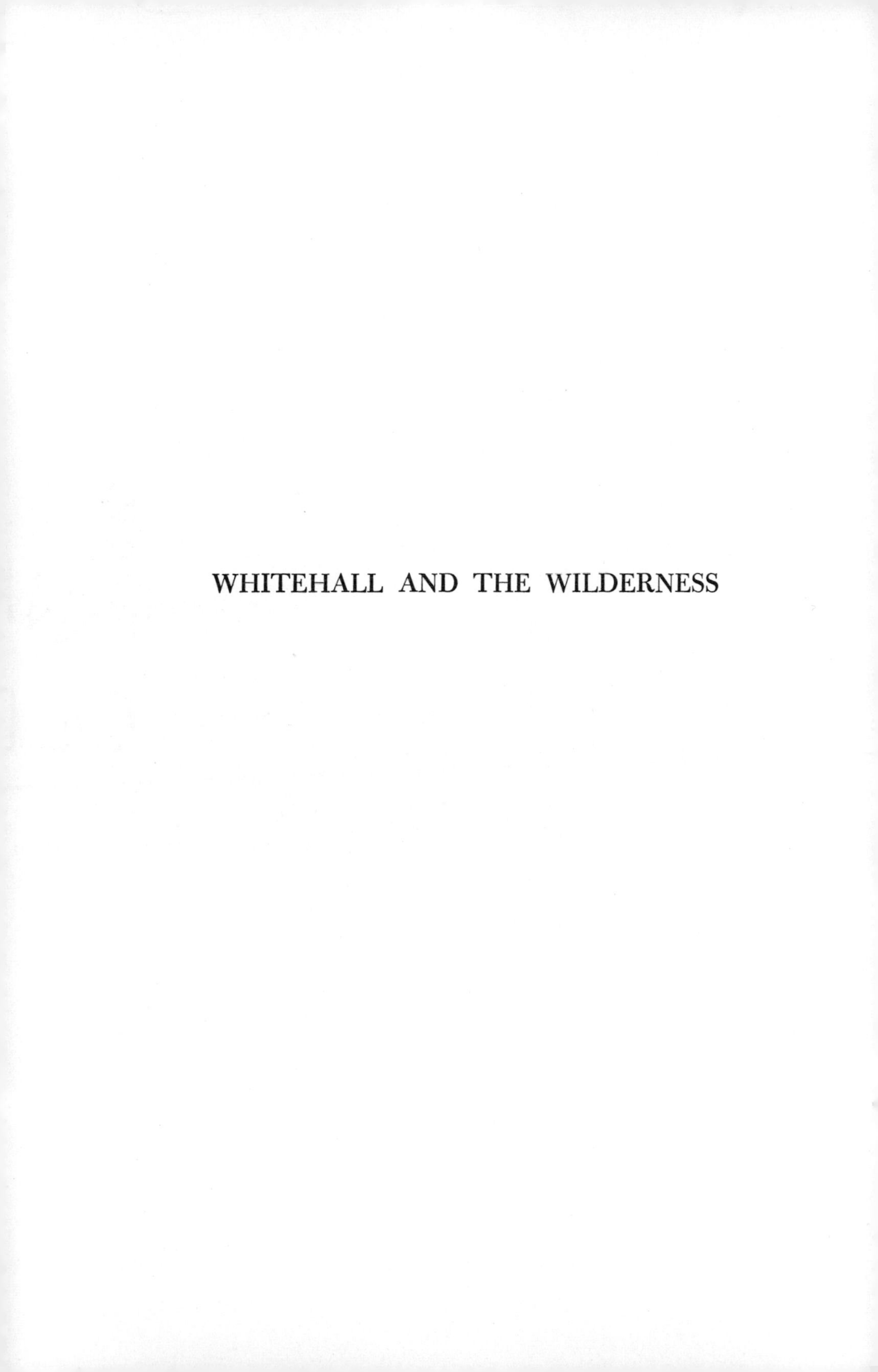

WHITEHALL AND THE WILDERNESS

JACK M. SOSIN

Whitehall and the Wilderness

The Middle West in British Colonial Policy, 1760-1775

UNIVERSITY OF NEBRASKA PRESS
LINCOLN 1961

The publication of this book
was assisted by a grant by the Ford Foundation.

Library of Congress catalog card number 61-10152.

MANUFACTURED IN THE UNITED STATES OF AMERICA.

FOR MY PARENTS

Preface

MORE than forty years ago Clarence W. Alvord in his *Mississippi Valley in British Politics* presented a systematic, original synthesis which brought together such hitherto diverse fields as eighteenth-century British politics and the American frontier. In many respects, Alvord's contribution was unique. One of the first to realize the factional basis of eighteenth-century British politics, Alvord offered a meaningful analysis of the relationship of these political groups to certain colonial questions. Specifically, he suggested that whenever British ministers deliberated the colonial problem, their primary concern was not with the revolutionary centers of the East, but rather with the evolution of policy for the interior acquired by the Peace of Paris of 1763. This was the first and last problem, and the decision to tax the colonists which frequently obscured this major issue was only a subsidiary phase of a broader program. Further, Alvord related the attitudes of English politicians to what he assumed to be their position on the Peace of Paris. Apparently he was led into this view by accepting the famous "Canada-Guadeloupe" pamphlet controversy as a real debate in which the pamphleteers represented specific political groups. The political faction which negotiated the treaty, in order to justify retaining Canada rather than Guadeloupe, was committed to a program of western expansion. Hence its opponents, the Whigs, were then forced to oppose development of the interior. "Thus it may be said with approximate truth," Alvord wrote, "that all future issues concerning the Mississippi Valley"—and hence, the American colonies—"were formed and the trend of partisan opinion determined during the critical period of peace negotiations." Finally Professor Alvord maintained that historians could only understand the successive plans of the English ministries for the newly acquired territories in so far as they approached these programs with an understanding of the political situation of 1763, and of the plan developed that spring and summer by the Earl of Shelburne, then President of the Board of Trade.[1]

Scholars subsequently have accepted the validity of these propositions and have accorded Professor Alvord a leading place on the rolls of imperial historians. The list of those who have generally adhered to or followed his early lead is long, and in some cases, distinguished.[2] Invariably he has been cited in general

1. Clarence W. Alvord, *The Mississippi Valley in British Politics: A Study of Trade, Land Speculation, and Experiments in Imperialism Culminating in the American Revolution* (2 vols., Cleveland, Ohio, 1917), I, 13–16, 45–46, 74, 157, 237; II, 254.

2. Among the more representative of these are Duncan McArthur, "The British Board of Trade and Canada, 1760–1774; I, The Proclamation of 1773 [*sic*]," Canadian Historical Association, *Annual Report for 1932* (Toronto, 1932), 97–113; Charles H. Metzger, "An Appraisal of Shelburne's Western Policy," *Mid-America,* IX (1937), 169–181; Robert W. Riddle, *Michigan under British Rule: Law and Law Courts, 1760–1796* (Lansing, Mich., 1926); Nelson V. Russell, *The British Regime in Michigan and the Old Northwest 1760–1796* (Northfield, Minn., 1939); Charles R. Ritcheson, *British Politics and the American Revolution* (Norman, Okla., 1954); Thomas P. Abernethy, *Western Lands and the American Revolution* (New York, 1937); and Louise P. Kellogg, *The British Regime in Wisconsin and the Northwest* (Madison, Wisc., 1935). Some question might be raised by including Ritcheson in this group but the present writer feels that his work shows little originality in the field of policy for the interior and that in the main he relied heavily on Alvord. Abernethy disagrees with Alvord on some points, but for the most part accepts the latter's dicta on British policy and politics.

texts as the authority in the field. The impact of Professor Alvord's writings [3] has been so great that very little has subsequently appeared to challenge his precepts or conclusions. The only significant exceptions are the limited articles which appeared more than twenty years ago by Robin A. Humphreys [4] and the brief treatment of the problem of the North American interior by Vincent T. Harlow in his study of the origins of the second British Empire.[5] These writings questioned one aspect of Alvord's work and revealed some inadequacies in his research and analysis which had hitherto escaped criticism.

On the basis of material not available to Alvord, and on a reevaluation of the data he did use, it is possible to suggest certain

3. In addition to his major work, Alvord's publications on this topic include "Party Politics and the British Empire," *Nineteenth Century,* XCVII (1925), 326–333; "Genesis of the Proclamation of 1763," *Michigan Pioneer and Historical Collections,* XXXVI (1908), 20–52; "Lord Shelburne and the Founding of British American Goodwill," *Proceedings of the British Academy,* XI (1924–1925), 369–396; *The Illinois Country, 1673–1818* (Springfield, Ill., 1920); and "The British Ministry and the Treaty of Fort Stanwix," Wisconsin State Historical Society, *Proceedings,* LVI (1909), 163–183. See also his introduction of the three volumes edited in collaboration with Clarence E. Carter, *The Critical Period, 1763–1765* (Springfield, Ill., 1905); *The New Regime, 1765–1767* (Springfield, Ill., 1916); and *Trade and Politics, 1767–1769* (Springfield, Ill., 1921), volumes X, XI, and XVI in *Illinois Historical Collections.*

4. Robin A. Humphreys, "Lord Shelburne and a Projected Recall of Colonial Governors in 1767," *American Historical Review,* XXXVII (1932), 269–273; "Lord Northington and the Laws of Canada," *Canadian Historical Review,* XIV (1933), 42–61; "Lord Shelburne and the Proclamation of 1763," *English Historical Review,* XLIX (1934), 241–264; and "Lord Shelburne and British Colonial Policy, 1766–1768," *ibid.,* L (1935), 257–277.

5. Vincent T. Harlow, *The Founding of the Second British Empire, 1763–1793* (London and New York, 1952). A. L. Burt's *The Old Province of Quebec* (Minneapolis, 1933) is a corrective to Alvord in part, but it is not specifically or primarily devoted to the policy bearing on the interior. Lawrence H. Gipson's *The Triumphant Empire: New Responsibilities within the Enlarged Empire, 1763–1766* (New York, 1956) touches briefly on the problem of the West and is evidently intended as the foundation for his later volumes. Carl B. Cone, reviewing this work in the *Journal of Southern History,* XXIII (1957), 112, has pointed out, however, that in his treatment of the Proclamation of 1763, Gipson delved no deeper than the views presented by Burt, Harlow, or Humphreys. None of these writers has shown that the Proclamation was the result of wartime experience and that it merely gave formal sanction to an already existing, *ad hoc* arrangement.

alternative views to those presented by Alvord. Not the least of these is one which may be useful in evaluating British measures for the colonies in general. That is, that British ministers were primarily administrators who arrived at particular solutions for specific problems as they arose, although they may have phrased their decisions in the terminology of mercantilist doctrine.

Historians have given the interior country and its relation to British colonial policy less than satisfactory treatment, so much so that one writer in recently discussing the literature of the subject has attempted to explain this deficiency in terms of the complexity of the topic. Phenomena based on particular occurrences, he points out, have made it easy for historians to mistake accident for principle.[6] This study is an attempt to describe the frames of reference governing the development of British policy. In view of the excellent study by Professor John Alden on the southern frontier [7]—a work which leaves little to be desired for an understanding of the problems faced in this area—this book will deal mainly with the Middle West. Nevertheless it should be noted that British policy was in general determined for the interior as a whole.

The author is grateful for the aid and encouragement of Professor John D. Barnhart of Indiana University, under whose direction this study was originally made. Professor Lawrence H. Gipson, Research Professor of History, Emeritus, Lehigh University, and Professor Ray A. Billington, Northwestern University, read the original manuscript and contributed valuable suggestions. I should also like to express my appreciation to the personnel of various libraries and repositories who have aided my research: the staffs of the Public Record Office and British Museum in London, the Illinois Historical Survey, the Library of Congress, the William L. Clements Library, the Henry E. Huntington Library, and the Historical Society of Pennsylvania. I am indebted also to the Earl of Dartmouth and Sir John Murray for

6. H. Hale Bellot, *American History and American Historians: A Review of Recent Contributions to the Interpretation of the United States* (Norman, Okla., 1952), 48–49.

7. John R. Alden, *John Stuart and the Southern Colonial Frontier. A Study of Indian Relations, War, Trade, and Land Problems in the Southern Wilderness, 1754–1775* (Ann Arbor, 1944).

permission to quote from the Dartmouth papers and the Grenville papers. My thanks also go to the Graduate School of Indiana University and the Research Council of the University of Nebraska for financial assistance to complete this study. The appendix to this volume originally appeared in a modified version in the *Pennsylvania Magazine of History and Biography*.

permission to quote from the Dartmouth papers and the Green-
ville papers. My thanks also go to the Graduate School of Indiana
University and the Research Council of the [illegible] of Nebraska for financial assistance, [illegible]
[illegible]
to the [illegible]

Contents

List of Maps

Times of tranquility are the most proper seasons for reviewing the state of the empire, improving its advantages, mending its defects, and preventing future evils . . . .

William Knox

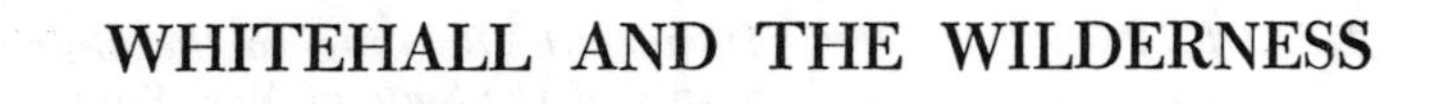

WHITEHALL AND THE WILDERNESS

KEY TO ABBREVIATIONS

AAE, Corr. Pol., Angl.	Archives des Affaires Étrangères, Correspondance Politique, Angleterre.
AAE, Mem. et Doc., Angl.	Archives des Affaires Étrangères, Mémoires et Documents, Angleterre.
Add. MSS	Additional Manuscripts, British Museum.
APSL	American Philosophical Society Library.
CHS	Connecticut Historical Society.
DRCHC	*Documents Relative to the Constitutional History of Canada.*
DRCHSNY	*Documents Relating to the Colonial History of the State of New York.*
HEHL	Henry E. Huntington Library.
HMC	Royal Historical Manuscripts Commission.
HSP	Historical Society of Pennsylvania.
IHS	Illinois Historical Survey.
LC	Library of Congress.
PAC	Public Archives of Canada.
PMHB	*Pennsylvania Magazine of History and Biography.*
P.R.O.; C.O.; W.O.; T.	Public Record Office; Colonial Office; War Office; Treasury.
SP, France; Spain	Public Record Office, State Papers, France; Spain.
WHS	Wisconsin Historical Society.
WLCL	William L. Clements Library.

CHAPTER I

Politics, Diplomacy, and the North American Interior

> There is a large Field before you, an opening in the back Country for Adventurers, where . . . an enterprising Man . . . may lay the foundation of a Noble Estate . . . .
>
> George Washington

LAND speculation and the idea of western settlement figured prominently in the plans of many an eighteenth-century American. The fertile soil of the upper Ohio Valley in particular attracted colonists, but France and her Indian allies controlled the area and contested British expansion across the Alleghenies. From the ensuing Anglo-French boundary dispute there developed the Seven Years' War.

At the onset the conflicts over the Ohio were defensive in nature, and although the international rivalries of England, France, and Spain may in some cases have resulted in the acquisition of extensive overseas territory, the original aim of these wars was limited. The British government's immediate concern was to protect the established seaboard colonies by eliminating

French power from the environs of the settled provinces. But competition for control of the wooded slopes of the upper Ohio Valley precipitated a war which extended to India, Africa, and Europe. Early military reverses conditioned British opinion to demand compensation for the heavy drain in men and treasure, and the original objectives were no longer sufficient. The fluid political situation in England, particularly during the unstable sequence of administrations following George III's accession in 1760, also was a decisive factor in arriving at terms for a peace.

While prosecuting the colonial war against the Bourbon powers, the successive British ministries derived certain lessons from the inadequacies of the defense system in North America. Because the conflict had been conducted primarily for the security of the provinces, they concluded that to insure the stability of the wilderness they would need to win the confidence of the Indian tribes; as a consequence, England emerged from the struggle with certain pledges to the natives. These commitments, more than any other factor, set the stage for the immediate policy of temporarily restricting the white population to the area east of the mountains, formulating an imperial system of Indian affairs, and preserving the security of the hinterland with royal garrisons.

This program—on whose points there appeared to be little division in ministerial circles—was to have a direct relation to the development of the American Revolution. The implementation of the policy by means of an American revenue such as the stamp tax was the first and perhaps the most decisive dividing force both in the colonies and in the mother country. The Stamp Act created an American issue in British politics and inaugurated the overt challenge to British authority which led to the independence of the colonies. The question of revenue intended for the support of the North American garrisons continued to affect policy for the interior country. With the repeal of the Stamp Act, all future British policy was concerned on the one hand with the cost of maintaining the garrisons in the wilderness and on the other with controlling the turbulent eastern colonies. As the revolutionary process developed, the need to keep the established provinces under the mother country overshadowed the original aim of garrisoning the West. When the alternative of diverse colonial control also proved inadequate, jurisdiction over the Old Northwest was given to the former French province of Quebec.

II

When the British ministers, responding to appeals from the legislatures of Massachusetts and Virginia, decided to defend the North American colonies, they pointed to French encroachments on the Ohio and elsewhere as their justification. These infringements would "endanger all the Northern colonies, and tend to the total Destruction thereof and their Trade." In explaining the ministerial resolution, the Duke of Newcastle wrote that the principal consideration on which he and his colleagues had acted was that "the Colonies must not be abandon'd." [1] This was a constant motive throughout the war. In December, 1756, the ministers informed Parliament through the King that the "succur and preservation of America" could not but constitute a primary object of the legislature's attention.[2] In 1756 with a French invasion feared and the home islands short of troops, Henry Fox, Secretary of State, wrote that England would have to do for herself since "America must not be given up, to avoid danger incurr'd only on Account of America." [3] Under the leadership of William Pitt the tide of the war turned in England's favor by 1758. One of the earliest victories was the capture of Louisbourg, a French fortress on Cape Breton Island. George II himself insisted that "we must keep Cape Breton, take Canada, drive the French out of America . . . ." The King seemed to view the French West Indian islands captured in the future merely as

1. See the memorandum of the cabinet meeting, June 26, 1754, in the Newcastle papers, Add. MSS 33029, f. 124; Newcastle to Horatio Walpole, June 29, 1754, Add. MSS 32735, f. 597.

2. William Cobbett, *The Parliamentary History of England from the Earliest Period to the Year 1803* (36 vols., London, 1812), XV, 772.

3. Fox to Devonshire, Jan. 31, 1756, Giles Stephen Holland Fox Strangways, Sixth Earl of Ilchester, *Henry Fox First Lord Holland, His Family and Relations* (2 vols., New York, 1920), I, 305.

equivalents in bargaining for losses in Europe: "We must conquer Martinique as a Set-off to Minorca." [4]

Any concrete war aims held by the various British ministers during the earlier years of the war were contingent on the extent of British military and naval successes. Until the fall of New France the primary object lay in securing a satisfactory frontier in North America which would provide for the security of the colonies. The entire cession of Canada was not a *sine qua non* at this point. Even after the capture of Quebec in 1759, Pitt, the Secretary of State for the Southern Department, felt that a line extending British possessions from Crown Point, Niagara, and the Great Lakes was necessary for any peace settlement. "These are essential to the security of our Colonies," he is reported to have said. Advocating the retention of the British conquests in Africa and Bengal, he seemed "indifferent" about the French sugar island of Guadeloupe. As to the rest of Canada, "Quebec, Montreal and even Louisbourg, they were to be treated upon," matters for negotiation, but not to be relinquished without compensation.[5]

The Duke of Newcastle, First Lord of the Treasury, was also thinking of the West Indian islands merely as bargaining points. He wrote the Earl of Hardwicke that Guadeloupe is "always a good thing to have on hand." The aims of Lord Chancellor Hardwicke were also limited.[6] But both men had influential advisors who contributed more specific, positive goals in prosecuting the war. James Douglas, Earl of Morton, argued that the

4. Quoted in Basil Williams, *William Pitt, Earl of Chatham* (2 vols., London, 1913), I, 379–380.

5. Thomas Hay, Earl of Kinnoull, to Newcastle, Oct. 30, 1759, Add. MSS 32897, f. 500. Kinnoull had access to a confidential memorandum for this statement. It was reported by the Spanish ambassador in London to his court, and then to Versailles, that Pitt proposed to return Quebec and Guadeloupe, but would demand a considerable part of the St. Lawrence River, and that France demolish all the forts on the Ohio built since the Peace of Utrecht. Marquis d'Ossun to the Duc de Choiseul, Feb. 22, 1760, Archives des Affairés Étrangères, Correspondance Politique, Espagne, 527: 273.

6. Newcastle to the Earl of Hardwicke, Oct. 31, 1759, Add. MSS 32897, f. 512. Newcastle to Hardwicke, June 14, 1759, Add. MSS 32892, f. 59; Hardwicke to Newcastle, Oct. 16, 1759, Add. MSS 32897, f. 135; Hardwicke to Pitt, Oct. 18, 1759, Add. MSS 35423, f. 192.

British holdings in North America should be expanded so that the French "should not have it in their Power to disturb our Settlements." Morton pressed for a revised Anglo-French boundary in North America which would leave Cape Breton, the Ottawa River, Lake Huron, Michillimackinac, Lake Michigan, the Illinois, and the Mississippi rivers to the Yazoo in British hands. The British should particularly retain the key French fortifications in the interior. The influential London alderman Sir William Baker presented similar views. While Guadeloupe might be more beneficial "in point of Trade," Canada would "serve for the Preservation of the Peace." The same theme appears in the recommendations of the experienced diplomat the Earl of Chesterfield. "We should keep Quebec and Canada as preventatives of a future war," he counseled. As for other conquests or objectives, the ministers might "scramble and negotiate" as best they could.[7]

This was the dominant view of the principal politicians and their advisors before the conquest of Canada as to the aims of the war in the western hemisphere. They sought to obtain a boundary between the French and British possessions which would eliminate the threat of the French to the English colonies.

Following the capitulation of New France with the capture of Montreal in the fall of 1760, Newcastle and Pitt conferred on possible peace terms to be offered France. The victory made possible increased British demands. The Secretary of State was willing to restore Guadeloupe and Goree in Africa, but would exclude the French from the Newfoundland fisheries. The alternatives presented by Pitt lay in demanding all Canada and Cape Breton, or merely a part of the French colony so as to bring the British possessions in America to the line of the Great Lakes. But Newcastle noted that opinions differed on the question of peace terms. While some would return Guadeloupe to France and

7. Copies of Morton's papers are in Add. MSS 32901, ff. 290–301, and Add. MSS 35910, ff. 19–23, LC transcript. Newcastle's memorandum for the King, containing Baker's arguments, dated October 14, 1760, Add. MSS 32913, f. 128. On Baker's part see Richard Pares, *War and Trade in the West Indies, 1739–1763* (Oxford, 1936), 225; and Chesterfield to Newcastle, Nov. 30, 1760, Bonomy Dobrée (ed.), *Letters of William Stanhope, Earl of Chesterfield* (6 vols., London, 1932), V, 2371.

retain all of Canada "as our Northern Colonies would never be quiet without it," others considered the West Indian sugar island "in reality, more advantageous . . . ." At this point Pitt did not attempt to impose his opinions. Indeed, he seems to have been undecided throughout the winter of 1760–1761. But by March, 1761, he had concluded that the reduction of all of Canada was of the *"utmost importance* to the Security of our *Colonies."* While Pitt recognized that the exigencies of war might force the British to give up all or part of Canada, he suggested further military operations against Martinique and the French coastal island of Belleisle so that Canada, Cape Breton, and the exclusive right to the Newfoundland fishery could be secured.[8]

Before the spring of 1761 there is little to show that the dominant ministers in the British cabinet held any fixed views on the peace or a choice of conquests. The one major exception was the restriction of the limits of Canada to alleviate the Bourbon threat to the British colonies in North America by guaranteeing English possession of the interior. As to a choice of conquests between North America and Guadeloupe, opinion tended to favor the retention of Canada for security reasons. In spite of the evidence available, historians have written extensively on the supposed Canada-Guadeloupe controversy. Scholars have emphasized this polemic and have cited the dubious Horace Walpole, who credited Pitt with having declared in the House of Commons late in 1760: "Some are for keeping Canada, some Guadeloupe; who will tell me which I shall be hanged for not keeping?" [9] The evidence that Pitt made this statement is slight, and even if he did, such rhetoric did not accurately reflect the sentiments he expressed to his colleagues in the cabinet. Pitt at that time was willing to return Guadeloupe, but he was undecided whether to accept all of Canada or merely part of the province—the area south of the Great Lakes. Shortly thereafter he planned an enlarged military campaign to insure the retention of the

8. Newcastle to Hardwicke, Dec. 3, 1760, Add. MSS 32915, ff. 270–271; Hardwicke to Newcastle, March 17, 1761, Add. MSS 32920, f. 271; Newcastle to Hardwicke, April 17, 1761, Add. MSS 32923, f. 19.

9. Horace Walpole, *Memoirs of the Reign of King George the Third,* G. F. R. Barker (ed.) (4 vols., London, 1894), I, 26.

entire colony. When peace negotiations commenced, the Secretary of State made up his mind. France must give up Canada.

The supposed controversy as between the merits of Canada and Guadeloupe resulted in a flood of pamphlets debating the relative value of the two conquests. Between 1759 and 1763 at least sixty-five different publications appeared on the subject.[10] Significantly, these tracts continued to come from the presses long after the ministers had made their decision in 1761, and it is important to bear in mind that the ministers, not the pamphleteers, made the choice. In reality, the pamphlet war had little or no influence on the decision of the responsible politicians. There is little to show that in 1760 any of the ministers held settled views on the choice between Canada and Guadeloupe, or that they tried to force any such opinion on their followers whether or not they might be pamphleteers. Long before the pamphlet controversy ceased, the ministers made their decision, and opinion as to their choice did not become an issue between Parliamentary factions.[11] In the final analysis there was

10. Vincent T. Harlow, *The Founding of the Second British Empire* (London, 1952), 162 n. 27. For a listing and textual description of the various publications see Alvord, *Mississippi Valley,* I, 55–56, II, 253–264; William L. Grant, "Canada *versus* Guadeloupe," *American Historical Review,* XVII (1912), 735–743; C. E. Fryer, "Further Pamphlets for the Canada-Guadeloupe Controversy," *Mississippi Valley Historical Review,* V (1917), 227–230; and Fred J. Ericson, "British Motives for Expansion in 1763; Territory, Commerce, or Security," *Papers* of the Michigan Academy of Science, Arts, and Letters, XXVII (1941), 581–594. Richard Pares, *War and Trade in the West Indies,* 223; Theodore C. Pease (ed.), *Anglo-French Boundary Disputes in the West, 1749–1763,* vol. XXVII in Illinois Historical Collections (Springfield, Ill., 1936), lxxxi n3; and Gerald S. Graham, *Sea Power and British North America, 1783–1820: A Study in British Colonial Policy* (Cambridge and London, 1941), 23 all tend to discount, or question, the significance of the pamphlets.

11. L. B. Namier, *England in the Age of the American Revolution* (London, 1930), 317–318. Professor Alvord attempted to link the question with Parliamentary groups (*Mississippi Valley,* I, 35–37, 74, 237, 246, II, 254) and further assumed a connection between the factions and the pamphleteers. He often stressed the connection between William Burke, who wrote several pro-Guadeloupe pamphlets, and the Whigs, and assumed that Burke's sentiments reflected the attitude of this Parliamentary group (*ibid.,* I, 58, 242). In the first place Burke at this time was connected with the Earl of Halifax, and not with Newcastle or the Whig magnates. Alvord's theory breaks down again, if one

little controversy as between Canada and Guadeloupe among those relatively few men who constituted the political nation in Great Britain, for the object of the war had been to obtain security for the North American colonies. Once France and England undertook concrete negotiations in the spring of 1761, the British ministry unanimously demanded the cession of Canada. Although the two powers, France and Britain, contended the boundaries of the province, they decided the general issue of Canada almost at once.

Due to the disastrous military situation, the French government had to accept the loss of its North American colony, but its foreign minister, the Duc de Choiseul, sought to minimize the damage by claiming that much of the North American interior fell within the province of Louisiana. Consequently, Choiseul was willing to accord to Great Britain the right bank of the Ohio to within ten leagues of the Wabash River. The watershed of the rivers flowing to the Atlantic and the Gulf of Mexico would delineate the other frontiers between the two powers. British victories in North America also reacted on the Spanish court in Madrid. Charles III, who came to the Spanish throne in 1759, had instructed his ambassador in London to notify Pitt that His Catholic Majesty could not disregard any military alteration in the balance of power in North America established in 1713 by the Peace of Utrecht. Exploiting this apprehension, Choiseul

---

notes that at the time Burke wrote a later pro-Guadeloupe pamphlet, *Considerations on the Approaching Peace* (London, 1762), he was connected with Henry Fox. Fox supported the treaty and managed the preliminary articles through the House of Commons, so that by Alvord's thesis, Burke should have written in favor of the retention of Canada. The attempt to relate the pamphlet war with factional attitudes breaks down in this case. The story of Burke's later pamphlet and the amusing reaction of Fox may be followed in Edmund Burke to Charles O'Hara, Aug. 20, 1762; William Burke to O'Hara, Oct. 9, 1762, and Nov. 20, 1762, Ross J. S. Hoffman (ed.), *Edmund Burke, New York Agent, with . . . Intimate Correspondence with Charles O'Hara* (Philadelphia, 1956), 285, 290, 291. William Burke was able to influence two votes in favor of the treaty for Fox in the session which ratified the peace settlement. Fox to the Earl of Sandwich, Nov. 12, 1763, Nanette Jucker (ed.), *The Jenkinson Papers, 1760–1766* (London, 1949), 413.

through his minister at Madrid warned of the danger of Spanish possessions posed by British control of the interior.[12]

These were the views of the major powers when the Duc de Choiseul initiated unilateral negotiations between Britain and France by dispatching a memorial on March 26, 1761. As a basis for negotiation Choiseul proposed the principle of *uti possidetis:* each nation to retain conquests made in Europe as of May 1; in America and Africa as of July 1; and in the East Indies as of September 6.[13] By a later exchange of notes in April, Pitt and Choiseul agreed on their respective envoys for talks to be conducted in London and Paris. With the machinery for negotiations now arranged, the British ministers had to come to a decision on their terms for peace. Pitt proposed by the capture of Martinique and Belleisle to confirm, among other points, the retention of Canada. Alderman Sir William Baker reinforced his arguments on Canada in a paper sent to the Duke of Newcastle. The benefits of Canada and the St. Lawrence River "as a means of security to our other dominions in America is so universally admitted," Baker wrote, that nothing more need be said on that score. If England were to retain any of her conquests, she should keep Canada "clearly and fully stated." Although less knowledgeable on Louisiana, Baker advised that the British ministers demand France's southern colony as well as all of her territory drained by the rivers emptying into the Gulf of Mexico. Such a settlement would fix the boundaries in North America so as to prevent French encroachments on the British colonies. Guadeloupe was not on a par with the North American territories; if the British must relinquish any conquest, "this Island seems the fittest," Baker concluded. Evidently impressed by these arguments, Newcastle sent Sir William's paper to Hardwicke, who considered it

12. See the proposal of Choiseul's advisor, Etienne de Silhouette in A A E, Mémoirs et Documents, Amérique, 24: 273–283, and Silhouette to Choiseul, Dec. 30, 1759, A A E, Mém. et Doc., Angleterre, 41: 395–396; Zenab Esmat Rashed, *The Peace of Paris, 1763* (Liverpool, 1951), 47; Choiseul to the Marquis d'Ossun, Jan. 6, 1760, A A E, Correspondance Politique, Espagne, 527: 12–13.

13. Choiseul to Pitt, March 26, 1761; the declaration of the French King; and the Memorial of the French court, of the same date are in Public Record Office, State Papers, 78, 251.

"very sensible and well drawn up . . . ." But for his part, Hardwicke would not bring "Louisiana upon the carpet." [14]

The ministers did hold differing opinions on the terms to be accorded to France. The primary question was not, however, as between Guadeloupe and North America, but whether to accord the Bourbon foe easy terms and thus end the expensive conflict, or to prolong the war by demanding maximum conditions in order to relegate France to the position of a minor colonial power. Harsh and dominating in his relations with his colleagues, Pitt favored the latter position.

At this point in the spring of 1761 domestic political factors influenced the situation. George III had succeeded to his grandfather's throne in October, 1760. Rigid and limited in his ideas, the young and immature King considered the politicians then in power—William Pitt and the Whig magnates associated with the Duke of Newcastle—unworthy of office. In contrast to these men against whom he had an almost personal grudge, George III placed his confidence in the Earl of Bute, an amateur in politics, who had played the father role in the King's formative years. Hoping eventually to have Bute head the ministry, the monarch appointed him Secretary of State for the Northern Department in March, 1761. Bute was no war minister. Were he to lead the government, as both he and the King desired, Bute must end the war as quickly as possible. Consequently Bute did not fully support Pitt in the latter's call for harsh terms to be imposed on France. Newcastle and the other Whig magnates who entertained little affection for Pitt were not less desirous for an early peace, which would eliminate the need for the "great Commoner" who alone seemed qualified to conduct an extended war. Furthermore, the task of raising the money to finance the war effort fell on Newcastle. Pitt had little understanding or sympathy for the problems of the First Lord of the Treasury. Resentful of Pitt's attitude, Newcastle, Hardwicke, and Bute called for the support of the Duke of Bedford at the meetings of the council held during

14. Newcastle to Hardwicke, April 17, 1761, Add. MSS 32923, f. 19; Hardwicke to Newcastle, April 18, 1761, Add. MSS 32923, f. 40; Baker to Newcastle, April 13, 1761, Add. MSS 33030, ff. 1–2; Hardwicke to Newcastle, April 17, 1761, Add. MSS 32922, f. 28.

April and May, 1761, to discuss terms for the negotiations. Of the major figures who played a part in the peace negotiations, Bedford was the most pacifically inclined and perhaps the most ludicrous of the politicians. If his opinions had prevailed Great Britain would have retained almost nothing. Yet even Bedford urged his colleagues to be firm in retaining those objects for which the nation had gone to war, "security of our possessions in America, and the West Indies . . . upon the *Uti possidetis.*" [15]

In agreement on these points the council on May 13 decided on the instructions for the British negotiator in Paris, Hans Stanley. As a basis for discussion the British accepted the proposals contained in the French memorial of March 26.[16]

In his discussions with Stanley in the French capital, Choiseul proposed the "entire" cession of New France with "une fixation des limites du Canada dans la partie de l'Ohio determinées par les eaux pendantes" so clearly defined by treaty as to avoid future disputes. But the British cabinet refused to allow the boundaries of Canada to be thus redefined. They demanded the whole province. In a rigid letter on June 26, Pitt rejected the French position on the southern limits of Canada, demanding the cession of the province "total and entire, not mutilated or dismembered." He termed the boundary of the Ohio River "insidious," put forth in the hope of reducing the extent of Canada and increasing the area of Louisiana. The French, he charged, were attempting to establish an inadmissible principle, namely, "that which is not Canada is Louisiana." Thus France would unjustly retain all the territory between the two provinces.[17]

15. Bedford to Newcastle, May 9, 1761, Add. MSS 32922, f. 451. To some extent Hardwicke shared Bedford's views. "There is one Thing upon which I have long thought as the Duke of B[edford] does," he wrote, "that it is possible for England to be overloaded with foreign Colonies." To retain Canada, Guadeloupe, and part of Louisiana, as some were advocating, would result in an excessive burden in garrisoning the area to subjugate the French populace. If the French settlers were evacuated, England and Ireland would be depopulated in the attempt to fill the void, for "the Swarms of German Emigrants seem to be at end." Hardwicke to Newcastle, May 16, 1761, Add. MSS 32923, ff. 123–128.

16. Stanley's instructions, dated May 18, 1761, are in S. P. 78, 251.

17. The so-called "little leaf" or "little Paper," dictated by Choiseul is in Stanley to Pitt, June 18, 1761, S. P. 78, 251. Charles Jenkinson to George Gren-

In the face of Pitt's uncompromising attitude, Choiseul played a clever game in negotiating. In his answers to the British notes, he seemed to give in to their demands, but in his private communications to his representative in London, François de Bussy, he continued to define Louisiana as broadly as possible. For example, in the French Memorial of Propositions of July 13, 1761, Choiseul agreed to the cession of Canada "such as it has been and in right ought to be possessed by France" and stipulated that the limits of the colony vis-à-vis Louisiana "shall be clearly and firmly established" so as to eliminate future boundary disputes with the British. But in a private note sent two days later Choiseul instructed Bussy that the Alabama, Tennessee, and Wabash rivers bounded Louisiana on the southeast. To the north Lakes Nipigon, Superior, and Michigan separated Canada from Louisiana.[18] Pitt emphatically rejected these French contentions in an interview with Bussy on July 26. No compensation was due France for the cession of Canada. England had possession by right of conquest. On July 29 the British presented an ultimatum which called for the total cession of Canada. Again Pitt rejected the French contention that all territory which did not belong to the northern province should be included in Louisiana. Furthermore, the tribes occupying the intermediary lands were to form a barrier between the possessions of the two powers. Neither directly nor indirectly were they to be under the influence of the French.[19]

---

ville, June 25, June 26, 1761, William J. Smith (ed.), *The Grenville Papers* (4 vols., London, 1838–1840), I, 372, 373; Newcastle to Devonshire, June 28, 1761, Add. MSS 32924, f. 322, cited in Namier, *England in the Age of the American Revolution*, 323; and Denys A. Winstanley, *Personal and Party Government: A Chapter in the Political History of the Early Years of the Reign of George III, 1760–1766* (Cambridge, 1910), 55; Pitt to Stanley, June 26, 1761, S. P. 78, 251

18. The French memorial of propositions, dated July 13, 1761, in S. P. 78, 251; A A E, Corr. Pol., Angl., 443: 358–359.

19. Bussy to Choiseul, July 26, 1761, A A E, Corr. Pol., Angl., 444: 65–66. The British Ultimatum, dated July 29, 1761, in S. P. 78, 251; also A A E Corr. Pol., Angl., 444: 87–88. A copy headed "Paper of Points to be delivered by Mr. Stanley to the Duc de Choiseul as containing the Ultimatum of the Court of Great Britain," in Stowe Collection, box 103b, Henry E. Huntington Library, San Marino, Calif.

Again Choiseul attempted to play a double game. In a French ultimatum of August 5 he seemed to agree in the main to the British demands, but five days later in a memorial to Bussy he proposed a line of demarcation between British and French possessions in North America extending in a near north-south line through the interior. Beginning at the mouth of the Perdido River between the bays of Mobile and Pensacola, it ran to the Alabama River, then to the western end of Lake Erie so as to include the Maumee River, and finally to the height of land towards Hudson's Bay near Lake Abitibi.[20] On learning of the new French boundary proposals, the British were convinced that the French were endeavoring "to chicane about the limits of Canada on the side of the Ohio." In conferring with Bussy, Pitt was so emphatic in rejecting Choiseul's proposal that the French envoy was convinced that the British sought all of the territory east of the Mississippi River. The British Secretary of State termed the Perdido River–Lake Abitibi line proposed by Choiseul as an "effrontery unparalleled," and on August 30 he demanded that France accord the province of Canada as surrendered by the Marquis de Vaudreuil at the capitulation of Montreal in 1760.[21]

Choiseul remained unyielding. By the third week of September, Stanley's dispatches from Paris conveyed the impression that there would be no peace at this time.[22] The Anglo-French negotiations, it seemed, were at an end. In spite of France's adverse military position, Choiseul placed his faith in a Spanish alliance. In August the Bourbon powers had signed the *Pacte de Famille*. In a secret convention, separate from this defensive treaty but dated simultaneously, Charles III agreed to declare war on Great

20. The French Ultimatum of Aug. 5, 1761, A A E, Corr. Pol., Angl., 444: 118–119; S. P. 78, 252. "Mémoire sur les limites a donner à las Louisiene du côté des colonies Angloises de côté du Canada en cas de cession de ce dernier pays," A A E, Corr. Pol., Angl., 444: 155.

21. Hardwicke to Royston, Aug. 22, 1761, Add. MSS 35352, f. 188; Bussy to Choiseul, Aug. 30, 1762, A A E, Corr. Pol., Angl., 444: 218–220; Pitt to Stanley, Aug. 27, 1761, S. P. 78, 252; A A E, Corr. Pol., Angl., 444: 233–235.

22. Newcastle to Bedford, Sept. 13, 1761, *Correspondence of John, 4th Duke of Bedford* . . . (intro. by Lord John Russell) (3 vols., London, 1842–1846), III, 44.

Britain by May 1, 1762, if by that date the two belligerents had not settled their disputes.[23] Suspecting the extent of the Bourbon alliance, Pitt favored a preventative war against Spain, but finding himself almost isolated in the cabinet he resigned early in October, 1761. The Earl of Egremont replaced him as Secretary of State for the Southern Department. The wartime coalition of ministers was finally broken, never to be repaired. Ironically, events proved Pitt correct, for faced with the refusal of the Spanish court to give satisfactory assurances as to its future intentions, the British ministers, including Bute, who had balked at Pitt's policy the previous fall, declared war on Spain on January 4, 1762. But disagreement between Bute and the Whig magnates as to the conduct of the now enlarged war and on the problems of negotiating a peace hampered the British effort.

Actually contact between London and Versailles had continued following the rupture of negotiations in the fall of 1761. Both Choiseul and Bute had kept in touch by means of the Sardinian ambassadors at their respective courts, the Baille de Breille and the Comte de Viry.[24] This partially secret channel served as the medium by which the two politicians arranged the preliminaries of the peace treaty. On a formal level diplomatic relations between the two courts remained open through a series of letters between Egremont and the French ministers—correspondence concerning the exchange of the French admiral, d'Estaing, who had violated his parole and had been recaptured. In time this open exchange merged with the negotiations conducted through Viry and Solar.[25]

23. When hostilities broke out between England and Spain in January, 1762, the Spanish foreign minister, the Marquis de Grimaldi, in order to mask Spain's hostile acts, suggested that the pact be altered so that it should appear to be the result, rather than the cause, of the failure of the peace negotiations. The secret convention was rewritten, and redated to February 4, 1762, after the British declaration of war of January 4, 1762. Samuel F. Bemis, *Diplomacy of the American Revolution* (New York, 1935), 6n.; Arthur I. Aiton, "A Neglected Intrigue of the Family Compact," *Hispanic American Review*, XI (1931), 389.

24. Max Savelle, *The Diplomatic History of the Canadian Boundary, 1749–1763* (New Haven, London, and Toronto, 1940), 127; Rashed, *Peace of Paris*, 118; and Pease, *Anglo-French Boundary Disputes*, cxxiii.

25. Egremont to the Duc de Choiseul, Feb. 22, 1762; Duc de Choiseul to Egremont, March 7, 1762; Egremont to the Duc de Choiseul, April 7, 1762; Duc

On March 18, 1762, the cabinet, including the Duke of Devonshire, Bute, George Grenville, Newcastle, and Hardwicke, discussed the draft of a letter concerning terms for peace to be transmitted by Viry. Despite some doubts by Grenville, they resolved to accept Canada as offered in the last French memorial of August 5, 1761. The letter was scheduled to be sent on March 23, but late in the evening of the 21st, the government received news of the British capture of Martinique. Consequently they delayed sending the note.[26]

The conquest of Martinique reopened the issue of the Caribbean islands, especially for Newcastle and Hardwicke. The latter wrote Newcastle that his grace knew "what had been debated in the pamphlets, whether we should keep Canada or Guadeloupe." But the acquisition of Martinique raised a graver question in the mind of Hardwicke: whether Great Britain "should restore to France all her Sugar-Colonies, or a great part of Canada." Emphasizing that the most material argument for the retention of Canada was the security of the North American colonies, Hardwicke insisted that, in the opinion of some, this objective could not be attained "without conquering Louisiana also . . . ." Others thought that some parts of Canada might serve as well as the entire province to insure the security of the British colonies on the mainland. The question was, Hardwicke reiterated, between "Canada, or a great part of Canada," and all the major French sugar islands. Listing the commercial advantages of the islands over the northern province, the former Lord Chancellor repeated his arguments of the previous year. The British isles could not populate the North American interior "in centuries to come . . . ." The mother country would have to support expensive garrisons to control the subversive French population. Yet Hardwicke was unable to resolve his doubts. He concluded by warning Newcastle: "Don't take this as an opinion, for I have form'd none." [27]

Whatever the final decision on Martinique, the capture of the

---

de Choiseul to Egremont, April 14, 1762; and Comte de Choiseul to Solar, April 16, 1762, Stowe Collection, box 103a, HEHL.

26. See Grenville's minute, headed "Thursday At Ld Egremonts March 18, 1762," Stowe Collection, box 103c, HEHL.

27. Hardwicke to Newcastle, April 2, 1762, Add. MSS 32936, ff. 310–311.

island interrupted the progress of the peace negotiations only momentarily. Through communications exchanged between the Sardinian ambassadors, both sides agreed to resume discussions on the basis of their official declarations of the previous August. Since Canada was the great object of the war, Choiseul conceded that it should go to the victorious power. He professed to see no difficulties on the boundaries of Louisiana.[28] But this point created dissension among the British ministers in a cabinet session on April 30. They first agreed to return Martinique if France would cede either Guadeloupe or Louisiana. After the meeting Bute, however, concluded that these terms were too harsh; consequently France would reject them and continue the war. On the pretext that many of the ministers had not expressed themselves earlier that day, Bute called another meeting and argued against the previous decision. He now proposed that England restore Martinique and Guadeloupe, while retaining the lesser West Indian islands except Marie Galente. In order to "secure in perpetuity our northern conquests from all future chicane," Bute put forth the Mississippi River as the boundary between the French and British possessions in North America. Newcastle and Devonshire agreed "heartily" to the proposal, although Egremont foresaw some difficulty in distinguishing between the French settlements in Louisiana and those of the Spanish in Florida.[29]

Egremont presented the British demands to Viry on May 1. The Sardinian envoy queried the Secretary of State for a specific explanation of the Mississippi boundary line, but the British minister refused to amplify the point. Viry then wrote "confidemment à une personne de credit" for further clarification.

28. "March 29, 1762. Minute of a Cabinet Council at St. James.," HMC *Tenth Report*, app., pt. I (London, 1885), 449–450, from the papers of Edward Weston, Under-Secretary of State; Viry to Solar, April 8, 1762, enclosing "Declaration de Sa Majeste le Roy de la Grande Bretagne," Shelburne Papers, 9: 100–107, William L. Clements Library, Ann Arbor, Michigan; Duc de Choiseul to Solar, April 15, 1762, *ibid.*, 9: 123.

29. Newcastle to Hardwicke, April 25, 1762, Add. MSS 32937, f. 349; Bute to Bedford, May 1, 1762, *Bedford Correspondence*, III, 74–75; Newcastle to Hardwicke, May 1, 1762, Add. MSS 32938, f. 10.

Bute was the minister in question. Through his brother, James Stuart Mackenzie, he secretly sent Viry a note defining the Mississippi boundary line. Since the river had several "embouchures," Bute specified the most easterly source by way of the Iberville River, Lake Maurepas, and Lake Ponchartrain.[30] Bute's ill-considered secret commitment to the French ministers had grave consequences. The French never relinquished the advantage they thus obtained. Fearing the possible exposure of his actions, Bute had to support the Choiseuls. His actions damaged British interests on two points. First, by retaining New Orleans, France held the back door to British possession in the interior. Second, the Iberville channel proved insufficient for navigation; and Great Britain had to depend on the French outlet at New Orleans. This was a precarious arrangement at best. For the sake of an early peace, Bute needlessly threw away a valuable point.

For the moment the Scottish favorite seemed to be in a more dominant position than ever. His relations with Newcastle had always been uneasy. The two had clashed on the issue of the German war, particularly when Bute proposed to terminate subsidies to Prussia. The Duke also feared Bute's influence and the threat to his own position; so much so that he resigned from the ministry on May 26. Bute became First Lord of the Treasury, while George Grenville assumed the post of Secretary of State for the Northern Department. During the summer even these two ministers were continually at odds, for Grenville constantly advocated peace terms more harsh than those Bute desired. If the British demands were too great, the French would terminate negotiations. With this possibility in mind, Bute feared the consequences of military success. In expectation of the capture of Havana he wrote: "I am afraid of the success even alienating the Spaniard, instead of prompting him to peace . . . ." A truly astonishing method of waging war! For his part, Grenville

30. Egremont to Viry, May 1, 1762, Shelburne Papers, 9: 175, WLCL; Viry to Solar, May 4, 1762, *ibid.*, 9: 182–183. The identification of Bute and Stuart Mackenzie is made possible by a letter from the Comte de Choiseul (then Duc de Praslin) to the Duc de Nivernois, Dec. 26, 1762, A A E, Corr. Pol., Angl., 448: 427. Bute's note, headed "Copie de la note au sujet de la limite du cours du Mississippi entre les deux nations," Shelburne Papers, 9: 183, WLCL.

advocated exacting some compensation for the restoration of Guadeloupe and Havana.[31]

The two ministers clashed during a cabinet meeting on July 26 when the administration members discussed a French *projet* of preliminary articles of peace. Article VI of the project based on Bute's secret commitment to Viry of May 4 stipulated that the Mississippi from its source to the sea—via the Iberville-Maurepas-Ponchartrain channel—was to be the boundary between the two powers in North America. The subjects of both nations would be free to navigate the river. France was thus granting Great Britain an outlet to the Gulf of Mexico. The Comte de Choiseul had warned, however, that this arrangement must be secret for the moment, for Spain objected to English penetration to the Gulf. These conditions aroused strong opposition in the cabinet, much to Bute's discomfort. Grenville pointed out that the French proposals fixed the English boundary by a questionable water passage to the sea. It would thus deny to Britain the navigation of the Mississippi. On this point the Duke of Bedford strongly opposed Grenville, arguing that the navigation of the Mississippi was "not worth having at all," for the river served only to delineate the boundary between the two nations. As was to be expected, Bute supported Bedford, while the Earl of Halifax inclined toward Grenville's views. Bedford held his ground by urging the "great impropriety" of demanding the right of navigation on both sides of New Orleans. There was neither "justice" nor "Conscience" to such a demand. The ministers ought not to pay any attention to "popular clamour" in this matter, but follow "the golden rule of doing as we wou[l]d be done by & not to ask things which were neither fit to be ask[e]d by one or granted by the other." Grenville, who was as stubborn but not as charitable as Bedford, insisted that the navigation of the Mississippi was essential for any future settlements established on the river. The ministers, he emphasized, knew nothing of the practicality of navigation by the Iberville channel.[32]

31. Bute to Grenville, May 30, 1762, William J. Smith (ed.), *The Grenville Papers, being the Correspondence of Richard Grenville . . . and . . . George Grenville* . . . (4 vols., London, 1838–1840), I, 443; Grenville Diary, *ibid.*, I, 450.

32. Choiseul to Solar, July 21, 1762, Shelburne Papers, 10: 369–374, WLCL;

Grenville won the argument, for the instructions to Bedford, the plenipotentiary appointed to negotiate a treaty with the French ministers in Paris, specified that if navigation by the Iberville channel should prove impractical for purposes of commerce, British subjects would have access to that branch of the Mississippi the French ordinarily used. Furthermore, both Grenville and Egremont insisted on further compensation for Havana in case British forces should capture that city before the conclusion of a peace treaty.[33]

By September 21, Bedford, the British plenipotentiary in Paris, reported that the difficulties over the draft article in the treaty on the Mississippi boundary "are pretty well over with the Ministers here." But a crisis developed over the issue of Havana since both powers, anticipating the capture of the city, attempted to provide for that eventuality. The Choiseuls proposed specifically mentioning the city in an article covering the restitutions of conquests that "may have been made, during the course of the Negotiations . . . ." When Bedford "objected very strongly" to such vague terminology, the French sought to reassure him that they "only meant it as . . . Bait for Spain . . . ."[34]

News of the actual capture of Havana presented the British with a diplomatic lever to force more favorable terms. They had

---

a copy of Article VI is in *ibid.*, 10: 374; copies of Article VI and Article XII, relevant to North America are also found in Grenville's papers, endorsed "Articles 6 & 12 R. from Count Viry 24 July 1762," Stowe Collection, box 103a, HEHL. The account of the cabinet debate is from Grenville's minutes of the meeting headed "At Ld Granvilles in Arlington Street Monday July 26. 1762," Stowe Collection, box 103c, HEHL. Bute to Egremont, July 26, 1762, Romney Sedgwick (ed.), *Letters from George III to Lord Bute, 1756–1766* (London, 1939), 127.

33. Egremont to Viry, July 31, 1762, Shelburne Papers, 11: 37–38, WLCL. Bedford's minute of his conversation with Bute on August 23, 1762, *Bedford Correspondence,* III, 96–97; also Grenville's notes, headed "At the Duke of Cumberlands lodgings Sept 3rd 1762," Stowe Collection, box 103c, HEHL. Bedford's instructions, dated September 4, 1762, *ibid.*, box 103b; and S. P. France, 78, 253.

34. Bedford to Egremont, Sept. 21, 1762, Stowe Collection, box 103c, HEHL. The draft of the article headed "K. Art. 6 Ce lui qui est dans Les Preliminaries," *ibid.;* Bedford to Egremont (secret), Sept. 24, 1762; Sept. 25, 1762 (most secret), *ibid.*

taken eleven Spanish ships of war as well as a million and a half in treasure in the assault on the Caribbean metropolis. Grenville was especially insistent on some equivalent for restoring the conquest. He even threatened to call in members of the opposition to the discussions in the council.[35] Grenville paid a price for his show of independence. Bute feared that he would exert pressure to bring the preliminary peace treaty before Parliament for approval before signing. Consequently he obtained the King's permission to replace Grenville with the less scrupulous but highly effective Henry Fox. Fox refused the seals of office but did consent to lead the administration forces in the House of Commons. Bute needed someone in the Commons who could stand up to Pitt, who was expected to attack the treaty, and Fox was just the man for this task. Bute retained Grenville in a minor office, for if he were a free agent, he could carry considerable strength in opposition and might disclose some of the embarrassing details of the peace negotiations.[36]

On the question of an equivalent for Havana, however, the majority of the cabinet sided with Grenville, maintaining that some additional territory was indispensable. Also anxious to know what compensation the English would demand, the French had offered Louisiana to Spain as an indemnity for whatever Spanish territory the British would ask.[37] On October 22 the British ministers decided to insist on either Florida or Puerto Rico as restitution for Havana. Egremont hoped that the loss of the Cuban city would "make the Court of Madrid seriously inclined to listen to Terms of Accommodation." [38] It did, especially in view of the secret French offer to cede to Spain New Orleans and that part of Louisiana west of the Mississippi. Great Britain received Florida. Bedford signed the preliminary treaty in Paris

35. Henry Fox to the Duke of Cumberland, Sept. 29, 1762, George Thomas Keppel, Earl of Albermarle (ed.), *Memoirs of the Marquis of Rockingham* (2 vols., London, 1852), I, 129–130.

36. Pares, *War and Trade in the West Indies,* 607–608.

37. Bute to Bedford, Oct. 14, 1762, *Bedford Correspondence,* III, 137; Bedford to Egremont, Oct. 11, 1762, Stowe Collection, box 103c, HEHL; Rashed, *Peace of Paris,* 181.

38. Egremont to Bedford, Oct. 26, 1762, *Bedford Correspondence,* III, 139; Egremont to Bedford, Oct. 10, 1762, Stowe Collection, box 103c, HEHL.

on November 3, and the next day Louis XV ceded Louisiana to his Bourbon ally. The British cabinet approved the preliminary treaty on November 10. The definitive treaty of February 10, 1763, did not differ significantly from the preliminaries with respect to the North American continent. By April 18, 1763, Egremont, the Secretary of State for the Southern Department, issued orders for the British evacuation of Guadeloupe, Martinique, and Havana, and for the occupation of Florida and Louisiana east of the Mississippi River.[39]

The long struggle was over; the ministers had achieved the object of the war—security for the North American colonists. By retaining territories in North America—the interior, Canada, and Florida—the administration sacrificed the more tangible economic benefits to be gained from the sugar islands in the West Indies. Some historians have seen an economic motive in this decision. While the evidence seems to point to the security issue as the deciding factor in this choice, scholars have argued that the retention of the American territories reflected a basic shift in British colonial and commercial policy. The ministers now sought colonies as markets for British manufactured goods rather than as sources of tropical raw materials. Scholars emphasize the fact that Bute's protégé, the young Earl of Shelburne, in defending the preliminary treaty in a speech in the House of Lords, stressed the importance of the North American interior as a potential market for the industrial output of England.[40] The fact that Shelburne used such an argument does not prove this motive behind the peace treaty, nor does it indicate that Shelburne was a western expansionist. The sentiments he expressed in December, 1762, are not at all in line with what he wrote to Egremont just five months before when he advocated moderate peace terms in order to end the war quickly. At that time he

39. Egremont to the Secretary-at-War, April 18, 1763, Joseph Reddington and Richard Roberts (eds.), *Calendar of Home Office Papers of the Reign of George III* (4 vols., London, 1878–1889), I, 274.

40. Shelburne Papers, vol. 165, unfoliated, WLCL. Harlow, *Founding of the Second British Empire,* 183, and Harold V. Temperly, "The Peace of Paris," in J. Holland Rose, A. P. Newton, and E. A. Benians (eds.), *The Cambridge History of the British Empire* (8 vols., London, 1929–1936), I, 504–505, accept the document in the Shelburne Papers as the notes of his speech.

demonstrated no interest in the North American interior and stressed a return to the *status quo* of 1754! The object of the war, he had stated, was "to defend not to acquire . . . ." [41] Shelburne's attitudes were not inconsistent as long as one recognizes his true motives. He was, in fact, perfectly consistent. As a protégé of Bute he had supported that minister in July, 1762, by advocating peace terms which would end the war. In December, 1762, he had the same political motive in defending the treaty negotiated by his mentor.

In reality there was little need to justify the treaty, for the opposition in Parliament proved very weak. One thing is certain. The Whigs did not condemn the ministry for retaining Canada or the North American interior, but for not having exacted further compensation or indemnities for the French West Indian islands after they were assured of the cession of Canada. For example, the day before Parliament considered the preliminary peace treaty, Newcastle indicated that the ministry had achieved the primary goal of the war. The elimination of the French from Canada provided security for the British colonists. But, he argued, there was no reason to have returned Guadeloupe or Martinique.[42] It is little wonder that the treaty provoked relatively little excitement in Parliament. In the Lords on December 9, 1762, there was not even a division. In the House of Commons only Pitt made a sustained attack on the peace. "Nobody besides him spoke a word . . . worth remembering" against the settlement negotiated by Bedford. Although he condemned the preliminaries on general grounds, Pitt commended the articles which related to the new acquisitions in America. He attacked the Bute ministry for not having exacted further cessions.[43] Pitt's efforts were to little avail, indeed, if he had so intended them to be. The Commons overwhelmingly supported the treaty by

41. Shelburne to Egremont, July 9, 1762, Shelburne Papers, volume labeled "Letters," unfoliated, WLCL.

42. Newcastle to Hardwicke, Nov. 29, 1762, Add. MSS 32945, f. 260.

43. Viscount Barrington to Andrew Mitchell, Dec. 13, 1762, quoted in Namier, *England in the Age of the American Revolution,* 459; James Hayes to Richard Neville, Dec. 10, 1762, *Bedford Correspondence,* III, 168. The speech attributed to Pitt in the *Parliamentary History,* XV, 1263–67, agrees with the accounts cited above.

a vote of 319 to 65. An extraordinary majority for the times.

With the conclusion of the definitive treaty, Bute resigned in April after forming a new cabinet headed by George Grenville as First Lord of the Treasury, and Halifax and Egremont as Secretaries of State. For purely domestic political reasons, Shelburne headed the Board of Trade,[44] but this administrative agency did not have as much influence in colonial affairs as it had previously enjoyed. The Grenville ministry was to be one of the most momentous in the history of the first British Empire. Its main concern, as both Bute and his advisor, James Oswald, indicated, was to be the "settlement" of America.[45] The new ministers were to implement certain policies adopted in the last months of the Bute administration for the new acquisitions. As Egremont wrote in March, 1763, to the Commander-in-Chief of the royal army in America: "A general Plan for the future Regulation of That Country . . . is now actually under Consideration . . . ."

British administrators had retained the North American conquests for the security of the American colonists and they now sought to insure this goal. Regular troops would protect the continent. During the winter of 1762–1763, the ministers had also considered an American tax for the support of this military establishment, but had postponed a final decision until they obtained further information.[46] The decision to adopt these measures marked a significant point in the history of the first British Empire; indeed, it was to lead to the disruption of that empire in the American Revolution. But practical administrative experiences in prosecuting the Seven Years' War lay behind the new program. Having waged the war in America for the security of

44. Bute to Grenville, April 1, 1763, *Grenville Papers,* II, 41.

45. Fox to Bute, March 17, 1763, Lord Edmund Fitzmaurice, *Life of William, Earl of Shelburne* (3 vols., London, 1875), I, 197; and Oswald to Bute, n. d., James Oswald, *Memorials of the public life and character of the Right Honourable James Oswald . . .* (Edinburgh, 1825), 410–412.

46. Egremont to Amherst, March 12, 1763, Public Record Office, Colonial Office, 5/214: 622, Library of Congress transcript; Welbore Ellis (Secretary-at-War) to Amherst, Feb. 12, 1763, Amherst Papers, packet 43, PAC transcript; the King to Bute, March 19, 1763, Sedgwick, *Letters from George III to Bute,* 201.

the colonies and acquired Canada, the interior, and Florida with this objective in mind, the ministers sought to preserve the goal by inaugurating a new arrangement for defense and Indian affairs. The lessons of the war determined the lines this project would follow.

CHAPTER II

Lessons of the War

THE Great War for Empire illustrated with almost disastrous results the shortcomings of Britain's colonial policy of "salutary neglect." Prior to this conflict the provincial governments had been responsible for their own defense and their relations with the Indian tribes. The British administrators appreciated the deficiencies of the traditional system, and following the war they promulgated the Proclamation of 1763 to correct the failures of the previous security arrangement. The program incorporated into the Proclamation was not based on mercantilist doctrine, nor was it the theoretical rationalization of any single individual. The proclamation of 1763 stemmed directly from the experience of British officials in prosecuting the war in America. The relevant factors contributing to the new defense program were raising and financing a military establishment and maintaining peaceful relations with the natives.

No sustained challenge had tested the effectiveness of traditional defense systems. Although of long duration, the conflict with the French and Spanish on the North American continent had been for the most part sporadic and localized. The Indian tribes had grudgingly withdrawn as the line of British settlement edged westward until it stood poised before the mountain barrier. But constant tension marred the relations of the English and the natives, for the land hunger of the whites threatened the Indian way of life. The French settlements did not pose such a menace.

Paradoxically, the implements of European civilization committed the Indians to the white culture. The acute Swedish observer Peter Kalm noted particularly to what extent the natives were dependent on the paraphernalia of the more advanced race. Since the Indians could only obtain utensils, weapons, and goods by trade, the tribes must go either to the French or to the British. The natives realized this. A Wyandotte told George Croghan, the Pennsylvania trader and Indian agent, that no Indian tribe could exist without the support of either of the white nations. They would not live as their ancestors had before the arrival of the Europeans. Consequently, the support of the tribes during the war depended to a large extent on the ability of the British or French to supply trade goods. Many whites recognized the political consequences of the Indian traffic. New York's Indian secretary, Charles Wraxall, described the trade with the natives as the foundation of the Indian alliances, "the chief Cement which binds us together." It should be the "first Principle of our whole System of Indian politics." [1]

For the most part the tribes chose to support the French in the colonial conflict. Most realized the threat presented to their way of life by the agricultural British settlements. In general, the French traders treated the natives more fairly than did their British rivals, who all too often practiced violence, deception, and fraud in their dealings with the Indians. The inability of the colonial governments to control the turbulent frontier or to institute a uniform, just system for managing Indian affairs made the situation worse.

Almost at the outset of the struggle the home government realized the inadequacy of the colonial system for defense and Indian affairs. In the summer of 1754 the Board of Trade under

1. Peter Kalm, *Travels into North America,* translated by John R. Forster, 2nd ed. (2 vols., London, 1772), I, 391–392; Nicholas B. Wainwright (ed.), "George Croghan's Journal, 1759–1763, from the Original in the Cadwallader Collection of the Historical Society of Pennsylvania," *Pennsylvania Magazine of History and Biography,* LXXI (1947), 357; Peter Wraxall, *An Abridgement of Indian Affairs . . . Transacted in the Colony of New York from the Year 1678 to the Year 1751,* ed. by Charles H. McIlwain (Cambridge, Mass., 1915), 153.

the Earl of Halifax presented a project of mutual defense for the colonies. The appointment by the Crown of a single authority to command permanent forts and troops and to direct Indian affairs was a step toward a more efficient system. But it was not enough. If the colonies themselves took no action, the Commissioners of Trade saw no other alternative "but that of an Application for an Interposition of the Authority of Parliament." [2] Here was an indication of future imperial policy should the colonies fail to respond adequately in the common war effort.

The project for a coordinated colonial defense system collapsed with the rejection of the formula devised at the Albany Congress in 1754. But the British ministry in the spring of 1755 took the first step in accepting responsibility for protection of the American frontier with the appointment of General Edward Braddock as Commander-in-Chief in North America and with the nomination of two imperial superintendents in charge of political relations with the tribes. This arrangement proved unsatisfactory during the war. The attempt to coordinate imperial and provincial contributions was cumbersome and in some cases completely inadequate. The requisition system by which the home government called on the colonies for men and money required over-all imperial direction but depended on the provincial governments for effective implementation.

As early as May, 1755, Edmund Atkin, the first Indian Superintendent for the Southern District, presented a report to the Board of Trade in which he condemned the management of Indian affairs as practiced by the separate colonies. If no remedy was forthcoming, he predicted, the British would lose the friendship of those few tribes left on their side. Some provinces had made no regulations for conducting the vital Indian trade. Such legislation as did exist often conflicted with the statutes of other colonies. At times the provincial assemblies left the conduct of Indian relations to traders who had no aptitude for public affairs —men who often had their own self-interest first in mind. Atkin predicted that the colonies could not cooperate to develop a uniform system for the regulation of the Indian traffic because

2. A copy of the board's representation, dated August 9, 1754, is found in the Shelburne Papers, 49: 259–265, WLCL.

of their varied interests and circumstances. Neither would they ever agree on a common fund to defray the cost of the general service. Consequently he recommended that Parliament establish general regulations obligatory on all the provinces and that the government in London appoint officials to execute such common rules.

Atkin was not alone in his evaluation. A year later Governor William Shirley of Massachusetts proposed imperial regulation of the Indian trade. Lieutenant Governor Robert Dinwiddie of Virginia was also concerned over the matter. In February, 1756, he informed the Board of Trade that the malpractices of the English traders were chiefly responsible for the desertion of the tribes from the British interest. Since the colonies could not be depended upon to manage Indian affairs effectively, Dinwiddie suggested that Parliament levy a poll tax for this purpose. Washington, who commanded a regiment of Virginia troops during the war, agreed to some extent with these conclusions. He suggested a general system so that the rules of one colony would not undermine the regulations of the others. Not the least of those advocating reformation of Indian affairs was Sir William Johnson, Superintendent for the Northern District. He appealed to the home government and to local military commanders in America for corrective action. The superintendents under the authority of the Crown should direct Indian affairs.[3]

3. Wilbur R. Jacobs (ed.), *The Edmund Atkin Report and Plan of 1755* (Columbia, S. C., 1954), 3, 8, 13–17, and 40. On Atkin, see Alden, *Southern Colonial Frontier,* 69; "Sketch of a System for the Management of Indian Affairs in North America under One General Direction," Charles H. Lincoln (ed.), *Correspondence of William Shirley Governor of Massachusetts and Military Commander in America, 1731–1760* (2 vols., New York, 1912), II, 373–377; Dinwiddie to the Board of Trade, Feb. 23, 1756, Robert A. Brock (ed.), *The Official Records of Robert Dinwiddie, 1751–1758,* Virginia Historical Society *Collections* (3 vols., Richmond, Va., 1882–1892), II, 338–339; Washington to Dinwiddie, May 30, 1757; Washington to Fauquier, Dec. 2, 1758, John C. Fitzpatrick (ed.), *The Writings of George Washington* (39 vols., Washington, 1931–1944), II, 313–314; Johnson to the Board of Trade, May 17, 1759, Edmund B. O'Callaghan (ed.), *Documents relative to the colonial history of the state of New York* (15 vols., Albany, 1856–1887), VII, 377; Johnson to Amherst, Dec. 8, 1759, James Sullivan *et al.* (eds.), *The Papers of Sir William Johnson* (12 vols., Albany and New York, 1921–1958), III, 183.

The imperial government appreciated these arguments. As early as November, 1757, the Commissioners of Trade admitted to the governor of South Carolina that the "only effectual method of conducting Indian affairs will be to establish one general system under the sole direction of the crown and its officers . . . ." The commissioners disapproved of regulations, however proper in themselves, imposed by any particular colony, for these must be, by their nature, "partial" and would probably conflict with the measures adopted by other provinces. At this time the board hoped to develop a general plan. For the moment it could not proceed for lack of information. In the interim the Board of Trade did allow the colonies on their own initiative to legislate for the correction of abuses.[4] While the war was in progress in North America, however, the imperial government took no definite step to impose an over-all system.

The Indian agents, superintendents, and colonial governors often stressed another source of difficulty with the tribes—one which further jeopardized the Indian alliance so necessary during the war. The natives were dissatisfied over fraudulent purchases of their lands by the whites. Governor Denny warned the proprietors of Pennsylvania that the injuries committed by individuals in his province, as well as in the neighboring colonies, would jeopardize any permanent peace settlement with the tribes. As early as 1756 Sir William Johnson cautioned that the natives were disgusted with extensive purchases of their lands.[5] Whether the whites acquired these lands fairly or by force and deception meant little to the Indians in the final analysis. The Onondaga council in 1756 told George Croghan that "in either case they would lose their Lands, & the consideration they got, was soon spent, altho' the Lands remained" with the whites. Repeatedly the agents had to assure the tribes that the English did not mean to dispossess them. Johnson frequently urged the imperial govern-

4. Board of Trade to Gov. Henry Littelton, Nov. 9, 1757, C. O. 5/403: 201–203; *Journal of the Board of Trade, 1759–1763,* p. 41.

5. Denny to the proprietors, April 9, 1757, Samuel Hazard, *et al.* (eds.), *Pennsylvania Archives* (9 ser., 138 vols., Philadelphia and Harrisburg, 1852–1949), 1st ser., III, 107. See also the complaints of the Indians at the conference at Easton, Pennsylvania, *DRCHSNY,* VII, 301; Johnson to the Board of Trade, Sept. 28, 1756, *DRCHSNY,* VII, 276.

ment to redress the grievances of the tribes over the large grants of land made by the provincial governments. These acts, he warned, were driving the Indians into the arms of the French.[6] Although the Board of Trade realized the extent to which colonial land practices alienated the Indians,[7] it did not adopt an official policy to halt encroachments on Indian lands until later in the war.

In 1758, the proprietary government of Pennsylvania took a significant step in repairing the alliance with the tribes on the upper Ohio when it re-ceded lands west of the mountains purchased four years earlier and pledged that it would make no further grants in that area. Following this initial example, several British military officials gave concrete assurances of a similar nature to the tribes. In December, 1758, Colonel Henry Bouquet, commandant at Fort Pitt, pledged in the name of the King that the English did not mean to deprive the Indians of their possessions. At a conference with chiefs of the Six Nations, Miami, Ottawa, Shawnee, Wyandotte, and Potawatami at Pittsburgh two years later, General Robert Monckton assured "all the Indian Nations, that His Majesty has not sent me to deprive . . . you of your Lands and Property . . . ." Jeffrey Amherst, the Commander-in-Chief, made a comparable pledge to the natives the following year.[8] By 1761, these imperial officials had established a definite boundary line to preserve Indian lands. The Board of Trade under the Earl of Halifax upheld these commitments, and following the war it incorporated the principle of an Indian

6. William West to Thomas Penn, Jan. 12, 1756, Loudoun Papers, LO 757, HEHL; Johnson to Amherst, Sept. 18, 1759, *Johnson Papers,* III, 138; Johnson to the Board of Trade, Sept. 10, 1756, May 28, 1756, Nov. 10, 1756, and May 17, 1759, *DRCHSNY,* VII, 87, 170, 377.

7. Board of Trade to Gov. Charles Hardy of New York, March 19, 1756, *ibid.,* VII, 77.

8. See the proceedings of the Easton conference, *Minutes of the Provincial Council of Pennsylvania, 1693–1776, Colonial Records of Pennsylvania, 1683–1790* (16 vols., Philadelphia, 1852–1853), VII, 199; "A Conference Held by Col. Bouquet With the Chiefs of the Delaware Indians at Pittsburg, Dec. 4, 1758," *Pennsylvania Archives,* 1st ser., III, 572; "At a Conference held by Gen. Monckton with the western Nations of Indians at the Camp before Pittsburg 12 Aug. 1760," *ibid.,* 1st ser. III, 745; *ibid.,* 1st ser., IV, 49.

reservation into the Proclamation of 1763. The inadequacy of provincial control over the frontier and the pressure of wartime expediency forced the imperial government to act.

The participation of the colonial governments in the defense of the frontier against French incursions also proved unsatisfactory. Under the requisition system, the home government periodically issued calls for men, money, and supplies to be voted by the provincial assemblies. On the whole, the colonies did contribute substantially to the war effort. Whatever the political or constitutional merits of the system, however, inconvenience, delay, and inefficiency entailed in operating through thirteen separate bodies imbued with a local outlook hampered the British cause.

It was difficult enough to get the various sections to agree on common aims and interests, let alone thirteen different colonies. For example, the New England colonies which usually fulfilled the quotas expected of them demanded in 1757 that the Commander-in-Chief specify beforehand how he would use their troops. The Earl of Loudoun remonstrated that he would employ them in the interests of the colonies as a whole. But the New England commissioners pleaded that "it will be a great discouragement to the Inhabitants of the Northern Colonies from Enlisting unless assurances can be given that they shall not march to the southward of certain limits . . . ." Shirley of Massachusetts faced the same problem. In 1755, he complained to the Secretary of State that it was impractical to raise a large number of New England troops without acquainting them beforehand "of their immediate destination . . . ." The command under which "they are to act, is likewise another very material point with them." The Virginians were unwilling to contribute to a northern campaign, while the assembly of Pennsylvania was unable to settle its disputes over instructions to its troops. Shirley despaired over the possibility of coordinating the efforts of the separate legislatures.[9] Governor Horatio Sharpe had a most dif-

9. Loudoun to the New England commissioners, Jan. 29, 1757; the commissioners to Loudoun, Jan. 31, 1757, "Fitch Papers," Connecticut Historical Society *Collections* (Hartford, Conn., 1860–1932), XVII, 279, 280; Shirley to Sir Thomas Robinson, June 20, 1755, *Shirley Correspondence*, II, 203–204;

ficult task in persuading the Maryland assembly to vote supplies and troops. Even when the legislatures did act, it was with a qualification as to the disposition of the forces. Needless to say, their strategy did not conform to the plans of Loudoun, the Commander-in-Chief at the time. Dinwiddie of Virginia, who took an active part in organizing the war effort, made perhaps the strongest comment on the legislatures. He had attempted to arouse the various provincial governments "from their Lethargic Stupidity," but they remained "obstinate." [10]

When the legislatures did vote money for the war effort, they often did so only for a limited period. The sums appropriated were frequently inadequate for an extended campaign. As a result, the pay of the colonial forces was in arrears. The assemblies of the two proprietary colonies, Maryland and Pennsylvania, habitually exacted political concessions from the proprietors and governors as the price for voting money for the war effort. So great was the reaction against the inadequacy of the requisition system that some of the governors, Dinwiddie, Shirley, and Denny, as well as private individuals recommended that Parliament impose taxes to insure a reliable defense establishment.[11]

Horatio Sharpe to John Sharpe, April 19, 1755, *Archives of Maryland,* VI, 197–198; Shirley to Sir Thomas Robinson, Feb. 4, 1755; Shirley to Henry Fox, May 6, 1756, *Shirley Correspondence,* II, 123, 433–434.

10. Sharpe to Pitt, May 26, 1757, *Archives of Maryland,* IX, 3; Dinwiddie to Halifax, July 24, 1754, *Dinwiddie Records,* I, 251.

11. Denny to the proprietors, April 9, 1757, *Pennsylvania Archives,* 1st ser., III, 116; Sharpe to Pitt, March 26, 1758, *Archives of Maryland,* IX, 153–154; Sharpe to Cecelius Calvert, March ?, 1756; Sharpe to John and William Sharpe, Nov. 25, 1755, *Archives of Maryland,* VI, 384, 310–311; Dinwiddie to Halifax, April 30, 1755, *Dinwiddie Records,* II, 17. At one time he recommended a poll tax. Dinwiddie to Halifax, July 24, 1754, *ibid.,* I, 251. Shirley to Robinson, Feb. 4, 1755; June 20, 1755, *Shirley Correspondence,* II, 123, 204. Denny to Pitt, April 9, 1757, *Pennsylvania Archives,* 1st ser., III, 106. See also Samuel Johnson to William Johnson, Jan. 10, 1756, Herbert W. and Carol S. Schneider (eds.), *Samuel Johnson, His Career and Writings* (4 vols., New York, 1929), I, 231; and Peter Collinson to Cadwallader Colden, June 9, 1755, *Letters and Papers of Cadwallader Colden . . . 1711–1775,* New York Historical Society *Collections,* LIV, 18. John Watts to Col. Isaac Barré, Feb. 28, 1762, *Letter Book of John Watts,* New York Historical Society *Collections,* LXI, 25. Cecelius Calvert to Horatio Sharpe, Jan. 19, 1760, *Archives of Maryland,* XXXI, 527.

When British and colonial forces captured immediate objectives in North America, some of the colonial assemblies reduced their contributions. The war was over for them. After the fall of Quebec in 1759, the Pennsylvania assembly voted to cut back drastically its appropriations. The practice was so widespread that in the spring of 1761 Amherst, the Commander-in-Chief, felt constrained to complain. With the elimination of the immediate French threat, the colonists complied even less with the requisitions sent them by the home government—quotas designed to carry on the war "for the general good of the King's Subjects" in other areas.[12] In spite of the surrender of Canada, British troops had to occupy the province as well as the interior posts in the Indian country. Victory brought new responsibilities for the British army. From the experience of the war, it was clear that a permanent, stable procedure for the defense establishment of North America must replace the requisition system.

The problem of garrisoning the forts in the wilderness illustrated this need. In the spring of 1760, before launching an attack against Montreal, Amherst stationed four hundred men at Niagara to secure his line of communications between Fort Pitt and the Lakes by garrisoning men at Venango, Presqu'isle, and LeBoeuf. At the capitulation of New France on September 8, 1760, the Marquis de Vaudreuil surrendered the western garrisons at Detroit, Michillimackinac, and the other interior forts. Five days after the fall of Montreal, Amherst dispatched Major Robert Rogers, the partisan leader, with two hundred rangers to the posts of Detroit, St. Joseph, Michillimackinac, and Ouiatanon to accept the surrender of the garrisons there. General Monckton, commanding in Philadelphia, supplemented Rogers' force with regular troops.[13] In order to replace the regulars dispatched to

12. *Minutes of the Provincial Council of Pennsylvania,* VIII, 425; Amherst to Pitt, April 6, 1761, C. O. 5/60: 416.

13. Amherst to Monckton, April 20, 1760, *The Northcliffe Collection* (Ottawa, 1926), 289. A line of smaller forts had been erected in 1756 by Pennsylvania to protect the frontier beyond the Kittaning hills following Braddock's defeat: see Gov. Robert Hunter to Shirley, Feb. 9, 1756, *Shirley Correspondence,* II, 388–390. These now served as communications between Fort Pitt and the East. See also Article II of the capitulation in Arthur S. Doughty and Adam Shortt (eds.), *Documents Relating to the Constitutional History of*

the western posts, Monckton called on the governors of Maryland, Virginia, and Pennsylvania to raise provincials for winter garrison duty along the Ohio and Lake Erie. But the assemblies of these provinces adjourned without taking any action. They left the problem to their successors. Since the winter season prohibited any large-scale garrisoning of the western posts at this time, Amherst was not particularly concerned, for the garrison at Detroit was sufficient for the moment. Yet the "backwardness" of the provincial assemblies in not furnishing the men Monckton requested would have jeopardized the defense system in other circumstances. They were not any the less to blame for their laxness.[14]

By the spring of 1761 the British army had a tenuous hold on the interior. It had not as yet taken possession of the French settlements in the Illinois country or at Vincennes, reputed to be part of Louisiana. In order to maintain "quiet possession of the whole" interior, Amherst planned to repair the forts and build small craft for communication on the Lakes. He strengthened the outposts by dispatching Major Henry Gladwin and three hundred troops to Detroit with instructions to explore the country and repair the fortifications. The Commander-in-Chief assigned "just enough" men at the lesser posts to maintain the lines of communication, for he thought there was "Nothing to fear from the Indians in our present Circumstances . . . ." [15] In the sum-

Canada, 1759–1791 (Ottawa, 1907), 21; the documents exchanged at the capitulation are also printed in the *Annual Register* (104 vols., London, 1759–1862), III (1760), 220–230; Amherst to Pitt, Oct. 4, 1760, G. S. Kimball (ed.), *Correspondence of William Pitt, when Secretary of State, with Colonial Governors, and Military and Naval Commanders in America* (2 vols., New York, 1906), II, 336. At the same time, he ordered Lt. Diedrick Brehm, an engineer of the Royal American regiment, to evaluate the fortifications. John C. Webster (ed.), *The Journal of Jeffrey Amherst* (Toronto and Chicago, 1931), 251.

14. Monckton to Sharpe, Oct. 17, 1760, *Archives of Maryland,* IX, 461; *Minutes of the Provincial Council of Pennsylvania,* VIII, 495; Sharpe to Monckton, Oct. 24, 1760, *Archives of Maryland,* IX, 463; Amherst to Monckton, Nov. 27, 1760, *Northcliffe Collection,* 116; Amherst to Monckton, Nov. 3, 1760, "Aspinwall Papers," Massachusetts Historical Society *Collections,* 4th ser., IX (1871), 348.

15. Amherst to Pitt, Feb. 27, 1761, Kimball, *Pitt's Colonial Correspondence,* II, 104; Amherst to Pitt, C. O. 5/61: 531–532; Amherst to Bouquet, March 2,

mer of 1762 he took further precautions by establishing outposts at Sault Sainte Marie and at Kaministiqua on the north shore of Lake Superior in order "to secure entirely that Frontier." He assured the Secretary of State that "everything is well in Canada and in the several Posts." [16]

By the end of the year, with the conclusion of hostilities, Amherst had almost nine thousand men in North America, dispersed in a line running from Nova Scotia and Newfoundland to Quebec, Montreal, Crown Point, and along the New York and Pennsylvania frontiers to the Great Lakes, Detroit, and its dependent posts. Yet the Commander-in-Chief was disturbed over the thin distribution of the army over so wide an area. Consequently he proposed to Egremont that the government establish settlements at Crown Point, Niagara, and particularly Detroit, to strengthen the British hold in the interior.[17]

Unknown to Amherst, the ministry in London had decided on a permanent defense establishment of twenty battalions for the

---

1762, Add. MSS 21634, f. 102, PAC transcript. The Cherokee war which had raged in the south since 1759 had been brought to an end by October, 1761, with the aid of regular troops requested by the government of Virginia. Amherst to Gage, Oct. 1, Oct. 25, 1761, Amherst Papers, 5:103, 110, WLCL. See the copy of the address of the Virginia House of Burgesses in Fauquier to Amherst, March 13, 1761, requesting aid against the Cherokees, Enclosure in Amherst to Pitt, April 6, 1761, C. O. 5/60: 587–588.

16. Amherst to Egremont, June 15, 1762, C. O. 5/62: 241–242.

17. "State of Disposition of His Majesty's Troops serving in North America Decem[r]: 1762," C. O. 5/62: 833–834. Forts Ontario, Oswego, and the posts to Schenectady were allotted five companies of troops; Crown Point and the posts to Albany, a similar complement. Fort William Augustus and Oswegatchie (on the St. Lawrence, thirty miles below Montreal) had four companies, while Niagara had three. Fort Pitt, Presqu'isle, Sandusky, and the lesser forts of Pennsylvania were assigned five companies, while Detroit and its dependencies (Michillimackinac, La Baye, Miamis, St. Joseph, and Ouiatanon) were allotted three companies and 141 rangers. The bulk of the troops was assigned to Quebec, Montreal, Trois Rivieres, Nova Scotia, Cape Breton, and Newfoundland. The frontiers of South Carolina and Georgia were allotted three independent companies and 150 rangers. This disposition was but slightly altered in the winter of 1762–1763 when an explosion destroyed the fort at Sault Sainte Marie, and the garrison was evacuated to Michillimackinac. *Amherst Journal,* 302. See also Amherst to Egremont, Nov. 30, 1762, C. O. 5/62: 593.

new acquisitions. The Secretary-at-War, Welbore Ellis, now ordered that the Commander-in-Chief submit a plan for the garrisoning of the recently acquired territories as well as a general program for the "future Defense of North America." Economy was an important consideration, for Ellis warned Amherst that his plan was to be "as little expensive as may be consistent with Safety and sound Policy." Amherst specified two principal areas as requiring the greatest number of troops, the Mississippi River boundary and Canada. Garrisons on the Mississippi—the only possible source of enemy incursions—would guard against invasion and also control the tribes. In addition, the principal forts on the Lakes and in the back country, Newfoundland, Cape Breton, St. John's Island, and Nova Scotia, as well as Florida, all required troops.[18] It is clear from the dispositions made by Amherst, his recommendations to the ministry, and the directives

18. Egremont to Amherst, Nov. 27, 1762, C. O. 5/214: 605; Welbore Ellis to Amherst, Feb. 12, 1763, Amherst Papers, packet 43, PAC transcript. Amherst received this letter by the packet *Halifax* on April 18, and dispatched his reply by the packet *Harriot* on April 26. This point is important in that it invalidates the claim of C. W. Alvord and C. E. Carter that the document printed by them in *The Critical Period, 1763–1765* (Springfield, Ill., 1905), 5–11 (endorsed, "Plan of Forts and Garrisons proposed for the Security of North America Q.59"), was based on Amherst's answer to Ellis's request. As shown by the endorsement of the letter from the Secretary-at-War, Amherst received this communication on April 18 and did not answer until April 26. This schedule is confirmed by the entry in Amherst's journal. The *Halifax*, bearing Ellis's letter of February 18, arrived on April 18. It was the last dispatch from the Secretary-at-War, and the ship carried no communication from the Secretary of State. *Amherst Journal,* 302. It was physically impossible for the document endorsed by the Board of Trade "Q.59" to have been sent by Amherst (if indeed it was) and to have arrived in London by May 5 when Egremont enclosed this document and others in a letter to the Board of Trade by which he initiated the correspondence culminating in the Proclamation of October 7, 1763. *Journal of the Board of Trade, 1759–1763,* pp. 362–363. Copies of the document, Q.59, are in the transcripts of Board of Trade Papers, Plantations General, vol. 18, unfoliated, Historical Society of Pennsylvania, Philadelphia, and C. O. 323/16: 169 ff. Illinois Historical Survey transcript. In fact Amherst's letter to Ellis of April 26, 1763 was received by the Secretary-at-War on June 8, 1763 and transmitted by him to Egremont the next day. See Ellis to Egremont, June 9, 1763. Egremont Papers, G. D. 47, P. R. O. 30/47/25: 14, and Amherst to Ellis, April 26, 1763, Amherst Papers, packet 44, PAC transcript.

sent him by the home government that British officials were concerned with the defense of the interior and the new acquisitions, and that they did not contemplate using the royal army on the seaboard to coerce the colonists as has recently been suggested.[19]

Actually the defense establishment for America was part of a "general Plan for the Future Regulation of That Country, which is now actually under Consideration," Egremont, the Secretary of State, notified Amherst in March, 1763. In subsequent letters that year, the Secretary of State, referring to this plan, informed the Commander-in-Chief that he had exchanged some correspondence with the Board of Trade on the matter.[20] This correspondence, initiated by Egremont on May 5, 1763, led to the Proclamation of October 7, 1763, by which the British ministry promulgated a formal program for the North American wilderness. It is important to recognize that, contrary to the usual interpretation, the British ministry began considering the program later issued in the Proclamation some months *before* it consulted, simply as a matter of procedure, the Earl of Shelburne—thought to be the author of the Proclamation—and the other Commissioners of Trade.

Actually, royal officials in America during the struggle against France had instituted those elements of the Proclamation of 1763 which related to the American wilderness—military occupation of the West, a reservation for the tribes, and regulated Indian trade.

British relations with the tribes led to this program. For some time Sir William Johnson had advocated the necessity of regulated trade with the natives as the most effective means of improving and extending alliances with the Indians. The ability of the British to retain the interest of the western tribes would depend to a great extent, if not entirely, on the equitable treatment accorded them by the commanders at the interior forts. Nothing could more effectively win over those tribes traditionally

19. Robert E. Brown, *Middle-Class Democracy and the Revolution in Massachusetts, 1691–1780* (Ithaca, 1955), 172, 193, 198–199.

20. Egremont to Amherst, March 12, 1763, C. O. 5/214: 618, 621–622; Egremont to Amherst, May 21, 1763, C. O. 5/214: 639–640. Egremont to Amherst, June 8, 1763, Aug. 13, 1763, C. O. 5/214: 647–648; 667–668.

sympathetic to the French than the establishment of "free and open Trade," carried on under "proper Regulations & Restrictions . . . ." Although Amherst hesitated to adopt such a program for fear it might conflict with instructions issued in England—he thought it "prudent to wait for Directions from home on that head"—he allowed Colonel Thomas Gage at Montreal to open the western posts so that the Indians might obtain supplies.[21] In the summer of 1761, Amherst sent Johnson to Detroit to pacify the western tribes, authorizing the superintendent to issue such instructions as he deemed necessary for conducting the Indian trade. At Detroit Johnson drew up a list of regulations which he then distributed among the western garrisons. These injunctions charged the commanding officers with maintaining good relations with the natives and protecting them from any injustices. It was the responsibility of the military to see to it that civilian traders adhered strictly to the prescribed regulations. No person could engage in the trade except at a garrisoned post, and all traders must show a passport or license issued by Johnson. In spite of complaints by some traders at Fort Pitt, Johnson's system prevailed at the outposts.[22]

This system coincided with the program favored by the Secretary of State. Just two months after he assumed office, the Earl of Egremont addressed himself to the problem of Canada and the interior country. He requested "a full & particular account of the newly occupied territories" from Amherst. At the same time he expressed the government's concern at the usual treatment

21. Johnson to Amherst, Feb. 12, 1761, *Johnson Papers,* III, 330; Amherst to Johnson, Feb. 22, 1761, *ibid.*, III, 343–345; Amherst to Gage, April 26, 1761, Amherst Papers, 5:72, WLCL.

22. Amherst to Johnson, June 24, 1761, *Johnson Papers,* III, 422–423. Johnson's report to the Board of Trade is printed in "Unbound Papers," *Acts of the Privy Council, Col.,* VI, 341–342. The minutes of the proceedings of the council at Detroit are found in *ibid.*, VI, 343–347. Johnson to Bouquet, Sept. 18, 1761, *Johnson Papers,* III, 529. A copy of Johnson's instructions, issued at Fort Detroit and dated Sept. 16, 1761, is printed in *ibid.*, III, 527–528. Bouquet to Monckton, July 24, 1761; Monckton to Bouquet, Aug. 24, 1761; and Bouquet to Monckton, Oct. 5, 1761, *Michigan Pioneer and Historical Collections,* XIX (1891), 97, 106, 114.

accorded to the tribes by the British traders. According to every report, they had made "no scruple of using every low trick and Artifice to . . . cheat those unguarded Ignorant people . . . ." Egremont hardly needed to observe that the government's best interest lay in "treating the Indians upon . . . principles of Humanity & proper Indulgence . . . ." [23] Amherst transmitted Egremont's request to the military commanders in Canada. Their reports were useful later when Egremont initiated a definitive policy for the new acquisitions. The analysis of Colonel Thomas Gage was particularly significant, for his seat of government, Montreal, controlled the route to the upper country by the St. Lawrence and Ottawa rivers.

Under the French regime, the Indian trade under governmental monopoly had been the source of some revenue. Because of the large number of commissaries and factors, however, much of the income had found its way into the hands of private persons. Furthermore, the enormous cost of presents for the Indians had constituted a considerable drain. The British had abolished this monopolistic system and had removed all "incumbrances" to the traffic. In the opinion of Gage, the French system was not "worthy of our imitation," for monopoly injured the trade, the Indians paid higher prices, and, since no one regulated the traffic, the traders abused the natives. Instead of duplicating the French practice, the government should designate certain posts in the interior as the only marts for the fur trade. Merchants operating at five posts—Kaministiquia, Michillimackinac, Baye des Puans on Lake Michigan, Detroit, and Ouiatanon on the Wabash—could supply all of the tribes who had formerly trafficked with the French.[24]

Egremont used this analysis when he developed his program for the American interior. The Secretary of State indicated the outlines of his project by reconciling the Indians in the southern district. Following the advice of Henry Ellis, former governor of Georgia, he ordered the governors of the southern colonies and

23. Egremont to Amherst, Dec. 12, 1761, C. O. 5/214: 486–491.

24. Gage's report is printed in *DRCHC,* 69–71; and in *Michigan Pioneer and Historical Collections,* XIX (1891), 16–19.

the newly appointed Superintendent for the Southern District, John Stuart, to reassure the natives of a prosperous trade and a redress of their grievances.[25]

The ministry had also been careful not to antagonize the tribes by prohibiting settlement on any soil they claimed. This was a difficult task because of concerted efforts by the colonists to expand onto these lands. With the elimination of the French threat on the Ohio, some American land speculators sought to take advantage of the situation. In July, 1759, Thomas Cresap of Maryland, acting for the Ohio Company of Virginia, approached Colonel Henry Bouquet, commander at Fort Pitt, with a tempting offer—25,000 acres of the company's land in return for Bouquet's services in procuring German and Swiss settlers. Bouquet doubted the propriety of such settlements since by the Treaty of Easton, a compact the imperial government had confirmed, the British had "engaged not to settle the Lands beyond the Allegheny." Bouquet interpreted this as meaning that not only Pennsylvania but Virginia and Maryland as well had pledged that no "settlement will be permitted upon the Ohio" until the Indians had given their consent. The Ohio Company made one more appeal to Bouquet through an old comrade-at-arms, Colonel George Mercer, and finally began a lobbying campaign in London.[26] Bouquet had already prohibited settlers from Virginia and Maryland from squatting on lands along the Youghiogheny River and Redstone Creek, tributaries of the Monongahela River. In October, 1761, he issued a proclamation at

25. Egremont's directive of March 16, 1763, follows very closely—almost verbatim—the advice sent him by Ellis. See Ellis to Egremont, Dec. 15, 1762, Egremont Papers, P. R. O., G. D. 47/30/47/14: 246–247. See also on this point, Alden, *Southern Colonial Frontier,* 181. Egremont sent a copy of his instructions to the Board of Trade as an enclosure to his letter of May 5, 1763, initiating a definitive policy. C. O. 323/16: 205–211.

26. Cresap to Bouquet, July 24, 1760, Add. MSS 21645, f. 188; Bouquet to Cresap, Sept. 12, 1760, Add. MSS 21653, ff. 32–33; Mercer to Bouquet, Dec. 27, 1760, Add. MSS 21645, ff. 340–341, PAC transcripts; Resolution of the Ohio Company, September 7, 1761, printed in Lois Mulkearn (ed.), *George Mercer Papers Relating to the Ohio Company of Virginia* (Pittsburgh, 1954), 151 and Committee of the Ohio Company to Robert Dinwiddie, Sept. 9, 1761, in Kate M. Rowland, *The Life of George Mason, 1725–1792; including his speeches, public papers, and correspondence* (2 vols., New York, 1929), I, 78.

Fort Pitt reinforcing his ban. The Treaty of Easton reserved the country west of the Allegheny Mountains to the Indians for their hunting grounds. To avoid giving the natives any cause for complaint, Bouquet forbade any British subject entering the area unless he could show written permission from the Commander-in-Chief or a colonial governor.[27]

Members of the Virginia council who were interested in western lands were disturbed by Bouquet's proclamation. Amherst supported the commander at Fort Pitt, and Lieutenant Governor Fauquier gave way, especially when the government in London supported the military.[28]

Many influential Virginians were members of land speculating organizations such as the Loyal Company and the Greenbriar Company. Veterans of the French war in Virginia also were interested in western lands. In an effort to stimulate enlistments, Lieutenant Governor Robert Dinwiddie, in February, 1754, had issued a proclamation setting aside 200,000 acres for volunteers in the Virginia regiments.[29] Following the evacuation of the upper Ohio Valley by the French in the fall of 1759, two of the ranking Virginia officers, George Washington and George Mercer,

27. Bouquet to Monckton, March 20, 1761, Bouquet to Major Gates, April 22, 1761, "Aspinwall Papers," Massachusetts Historical Society *Collections*, 4th ser., IX, 397, 408. Bouquet's proclamation is in Add. MSS 21657, f. 10, PAC transcript.

28. Journal of the Virginia Council, Jan. 16, 1762, printed in *Virginia Magazine of History and Biography*, XVI (1908), 141–142; Amherst to Bouquet, Feb. 28, 1762, Add. MSS 21634, ff. 100–102; Fauquier to Bouquet, March 12, 1762, Add. MSS 21648, f. 75, PAC transcripts.

29. The Loyal Company had obtained a conditional grant of 800,000 acres along the southern Virginia frontier before the war. Its members included John Lewis, Dr. Thomas Walker, and several of the Washington family. There were no fixed boundaries between the lands claimed by this company and those of the Ohio Company; consequently the rivalry between the two groups was intense. T. P. Abernethy, *Western Lands and the American Revolution* (New York, 1937), 7–8. The Greenbriar Company was organized by John Robinson, speaker of the House of Burgesses, and by Thomas Nelson, President of the Virginia Council. Dinwiddie's proclamation dated February 19, 1754, is in C. O. 5/1348: 334–336 and Draper Collection, 1JJ20–22, Wisconsin Historical Society, Madison, Wisconsin; printed in Kenneth P. Bailey (ed.), *The Ohio Company Papers, 1753–1817, Being Primarily Papers of the "Suffering Traders" of Pennsylvania* (Arcata, Calif., 1947), 25–26.

sought to take advantage of Dinwiddie's promise. In response to a proposal from Washington, Mercer agreed to meet his fellow officer at Williamsburg in November. ". . . we will leave no stone unturned to secure to ourselves this Land," Mercer predicted.[30] The Virginia governor himself took up the matter with the home government when he broached the general question of land policy in a letter to the Board of Trade in December, 1759. Since the area between the mountains and the waters of the Ohio is "now cleared of the Enemy, people seem to be very desirous to settle on the fine fertile lands" to the West. Would the Crown now renew the large grants for western lands the government had made before the war? [31]

Due to the interdiction of French privateers, this letter of December 1, 1759, never arrived in London. Some time later, Fauquier dispatched a copy. In the interim, on March 13, 1760, Fauquier again wrote to the Commissioners of Trade requesting instructions on the point he had raised in his earlier letter which, unknown to him, had never reached its destination. The Virginia officers, including Washington and Mercer no doubt, were "pressing" that the lands about Fort Pitt be surveyed so that they might "be possessed of them . . . ." The governor had offered objections to their solicitations, however, for it was uncertain whether the lands lay in Virginia or Pennsylvania. Furthermore, it "is confidentially said," he reported, that by a treaty negotiated by General John Forbes after the capture of Fort Duquesne, the government had promised that these lands would not be opened to white settlement. General John Stanwix reportedly had confirmed this agreement, but whether these rumors "are so or not," Fauquier confessed, "we are not certain, as we have not received a Copy of either Treaty . . . ." Uncertain or not, he again pressed the matter in another letter in May, 1760. "The affair of granting the Lands on the Ohio grows every day of more importance . . . ." [32]

30. Mercer to Washington, Sept. 16, 1759, Stanislaus Hamilton (ed.), *Letters to Washington and Accompanying Papers* (5 vols., Boston, 1898–1902), II, 159.

31. Fauquier to the Board of Trade, Dec. 1, 1759, C. O. 5/1330: 51–52.

32. Fauquier to the Board of Trade, March 13, 1760, C. O. 5/1329: 399–401; Fauquier to the Board of Trade, May 12, 1760, in Henry R. McIlwaine and

By June, the Board of Trade had received Fauquier's communication of March 13, but not his earlier letter of December 1, lost en route. Consequently, Halifax and the other Commissioners of Trade could not "guess upon what grounds and Motives" Fauquier had urged "the Necessity of Settling those Lands . . . ." There was no reason at this time, they maintained, to enter into general considerations of either the propriety or the policy of the government's encouraging western settlement before the war. It was sufficient now to observe that no conflict then existed with a foreign power over the dominion of that area; nor was it then understood that the Indians claimed the lands west of the mountains. These "Questions have since envolved us in a very bloody and dangerous" war. Moreover, the tribes seemed to have ended hostilities "solely upon Our having engaged . . . not to Settle upon their hunting Grounds . . . ." Any attempt to settle on these lands—"a Measure of the most dangerous Tendency"—would constitute an "open Violation of our late solemn Engagements" with the Indians and would "infallibly" provoke them. The commissioners concluded by ordering Fauquier to take no action for settling "any Lands upon the waters of the Ohio, untill His Majesty's further pleasure be known." [33]

Halifax had explained the situation clearly, but Fauquier, who by this time had already transmitted copies of his original letter of December 1, 1759, was persistent. He had hesitated to raise the question of western lands, so he informed the Board of Trade; so much so that he had incurred the displeasure of the Virginia officers, who had allegedly registered their claims with Governor James Hamilton of Pennsylvania. Perhaps he was unduly concerned for the Virginians, but the governor persisted. "There is a Doubt arisen here" whether the Commissioners of Trade had meant to include lands on the Greenbriar and New (Kanawha) rivers in their orders prohibiting settlement. These had been "tolerably seated for some time" but the settlers had been driven off during "the late Disturbances . . . ." [34]

John P. Kennedy (eds.), *Journals of the House of Burgesses of Virginia* (13 vols., Richmond, 1905–1913), *1758–1761*, p. 284.

33. Board of Trade to Fauquier, June 13, 1760, C. O. 5/1367: 409–412.

34. Fauquier to the Board of Trade, Sept. 1, 1760, *Journal of the Virginia*

The Board of Trade avoided the dilemma raised by the fact that the settlers on the Greenbriar and Kanawha claimed their lands by legal titles granted before the war. Insufficient information prevented them from giving "any explicit Opinion," but the commissioners again stressed the principle that "whatever may in any degree, have a tendency" to alarm the Indians, or to compromise the commitments made to redress their grievances, "cannot fail of being attended with fatal Consequences." If any of the tribes claiming these lands considered settlements on them as a violation of Indian rights, then, in the opinion of the Commissioners of Trade, it would be "imprudent in the highest degree" to promote or encourage such settlements. Admittedly, if the natives relinquished title to their lands through valid negotiations, settlement on western lands would greatly benefit the security of Virginia. But the governor should make no further grants until he had informed the Board of Trade of the claims of the Indians and had received further instructions.[35]

Here is the clearest statement of the motive for channeling and controlling westward expansion. The Commissioners of Trade were not concerned with any rigid doctrine of mercantilism, nor were they operating on any abstract, theoretical principle. Practical experience with the tribes during the war conditioned their attitude. Only by reassuring the Indians of their lands could the British maintain the peace and stability of the frontier.

The policy of controlling expansion on the frontier did not apply only to Virginia, Pennsylvania, and Maryland. The colonists to the north had exerted similar pressure to open lands,

---

Burgesses, 1758–1761, p. 289; Fauquier to the Board of Trade, Dec. 6, 1760, C. O. 5/1330: 67.

35. Board of Trade to Fauquier, Feb. 17, 1761, C. O. 5/1368: 12–15. Amherst, later appointed absentee governor of Virginia, was instructed by an Order-in-Council of May 15, 1761, that, concerning the 74th article of the former general instructions "whereby the Governor was authorized to make Grants of Lands to the Westward of the great ridge of Mountains, it having been found by experience, that the Settlements made in those parts on Lands which the Indians conceived to have been reserved to them for Hunting Grounds, have been the principal Cause of those merciless Devastations which have greatly distressed the Western Frontiers of this and the other Neighbouring Colonies . . . ." C. O. 5/23: 26.

particularly along the New York frontier. During the successful campaign against the French in Canada, many officers serving under Amherst, mostly colonials, proposed projects for settlements along the northern frontier of New York.[36] In December, 1759, Amherst approved these requests and forwarded them to the proper authorities in London.[37] The Commissioners of Trade early the next year gave their qualified consent, since settlements would recompense the troops who had fought in America, and at the same time contribute to the defense of the frontier. Yet the board warned that in executing the projected settlements, the authorities must give "proper Regard to our Engagements with the Indians," in this case the powerful Six Nations, who might claim the lands in question as their hunting grounds reserved to them by "the most solemn Treaties . . . ." Four months later the board in principle approved further grants on the New York frontier, "provided such Settlements do not interfere with the Claims of Our Indian Allies . . . ." [38] At this point a conflict of motives and authority is evident. Since, in the opinion of the Commander-in-Chief in America, expansion to the north could not "but prove of the greatest Advantage," Amherst himself proposed to Lieutenant Governor Cadwallader Colden that he invite settlers into the district and assure them of a "Quiet and Peaceable Abode in their Habitations." The New York council, composed of great landowners speculating in frontier lands, considered the general's suggestion in September, and thereafter issued a proclamation opening the frontier area.[39] The New Yorkers rushed to settle on Mohawk lands in the spring and summer of 1761. The Indians were not long in complaining.

The government in London reacted quickly. On November 11,

36. See the memorial of Major Philip Skene, dated at Crown Point, Nov. 10, 1759, printed in "Colden Papers," New York Historical Society *Collections,* LIV, 303, and the memorial of General Phineas Lyman, dated Nov. 10, 1759, printed in "Fitch Papers," Connecticut Historical Society *Collections,* XVIII, 30–32.

37. Amherst to the officers, Nov. 10, 1759, *ibid.,* XVIII, 32.

38. Board of Trade to Pitt, Feb. 21, 1760, C. O. 5/7: 200–203; Board of Trade to DeLancey, June 13, 1760, *DRCHSNY,* VII, 437.

39. Amherst to Colden, Aug. 26, 1760, "Colden Papers," New York Historical Society *Collections,* LIV, 331.

1761, the Board of Trade issued a report on the situation in the Mohawk Valley. Refusing to accept the abstract principles of the policy undertaken by the government of New York, the Commissioners of Trade on practical grounds condemned its land practices as "dangerous to [the] Security" of the colonies. In the past, the Indians had taken up arms against the colonists. The primary causes for their dissatisfaction were the violations of treaties guaranteeing the tribes their hunting grounds. Consequently, the practice of granting lands before the claims of the natives had been ascertained was "a measure of the most dangerous tendency . . . ." [40]

This report led to a general ban extending to all the royal colonies. On December 3 the Privy Council issued instructions prohibiting the governors in such American colonies as were under the King's "immediate Government and where the property of the Soil is in His Majesty" from passing grants or encouraging settlements on lands "which may interfere with the Indians bordering" on these provinces. For the future, the governors must refer all applications for Indian lands to the Board of Trade.[41]

The imperial government had taken a clear stand. It held to this position in spite of pressures from the colonial governments. In attempting to controvert this policy, Fauquier based the claims of Virginia on treaties negotiated by that colony with the Indians prior to the war. To facilitate western settlement, it would be necessary to ascertain which colony had jurisdiction over the Ohio Valley. Consequently, Fauquier proposed that

40. The representation, dated November 11, 1761, is printed in "Aspinwall Papers," Massachusetts Historical Society *Collections,* 4th ser., IX, 441–447, where it is mistakenly called a Privy Council report.

41. *Acts of the Privy Council, Col.,* IV, 494–496, 500. The Order-in-Council of November 23, is in *DRCHSNY,* VII, 472–475. The circular letter to the governors is in C. O. 324/17: 164–171; printed in *DRCHSNY,* VII, 478–479 and in Frederick W. Ricord and William Nelson (eds.), *Archives of New Jersey* (36 vols., Newark, 1880–1941), 1st ser., IX, 321–328. A copy was also sent to Amherst; "Copy of an Instruction for the Governors of Nova Scotia, New Hampshire, New York, Virginia, North Carolina, South Carolina, and Georgia, forbidding them to Grant Lands or make Settlements which may interfere with the Indians bordering on those Colonys," P. R. O. War Office, 34/72: 337.

the home government appoint commissioners to determine the Virginia-Pennsylvania boundaries as a joint project with the survey of the Maryland-Pennsylvania line then under way.[42]

By this time a new Board of Trade, under Lord Sandys, had taken office, but the recently appointed commissioners followed the policy Halifax had laid down earlier. Men familiar with the situation in America supported them in testimony given during the week of April 1–8, 1762. For example, Thomas Penn, proprietor of the Quaker colony, testified that he had no intention of extending the southern boundary line of Pennsylvania into the Indian country for fear of antagonizing the natives. General John Stanwix, a veteran of the American campaigns, supported him. Founding "settlements upon the lands to the westward of the Allegheny Mountains would infallibly irritate and provoke the Indians, and might be attended with fatal consequences." [43] These sentiments confirmed the arguments Halifax had previously taken and consistently maintained. In rejecting the Virginia claims, Sandys and his fellow commissioners specifically cited Halifax's previous orders. They rejected the Virginia position by dismissing the concession "a few Indians" had made before the war. The treaties signed by the Six Nations and the Delaware at Lancaster in 1744 and at Logstown on the Ohio in 1752 were "vague and void of precision." By way of contrast, the Easton Treaty of 1758 and the commitments made since then by the King's generals were such "strong pledges on the part of the Crown and of those who hold or act under its Authority" that any new settlements would constitute a flagrant violation of the government's word. In fairly blunt terms the board ordered that for the present there were to be no further grants of Indian lands.[44]

The highest executive body in the imperial government confirmed this position. The following March, the Privy Council accepted a representation of the Board of Trade regulating the boundary between the Carolinas. The line terminated at the eastern limits of the territory claimed by the southern tribes.

42. Fauquier to the Board of Trade, Nov. 30, 1761, C. O. 5/1330: 189–193.
43. *Journal of the Board of Trade, 1759–1763,* pp. 268–269, 271.
44. Board of Trade to Fauquier, April 8, 1762, C. O. 5/1368: 199–201.

Those lands could not be settled until a final adjustment of the claims of the Indians.[45]

A complicated dispute between Connecticut and Pennsylvania threatened to undo this program. In 1753, land speculators in Wyndham, Connecticut, had formed the Susquehanna Company and had selected the Wyoming Valley of northern Pennsylvania as a site for their settlements. The following year at the Albany Congress, they had obtained a questionable deed for the land from the Six Nations. The war prohibited actual settlement, but following the cessation of hostilities, families from Connecticut planned to migrate to the Wyoming district. Such a step would violate the terms of the Treaty of Easton. When the governor of Connecticut refused to intervene, Richard Peters, the Secretary of Pennsylvania, put the matter before Amherst, the Commander-in-Chief, and Sir William Johnson, Indian Superintendent for the Northern District. The important question was not whether people from Connecticut or Pennsylvania had a right to the lands in question. A treaty confirmed by the imperial government had reserved the area to the Delaware Indians. This fact made "it a national not a provincial Cause," Peters argued. Consequently, the controversy was "not between Subject and Subject, but between Indians & Englishmen." [46] Amherst agreed. In view of the recent pledges given the tribes, the ministry would "undoubtedly be astonished to see two Provinces at this Junction disputing their Rights" and at the same time "alarmed at the Consequences" if the projected settlement would arouse the natives.[47]

The Indians reacted to the projected settlement on their lands. In the spring of 1762 Sir William Johnson conferred with the Six Nations. He reported that they were particularly uneasy over the rumor that one thousand families from Connecticut were planning to migrate to the Wyoming Valley.[48] At this point the

45. *Acts of the Privy Council, Col.*, IV, 553–554.

46. Peters to Johnson, May 18, 1761, *Pennsylvania Archives*, 1st ser., IV, 57.

47. Amherst to Hamilton, May 17, 1761, *Pennsylvania Archives*, 1st ser., IV, 51; Amherst to Fitch, May 17, 1761, Connecticut Historical Society *Collections*, XVIII, 126.

48. Johnson to Amherst, May 19, 1762, *Johnson Papers*, III, 743.

ministry in London intervened. Egremont explained the government's position to the Commander-in-Chief. In order to prevent an Indian war, the ministry was attempting "to conciliate . . . the Indian Nations, by every Act of strict Justice, and by affording them . . . Protection from any Incroachments on the Lands they have reserved to themselves, for their hunting Grounds . . . ." The Secretary of State then informed Amherst that "a Plan, for this desireable End, is actually under Consideration." [49]

This letter, written in January, 1763, proves that the British ministry was forming the basic elements of the Proclamation of 1763 some months *before* the Earl of Shelburne—the man traditionally thought responsible for that document—came to office. From the evidence noted, it is also clear that the basic elements of the Proclamation stemmed from the experiences of royal officials in America during the war in their effort to win and hold the Indian alliances, and to maintain peace on the frontier. In fact, the military in America during the war had put into operation the basic features of the Proclamation issued in October, 1763. The inadequacies of the requisition system had demonstrated the need for royal troops to garrison the wilderness and the new acquisitions. In order to pacify the Indians, Amherst and Johnson had instituted an *ad hoc* program for regulating trade at the posts. For the moment, this arrangement had replaced the system of diversified colonial regulation which had proved ineffective. Finally, the need to alleviate the resentments of the tribes over white encroachments on their lands had led to the establishment by the military of an Indian reservation beyond the mountains. The Board of Trade and the Privy Council had sanctioned this development. All that remained for the home government was to give formal expression to these measures within a comprehensive program, once the definitive Treaty of Paris legally transferred the new territories to the British Crown.

49. Egremont to Amherst, Jan. 27, 1763, "Fitch Papers," Connecticut Historical Society *Collections,* XVIII, 224; Egremont to Fitch, Jan. 27, 1763, *ibid.,* XVIII, 224–225.

CHAPTER III

A Program for the Wilderness

THE promulgation of the Proclamation of 1763 provides the historian with an insight into the operation of the governmental machinery of the first British Empire. Often scholars have written in terms of the formalistic functioning of administrative institutions such as the Board of Trade or the Privy Council. Historians have also viewed British policy for the colonies simply as a reflection of a prevailing economic doctrine, mercantilism. In so doing, they have merely examined the end product of the administrative process, the formal reports of the Commissioners of Trade, or the judgments of the Privy Council, without investigating the undercurrents of personalities and politics which operated to produce a particular program. Neither have scholars attempted in many cases to establish the origins of measures for the colonies in terms of the concrete experiences of the men who participated in policy decisions. The formulation of the Proclamation of 1763 may shed some light on the proposition that eighteenth-century British politicians were primarily administrators who arrived at particular solutions for specific problems as these issues arose. These ministers did not necessarily have any doctrinaire frame of reference, although they may have couched their decisions in the language of mercantilism. As an analysis of the Proclamation of 1763 shows, the ministers simply expressed in formal terms the practical lessons of the French and Indian War.

The various components of the program incorporated into the Proclamation—at least those relating to the North American interior—were already in operation. But when the definite Treaty of Paris confirmed the retention by Great Britain of Canada, Florida, and the Ohio Valley, the ministers had to give legal sanction to the *ad hoc* measures of the war.

Shortly after the conclusion of the treaty in February, 1763, the two Secretaries of State, Halifax and Egremont, began to consider the formal status of the newly acquired territories. In the course of their deliberations, they mentioned to William Murray, Lord Mansfield, "the necessity of a letter to the Board of Trade for their advice how the new acquisitions were to be settled . . . ." Mansfield objected to this procedure. Instead he recommended that the two secretaries devise a plan beforehand which they would then circulate among those usually consulted on policy matters. Egremont and Halifax would then send the Commissioners of Trade a public letter requesting their opinion, but instruct them privately what the commissioners were to report. Lacking sufficient information, the board might otherwise submit an "improper" plan. The result might lead to "a very unpleasant affair . . . ." Egremont did have a program for the North American wilderness; [1] whether or not he followed the

1. The King to Bute, March ?, 1763, Sedgwick, *Letters from George III to Bute,* 202–203. Among the Grenville papers in the possession of Sir John Murray, London, is a letter from Egremont to Grenville, dated March 11, 1763. Egremont wrote, "I send you a map with the forts, & divisions of Governments marked upon it; as according to the best ideas I have been able to collect, I should prepare for a rough idea of the new settlement of North America, & the West Indies after the Peace. I will be ready to explain it to you whenever you please: & shall be glad to know when I can have the honour to attend you about that . . . ." In a paper sent to Egremont on February 15, 1763, John Pownall, secretary to the Board of Trade, stated that the board was incompetent to make policy decisions and that decisions as to the new acquisitions should be referred to a select committee of the Privy Council consisting of the two Secretaries of State and the first Lord of Trade in addition to the Crown Law Officers. See Pownall's paper entitled "Questions," Egremont Papers, G. D. 47, P. R. O. 30/47/14: 236–237.

procedure Mansfield recommended we cannot determine specifically. But the evidence suggests that he did exactly as Mansfield suggested.

Certainly there was little to qualify Shelburne, President of the Board of Trade, for the task of devising colonial policy. By his own admission, he had little education, no experience, and no information at his disposal except what he might have acquired by slight observation or by chance.[2] Bute had placed Shelburne at the head of the Board of Trade purely for a set of particular political circumstances. The Scottish favorite needed someone to assure the ministry of Henry Fox's followers, and the erratic behavior of Charles Townshend made the post available to Shelburne at the last moment. With the exception of John Pownall, secretary to the board, there was nothing outstanding about the personnel of the board.[3] Except for a short interval in 1761, Pownall had served as clerk and secretary since 1745. Devoted to Halifax, he became under-secretary of state for the colonies with the creation of an American Department in 1768.

Whatever his qualifications (or lack of them), Shelburne certainly resented the minor role assigned to him. Historians have been wrong in thinking he had equal weight in colonial affairs with Egremont. Nor did Shelburne as First Lord have the power that Halifax had enjoyed when he headed the board from 1754 to 1761. An Order-in-Council of May, 1761, deprived the commissioners of the right to nominate colonial officials, and they now shared responsibility for colonial correspondence with the Secretary of State.[4] Shortly after assuming office, Shelburne complained bitterly to Bute of his inferior position. He even threatened to resign, but Bute dissuaded him. A politician as young as

2. *Life of Shelburne,* I, 11.

3. For the political connections and background of the other members of the board, see Namier, *England in the Age of the American Revolution,* 197n2, 204, 448, 457, 461, 463; and L. B. Namier, *The Structure of Politics at the Accession of George III* (2 vols., London, 1929), I, 134, 137n2, 315.

4. R. A. Humphreys, "Lord Shelburne and the Proclamation of 1763," *English Historical Review,* XLIX (1934), 243, disproves the contention of Alvord, *Mississippi Valley,* I, 140, 154, that Shelburne had full power.

Shelburne should not be "concerned at want of information or the little paltry trappings of Ministry." [5]

It is difficult to escape the conclusion that Shelburne's dissatisfaction stemmed in great part from his minor role, and that Egremont determined policy, often merely going through the formal procedure of consulting the Board of Trade. The evidence strongly suggests that Egremont laid down a preconceived program to the Commissioners of Trade when the disposition of the North American wilderness was under consideration. The Secretary of State's letters to the Commander-in-Chief prove that he was contemplating the main aspects of his program before Shelburne assumed office. Furthermore, every facet of this program was either in operation or left to the consideration of some other executive department. Shelburne and the other Commissioners of Trade had little to decide concerning the North American interior.

On May 5, 1763, less than three weeks after George Grenville had succeeded Bute as First Lord of the Treasury, Egremont sent an open directive to the Commissioners of Trade, ostensibly requesting them to report on the newly acquired territories. From the contents of this letter and from Egremont's correspondence with Jeffrey Amherst, it is clear that the Secretary of State had already decided on a comprehensive program for the American interior. Indeed, this program was already in operation. Egremont was not asking the board for a policy statement; at best, he was merely requesting the commissioners simply to contribute the details within the framework of his directive of May 5.

The Secretary of State presented three topics specifically relating to North America: the establishment of governments for the recently acquired territories, the disposition of the garrisons for defense of the continent, and, finally, the method "least Burthensome and most palatable" for the colonists in contributing to the cost of this defense system. The second point, the "Security of North America," involved protecting the area against any European power, and the preservation of internal peace

5. Shelburne to Bute, April 26, 1763, *Life of Shelburne,* I, 269–273; Bute to Shelburne, June 23, 1763, *ibid.,* I, 276.

against any Indian disturbances. The latter was the more urgent of the two; consequently, it would be necessary to maintain posts in the Indian country with the consent of the natives. But the British would conciliate the tribes by protecting their property and guaranteeing their possessions. It was essential to guard "most cautiously" against "any Invasion or Occupation of their Hunting Lands . . . ." The government could acquire their soil "by fair Purchase only . . . ." [6]

In addition to this specific directive, Egremont sent thirty-one enclosures [7] containing data on the new acquisitions from which the board might draw a definite policy. Egremont had collected this information since entering office in 1761. The list included his letter to the governors of the southern colonies on conciliating the Indians in that district and the reports of the military governors of Canada. Grenville had received copies of two especially important documents. The first, called "Plan of Forts and Garrisons proposed for the Security of North America," [8] assigned troops to specific garrisons in the new acquisitions and along the strategic waterways of the interior. Most important of all was the document entitled "Hints relative to the Division and Government of the Conquered & newly acquired Countries in America." Egremont's colonial advisor, Henry Ellis,[9] probably wrote

6. Egremont to the Board of Trade, May 5, 1763, Shelburne Papers, 49: 283–290, WLCL; printed in *DRCHC,* 93–96, *DRCHSNY,* VII, 519–520.

7. For the entire list see C. O. 323 vols. 15–16.

8. The Board of Trade copy endorsed "Q.59," C. O. 323/16: 169–185, is printed in Alvord and Carter, *Critical Period,* 5–11. Grenville's copy, entitled "Plan of Forts & Garrisons proposed for the Security of North America and the Establishment of Commerce with the Indians—The Number of Regiments, Their Stations & in what Manner the Garrisons necessary in each Fort; is to be kept up, by Detachments from the said Regiments," in Stowe Americana, Miscellaneous file, 1670–1813, HEHL.

9. MSS copies in C. O. 323/16: 189–201; Shelburne Papers, 48: 543–558, WLCL; and Stowe Collection, box 103b, HEHL. The document is printed in Verner W. Crane (ed.), "Hints Relative to the Division and Government of the Newly Acquired Countries in America," *Mississippi Valley Historical Review,* VIII, (1922), 370–373. Crane holds that Ellis was the author. He is supported by Charles Lock Mowat, *East Florida as a British Province, 1763–1784* (Berkeley, Calif., 1943), 10–12, who argues that William Knox supplied the pertinent information concerning Florida. So great was the influence of Ellis at this time that Francis Maseres, later an agent for the Canadians in London, was con-

this paper, which closely paralleled the plan the Secretary of State had previously revealed to Amherst. It called for a "Western Boundary to our ancient provinces" beyond which there was to be no settlement for the present. Migration to Nova Scotia and the South would accommodate future increase in colonial population. The officers commanding at the interior posts would have jurisdiction over the territory west of the mountains, but the courts in any of the neighboring colonies could settle disputes between civilians in the Indian reservation cognizable by law. The new governments would consist of an east and west Florida and an upper and lower Canada with the capitals at Montreal and Quebec.

The program delineated in this document and Egremont's directive of May 5 was not unique. It merely reflected the *ad hoc* measures the military commanders and the Indian superintendents had instituted in America some time before. Egremont had already described the basic aspects of this plan to the Commander-in-Chief in America. It is highly improbable that the Board of Trade would deviate from the Secretary of State on any major point of consideration. Consequently, we may infer that Egremont had privately informed the board of the policy expected, or that he merely allowed the Commissioners of Trade to fill in the details of the program already developed during the war.

There is little to indicate that Shelburne was able to undertake an independent policy. He was not qualified for such a task. The evidence from which to glean an understanding of his ideas on the colonial problem in 1763—if indeed he had any—is scanty. The only significant document in his own hand found among his papers merely paraphrases the language of Egremont's directive of May 5.[10] At this time Shelburne's knowledge of the

vinced that Ellis drew up the Proclamation of 1763. Maseres to Fowler Walker, Nov. 19, 1767. William S. Wallace (ed.), *Maseres Letters, 1766–1768* (Toronto, 1919), 62. It was later said in Quebec that a copy of the Proclamation, in Ellis's handwriting, was seen before it was published, and that at the time, Ellis was the "oracle of the ministry for all American matters." Maseres to Walker, Aug. 11, 1768, *ibid.*, 99.

10. Shelburne Papers, 50: 37–41, WLCL. It is headed in a different hand,

colonies was largely derived from information he received after his appointment to the Board of Trade.[11] Almost certainly, Egremont supplied the information relating to the Proclamation of 1763.

The Board of Trade had little to decide concerning the North American interior. Under the supervision of George Grenville, the Treasury was dealing with the question of revenue for the defense establishment. The ministry had already approved of the *ad hoc* arrangement for regulating the Indian trade, and it had accepted the prohibition of settlement west of the mountains. In July, 1763, the Secretary-at-War informed Shelburne that the Commander-in-Chief in America, not the Board of Trade, would determine the disposition of the garrisons. Amherst was much better qualified than any of the ministers in London for this task.[12] What was there for Shelburne and the other Commissioners of Trade to decide? Every major point raised by Egremont in his directive either lay with some other department or was then in operation. It is little wonder that the Board of Trade took such a short time in considering an answer to Egremont's letter, for on May 27, after only three weeks, it decided on a representation. Before the end of the month, John Pownall drew up a draft of their report.[13]

---

probably Lauchlin MacLeane's, later his secretary, "Ld. Shelburne's Remarks on the Cession made by France and Spain, and the commercial advantages that maybe [*sic*] derived therefrom."

11. Humphreys, "Shelburne and the Proclamation," *English Historical Review,* XLIX (1934), 244. There are several unsigned and undated documents in Shelburne's papers bearing on the problem of the new acquisitions at this time, but it is extremely improbable that they originated with the President of the Board of Trade. The paper entitled "Hints respecting the civil establishments in the American colonies" (Shelburne Papers, 48: 518–520, WLCL) argues for a restriction of settlement and an imperial system of regulated Indian trade. In a similar vein is "Hints respecting the Settlement of our American Colonies," *ibid.,* 48: 475–487, and the appended "Hints respecting the Military Establishment for the American Colonies," *ibid.,* 48: 488–499. The document "Some thoughts on the Settlement and Government of our Colonies in North America," *ibid.,* 48: 525–542, dated March 10, 1763, predates Shelburne's entry into office.

12. Ellis to Shelburne, July 31, 1763, Shelburne Papers, 49: 609–611, WLCL.

13. *Journal of the Board of Trade, 1759–1763,* p. 368.

There was nothing startling in what Pownall wrote. After all, as secretary to the board, he had drafted letters for Halifax on this very problem. He cited the various commitments made to the tribes by the Treaty of Easton, the pledges given by the military at Fort Pitt, and by Sir William Johnson at Detroit in 1761. Any settlements in the interior would constitute a breach of these engagements with the Indians, and would "naturally excite in them a Jealousy and Disgust that might prove of fatal Consequence . . . ." For the present, white settlement must not, therefore, extend beyond the sources of those rivers discharging directly into the Atlantic and the Gulf of Mexico. The area west of the mountains "should be considered as Lands belonging to the Indians," and protected by military garrisons. Under a uniformly regulated system, all British subjects would have the right to trade with the tribes.

For the moment Pownall deferred a detailed consideration of Indian trade regulations and the military establishment. Actually, the Board of Trade need not have concerned itself with the defense problem, for, as Welbore Ellis, the Secretary-at-War, notified Shelburne, the ministry had left this question to the discretion of the Commander-in-Chief in America.

Although Pownall had laid down a general statement for restricting settlement at the mountains, he noted a few exceptions. Some tribes claimed lands east of the barrier, while the whites under the jurisdiction of Virginia had occupied land between the forks of the Ohio and the Great Kanawha before the war. Admitting that he had little knowledge of the Gulf district, he concurred with Egremont's proposal to establish two colonies in Florida and recommended a survey to ascertain the claims of the Indians in that area. For financial reasons, Pownall took exception, however, to Egremont's plan of creating two separate provinces in Canada. He would create one government, Quebec, and would limit that new colony on the west and southwest at the sources of the streams flowing into the Ottawa River.[14]

14. "Mr Pownal[l]'s Sketch of a Report concerning the Cessions in Africa and America at the Peace of 1763," Shelburne Papers, 49: 333–363, printed in Humphreys, "Shelburne and the Proclamation," *English Historical Review,* XLIX (1934), 258–264.

An analysis of Pownall's draft report for the Commissioners of Trade shows that the secretary had merely buttressed the general policy laid down in Egremont's directive of May 5 and the enclosed "Hints." Delineating a specific boundary line agreed upon with the tribes during the war, he differed with Egremont only on the division of Canada into two governments.

The Commissioners of Trade did not tarry long on their report. By June 3 they had agreed on a draft. Apparently Maurice Morgann, Shelburne's private secretary, aided in composing the final document, which was signed on June 8. It was merely an enlarged and revised version of Pownall's "Sketch." The commissioners had added a lengthy preface on the advantages of the new acquisitions, especially an expanded fur trade conducted under regulations enforced by the military. As was to be expected in dealing with the North American interior, the Board of Trade did approve maintaining the wilderness as an Indian reservation. The line of the Ottawa River and Lake Nipising would limit Canada so as to leave the tribes in possession of the upper country under the protection of royal garrisons. In addition to Canada, the Floridas and the West Indies required established governments. Population could flow into these new colonies. Under the proper regulations, all British subjects could trade with the tribes at the garrisoned posts in the Indian country. This system would protect the trade, insure good treatment for the natives, uphold British sovereignty, and aid in the defense of the continent. For the present, the commissioners deferred dealing with the questions of specific regulations for the Indian trade, troop dispositions, and revenue to finance the new establishment. Well they might, for the last two points were not their concern. On only two minor points did they disagree with the program Egremont had presented. They would establish only one government in Canada instead of the two proposed by the Secretary of State, and they would not grant to any province the civil jurisdiction over the Indian country as he had recommended.[15]

15. *Journal of the Board of Trade, 1759–1763,* p. 368; Humphreys, "Shelburne and the Proclamation," *English Historical Review,* XLIX (1934), 250; C. O. 324/21: 245–290; Shelburne Papers, 49: 365–395, WLCL, printed in *DRCHC,* 97–107.

Little more than an elaboration of the program presented by Egremont, this report of June 8, 1763, logically followed from the policy evolved during the war as outlined by the Secretary of State and further delineated in the draft by Pownall, who was familiar with the program sanctioned by Halifax several years before. Consequently, Egremont's general response to this document on July 14 was favorable.[16] Yet, he noted, "great Inconveniences might arise" in leaving the interior outside "the Civil Jurisdiction" of some government. Fugitives from the law might escape into the area, or foreign powers could lay claim to the territory as "derelict lands." Unless the board could suggest some other arrangement, he proposed assigning Canada civil jurisdiction over the interior but reserving the exclusive use of the land to the tribes. The policy of restricting white settlement on Indian territory offered no difficulty. At this time Egremont ordered the Commissioners of Trade to prepare instructions for the governors of "ancient Colonies" prohibiting them from passing grants for lands beyond the boundary. In order that the board might develop a permanent plan for Indian affairs, Egremont granted the commissioners permission to correspond with the superintendents in America, but he denied their request to correspond with the Commander-in-Chief on the military establishment.[17]

On August 5, the commissioners dispatched instructions to the superintendents to correspond regularly with them concerning Indian affairs.[18] At the same time, they submitted a further report to the Secretary of State objecting to his proposal for assigning any established colony, especially Canada, jurisdiction over the Indian country. This procedure might confirm the suspicions of the Indians that the British claimed the territory only on the basis of the cession by France. For the sake of British

16. It should be noted that Egremont came to a cabinet meeting on July 8 with a prepared draft of his reply to the Board of Trade report. His answer was approved by the cabinet without alteration. See the minute headed "At the Duke of Cumberlands late Lodgings," July 8, 1763, Grenville-Murray papers.

17. Egremont to the Board of Trade, July 14, 1763, C. O. 323/16: 319–325; Shelburne Papers, 49: 319–322, WLCL, printed in *DRCHC*, 108–109.

18. Board of Trade to Johnson, Aug. 5, 1763, C. O. 5/1130: 215.

prestige, it was imperative that the tribes be disabused of this notion. Furthermore, if the government of Quebec exercised legal jurisdiction over the interior country, the Canadians would enjoy an unfair advantage in the fur trade. Finally, by the proposal put forth by Egremont, the governor of Quebec would become virtual commander-in-chief, since he would exercise authority over the troops and garrisons. Consequently, the Commissioners of Trade recommended empowering Amherst by royal commission to send fugitives and criminals to their respective colonies for trial. They also proposed issuing a proclamation to assure the Indians of the government's intention to protect their rights by restricting settlements on their lands and providing an equitable trade program.[19]

Thus having fulfilled their duty in submitting this supplementary report of August 5, the Commissioners of Trade proceeded on their summer holiday, in spite of the fact than an Indian war—Pontiac's rebellion—was then raging in America.

There was no rest for Shelburne, however. Discontented with his inferior role, he promptly began intriguing to upset the ministry and thus better his own position. George III had justifiably referred to him as a man who "when dissatisfy'd will go any lengths . . . ." [20] Shelburne's future looked all the more bright when Egremont died of an apopletic stroke on August 21. With the cabinet post now vacant, Shelburne "postule le ministere," but, as one wit put it, he ought to be given the position "as you marry boys under age, and then send them to travel till they are ripe!" [21] Shelburne's hopes lay with the formation of a new ministry under William Pitt. But the King would not accept Pitt's excessive demands. Grenville now had the upper hand, but he did not immediately learn the full details of Shelburne's attempt to

19. The board's representation, dated August 5, 1763, in C. O. 42/24: 107–111, PAC transcript; in the Shelburne Papers, 49: 327–332, under the title "A Report from the Lords of Trade concerning that part of North America which lies to the West of the Old Colonies and which was acquired at the Peace in 1763," printed in *DRCHC,* 110–111.

20. The King to Bute, June 18, 1762, Sedgwick, *Letters from George III to Bute,* 117–118.

21. Horace Walpole to Sir Horace Mann, Sept. 1, 1763, Mrs. Paget Toynbee (ed.), *Letters of Horace Walpole* (16 vols., Oxford, 1903–1905), V, 364.

replace the ministry. Anticipating that Grenville would uncover his role in the political crisis, Shelburne resigned early in September. In the realignment that followed, the Earl of Hillsborough took the post vacated by Shelburne, while the Earl of Sandwich replaced Halifax, who had assumed Egremont's duties.

After a month's interruption, the reconstituted administration was ready to resume the affairs of state. According to Sandwich, the ministers felt "fully prepared to stand examination" regarding that "important and extensive branch of Business," the colonies. They would immediately issue a proclamation on the new acquisitions. If there had been any delay, "it will appear that it was chiefly owing to . . . Shelburne's intriguing disposition," and to the fact that, as First Lord of Trade, he "chose rather to draw up representations that might occasion contest and differences of opinion" with Egremont.[22] Shelburne now had to reap the seeds of discord he had sown.

The cabinet ministers now acted quickly to complete the program for the new acquisitions. On September 16, they voted almost unanimously to issue a proclamation. Only Grenville raised a minor objection.[23] Three days later, Halifax incorporated their decision in a letter to the Board of Trade. The cabinet had accepted the arguments of the board in their representation of August 5, against extending the jurisdiction of Quebec over the Indian country. In other respects, the proclamation would follow the points previously determined. Whites could neither settle on nor privately purchase Indian lands. Under licenses and proper security, all British subjects could engage

22. Sandwich to Holland, Sept. 26, 1763, [Giles Stephen Holland Fox-Strangways] Earl of Ilchester, *Letters to Henry Fox Lord Holland with a few Additional to his Brother, Stephen, Earl of Ilchester* (London, 1915), 181.

23. See the minute of the cabinet dated Sept. 16, 1763, Grenville-Murray papers. Attending were the Lord President, Grenville, and the Earls of Halifax, Gower, Sandwich, and Egmont. A revealing marginal note on this document reads as follows: "Some Objections were made to this Plan of not including all the Territory ceded by the late Treaty to Great Britain in Some of ye Governments & likewise to the line beyond which the Lands *for the Present* are reserved to the Indians which is to be declared by Proclamation issued *here* but as these were doubts rais[e]d by Mr Grenville only agst. Ld Halifax's Opinion as well as that of ye other Lords they were no further insisted upon."

in a regulated trade. Military officials and Indian agents could return criminals and fugitives from the Indian country to the seaboard colonies for legal judgment. For the present, however, the Commander-in-Chief would not receive a commission under the Great Seal to exercise jurisdiction over the interior. The government might take such a step later should it prove necessary. Finally, Halifax instructed the commissioners to begin formulating specific regulations for the Indian trade.[24]

Under Hillsborough the board acted quickly. The commissioners read Halifax's letter at their initial meeting under the new first lord. Within three days they transmitted a draft document to the Attorney General. After some slight verbal alteration, the Privy Council approved the proclamation on October 5, and it received the royal signature two days later.[25] The Board of Trade transmitted copies to officials in the colonies on October 11 by the New York packet.[26] Thus the British ministry hoped by a formal policy to preserve the peace of the frontier by conciliating the Indians. The provisions of the proclamation were entirely compatible with the policy Egremont had outlined in May. The sequence of documents exchanged by the governmental

24. Halifax to the Lords of Trade, Sept. 19, 1763, *DRCHC,* 112–113; *Calendar of Home Office Papers, George III,* I, 303–304.

25. *Journal of the Board of Trade, 1759–1763,* pp. 381, 384–385; *Acts of the Privy Council, Col.,* IV, 573. The text of the Proclamation is printed in *DRCHC,* 119–123; and in *Annual Register,* VI (1763), 208–213.

26. Board of Trade to Hillsborough, Oct. 10, 1763, C. O. 324/17: 303. The circular letter from the Board of Trade, dated October 10, 1763, is in C. O. 324/17: 304–305. It should be noted for later reference that Governor Fauquier wrote to Halifax on Jan. 31, 1764, C. O. 5/1345: 115–117 acknowledging receipt of the Proclamation.

Alvord argued that Shelburne was the official most responsible for the formation of policy but that his was not the pen that wrote the final pronouncement. He further charged that, due to changes in Shelburne's policy effected by Halifax, the latter must assume the responsibility for blunders written into the document. *Mississippi Valley,* I, 195, 199. In the first place, it has been shown that Egremont was responsible for policy, and that there was no break in continuity or consistency in the documents issued between May and October, 1763. Finally, Humphreys, "Shelburne and the Proclamation," *English Historical Review,* XLIX (1934), 242, has demonstrated that if there were any blunders in drafting the Proclamation after his resignation, Shelburne was not aware of them, but accepted the policy.

North America and the Proclamation of 1763. From *The Annual Register*, 1763, 5th ed., London, 1782.

departments discloses no major inconsistency. Further, Egremont had already indicated the basic provisions for the plan in his letters to Amherst as early as January, 1763. Indeed, the provisions of the proclamation relating to the American wilderness formally sanctioned the commitments made to the tribes during the French and Indian War—commitments which were actually in operation during the last years of the conflict.

Yet the royal pronouncement only partially fulfilled the policy initiated by Egremont. The most pressing problem in the fall of 1763 was restoring the British alliance with the natives broken by the Indian uprising under Pontiac earlier that year. Halifax was hopeful that the "Measures of Equity and Moderation" contained in the proclamation would accomplish this by restraining "unjust Settlement and fraudulent Purchase" of Indian lands and suppressing "unfair Practices in the trade." The Board of Trade was considering a uniform plan for free trade at the posts, he informed Amherst, the harried commander in America. These measures, in conjunction with the ten thousand troops, would, Halifax felt, insure "the internal Peace and Security of that Continent." [27]

As long as the Indians remained hostile, however, Amherst could make no permanent arrangement for the defense of America.[28] Furthermore, Pontiac's rebellion made a deep impression on British military officers, and these men were influential later in determining policy for the wilderness.

It is impossible to determine with certainty the causes of the widespread outbreak among the northern and western tribes in the spring and summer of 1763. The Indians themselves left no reliable records. Consequently, the historian must reconstruct the narrative from the impressions of whites, many of whom were partisan. They offered many reasons for the Indian rebellion. During the height of the crisis, Lieutenant Governor Fauquier of Virginia maintained that the tribes had revolted in resentment over unauthorized settlements on their lands. He had heard that a proposed interior colony, New Wales, advertised in the *Pennsylvania Gazette* that April, "gave great offence to the In-

27. Halifax to Amherst, Oct. 11, 1763, C. O. 5/214: 689–690.
28. Ellis to the Board of Trade, Oct. 19, 1763, C. O. 323/17: 17.

dians." At Detroit, Major Henry Gladwin was under the impression that disaffected Canadians and French traders inspired the uprising. Amherst himself thought it not impossible that the French traders had gone to great lengths in attempting to engross the fur trade by excluding their British rivals. From Montreal, Gage reported that the French, Canadians, and Spaniards had stirred up the Indians by circulating rumors that the English planned to deprive the natives of their lands.[29] Apparently the ejection of the French and Spanish from the eastern half of the continent acted as a catalyst to Indian resentment. Governor Thomas Boone of South Carolina reported that the southern tribes were restless over the elimination of the Bourbons. The natives refused to recognize the right of the British to take over Spanish and French holdings which the tribes had never ceded. In the north, George Croghan related a similar attitude: the Indians were complaining that the French had no right "to give away their country . . . ."[30]

Rumors of an Indian outbreak found the Commander-in-Chief in America in an awkward position. Amherst had not as yet received final word as to the number of troops at his disposal.[31] Consequently, he could not make final arrangements for the occupation of the frontier posts.[32] Liaison between officials in

29. Fauquier to the Board of Trade, July 8, 1763, C. O. 5/1330: 511–512; Fauquier to Egremont, July 27, 1763, C. O. 5/1345: 87. For the details of the ambitious, but ill conceived, colony of New Wales see the *Pennsylvania Gazette* for April 21, 1763. The scheme was suppressed by Amherst within a week. See W. Hicks to Benjamin Franklin, n.d., Carl Van Doren (ed.), *Letters and Papers of Benjamin Franklin and Richard Jackson, 1753–1785* (Philadelphia, 1947), 207, and Franklin to Jackson, June 10, 1763, *ibid.*, 105. See also John C. Webster (ed.), *The Journal of Jeffrey Amherst* (Chicago and Toronto, 1931), 315, and Gage to Egremont, Aug. 28, 1763, C. O. 42/24: 192, PAC transcript.

30. Boone to Egremont, June 1, 1763, Shelburne Papers, 49: 255–257, WLCL; Croghan to Amherst, April 30, 1763, Add. MSS 21634, f. 235, PAC transcript; Croghan to Johnson, March 12, 1763, Ayer Collection, the Newberry Library, Chicago.

31. On April 7, 1763, Lt. Col. James Robertson wrote Loudoun that "The establishment to be made here, is Unknown to Sir Jeffrey . . . ." Loudoun Papers, LO 6332, HEHL.

32. Bouquet to Sharpe, May 21, 1763, Add. MSS 21634, f. 262, PAC transcript; Amherst to Bouquet, May 15, 1763, Add. MSS 21634, f. 247, PAC transcript.

England was poor. Not until May 10 did the Secretary-at-War send orders to the commanders in Guadeloupe and Havana to embark their troops for New York and the Gulf Coast.[33] In America the only reserves available to meet the crisis were those quartered on Long Island, three depleted regiments previously sent from Havana "to save the trouble of burying them there." These men were "but convalescents" and only about five hundred were fit to march.[34] As late as June 18, Egremont was still unable to inform Amherst of the final decision on the American military establishment. He promised to do so by the next packet,[35] but this was little consolation to the harassed Commander-in-Chief.

By the middle of June, as one isolated post after another fell before the Indian onslaught, Colonel Henry Bouquet warned Amherst that "The Panic appears general on the Frontiers."[36] Having committed the last of his reserves to the Pennsylvania frontier by June 25, Amherst informed the governors of Pennsylvania, Rhode Island, Connecticut, and New Hampshire of the situation, requesting that their assemblies raise troops for garrison duty so that the regulars might be relieved for the protection of the upper country.[37] In order to deprive the Indians of munitions, Amherst and Gage imposed an embargo on the Indian trade.[38] But these measures had little immediate effect. On July 7, Amherst learned that Presqu'isle had been sur-

33. Welbore Ellis to Dalrymple, May 10, 1763; Ellis to Keppel, May 10, 1763, Shelburne Papers, 49: 613, 621, WLCL. As late as the final week in June the last orders received in New York concerning the troops at Havana were dated March 19. Robertson to Loudoun, June 25, 1763, Loudoun Papers, LO 6337, HEHL.

34. Robertson to Loudoun, June 25, 1763, Loudoun Papers, LO 2337, HEHL.

35. Egremont to Amherst, June 18, 1763, Amherst Papers, 1:19, WLCL.

36. Bouquet to Amherst, June 16, 1763, Add. MSS 21634, f. 282, PAC transcript.

37. A copy of Amherst's circular letter, dated June 17, 1763, is printed in "Fitch Papers," Connecticut Historical Society *Collections,* XVIII, 241–242.

38. Amherst to Bouquet, June 29, 1763, *Michigan Pioneer and Historical Collections,* XIX (1891), 203; Gage to Egremont, Aug. 28, 1763, C. O. 42/24: 193, PAC transcript. By September, however, the trade in the south was resumed by order of Lt. Col. James Robertson at St. Augustine. John Stuart to Amherst, Oct. 6, 1763, Amherst Papers, 3:60, WLCL.

rendered, Venango destroyed, and LeBoeuf evacuated.[39] He now sent a sharp letter to the governor of Pennsylvania describing the plight of the "Poor Families, who have Abandoned their Settlements," and stressing the "Danger that the whole Province is Threatened with." He urged that the assembly "Exert Themselves *like* Men" and raise a garrison for the frontier while the regulars undertook a punitive expedition against the tribes. Amherst was "persuaded that fear is the only motive" which would keep the Indians in line. His honor and military reputation at stake, he was determined "to take Signal Satisfaction for their unprovoked insults." [40] These were but empty words. The worst was still to come. Almost all of the upper posts, Michillimackinac, Ouiatanon, Sandusky, and St. Joseph had fallen in the first onslaught.[41]

The expected reinforcements proved to be of little value. On July 20, Amherst learned that four of the West Indian regiments had been sent to garrison the Gulf Coast. The five regiments from the Caribbean sent to New York consisted mainly of invalids and men entitled to discharge. He then transferred the bulk of these to the Canadian garrisons, in spite of the fact that the Indians in the Montreal district up to this time had not taken part in the insurrection. Weakened by disease, the West Indian forces were not fit for strenuous duty. Amherst might have felt that the French, whom he suspected of instigating the tribes, needed watching.[42]

39. *Amherst Journal,* 310.

40. Amherst to Hamilton, July 7, 1763, *Bouquet Papers,* 21634, p. 211; Robertson to Loudoun, June 25, 1763, Loudoun Papers, LO 6337, HEHL.

41. *Amherst Journal,* 314–316. For the disposition of the troops in August see Amherst's report endorsed as dispatched on August 13: "Disposition of His Majesty's Forces in North America, Aug: 1763," Amherst Papers, 3:81, WLCL. A copy taken from C. O. 323/17: 45–46 is printed without date in Alvord and Carter, *Critical Period,* 14–17.

42. *Amherst Journal,* 311, 314, 317; Gage to Egremont, July 21, 1763, C. O. 42/24: 142, PAC transcript. The poor condition of the West Indian troops probably accounts for the fact that Amherst stationed them in the Canadian maritime provinces rather than employing them against the tribes. This would seem to be a more plausible explanation than that given by Charles S. Grant, "Pontiac's Rebellion and the British Troop Moves of 1763," *Mississippi Valley Historical Review,* L (1953), 83, to the effect that

Relief did not come to the harried commander until the last week of August, 1763, when he learned that Colonel Henry Bouquet, leading a relief expedition to Fort Pitt, had won the decisive battle of Bushy Run on August 5.[43] More determined than ever to crush the Indians, Amherst threatened to take measures "that in the end will put a most effectual stop to their *very being.*"[44] His attitude toward the tribes now conditioned the plans he made for the disposition of the military forces in America. Before the outbreak of the Indian war, Amherst had decided to demolish the smaller forts, but he was now determined "not to give up a Single Post" that would enable the British to control the Indian country. Once the uprising had been put down, the army would reoccupy all the area lost to the incursions of the tribes.[45] But with the approach of autumn, the opportunity for a large-scale operation was limited. After some procrastination, Amherst finally issued calls for colonial troops to undertake a campaign the next season. For some reason, he neglected to call on the New England provinces. This oversight later proved embarrassing to his successor as Commander-in-Chief, General Thomas Gage, for the middle colonies could refuse to fulfill the quotas expected of them on the grounds that the New Englanders were contributing nothing.

In general, the response of the colonial legislatures to the call for troops to put down the Indian rebellion was far from satisfactory. To British officials, it confirmed the need of royal garrisons to defend the frontier. For example, the laxness of the colonial assemblies in raising soldiers distressed Halifax, who ordered Amherst to press the issue with the governors. But the Commander-in-Chief was not to give the assemblies "the least hope or Expectation" of any reimbursement for the expenditures

---

Amherst's action in this respect stemmed from his underestimating the Indian threat.

43. *Amherst Journal,* 316–317.

44. Amherst to Johnson, Aug. 27, 1763, *DRCHSNY,* VII, 545.

45. Amherst to Johnson, Sept. 10, 1763, *Johnson Papers,* IV, 202; Amherst to Bouquet, Aug. 7, 1763, *Bouquet Papers,* 21634, p. 238; and Amherst to Gage, Nov. 17, 1763, Clarence E. Carter (ed.), *Correspondence of General Thomas Gage* (2 vols., New Haven, 1931–1933), II, 211.

they would make "for their own defence . . . ."[46] Amherst did not have to deal with the vexatious problem of securing colonial aid or subduing the Indians, for the approaching winter temporarily halted military operations. After leaving instructions for his successor,[47] Amherst departed from America in November, never to return. His inability to cope with the native uprising had tarnished the glory he had won by the conquest of New France. He left the colonies embittered toward the tribes. In the years to come, however, he played an important part in determining policy for the American interior.

The task of raising troops to take the field against the tribes in 1764 fell to General Thomas Gage, who soon encountered resistance by many colonial legislatures. Facing no immediate danger themselves, some of the provincial assemblies were extremely adverse to complying with the demand for men to campaign on the frontier. Amherst had neglected to call on the New England legislatures; consequently, the assemblies of New York and New Jersey deferred action until the northern colonies made their contributions.[48] Repeating the call for men, Gage received only a limited response. New York agreed to raise half the troops requested, while New Jersey reluctantly contributed a proportionate number.[49] At first Connecticut refused any aid. The

46. Halifax to Amherst, Oct. 19, 1763, Amherst Papers, 6:99, 101, WLCL; Halifax to John Penn, Oct. 18, 1763, C. O. 5/1280: 269–270; Halifax to Fitch, Oct. 19, 1763, "Fitch Papers," Connecticut Historical Society *Collections,* XVIII, 256–257.

47. Amherst to Gage, Nov. 17, 1763, *Gage Correspondence,* II, 216; Gage to Horatio Sharpe, Nov. 25, 1763, Huntington Miscellaneous, HM 25041, HEHL.

48. William Franklin to the Board of Trade, Dec. 5, 1763, *Archives of New Jersey,* 1st ser., IX, 398–399; John Watts to Sir William Baker, Nov. 15, 1763, "Watts Letter Book," New York Historical Society, *Collections,* LXI, 196.

49. Watts to Monckton, Dec. 10, 1763, "Watts Letter Book," New York Historical Society *Collections,* LXI, 206. It was only by the pressure of Governor Franklin that the New Jersey Assembly was prevailed upon to delete a clause in the enabling act which would have restrained their grant until a majority of the eastern colonies had agreed to contribute troops. As it was, the legislature made its grant contingent on the action of New York. Franklin to Halifax, March 6, 1764, *Archives of New Jersey,* 1st ser., IX, 431.

danger to the colony was remote, and according to rumor, the tribes were already suing for peace.[50] By the spring of 1764, Connecticut, New York, and New Jersey had offered some troops, but, as a member of the New York council bitterly complained, "all to the Southward" there was "a clear Blank . . . ."[51]

Gage implored the governors of Maryland, Pennsylvania, and Virginia to raise colonials for garrison duty so that the regulars might be free to take the offensive. But even when they did enroll, provincial troops were unreliable.[52] Bouquet noted sarcastically that of the 950 men sent by Pennsylvania to take part in the campaign of 1764, 200 had deserted even before operations had begun. The provincials continued to desert even on the march with the additional loss of the horses and arms which they carried off with them. Bouquet swore he would never again "depend upon new[ly] raised troops."[53]

In spite of the handicaps faced by the British command in coordinating the colonial and English forces, in the final analysis Indian resistance proved remarkably ineffective. The tribes were unable to unite for a sustained war and lacked sufficient munitions. In the fall of 1764, one British column headed by Bouquet operated along the Ohio. Another under the command of John Bradstreet toured the Lakes to Detroit. Of the two, Bouquet was the more effective in chastising the natives, but no major engagement was necessary to reoccupy the western forts. To all intents,

50. See the report of the committee of the General Assembly dated Jan. 19, 1764, "Fitch Papers," Connecticut Historical Society *Collections,* XVIII, 274–275; also Fitch to Halifax, March 23, 1764, *ibid.,* XVIII, 279–280.

51. Watts to Monckton, April 14, 1764, "Watts Letter Book," New York Historical Society *Collections,* LXI, 243. That summer, Bouquet in Philadelphia complained that, while the Virginians, who did not have nearly as much at stake, were volunteering in great numbers, "not a single man of this Province has hitherto offered himself." Bouquet to John Harris, July 29, 1764, *Michigan Pioneer and Historical Collections,* XIX (1891), 268.

52. Gage to Penn, April 3, 1764, *Pennsylvania Archives,* 1st ser., IV, 171–172; Gage to Sharpe, April 4, 1764, *Maryland Archives,* XIV, 153; Gage to Bouquet, Aug. 18, 1764, *Michigan Pioneer and Historical Collections,* XIX (1891), 269.

53. Bouquet to Penn, Aug. 22, 1764, *Pennsylvania Archives,* 1st ser., IV, 206; Bouquet to Gage, Sept. 5, 1764, *Michigan Pioneer and Historical Collections,* XIX (1891), 273.

the Indian rebellion was at an end. No matter how futile had been the attempt of the western tribes to drive the British out of the interior, their brief but savage uprising had a marked effect on British military officers and other officials. These men were later influential in determining policy for Indian affairs and the disposition of the garrisons in the wilderness.

Because the Indians had been relatively successful in bypassing the forts—the keystone to the defense system established and retained by Amherst—Gage now argued that the government should establish a series of military colonies on the frontier, especially at Niagara and Fort Pitt. "We may by such means," he advised Halifax, "become formidable on the Ohio . . . ." Bouquet concurred. "I wish the Plan of a Military Frontier could be put into Execution," he wrote Benjamin Franklin.[54] The lessons of the Indian war were not lost on other influential officers. The system of garrisoned forts seemed to have been almost completely ineffective in controlling the tribes. Colonel William Eyre, chief military engineer in America, on returning from Niagara in 1764, advocated a partial withdrawal of the exposed garrisons. Particularly bitter about the French in the interior, Eyre wanted to "remove every Canadian" from the outposts to the inhabited "Parts of Canada . . . to prevent their doing Mischief . . . ." Sir William Johnson agreed with him on almost every point.[55] Others shared their sentiments. So great was the reaction of some officials against the French for their imagined perfidy during the Indian uprising that Governor James Murray of Quebec actually proposed to Halifax evacuation of the thousand families from the interior and settling them on lands in Quebec. The Secretary of State transmitted this drastic

54. Gage to Halifax, April 14, 1764, *Gage Correspondence,* I, 24–25. A copy of this letter was sent to the Board of Trade on May 23, 1764, C. O. 323/19: 581–582; see also Gage to Bouquet, May 14, 1764, *Michigan Pioneer and Historical Collections,* XIX (1891), 257–258, and Gage to Johnson, May 16, 1764, *Johnson Papers,* IV, 425. See also Bouquet to Franklin, Aug. 22, 1764, Franklin Papers, I, 2, no. 94, APSL.

55. Eyre to Johnson, Jan. 7, 1764, Stanley M. Pargellis (ed.), *Military Affairs in North America, 1748–1765: Selected Documents from the Cumberland Papers in Windsor Castle* (New York, 1936), 455–457. Johnson to Eyre, Jan. 19, 1764, *ibid.,* 458.

scheme to the Board of Trade,[56] but the imperial government could not adopt this harsh expedient simply because the French inhabitants held their lands by titles issued during the French regime. By the terms of the Treaty of Paris of 1763, the British Crown had recognized the property rights of the new subjects. Whether or not the French inhabitants had played a part in instigating the Indian revolt of 1763, the British ministry had to evolve some defense system for the interior while tolerating the French in the vicinity of the forts.

Pontiac's rebellion had disrupted the troop dispositions Amherst had established. While other military officials recognized the inadequacy of his defense arrangement, Amherst had insisted that Gage reoccupy the posts and forts in the Indian country. In spite of the Indian war, for the present the military in America confirmed the defense program which had formed one aspect of the policy Egremont had instituted in 1763.

The ministry had left unfinished another facet of Egremont's program for the interior when it issued the Proclamation in October. The Board of Trade still had to devise a detailed program for managing Indian affairs—a problem made all the more acute by the Indian uprising of 1763. Many colonial officials, including the Indian superintendents, Sir William Johnson and John Stuart, had repeatedly urged the adoption of a unified imperial system. Halifax and the Board of Trade had accepted the framework of such a program in 1763. British subjects could trade at the garrisoned posts under the inspection of the military, only after acquiring a license from a colonial governor and posting bond that they would observe such regulations and prices as should be thought necessary to prevent them from defrauding the Indians.[57]

The Commissioners of Trade began evaluating material for

56. Murray to Halifax, March 9, Oct. 29 (private), 1764, C. O. 42/25: 58, 165; Halifax to the Board of Trade, May 21, 1764, C. O. 42/1: 128, and Murray to the Board of Trade, Sept. 8, 1764, C. O. 42/1: 400–402, PAC transcripts.

57. Board of Trade to Johnson, Sept. 29, 1763, *DRCHSNY,* VII, 567; Halifax to Amherst, Oct. 19, 1763, Amherst Papers, 6:98, WLCL. See also Gage to Halifax, Jan. 7, 1764, and Halifax to Gage, Jan. 14, 1764, *Gage Correspondence,* I, 11; II, 10.

a comprehensive plan [58] during the first week of December, 1763. They continued their deliberations throughout the following month.[59] In February, George Croghan, Johnson's deputy, arrived in London on private business, but he was able to confer with Halifax and the Board of Trade on the problem throughout the spring. It was soon evident that the cost of an imperial system of Indian affairs was a crucial point. Extremely conscious of the financial burden on Great Britain, the Treasury would allow the Board of Trade only £15,000 for surveying and the Indian establishment.[60] Due to the press of political matters, the Commissioners of Trade were not able to accomplish much that spring. But with the end of the Parliamentary session, they turned once more to the problem of regulating Indian affairs. In June they dealt at length with a comprehensive paper by Johnson on

58. With the details of the plan now under consideration, Sir William Johnson sent a lengthy report to the Board of Trade setting forth the situation in his department and arguing for a continuation of the policy of subsidizing the tribes by means of presents, and that a fair trade be accorded at the chief posts under regulation and price control. He also advocated delineating a specific boundary to separate the lands of the Indians from those of the whites. In this respect, however, he was guilty of a serious error of judgment, for in stating the territorial claims of the tribes, he held that the Six Nations, by right of conquest, had title to all of the land from the mountains as far west of Virginia as the Kentucky River and then by the Ohio and Mississippi to the Great Lakes and the Ottawa River. Johnson maintained that no settlement should be made in this area until the Six Nations had relinquished their rights. Johnson to the Board of Trade, Nov. 18, 1763, Board of Trade Papers, Plantations General, vol. 20, unfoliated, Historical Society of Pennsylvania, Philadelphia; misdated Nov. 13, 1763, in *Pennsylvania Archives,* 2nd ser., VI, 640–653, and *DRCHSNY,* VII, 572–581. This was an unrealistic view, for the criterion Johnson should have used was actual possession of the land, not claims based on long past conquests, no longer recognized but contested by the southern and western tribes. Johnson was to support the Six Nations in these claims, however, with decidedly adverse consequences in the future.

59. *Journal of the Board of Trade, 1759–1763,* pp. 417–418; *ibid., 1764–1767,* pp. 4, 8.

60. Croghan to Johnson, Feb. 24, March 10, April 14, May 11, 1764, *Johnson Papers,* IV, 339, 362–363, 396–399 and 419–420; Gage to Halifax, April 2, 1764, *Gage Correspondence,* I, 21; Charles Jenkinson to Hillsborough, Jan. 14, 1764, Add. MSS 38304, f. 7.

the problem.[61] The Superintendent for the Northern District would station interpreters, smiths, and deputy agents at the principal forts where traders could sell supplies to the Indians at prices set by the superintendents. On June 8, Croghan attended a meeting of the board where he presented a long memorandum outlining his own views in support of those of his superior.[62] Seeking to obtain further information, the commissioners heard the testimony of Thomas Penn and reviewed the correspondence of Gage and Stuart on the question of Indian affairs. On June 13 they decided to incorporate the various proposals into a formal plan, and two days later ordered copies sent to the superintendents and the colonial governors by a circular letter. On July 10 they completed the document.[63]

In their circular letter to officials in America, the Commissioners of Trade indicated clearly the principles behind the plan of July 10, 1764. They sought to regulate Indian affairs, both commercial and political, through one general system under the direction of officers appointed by the Crown, so as to eliminate all local interference by individual colonies. This interference, they charged, has been "one great Cause of the distracted State of Indian Affairs . . . ." [64] Thus the Board of Trade was applying the lessons of the late war with the French. To a great extent, the commissioners had followed the proposals advanced by the Indian superintendents. British subjects could traffic with the Indians only at specified locations, the Indian towns in the southern

61. A transcript, dated Nov. 18, 1763, is to be found in the Board of Trade Papers, Plantations General, vol. 20, unfoliated, HSP.

62. The memorandum is printed without date in *DRCHSNY,* VII, 602–607, and in *Pennsylvania Archives,* 2nd ser., VI, 659–665. Transcript in Board of Trade Papers, Plantations General, vol. 19, unfoliated, endorsed "Letter from Mr. George Croghan to the Board of Trade without Date—containing his Sentiments of the proper methods to be used for giving lasting Peace to His Majesty's Colonies in North America, Read June 8. 1764 R.54."

63. *Journal of the Board of Trade, 1764–1767,* pp. 66–69; *ibid., 1764–1767,* p. 98; Croghan to Johnson, July 12, 1764, *Johnson Papers,* IV, 462–463.

64. Board of Trade to Stuart, July 10, 1764, C. O. 324/17: 416. The letter to the superintendents is printed in *Pennsylvania Archives,* 1st ser., IV, 189–191, and *DRCHSNY,* VII, 636.

district, and the military posts in the north. The trade was open to all under imperial regulation. The plan required persons engaging in the trade to take out licenses from the colonial governors and to post bond for their good behavior. Deputies appointed by Johnson and Stuart were to act as justices of the peace in the Indian country. Finally, the commissioners proposed the repeal of all colonial laws dealing with the traffic.[65]

The Board of Trade faced a difficult problem in financing the imperial plan. Both Johnson and Stuart had advocated a tax on furs, but the commissioners thought that such a levy would be difficult to collect and would be inconsistent with that "Freedom which is one of the first Principles of Commerce . . . ." In view of the difficulty of providing revenue to finance the system, the board deferred submitting a bill to Parliament incorporating the plan of 1764 until the next legislative session. In the meantime, they referred the imperial plan to the superintendents and colonial governors for further consideration and recommendations.[66] Throughout, the commissioners had shown an ability to appreciate the lessons learned during the war. Further, in drafting their plan, they had relied on the judgment of men with practical experience in dealing with the natives.

In general, the response of the colonial governors to the plan was favorable.[67] But Governor James Murray of Quebec sounded a dissenting note. He objected strongly to the jurisdiction exercised by the superintendents and advocated regulation of the Indian trade by the colonies through provincial officers who would coordinate their actions at a colonial congress.[68] In contrast, Sir William Johnson advocated even more control by the

65. The plan of 1764 for the future management of Indian affairs is printed in *Pennsylvania Archives,* 1st ser., IV, 182–189, and *DRCHSNY,* VII, 637–641.

66. Board of Trade to Stuart, July 10, 1764, C. O. 324/17: 417–419.

67. The correspondence of the governors and Indian superintendents with the Board of Trade on this subject are in C. O. 323/20.

68. "Governor Murray's Views on the Plan of 1764 for the Management of Indian Affairs: 26th October 1764," C. O. 323/20: 3–9; edited by R. A. Humphreys in *Canadian Historical Review,* XVI (1935), 166–169.

personnel of the Indian department, while Stuart wanted the superintendents, not the governors, to license the traders.[69]

In spite of the general approval registered in favor of the plan by most colonial officials, the Board of Trade had to defer action until the administration could find a source of revenue to finance the imperial system. Revenue for the Indian department, moreover, was directly related to the funds for the army stationed in America, for the Commander-in-Chief paid the expenses of the superintendents out of the military budget. Until the ministry could provide a permanent source of revenue, the imperial plan of 1764 lay dormant. In the meantime, Gage and Johnson together evolved an *ad hoc* system for conducting the Indian trade[70] which in substance embodied the regulations of 1764 and continued the program instituted by Johnson in the last years of the war.

In its program for the North American wilderness during 1763–1764, the Grenville administration had merely posed in formal terms the lessons of the great war for empire—lessons which had led Amherst, Johnson, Bouquet, Monckton, and other officials to institute temporary measures during the conflict in order to win and retain the confidence of the natives so that they might insure the peace of the frontier. Pontiac's rebellion of 1763 confirmed the need for imperial supervision of the wilderness. Neither the rigid economic doctrine of mercantilism nor the theoretic views of the Earl of Shelburne counted for much in the final analysis. Practical experience did. By the Proclamation of 1763 and the plan of 1764 for the management of Indian

69. Johnson to the Board of Trade, Oct. 8, 1764, *DRCHSNY,* VII, 657–660. See also Johnson's "A State of the Indian Trade, and a Scheme for raising a fund by Duties thereon," *Johnson Papers,* IV, 556–563. Stuart's observations on the plan of 1764, C. O. 323/20: 199–218, are edited by Clarence E. Carter in "Observations of John Stuart and Governor James Grant of East Florida on the Proposed Plan of 1764 for the Future Management of Indian Affairs," *American Historical Review,* XX (1915), 815–831.

70. Gage to Johnson, June 24, 1764, Alvord and Carter, *Critical Period,* 268; see also Gage's "Orders to the officers Command[ing] to the Westwards regard[in]g Trade," Headquarters, New York, January 16, 1765, printed in *ibid.,* 400.

affairs, Egremont and Halifax simply sanctioned the program initiated and established by the military during the French and Indian War. But would the program work? The answer depended to a great extent on two further questions. Would the ministry be able to raise the revenue necessary to finance the imperial establishment? Would the colonists accept imperial regulation? As it happened, the fate of the first British Empire rested on these questions.

CHAPTER IV

Politics and an American Revenue

REVENUE to defray the cost of the military establishment was essential to every aspect of the imperial program the Grenville ministry had adopted for the American wilderness. The army garrisoned the Indian country, enforced the boundary line, and bore the expenses of the Indian department and the cost of the civil governments of such "infant" colonies as Nova Scotia, Georgia, and the Floridas.[1] As early as 1754, the Board of Trade

1. By indiscriminately linking the Grenville tax program with Charles Townshend's later measures of 1767 for an American revenue to finance the colonial civil establishment, O. M. Dickerson, *The Navigation Acts and the American Revolution* (Philadelphia, 1951), 162, contends that in 1763 Grenville was responsible for raising a revenue to make the colonial governors financially independent of the provincial legislatures. Professor Dickerson offers no evidence to support this view. Townshend at this time probably was contemplating an American revenue for such a purpose, as Professor Namier has recently pointed out, but it is clear that in the debates in the House of Commons in March, 1763, Grenville contested Townshend on the subject of American duties (Sir Lewis B. Namier, *Charles Townshend His Character and Career*, The Leslie Stephen Lecture, 1959 [Cambridge, England, 1959], 17, 19, 20).

Allen S. Johnson (see his unpublished dissertation, "The Political Career of George Grenville," Duke University, 1955, p. 259 and his "The Passage of the Sugar Act," *William and Mary Quarterly*, 3rd ser., XVI [1959], 509) had realized that a permanent defense system for North America required a stable source of revenue for its support. At that time the commissioners had recommended that Parliament should levy some tax if the colonies should prove negligent in providing money. During the French and Indian War many of the colonial

---

charges that the Treasury under Grenville for some months considered applying an American revenue to the colonial civil list, but finally dropped the idea. Johnson's evidence is slight and misleading. He cites a letter from Jasper Mauduit, colonial agent for Massachusetts, by which Grenville is supposed to have declared that he desired America "should bear the charge of its own government and defence, and nothing more" (Mass. Historical Society *Collections,* 1st ser., VI, 194). Johnson further states that on January 23, 1764, the Treasury considered estimates of the civil establishments of *all* the colonies. But the evidence he cites (Public Record Office, Treasury Board papers, T. 1/423: 11–16) includes the estimates *only* for Georgia, East and West Florida. Evidently Johnson was unaware that the military budget carried the civil list of these "infant" colonies. (A notation on the list for the American civil establishment drawn up in preparation for the Townshend law of 1767 reads: "Nova Scotia, Georgia, and West Florida, are inserted in the Military Establishment," Shelburne Papers, 57: 263, WLCL.) The relatively small population of these new provinces could not bear the cost of the salaries of executive and judicial officials. There is no reason to assume on the basis of Johnson's evidence that the Treasury in 1763 used estimates for the civil lists because it desired to pay them by an American tax. Grenville expected the colonists to assume part of the burden of financing the military establishment by paying additional taxes. To determine if they were capable of bearing such new taxes, he first had to ascertain the annual expenditures of their governments. These included the cost of their civil establishments and the sums they spent annually to retire their war debts. Charles Garth, agent for South Carolina, noted that when Grenville opened his proposal for a stamp duty in the House of Commons in February, 1765, he produced accounts of the sums raised by each colony for its own civil list (totaling roughly £75,000 annually) and the debts still charged for the retirement of their war expenditures (£900,000), all to be paid off before 1769. Consequently, Grenville concluded that "it was but reasonable the Colonys should contribute at least to take off that part of the burthen from the Mother Country which concerned the protection and defence of themselves." (Garth to the South Carolina Committee of Correspondence, Feb. 8, 1765, L. B. Namier, "Charles Garth, Agent for South Carolina," *English Historical Review,* LIV [1939], 649–650.) Copies of these estimates are in C. O. 324/17: 497, 498. The continental colonies had expended almost £2,500,000 during the war, but Parliament had reimbursed them to the extent of over £1,500,000.

assemblies had been lax in voting money. Consequently, the provincial governors most active in prosecuting the war effort had agreed with the Board of Trade in the need for Parliamentary taxation. Because of the great financial burden imposed on Great Britain by the war and the increased responsibilities of the army in America, the Bute ministry in the winter of 1762–1763 decided to impose an American tax. But Bute had postponed levying any specific measure until the ministry received more information.[2] The task of finding an appropriate tax fell to George Grenville, who became First Lord of the Treasury, and Chancellor of the Exchequer in April, 1763. Subsequent action by Grenville's Treasury Board illustrated the need for additional revenue. In the fall of 1763, the board submitted a memorial to the Privy Council, asking that it issue orders to the various executive departments to tighten up on the collection of revenue provided by existing legislation. Such enforcement was all the more indispensable when the military establishment in the colonies required "a large Revenue to support it," in view of "their vast Increase in Territory . . . ." [3] The Treasury was too sanguine when it asked for £260,000 in placing the estimate for the American army before Parliament that winter. The amount was insufficient, and on February 5, 1765, Parliament voted an additional sum of over £400,000 for the extraordinary expenses incurred by the land forces which the legislature had not previously appropriated.[4]

2. The King to Bute, March ?, 1763, Sedgwick, *Letters from George III to Bute,* 201–202.

3. *Acts of the Privy Council, Col.,* IV, 569. The difficulty faced by Grenville was compounded by the fact that the cost of provisioning the troops in America had risen considerably. The last contract for supplying the troops by Quebec had been made with Sir James Colebrook and Company in 1760. Grenville, in order to review the situation, contacted the army contractor, Moses Franks, who sent him a statement of the cost of provisions as they had been set in 1760. Franks pleaded that, due to the rise in prices, it was impossible to maintain this rate if the contractors were to make a "fair, reasonable advantage on the transaction." Franks to Grenville, March 9, 1764, Stowe Collection, box 101, HEHL.

4. *Journal of the House of Commons,* XXIX, 681. The figure given for the forces serving in the plantations was £372,774. The above cited figure is arrived at by subtracting the estimated charges for the forces at Gibraltar and Minorca. The American establishment was set at £11,000 for each

This action was frequently necessary as the expenses of the American army mounted because of contingent and extraordinary outlays charged to the interior garrisons and the Indian services. Parliament periodically voted money in addition to the regular appropriations.[5] As it was put by Thomas Whately, joint secretary to the Treasury under Grenville, the American military "Service is not only more extensive than formerly, but some Parts of it cannot yet be thoroughly understood; and therefore the Extraordinaries cannot be calculated . . . ."[6]

It was difficult for Great Britain to bear even the cost of the original estimates of the American military establishment. As a result of the late war, the national debt had risen from £73,000,000 to £137,000,000. The funds borrowed at three to four percent to finance the war effort drew an interest of nearly £5,000,000 annually. At the same time, the yearly national budget was only £8,000,000.[7] With the mother country so burdened with debt, could the colonies help pay part of the cost of their own defense? Grenville thought they could, in view of their relatively

---

regiment of 500 men, with the exception of the Royal American, requiring £22,000 for a complement of 1,000 men. *Parliamentary History,* XV, 1419–1420; XVI, 59–60.

5. On April 14, 1766, almost £300,000 was voted to make good a deficiency for the grant for the services in 1765. *Ibid.,* XVI, 217–218. The base rate for the military establishment in America for 1765 amounted to £201,712. This included the pay and provisions for 15 battalions of 7,500 men, garrisons and staff, and contingent expenses. "Charge of the Military Establishment in North America In the year 1765," P.R.O. Treasury Board Papers, Class I, bundle 433, f. 404, LC transcript. On February 9, 1767, £316,000 was required for the extraordinaries incurred the previous year. *Parliamentary History,* XVI, 365–366. At the same time, the expenses for the forces in the plantations (including North America, Minorca, Gibraltar, the ceded islands, and Africa) had risen to £405,000. *Ibid.,* XVI, 363–364. Even so, an additional grant of £200,000 was necessary on June 28, 1768, to cover the extraordinaries, *ibid.,* XVI, 415–416, while £238,000 was necessary the following year, *ibid.,* XVI, 623–624.

6. [Thomas Whately], *Considerations of the Trade and Finances of this Kingdom, and on the Measures of Administration with respect to those great National Objects since the conclusion of the Peace* (3rd ed., London, printed for J. Wilkie, 1769), 79.

7. T. 1/434: 1–2.

slight financial obligations. According to estimates compiled by the Treasury, the annual colonial expense for their governments was £75,000. Although the colonies had spent £2,500,000 during the war, Parliament had reimbursed £1,500,000 of this sum. The colonies were retiring the remaining war debt at the rate of twenty percent a year so that they would be entirely free of debt by 1769.[8] Under these circumstances, they could bear additional taxes to assume part of the charges on the mother country for the North American military establishment.

When Grenville and the two Under-Secretaries of the Treasury, Charles Jenkinson and Thomas Whately, undertook to solve the revenue problem, they devised several measures. Stricter enforcement of the trade and revenue laws would bring in some money. But this was not enough. They had to find another source of revenue, new taxes. On September 23, 1763, the Treasury ordered the English Commissioners of Stamps to prepare "a Draft of an Act for imposing proper Stamp Duties upon his Majestys Subjects in America and the West Indies." [9] Certainly the idea of stamp taxes was not new. Such duties had existed in England for some time, and many had previously suggested extending the stamp laws to the colonies. Grenville opened the first of his colonial financial measures in the House of Commons on March 9, 1764. After reviewing the financial situation, he apparently convinced the House that it was necessary for every "part of the Government to contribute the utmost to lighten the publick burden." Needless to say, the House adopted the Treasury's solution to the revenue problem. One of the resolutions it adopted declared the propriety of imposing stamp duties on the Americans. But the administration did not introduce a stamp act at this session. According to the colonial agent for Massachusetts, Jasper Mauduit —his brother, Israel, had conferred with the secretaries at the Treasury—Grenville had postponed the stamp bill, "being willing

8. For the estimates of the colonial civil establishment and war debts see C. O. 324/17: 497, 498. Grenville used these estimates in presenting the stamp bill in the House of Commons in 1765. See Charles Garth to the South Carolina Committee of Correspondence, Feb. 8, 1765, Namier, "Garth, Agent for South Carolina," *English Historical Review,* LIV (1939), 649–650.

9. Jenkinson to the Commissioners of Stamps, Sept. 23, 1763, T. 27/28: 432.

to give to the Provinces their option to raise that [*sic*] or some equivalent tax [*sic*], Desirous as he express'd himself to consult the Ease, the Quiet, and the Good will of the Colonies." [10] He preferred this tax because the government might raise stamp duties without any great burden to the Americans, and it could collect them with the fewest officers.[11] It is clear, however, that one reason Grenville deferred the Stamp Act for a year was that the Treasury did not have sufficient information on taxable items in America to draft the law.[12] But in the House of Commons the member for Malden, John Huske of New Hampshire, argued that since the imposition of stamp duties was a "peculiar step," the colonies ought to have notice of the proposed tax measure beforehand and, by their agents, have an opportunity to present their objections to the measure.[13] Of all the known accounts of the debate in the House of Commons that day, only that of the Virginia agent, Edward Montague, indicates that Grenville might have made his option to the Stamp Act in terms of a requisition to the colonial assemblies. According to Montague, Grenville suggested that "it would be satisfactory to him if the several provinces would among themselves, and in modes best suited to their circumstances, raise a sum adequate to the expence of their own defence." Yet Grenville also expressed the hope that no one would dispute the right of the British legislature to tax the colonies, as had been hinted outside of Parliament. At the time the members seemed surprised that such a doubt even existed.[14]

Whether or not Grenville posed his option in the form of the traditional requisition is important in view of the charge made

10. Jasper Mauduit to the speaker of the Massachusetts House of Representatives, March 13, 1764, Massachusetts Archives, XXII, 359; Israel Mauduit to ?, March 10, 1764, *ibid.*, XXII, 357.

11. [Edward Montague to the Virginia committee of correspondence], April 11, 1764 (extract), *Virginia Gazette* (Purdie and Dixon), October 3, 1766.

12. Jenkinson to Grenville, July 2, 1764, *Grenville Papers,* II, 373.

13. Cecelius Calvert to Governor Horatio Sharpe, April 3, 1764, W. H. Browne, *et al.* (eds.), *Archives of Maryland* (65 vols., Baltimore, 1883–1952), XIV, 144. Calvert wrote "Hurst," but there was no M.P. by that name. See the list of members in Gerrit P. Judd, IV, *Members of Parliament 1734–1832* (New Haven, 1955).

14. *Virginia Gazette* (Purdie and Dixon), October 3, 1766.

recently that, in a subsequent interview with the colonial agents on May 17, 1764, Grenville spuriously offered the colonies an opportunity to raise the money themselves. But the option was meaningless, since he did not give them specific sums or quotas. Without knowing the exact amounts each colony was to raise or the portion of the total required of an individual province, the colonial assemblies could not vote appropriations.[15] The charge against Grenville is valid only if his option was actually in the form of a requisition and not for some other tax. The sum raised by each colony would have varied with the method of taxation. A duty on slaves, furs, land, persons, or stamps would have affected various colonies in different proportions. There were many accounts of this interview on May 17, 1764, between Grenville and the colonial agents. Most were written some time after the event, and their versions of what occurred are garbled. The most extensive account, written at the time by an agent who was present, is that of Charles Garth. The narrative of the South Carolina agent makes it clear that Grenville did not pose his option in terms of a requisition to the colonial assemblies. Indeed, Grenville specifically objected to any form of requisition, holding that the raising and appropriating of money by the colonies "would have been attended with very many difficulties even if it could be suppos'd that 26 colonies (including the Continent and West India Islands) would have all adopted such a recommendation, and which, in case of refusal to enforce the power of Parliament, must have had recourse to . . . ." By delaying the Stamp Act for a year, it was Grenville's intention to "have the sense of the Colonies themselves upon this matter, and if they could point out any system or plan as effectual and more easy to them" he was "open to every proposition . . . ." [16]

Grenville's option on the Stamp Act was not "hollow," as has been charged, for he was offering an alternative in the form of

15. Edmund S. Morgan, "The Postponement of the Stamp Act," *William and Mary Quarterly*, 3rd ser., VII (1950), 353–392 and *The Stamp Act Crisis: Prologue to Revolution* (Chapel Hill, 1953), 60–61.

16. Garth to the South Carolina Committee of Correspondence, June 5, 1764, Namier, "Garth, South Carolina Agent," *English Historical Review*, LIV (1939), 647.

some other tax, not a requisition by which the colonies needed to know specifically how much each colony was to raise or the proportion of the whole sum each was to contribute. In fact, Grenville had pointed out the impracticality of specific quotas since the capacity of the various colonies to pay would in time vary. There was nothing deceitful in asking the agents if they could suggest quotas, since the agents themselves had previously agreed at the Treasury on the division of Parliamentary grants to the provinces for various military outlays. Only a requisition need be made to the provinces through the "regular" channel of the Secretary of State. As head of the Treasury, Grenville could make his proposal through the agents. John Huske had suggested this procedure in the House of Commons in March, and it was common practice in the Grenville ministry for executive boards to consult with the agents on American business.

Grenville had postponed the Stamp Act to allow the colonists to register their objections to the stamp duties or to present alternative forms of taxation. He also had to give the Treasury time to collect additional information. By the end of the year, Whately had collected the information from the American governors and the Treasury had approved his stamp bill.[17]

What of the colonial legislatures who had been given time to register their reactions to the stamp measure and to present practical alternatives? Although they were almost unanimous in rejecting the proposal, none made any positive suggestions. The Pennsylvania assembly instructed its agent to remonstrate against a stamp duty laid by Parliament as "repugnant to our Rights and Privileges as Freemen and *British* Subjects." They would transmit a suitable alternative tax measure later. The South Carolina legislature also objected to the proposed stamp duty, or any other tax imposed by Parliament, as contrary to the inherent right of every British subject not to be taxed except by his own consent or that of his representatives. The Virginia House of Burgesses came out against the proposed stamp duties on more narrow grounds: they were "internal" or "Inland" taxes. If money must be raised, the burgesses asked, why not by the old requisition system to which they had "always with the greatest Chear-

17. T. 1/430: 175–291; and Add. MSS 35910, ff. 310–323.

fullness submitted . . . & comply'd . . . ?"[18] This had hardly been the case, for the Virginians had not wholeheartedly supported the requisition system, particularly during the early years of the war.

These responses were typical of the reactions of the other colonial legislatures to Grenville's option to the Stamp Act. But when the assemblies of New York and Massachusetts not only denied the right of Parliament to tax the Americans, but called on the other provinces for joint action, the government in London took action. In December, 1764, the Board of Trade, under the Earl of Hillsborough, charged that the Massachusetts House had treated "the acts and Resolutions of the Legislature of Great Britain . . . with the most indecent disrespect . . . ." Massachusetts had "openly avowed" principles of the "most dangerous nature and tendency," and had invited the assemblies of the other colonies "in a most extraordinary manner" to adopt the same opinions. In another report the following month, the board accused the New York assembly of seeking to "excite a combination in the several colonies to oppose particular Acts and resolutions" of Parliament.[19] The representations of the Commissioners of Trade confirmed the decision to pass the Stamp Act. According to Edward Sedgwick, Under-Secretary of State, the Privy Council directed the Board of Trade to lay before Parliament the resolutions of the assemblies in which they "almost deny or strongly remonstrate against the Right of Parliament to tax them." It was now necessary "to establish that Right by a new execution of it, and in the strongest instance, an internal Tax, that of the Stamp Duty."[20]

18. *Pennsylvania Archives,* 8th ser., VIII, 5635, 5643–5645; South Carolina Committee of Correspondence to Charles Garth, Sept. 4, 1764, Robert Wilson Gibbes (ed.), *Documentary History of the American Revolution, 1764–1776* (3 vols., 1853–1857), II, 2; *Virginia Magazine of History and Biography,* IX (1902), 353–354; XII (1904–1905), 9–11.

19. *Journal of the Board of Trade, 1764–1767,* p. 139. The representations on Massachusetts and New York, dated Dec. 11, 1764, and Jan. 17, 1765, respectively, are in C. O. 5/1130: 270, 275.

20. Sedgwick to Edward Weston, Feb. 14, 1765, Royal Historical Manuscripts Commission, *Tenth Report,* appendix, pt. I, 382. See also the similar explanation given by Charles Lloyd, Grenville's private secretary, in *The*

Thus the entire emphasis behind the Stamp Act had shifted. What had originated as a measure to help defray the cost of the American defense system had now become an essential measure to affirm the legislative supremacy of the British Parliament over the colonies. The Stamp Act heralded the prologue of the American Revolution.

While the original motive was now secondary, the Stamp Act was still necessary to help defray the cost of the defense establishment for the American wilderness. Grenville had given the Americans a year in which to present an option to this tax. The agents had warned their constituents that neither the First Lord of the Treasury nor Parliament would accept the argument that the British legislature could not tax the colonists. But there was little the agents could now do, for the colonial assemblies had left them no alternative other than to oppose the Stamp Act. The assemblies had offered no other means of raising money than by the requisition system, which Grenville again rejected as impractical in an interview with the agents on February 2, 1765. He asked representatives of the colonial legislatures if they could agree on quotas for each province under such a system. When they could not, he pointed out that no one in England could either. But even if they did agree on specific quotas, there was no guarantee that the colonies would meet these. Nor would the quotas set now be valid in the future, for the separate colonies were developing their commercial and financial potentials at uneven rates. Convinced of the advantages of the stamp bill, which would recognize such future contingencies, Grenville left it to the agents to present further objections to the act in Parliament.[21]

In opening his proposal to impose stamp duties on the Americans before the House of Commons on February 8, 1765, Grenville spoke of the colonists in "Terms of great Kindness & Regard

---

Conduct of the Late Administration Examined (London, printed for J. Almon, 1765), 15.

21. Garth to the South Carolina Committee of Correspondence, Feb. 8, 1765, Namier, "Garth, Agent for South Carolina," *English Historical Review*, LIV (1939), 649; Jared Ingersoll to Thomas Fitch, Feb. 11, 1765, Connecticut Historical Society *Collections*, XVIII, 324–326.

& in Particular assured ye House that there was no Intention to abridge or alter any of their Charters." By emphasizing the relatively slight financial obligations of the colonies, Grenville argued that they could afford to pay the additional stamp taxes he now proposed. He also argued in favor of the constitutionality of the measure—the incontestable right of Parliament to levy a tax—without referring to the addresses of the New York and Massachusetts assemblies which had confirmed the intention of the imperial government to pass the stamp bill.

Grenville easily had his way. Although some members of Parliament, Sir William Meredith, Richard Jackson, Isaac Barré, Alderman William Beckford, Garth, and General Henry Seymour Conway, spoke out against internal duties, they did not press the issue. The Americans' proponents sought to obtain the sense of the House by moving for adjournment, but they lost the vote, 245 to 49.[22] This indicated in convincing fashion the strength of the ministry. The Stamp Act easily passed the House of Commons. There was not even a division in the House of Lords. The passage of the Stamp Act was not a controversial issue in British politics at the time: the revenue measure soon became one.

Grenville thought that he had solved the problem of financing the defense establishment for the territories acquired from France and Spain. To insure that the money raised in America would remain in the colonies to be disbursed by the army for the defense of the North American continent and the West Indies, the Treasury issued specific orders that all money raised in America by acts of Parliament be turned over to the deputy paymaster of the forces in the colonies.[23]

This order was almost the last act of the Treasury under Gren-

22. Ingersoll to Fitch, Feb. 11, 1765, Connecticut Historical Society *Collections,* XVIII, 321, 334; Richard Jackson to Fitch, Feb. 9, 1765, *ibid.,* XVIII, 316–317; Garth to the South Carolina Committee of Correspondence, Feb. 8, 1765, *English Historical Review,* LIV, 650; Thomas Whately to John Temple, Feb. 9, 1765, John Temple Correspondence, Stowe Americana, Stowe Collection, HEHL.

23. J. M. Sosin, "A Postscript to the Stamp Act. George Grenville's Revenue Measures. A Drain on Colonial Specie?" *American Historical Review,* LXIII (1958), 918–923.

ville. Having achieved a major innovation in colonial policy by the Stamp Act, the Grenville administration was to endure but briefly. Although a resourceful and capable minister, by his independent attitude and domestic policies, Grenville had made himself unacceptable to the King. He was dismissed in July. But the consequences of his Stamp Act remained to plague the succeeding British administration, particularly in view of the peculiar weakness and composition of that ministry. For this reason it is worth noting briefly the circumstances which led to the formation of the new government.

With the failure of William Pitt—the King's first choice—to form a ministry, George III as a temporary expedient turned to the Whig magnates. The Marquis of Rockingham headed a new government as First Lord of the Treasury. Although Rockingham at one point considered Charles Townshend as one of the Secretaries of State, these posts finally went to the Duke of Grafton and General Henry S. Conway. Hillsborough left the Board of Trade, but only for political expediency. The King promised that he would be brought into office again at the first favorable opportunity.[24] After the younger Earl of Hardwicke and Shelburne rejected the appointment, Rockingham finally prevailed upon the Earl of Dartmouth to become First Lord of Trade. Another important office presented some difficulty. When Charles Townshend also refused the Chancellorship of the Exchequer, William Dowdeswell filled the office. These five important positions were held by men who had never occupied public office before. This was an astonishing situation. Edward Gibbon considered the case "unparalelled [*sic*] in our history," and hoped that in these circumstances "genius will supply the place of experience." [25] Unfortunately, the Rockingham ministry—called by Townshend "a lutestring ministry; fit only for the summer" [26] —lacked both, in addition to political courage. The Whigs re-

24. Hillsborough to the King, July 23, 1765, Sir John Fortescue (ed.), *The Correspondence of King George the Third* (6 vols., London, 1927), I, 160.

25. Gibbon to Stanier Porten, July 21, 1765, J. E. Norton (ed.), *The Letters of Edward Gibbon* (3 vols., London, 1956), I, 198.

26. Chesterfield to his son, Aug. 17, 1765, Dobrée, *Chesterfield Letters,* VI, 2661.

quired these qualities in the face of the major political and imperial crisis brought about by the Stamp Act.

When news of the passage of Grenville's last revenue measure reached America, widespread rioting and resistance to imperial authority broke out in the urban centers. This marked the first step in the revolutionary process leading to the disruption of the first British Empire. Resistance to the Stamp Act almost immediately affected imperial policy for the interior and the British political scene. Up to this point, there had been little division among the various factions in London on American policy.[27] Prior to the summer of 1765, almost everyone in political life had agreed to the principle that the colonists should help pay for the cost of the royal garrisons protecting the new acquisitions. Hereafter, the issue of America became a divisive force which impinged on political alliances and made it all the more difficult to form a stable government at a time when the developing imperial crisis made it necessary for the home government to take a decisive, consistent stand.

The reaction of the colonists to the passage of the Stamp Act also had an immediate and continuing effect on British policy for the North American wilderness. As opposition to the tax measure increased, many of the colonial governors feared that they would be unable to maintain order with the resources immediately available. Consequently, Colden of New York, Franklin of New Jersey, and Sharpe of Maryland, among others, wrote to General Thomas Gage requesting the aid of regular troops.[28] These appeals raised a basic constitutional issue, for, as the Commander-in-Chief pointed out, the military could do nothing by itself, but must act solely in obedience to the civil authority. As Gage was well aware, the calls from the governors created an additional problem, one impinging on western policy, for the troops were "at a great distance and a good deal Dispersed." Under the current disposition of the garrisons as set by Jeffrey Amherst after the Indian rebellion of 1763, it would take time

27. Keith Feiling, *The Second Tory Party, 1760–1832* (London, 1938), 83.

28. Colden to Gage, Sept. 2, 1765, *DRCHSNY*, VII, 758; Franklin to Gage, Sept. 14, 1765, *New Jersey Archives*, 1st ser., IX, 495; and Sharpe to Gage, Sept. 6, 1765, *Archives of Maryland*, XIV, 57.

to collect the forces for duty on the seaboard.[29] Gage would need at least a month to gather the troops, and he would only be able to comply with the call from the governors by "almost deserting the Posts in the upper country." [30] Nevertheless, the Commander-in-Chief was willing for the moment to make available small detachments from Fort Pitt and other posts, should the civil authorities request them for use in the eastern cities.[31] Already over-extended in garrisoning the interior, British forces were in time to become further depleted. The process by which the western garrisons were drained was intensified as the revolutionary drama unfolded in the urban centers in the years ahead. In time, the need for troops on the revolutionary seaboard loomed larger in the minds of the British ministers than did the necessity for maintaining control of the interior by military force. At that point, the ministers had to come to a basic decision on the West.

In the fall of 1765, however, the young and inexperienced Rockingham ministry faced a more immediate colonial problem. At the onset of the new administration, the Duke of Newcastle drew up a memorandum for the First Lord of the Treasury. Heading the list of measures under consideration were the Stamp Act and the question, "What is intended to be done, about the Settlement of our New Acquisitions in America . . . ?" [32] The disturbances caused by the revenue measures and colonial demands for their repeal were the most pressing issues. Many in London were shocked by the totally unexpected violence of the American reaction. ". . . dreadful News from America," wrote one of the Duke of Newcastle's associates. "Nothing less than a Rebellion at New York." [33] Rockingham, who had hoped to minimize, or at least play down, the colonial reaction to the

29. Gage to Colden, Aug. 31, 1765, "Colden Papers," New York Historical Society *Collections,* LVI, 57–58.

30. Gage to Francis Bernard, Sept. 29, 1765, Edward Channing and A. C. Cooledge (eds.), *Barrington-Bernard Correspondence* (Cambridge, Mass., 1912), 230.

31. Gage to William Franklin, Sept. 16, 1765, *New Jersey Archives,* 1st ser., IX, 495–496; Sharpe to Gage, Sept. 23, 1765, *Archives of Maryland,* XIV, 228.

32. "Mems for Lord Rockingham," dated Sept. 9, 1765, Add. MSS 32969, f. 343.

33. George Onslow to Newcastle, Dec. 11, 1765, Add. MSS 32972, f. 202.

Stamp Act, complained that the news of the New York disturbances "will oblige us to mention N[orth] A[merica] by Name" in presenting the administration's program at the opening of the Parliamentary session that winter.[34]

The colonial agents were diligently lobbying to secure repeal of the Stamp Act. In his campaign, Dennys De Berdt, agent for the Massachusetts House of Representatives, quite properly linked the revenue law with the Grenville program for the newly acquired territories. But he sought to undermine the need for revenue to support the army by ridiculing the proposition that a royal garrison was necessary to defend North America. Stationing troops in America, he wrote to the President of the Board of Trade, "is as absurd as it is needless." To prove this contention, he now presented a most inaccurate analysis of the origins or prosecution of the late war in America. The colonists had been able to defeat the French in 1755, and, if supported in time by the home government, would have been able to drive the French from Canada. Thus the British government would not have incurred the great expense of which the Grenville ministry had complained. Indeed, the Massachusetts agent charged, most inaccurately, the large debt contracted in prosecuting the French and Indian War was due to "the supine neglect & timmid [*sic*] efforts of the ministry" during the conflict. With the French menace now eliminated, De Berdt asked, could not the colonists protect themselves from Indians whom they had successfully resisted for over a century? He concluded his polemic by a direct and unfair assault on the existing defense program. Since the troops now stationed in America were consequently unnecessary, "it is creating a large expence to carry & support an useless, nay . . . a disolute sett of Men to lie in Idleness" among the Americans.[35] The officers and men of the British army in America who had fought and died in the Indian uprising of 1763 would have disagreed with this unjust charge. So would the governors of

34. Rockingham to Newcastle, Dec. 12, 1765, Add. MSS 32972, f. 214.

35. De Berdt to Dartmouth, Sept. 5, 1765, Dartmouth Papers, II, 81, William Salt Library, Stafford, England, printed in Albert Mathews (ed.), "Letters of Dennys De Berdt, 1757–1770," Publications of the Massachusetts Colonial Society, *Transactions,* XIII (1910–1911), 435.

the southern colonies. In 1760, during the Cherokee war, they had asked that British regulars be used against the Indians. Governor Fauquier of Virginia was convinced that "Provincial Troops alone cannot Effectually finish this Affair . . . ."[36]

The fanciful contentions of De Berdt were basically inaccurate, but they were significant in that they presaged the line of argument subsequently used by more influential people against imperial taxes for defraying the cost of the North American defense system. Benjamin Franklin, agent for Pennsylvania, took the same line in his famous and well advertised performance before the House of Commons in January, 1766, in testifying for repeal of the Stamp Act. Part of Franklin's evidence dealt with the use of troops to protect the North American continent. He held that the royal garrisons were not necessary. In response to a series of questions, the Pennsylvania agent—considered by some as the spokesman for the colonists—denied that the French and Indian War had been fought for the benefit of the colonists. The British had waged war for their own commercial interests—it was "really a British war," Franklin contended. It had never been necessary to send British troops to defend the colonies.[37] Hence, there was no need for the Stamp Act to finance a useless army.

To those familiar with the motives of the successive British ministries in prosecuting the French and Indian War and in negotiating the peace, Franklin's performance must have been galling—to all those except William Pitt, who could at times resolve almost any contradiction. But this was not the case with the member for Bristol, Robert Nugent (Lord Clare) when he heard Franklin's testimony. Clare made a violent speech attacking the Americans for their ingratitude. "We have fought, bled, and ruined ourselves, to conquer for them; and now they come and tell

36. Fauquier to Amherst, Dec. 13, 1760, *Journals of the House of Burgesses of Virginia, 1758–1761*, p. 267.

37. *Parliamentary History*, XVI, 154–155. A pointed rebuttal was printed by William Knox, *The Controversy Between Great Britain and her Colonies Reviewed* (London, 1769), 111–136. Citing the records of the Massachusetts and Virginia legislatures, as well as the Albany Congress, Knox argued that the colonists had requested British aid to defend provincial interests against the French.

us to our noses . . . that they were not obliged to us . . . ."[38]

In fact, the fate of the Stamp Act was not resolved on the merits of any constitutional or historical argument, but on the basis of political expediency. The violent reaction of the Americans to the revenue measure had intimidated the relatively young and inexperienced Rockingham. He simply was not strong enough to enforce the Act. He staked his whole administration on repeal. If the administration should be successful in revoking the measure, he wrote, "we shall then show *how* we stand," for he could wish no man "so great a curse" as to head a ministry and "be obliged to enforce" the Stamp Act.[39] Having so committed themselves against the Stamp Act even before they had actually concluded to repeal the measure, in the final analysis the Whigs had no other choice.[40]

What were the implications for western policy of the repeal of the revenue measure designed to defray one-third of the expenses of the army stationed in America? One writer has stated that, by their repeal of the Stamp Act, the Whig administration undermined the Grenville program. Consequently, they were forced to seal off the North American interior by making permanent the provisions of the Proclamation of 1763 which established the Indian reservation.[41] This overstates the case. At least the Whigs could maintain the present situation in America, but they were also considering an alternative to the Stamp Act—requisitions to the colonial assemblies to raise money for the support of the troops. The second Earl of Hardwicke suggested that the ministers take this step "whenever we have the good fortune to have a settled Administration." If the colonists should prove obdurate, then Hardwicke would recall the troops, but he considered this " a very unwise measure" in other respects.[42] As it

38. Carl Van Doren (ed.), *Benjamin Franklin's Autobiographical Writings* (New York, 1945), 153.

39. Rockingham to Charles Yorke, Jan. 25, 1766, Add. MSS 35430, ff. 7–8.

40. Carl B. Cone, *Burke and the Nature of Politics, The Age of the American Revolution* (Lexington, Ky., 1957), 85.

41. Charles Ritcheson, "The Preparation of the Stamp Act," *William and Mary Quarterly*, 3rd ser., X (1953), 545n3.

42. Hardwicke to Charles Yorke, Feb. 24, 1766, George Thomas Keppel,

developed, the Whigs did not have sufficient time to develop a policy for the interior.

During the early years of the reign of George III, few politicians were fortunate enough to create a "settled Administration," or to evolve long-range policy. The Rockingham Whigs were not exceptional. In fact, they were living on borrowed time. George III had originally accepted them in office only as a temporary expedient.[43] In the spring of 1766, he had already decided to dismiss them and he had waited merely "till the arduous business of the American colonies" was over—the repeal of the Stamp Act—before dismissing the ministry. On learning that Pitt was ready to form an administration independent of any party or faction, the King seized the opportunity in the summer of 1766.[44] Now raised to the peerage as Earl of Chatham, Pitt headed a new government. Townshend accepted office as Chancellor of the Exchequer, while Shelburne and Conway became the Secretaries of State. The Treasury went to the Duke of Grafton. Hillsborough finally accepted the presidency of the Board of Trade, but only on the stipulation that it be altered from a board of representation to a board of report only. He insisted that all executive affairs revert to the proper departments. Shelburne met these conditions.[45] Why Hillsborough insisted on a reduction in the powers of his own board is not clear, but in any case he did not serve long as First Lord of Trade. For reasons relating to the

Sixth Earl of Albermarle, *Memoirs of the Marquis of Rockingham and his Contemporaries* (2 vols., London, 1852), I, 310–311. It was not until January 27 that the cabinet discussed the accounts of the annual expenses of government in America. Grafton at that time ordered lists of the civil and military officers to be prepared. See the minute of the cabinet meeting dated Monday, Jan. 27, 1766, Dartmouth Papers.

43. The King to the Earl of Egmont, Jan. 11, 1766, Fortescue, *Correspondence of George III,* I, 220.

44. The King to Bute, July 12, 1766, Sedgwick, *Letters from George III to Bute,* 251–253.

45. James Grenville to Pitt, July 27, 1766, W. S. Taylor and J. H. Pringle (eds.), *Correspondence of William Pitt, Earl of Chatham* (4 vols., London, 1838–1840), II, 466–467; Dowdeswell to Chatham, July 31, 1766, Dowdeswell Papers, WLCL; Hillsborough to George Grenville, Aug. 6, 1766, *Grenville Papers,* III, 294–296; and Shelburne to the Board of Trade, Aug. 26, 1766, *Calendar of Home Office Papers, George III,* II, 70.

domestic political situation, Robert Nugent (Lord Clare) replaced him at the board. Clare had vigorously opposed the repeal of the Stamp Act.

Thus constituted, the ministry was weak, for Chatham had chosen men who had supported measures diametrically opposed to his own,[46] particularly on the American revenue issue, where he had insisted on the right of Parliament to legislate for the colonies in all cases except internal taxation. Consequently, there was no unifying element in the administration. William Dowdeswell aptly described the ministers as "discordant Atoms." [47]

Pitt had further weakened his position by accepting a peerage. As the Earl of Chesterfield observed wisely, "He is now certainly only Earl of Chatham, and no longer Mr. Pitt, in any respect whatever." [48] In the mind of the public, Pitt's prestige had diminished considerably. In time, Chatham might regain public favor, but as David Hume predicted, he would never recover his former weight on leaving that "great scene of business," the House of Commons.[49] In the lower house he had been able to sway men by the force and brilliance of his rhetoric. With Chatham sitting in the House of Lords, Henry Conway became the administration leader in the Commons. The Secretary of State for the Northern Department proved a weak figure in that most important of all political arenas where the Great Commoner had shown to such advantage and where he had derived his greatest strength. The inability of the administration effectively to control the House of Commons and the struggle in that body between Townshend and Conway had decisive consequences for colonial policy. This conflict between the two ministers arose on the question of the budget for the American army. In view of the adverse financial situation confronting the British government, Grenville had introduced the Stamp Act to defray one-third of the cost of this military establishment. The repeal of the revenue act by the

46. See the analysis of Denys A. Winstanley, *Lord Chatham and the Whig Opposition* (Cambridge, 1912), 55.

47. Dowdeswell to ?, July 30, 1766, Dowdeswell Papers, WLCL.

48. Chesterfield to his son, Aug. 1, 1766, Dobrée, *Chesterfield Letters,* VI, 2752.

49. Hume to the Marquise de Barbentane, Aug. 29, 1766, John Y. Greig (ed.), *The Letters of David Hume* (2 vols., Oxford, 1932), II, 85.

Rockingham ministry may have temporarily quieted the colonists, but it did nothing to remedy the financial situation. The army budget continued to plague the succeeding administrations. There was to be no easy solution to the problem. Grenville's political pamphleteers had closely linked the revenue question with that of the North American interior and had brought them into the limelight of British politics.[50] While the Chatham ministry undertook a review of the previous policy for the interior, there was no way of returning to the prewar situation, for significant alterations had taken place on the frontier. Just as the colonists had challenged the right of the Parliament to tax, so they disputed the imperial program for the wilderness.

50. [Thomas Whately], *Considerations on the Trade and Finances of this Kingdom, and on the Measures of Administration, with respect to those great national objects since the conclusion of the peace* (London, 1766), 27.

CHAPTER V

The Challenge to Imperial Control

EIGHTEENTH-CENTURY Americans were a highly individualistic breed. Jealous of their rights and privileges, but not overly concerned perhaps with their responsibilities, they tended to resent any restrictions imposed on them by a distant government. Just as they challenged the right of the imperial government to tax them, so they questioned the program that government had imposed to preserve the stability of the frontier by redressing the grievances of the native tribes. Perhaps they were shortsighted or interested only in their own immediate gain, but some colonists saw little reason for not exploiting the fur trade and settling Indian lands, or for contributing money for the support of British garrisons to maintain peace in the wilderness. Their negative reaction jeopardized the imperial program, tenuous as it was. The garrisons in the West were essential to the imperial program; in view of the financial situation in Britain, the military establishment could only be continued by adequate revenue.

While the controversy over American taxes raged in London, the management of Indian affairs and the other aspects of the imperial program for the wilderness suffered. Uncertain of an assured revenue, the Grenville ministry had to apply a policy of strict economy. Under these conditions, Gage, Johnson, and

Stuart faced a difficult task. As the Commander-in-Chief stressed to the Treasury officials, the problems confronting the military and Indian services in the wilderness were more complex than ever after the war. They must administer an extensive territory ranging from the St. Lawrence to the Mississippi. Involved in an Indian war, the army also had to support the infant colonies. At the same time, the officers were attempting to conciliate the various tribes and to prevent the extension of hostilities. All of these activities, Gage emphasized, "required heavy expenditures." [1]

The Treasury Board did not make the task of the Commander-in-Chief any easier when, in November, 1764, it imposed strict controls over the expenditures of the army in America.[2] Until the commissioners could appropriate a specific fund for the Indian department, however, the government had to employ some other method in carrying on this service. Although the Treasury granted Gage some latitude in using funds for emergencies, their restrictions on expenditures were so confining that Gage complained of the "great Difficulties" he experienced in maintaining the Indian departments.[3] Although the Indian superintendents continued to spend large sums of money, the termination of hostilities with the Indians eased the situation somewhat by the end of 1764.

But the successful conclusion of Pontiac's rebellion immediately reopened the issue of regulating the Indian trade. During the outbreak, the military had closed the traffic in order to deprive the tribes of munitions. Since the Indians normally depended on the goods supplied by the whites, it was essential that the trade be opened again. But on what grounds? Gage was anxious to learn what the governors of the various colonies intended doing, for they were the officials who issued the licenses to the traders. For his part, the Commander-in-Chief wanted to establish uniform instructions at the forts in the Indian country

1. Gage to Thomas Whately, Nov. 7, 1764, *Gage Correspondence,* II, 246.

2. The minute of the Treasury Board, dated Nov. 28, 1764, is printed in *ibid.,* II, 269n32; and *Barrington-Bernard Correspondence,* 223–224.

3. Gage to Johnson, March 10, March 31, 1765, *Johnson Papers,* IV, 667–668; 702.

to insure that the traders complied with the terms of their licenses.[4] Sir William Johnson, Superintendent for the Northern Department, was equally concerned. Favoring the imperial plan of 1764 for managing Indian affairs, he hoped to receive this set of regulations from the home government before the traders set out for the upper country.[5] In the interval, it would be sufficient if the governors would issue licenses binding the traders to observe such rules as the local military authorities at the forts would impose.[6] Gage took matters in his own hands in January, 1765, by issuing instructions to the military commanders at the forts. They were to insure that the traders complied with the passes granted by the governors and did not defraud the Indians.[7] This was simply a continuation of the *ad hoc* system in existence before Pontiac's rebellion.

Several factors complicated imperial administration of the program. In view of the recent Indian depredations, the frontiersmen naturally resented the traders' supplying the tribes with weapons which they could use against the settlers on the frontier. On the other hand, the Indians depended on the trade for essential items, and if the British would not supply these, they would turn to the French still seated across the Mississippi River. If this should happen, the French would win back the support of the tribes and once again threaten the peace of the frontier. Gage recognized that it was essential to reopen the trade with the tribes, since it was common knowledge that the French were sending goods to the Illinois country from New Orleans. For political as well as military reasons, it was all the more urgent

4. Gage to Sharpe, Dec. 7, 1764, *Archives of Maryland,* XIV, 185.

5. On Feb. 18, 1765, the Board of Trade did consider the plan referred to the colonial officials the previous July. Their answers were discussed that day and again in the following month. *Journal of the Board of Trade, 1764–1767,* pp. 149, 162. No definite action was possible, of course, until a source of revenue could be found.

6. Johnson to Cadwallader Colden, Dec. 18, 1764, "Colden Papers," New York Historical Society *Collections,* LV, 398–399.

7. "Orders given out at Headquarters in New York, 17 January 1765," Board of Trade Papers, Plantations General, 20:309, HSP transcript. For the regulations imposed by Stuart in the southern district see Alden, *Southern Colonial Frontier,* 341–343.

for the British to re-establish commercial relations with the natives, for "the Indians will soon discover where supplys are to be had, & we shall drive them again into the Arms of the French." [8] Thus, as both the Commander-in-Chief and Sir William Johnson emphasized in 1765, competition from the French situated on both sides of the Mississippi complicated a definite settlement of Indian relations.[9]

Even after the occupation of the Illinois country by units of the British army, the influence of the French did not subside. And the success of their traders in engrossing the traffic with the Indians aroused the resentment of the traders and merchants of Canada. Under the regulations Gage had issued, they were forced to operate at the forts, while the French west of the Mississippi could cross the river and deal directly with the Indians at the native villages. Consequently, their French rivals could send furs to New Orleans via the Illinois country, and the volume of peltry handled by the Canadian and other British traders diminished.[10] In the summer of 1765, Sir William Johnson began to respond to the arguments of the Canadians. He suggested to the Commander-in-Chief that in some instances the traders might be allowed to leave the posts to conduct their trade. Gage was not inflexible. He was willing to consider the proposal if after investigation it should prove to have any merit.[11] In order to hold the allegiance of the remote tribes who had requested traders to come into their country, British officials in America granted some concessions to traders operating in the area north of Michillimackinac. But in London, Fowler Walker, agent for the Canadian merchants, complained to the ministry that the commandant at Michillimackinac was indulging in favoritism by allowing a few

8. Gage to John Penn, June 16, 1765, *Minutes, Provincial Council of Pennsylvania,* IX, 268.

9. Johnson to the Board of Trade, May 24, 1765, *DRCHSNY,* VII, 716; Gage to Halifax, Aug. 10, 1765, *Gage Correspondence,* I, 63.

10. See the petitions of the Quebec, Montreal, and London merchants in C. O. 42/2: 277–280, 128, 130–131, PAC transcripts, and Gage to Johnson, Sept. 1, 1765, *Johnson Papers,* V, 368.

11. Gage to Johnson, Aug. 18, 1765, Clarence W. Alvord and Clarence E. Carter (eds.), *The New Regime, 1765–1767,* XI, *Collections* of the Illinois State Historical Library (Springfield, Ill., 1916), 76–77.

traders to traffic at the Indian villages. Henry Conway, the Whig Secretary of State, simply referred the matter to the Commander-in-Chief in the spring of 1766. Gage explained that the concessions at Michillimackinac were merely exceptions to the general rule. In justifying the general policy of regulating the trade with the tribes, the Commander-in-Chief charged that the "scandalous practices" of the British traders who had cheated and defrauded the Indians had been one of the principal causes of the defection of almost every tribe during Pontiac's rebellion. To prevent a recurrence of such practices, the Commander-in-Chief and the Superintendent of Indian Affairs had designated the forts in the interior as "marts" for the trade. The governors, by the terms of the licenses they issued to the British traders, had restricted them to the posts where the military officers would enforce the regulations prescribed by the imperial officials. The arrangement was just, Gage argued, for after all, it protected the whites from the vengeance of the natives as much as it prevented the traders from cheating the Indians.[12] Yet Gage's straightforward explanation did not satisfy the Canadians. Fowler Walker tried another line by attacking a supposed monopoly of the trade arising from a grant made during the French regime.[13] Under the British system, trade was supposedly open to all subjects.

In the last year of French rule in Canada, the Marquis de Vaudreuil had obtained an exclusive right to trade at Baye des Puans (Green Bay), and following the war, he had sold this concession to William Grant, a merchant of Montreal. In the summer of 1766, Grant's agents took possession of the area, claiming an exclusive right to trade on the basis of the Vaudreuil grant. The Canadian merchants were quick in protesting to Sir William Johnson. Since the Superintendent of Indian Affairs felt that such a monopoly would have an adverse effect on the trade and consequently damage Indian relations, he wrote to the Board of Trade in support of the Canadian merchants.[14] Gage took the

12. Gage to Conway, June 24, 1766, *Gage Correspondence*, I, 96–97.

13. *Journal of the Board of Trade, 1764–1767*, p. 308.

14. Johnson to the Board of Trade, March 22, 1766, *DRCHSNY*, VII, 817–818.

same attitude with the current Secretary of State, the Earl of Shelburne. If the government should acknowledge Grant's right, it would merely invite more claims of the same nature, since the French colonial regime had divided the interior into districts and sold the exclusive right of trade to private individuals. While Gage acknowledged that the French system had some benefits—for one, it produced revenue—he feared that such monopolies would "occasion Clamours" from the British traders that the traffic was not open to all. Many were of the opinion, he informed the Secretary of State, that the practice of confining the traders to the posts was the only method of preventing them from imposing on the Indians and of averting quarrels. On the other hand, the tribes incessantly demanded that the whites send goods directly to their country. In supporting the Indians in this demand, the traders asserted that they could obtain a greater quantity of peltry if the government did not confine the trade to specified locations. Prohibiting the British traders from trading directly with the Indians in their own territory gave an undue advantage to the French operating from the right bank of the Mississippi River. Gage, rejecting the arguments of the Canadians, advocated the passage of stringent legislation to force the traders to observe the regulations he had imposed. Furthermore, the government ought to invest the commandants at the forts with sufficient powers so that they might enforce the law.[15]

15. Gage to Shelburne, Nov. 11, 1766, *Gage Correspondence,* I, 113–114. The interior posts served many functions, and not the least of them was to maintain legal authority in the West. The provisions of the Proclamation of 1763 had not provided for the exercise of legal jurisdiction by the commanding officers at the forts, and Gage had represented to Halifax the need for reinforcing this power by an extension of the provisions of the Mutiny Act to America. In March, 1765, Halifax had informed the Commander-in-Chief that directions had been given to bring into Parliament a supplemental bill for this purpose. Halifax to Gage, March 9, 1765, *ibid.,* II, 24. Since Welbore Ellis, the Secretary-at-War who was to prepare and introduce the bill, was under the impression that all of the continent was under some civil jurisdiction, and that additional clauses in the Mutiny Act were not necessary, Halifax sent him the relative extracts of the Proclamation demonstrating that the territory reserved for the Indians was not within the civil jurisdiction. Although the Proclamation provided for the apprehension and extradition of criminals and fugitives from the colonies, there was no way to punish

The imperial government accepted the argument of the Commander-in-Chief and the superintendent against any monopolistic organization of the Indian trade. Although Shelburne deemed it necessary to review the whole question of Indian affairs, eight days after he received Gage's report he ordered the Board of Trade to examine the validity of the Vaudreuil grant and to determine what compensation the government must award to keep the claimants from exercising a trading monopoly at Baye des Puans.[16]

Local interests in America, in this case, the fur traders, had thus challenged one element of the ministry's Indian policy. There was another aspect of this program which demanded attention, for frontiersmen and land speculators were violating the Indian boundary. The line delineated in the Proclamation of 1763 was merely a temporary expedient; it reflected neither the actual state of settlement nor respective claims of the tribes or whites who had interests on both sides of the Allegheny Mountains. A more accurate boundary was necessary. Recognizing the need to negotiate a more equitable line, in the spring of 1765, Sir William Johnson and his deputy, George Croghan—if only for their own interests in land speculation—had broached the question with chiefs of the Six Nations and Delaware tribes. Not having full power from the ministry to treat on the subject, Johnson had only tentatively proposed purchasing additional Indian territory.[17] Although he was apprehensive over the cost involved in extending the boundary westward, Gage supported Johnson on this point with the ministry.[18] By squatting on In-

---

crimes committed in the interior. Halifax to Ellis, March 11, 1765, *Calendar of Home Office Papers, George III,* I, 534. Gage had suggested an addition to the 60th clause of the Mutiny Act providing that for crimes committed where civil jurisdiction had not been established, accused persons were to be tried by court martial, *Gage Correspondence,* II, 266. The Mutiny Act of 1765 (5 Geo. III, c. 13) merely provided for the officers to apprehend criminals and send them to the colonies for civil trial.

16. *Journal of the Board of Trade, 1764–1767,* p. 355; Shelburne to the Board of Trade, Dec. 30, 1766, *Calendar of Home Office Papers, George III,* II, 103.

17. Johnson to the Board of Trade, May 24, 1765, *DRCHSNY,* VII, 711–712.

18. Gage to Halifax, June 8, 1765, *Gage Correspondence,* I, 61.

dian lands, the frontiersmen had antagonized the natives, and it was necessary to adjust the boundary. Acutely aware of the problem of revenue for America after the repeal of the Stamp Act, the Whig ministry could give Johnson and Gage little satisfaction on any proposal of this nature which would mean an additional outlay of money. The Board of Trade avoided the issue of negotiating a new boundary line entirely, and Conway, the Secretary of State, took almost two months to inform Gage that insufficient time and information as to the estimated expense of such a negotiation made it impractical for the Earl of Dartmouth and the other Commissioners of Trade to arrive at any decision.[19] For reasons of economy, in April, 1766, the Commissioners of Trade also deferred any judgment on the plan of 1764 for the management of Indian affairs.[20] In spite of warnings by both Johnson and Gage that an Indian war would soon erupt unless the government could control the frontiersmen,[21] Conway gave the Commander-in-Chief in America little comfort. He was properly shocked by the "rash" and "most unjustifiable Behaviour of some of our Settlers on the Borders," but was confident that the governors and magistrates of the colonies would join Gage in punishing the frontiersmen for their "scandalous Disorders . . . ."[22]

The difficulty on the frontier was due in part to the fact that the boundary line set by the Proclamation of 1763 did not reflect the actual state of settlement in North America. Some of the settlers west of the mountains were legally entitled to their lands under grants made by Virginia before the outbreak of the French and Indian War.[23] In all fairness to the settlers, it is important to note that the imperial government was inconsistent in its

19. Conway to the Board of Trade, July 27, 1765, Board of Trade Papers, Plantations General, 20: 289, HSP transcript; *Journal of the Board of Trade, 1764–1767*, pp. 192, 193; and Conway to Gage, Oct. 24, 1765, *Gage Correspondence*, II, 27. See also "Notes on some papers in the Year June 1765–1766," Dartmouth Papers.

20. *Journal of the Board of Trade, 1764–1767*, pp. 271–273.

21. Johnson to Conway, June 28, 1766, *DRCHSNY*, VII, 836; Gage to Halifax, June 8, 1765, *Gage Correspondence*, I, 61.

22. Conway to Gage, Oct. 24, 1765, *ibid.*, II, 27.

23. Fauquier to the Board of Trade, Feb. 13, 1764, C. O. 5/1330: 589–591.

attitude. By the terms of the Proclamation of 1763, it denied their claims, but as late as 1766, the Auditor General for the Plantations, Robert Cholmondeley, insisted that they pay quit-rents for the same lands. Although the Privy Council referred the legal dilemma to the Board of Trade,[24] only an adjustment of the boundary line could resolve the matter.

Covert and illegal violations of the boundary by land speculators created further difficulties. George Washington and Thomas Walker of Virginia, and William Crawford of Pennsylvania, among others, secretly marked out lands on the Monongehela, Greenbriar, and New rivers in violation of the Proclamation of 1763, which Washington dismissed as merely a "temporary expedient to quiet the minds of the Indians." [25] Had they known of his activities, would the tribes have remained quiet for long? If the highborn and well-to-do so cavalierly dismissed the royal proclamation, it was little wonder that the more humble frontiersmen resorted to acts which embroiled them in open conflict with the Indians and earned for them, in Gage's words, the name of "Lawless Banditti." What aggravated the turbulent situation all the more was the difficulty the authorities experienced in trying to punish transgressors. The basis of the disorders, Gage felt, lay in the "Weakness of the [colonial] Governments to enforce obedience to the Laws." [26] Governor Francis Fauquier of Virginia agreed. He informed Halifax that the frontiersmen were "most publickly and notoriously" violating treaties the imperial officials had negotiated with the tribes. The provincial au-

24. See Cholmondeley's memorial to the King in Council, April 17, 1766, C. O. 323/24: 15–17; and *Journal of the Board of Trade, 1764–1767*, pp. 337, 345.

25. Washington to Crawford, Sept. 21, 1767, and Crawford to Washington, Sept. 29, 1767, Consul W. Butterfield (ed.), *Washington-Crawford Letters. Being the Correspondence Between George Washington and William Crawford, from 1767 to 1781 concerning western lands* (Cincinnati, 1877), 3–4, 8–9. See also P. Henry Jr. to Capt. William Fleming, June 10, 1767, Draper Collection, 15ZZ3, WHS. Not long before, the proprietors of Pennsylvania and Maryland had disapproved of continuing the boundary line between the two provinces in this general area "as they wou'd by no means give the least umbrage to the Indians . . . there at this Critical Juncture." Hugh Harmsley to Sharpe, Nov. 8, 1766, *Archives of Maryland*, XIV, 342.

26. Gage to Johnson, May 5, 1766, *Johnson Papers*, V, 201.

thorities were "set at open Defiance" since they did not have sufficient strength to enforce order.[27] No sooner had Sir William Johnson established peace with the tribes after Pontiac's rebellion than the frontiersmen on the borders of Pennsylvania, Maryland, and Virginia with no authorization began to migrate across the Allegheny Mountains. Such illegal settlement, Fauquier warned, would "certainly give umbrage to the neighbouring Indians." [28]

By the summer of 1765, confronted with widespread, overt violations of the prohibition against settlement which threatened to bring on an Indian war, the Whig ministry had to act.[29] On August 27, the Commissioners of Trade formally condemned the illegal settlements as dangerous to the peace of the frontier and recommended that the government immediately evacuate the squatters.[30] But it was not until October 18 that the Privy Council approved additional instructions to the governors of Virginia and Pennsylvania implementing this recommendation. Not only were the governors to remove all settlers on lands contiguous to the Ohio River, but they were to suppress any outrages committed against the Indians. If necessary, they were to apply to the Commander-in-Chief for royal troops to execute these orders.[31]

These orders had little effect. No matter how great the provocation, the British army hesitated to use naked force, and the law enforcement agencies in the colonies were inadequate.

Gage accurately reported the situation to Conway. The inability of the government to punish the "lawless Ruffians" merely encouraged other frontiersmen "to every Excess." Tried in one colony, they escaped to another, and "If by chance apprehended," they were either rescued from the law or faced an inconsequential trial, for "No Jury wou'd condemn them for murdering

27. Fauquier to Halifax, June 14, 1765, C. O. 5/1345: 159–160, LC transcript.

28. Fauquier to the Board of Trade, May 26, 1765, C. O. 5/1331: 9–10.

29. *Journal of the Board of Trade, 1764–1767*, pp. 190–192.

30. C. O. 5/1368: 261–264, LC transcript.

31. *Journal of the Board of Trade, 1764–1767*, pp. 211–212; *Acts of the Privy Council, Col.*, IV, 729–730. See also "Notes on some papers in the Year June 1765–1766," Dartmouth Papers. The additional instructions to Fauquier, dated Oct. 10, 1765, are found in C. O. 5/1368: 282–283, LC transcript.

or ill treating an Indian." Gage concluded that "the Reins of Government are too loose to enforce an Obedience to the Laws . . . ." [32] To make matters worse, George Croghan reported that some magistrates, rather than preserving peace on the frontier, actually encouraged whites to kill Indians.[33] The tribes were now thoroughly aroused. Unless the authorities removed the settlers from Red Stone Creek (a tributary of the Monongahela) and settled a new boundary line, the British would be "involved in all the Calamitys of another general War." [34] Sir William Johnson agreed with the sentiments of his deputy in warning the Commissioners of Trade that the chiefs could no longer hold back the warriors from making reprisals. The provincial governments were too weak to remedy the situation and, under the present circumstances, the Indian superintendent could do little.[35] Fauquier of Virginia confirmed the situation. He had done everything in his power to evacuate the settlers, but with little effect. "Perhaps the leaving them to the Mercy of the Indians," he conjectured, "may be the best if not the only Way to restrain them." [36] Not yet ready to adopt such a drastic step, Gage offered Governor John Penn the assistance of troops from Fort Pitt to remove squatters from Red Stone Creek. He reminded the Pennsylvania executive that settlement of lands west of the mountains by the whites was the "Chief Occasion of the defection of the Indians" at the outbreak of the French and Indian War.[37] Both Penn and Fauquier issued proclamations recalling the squatters, but with no results. The Virginia governor despaired that he did not "know what more can be done on our side . . . ." [38] Without resorting to violence, royal troops finally evacuated the illegal settlers on Red Stone Creek, but since no one punished the frontiersmen for their transgressions, they

32. Gage to Conway, May 6, 1766, *Gage Correspondence,* I, 91.

33. Croghan to Gage, June 17, 1766, Ayer Collection, Newberry Library.

34. Croghan to Gage, May 26, 1766, *Minutes, Provincial Council of Pennsylvania,* IX, 323.

35. Johnson to the Board of Trade, June 28, 1766, *DRCHSNY,* VII, 837–838.

36. Fauquier to the Board of Trade, July 26, 1766, C. O. 5/1331: 306.

37. Gage to Penn, July 2, 1766, *Minutes, Provincial Council of Pennsylvania,* IX, 321–322.

38. Fauquier to Penn, Dec. 11, 1766, *ibid.,* IX, 349.

simply returned to their illegal holdings in greater numbers than ever.[39]

The attempt by officials in the colonies to enforce the boundary line set by the Proclamation of 1763 proved fruitless.[40] This aspect of the program of 1763 was undermined. But the use of royal troops to enforce the boundary line further weakened another element of the imperial policy—military occupation of the interior.

During the Indian uprising of 1763, General Jeffrey Amherst had assigned garrisons to all of the forts in the wilderness in an effort to control the natives. While his resentment against the tribes had clouded Amherst's military judgment, Gage, his successor, had no illusions concerning the effectiveness of the isolated outposts in the face of a concerted Indian attack. In preparing for the offensive against the tribes in the spring of 1764, Gage had confided to Sir William Johnson that he did not plan to reoccupy all of the interior forts.[41] Gage's decision did not mean, however, that he would require fewer troops for the interior. He had to use every available man in view of the "small assistance" given by the colonies during the Indian war.[42]

The disposition of the troops in the interior which Amherst had advocated had certain disadvantages. Gage, his successor, pointed out to Conway that the garrisons "were greatly scattered and divided, over this vast Continent," and "very few could be collected in case of sudden Emergencies" except in Canada.[43] To remedy the situation, the Commander-in-Chief proposed evacuating several of the smaller posts and leaving such garrisons as were absolutely necessary for the defense of the larger installations.[44] Extremely conscious of the revenue problem, Conway, the Whig Secretary of State, speculated that the arrangement Gage had in

39. Gage to Penn, Dec. 7, 1767, *ibid.,* IX, 403.

40. Gage to Penn, Dec. 7, 1767, *ibid.,* IX, 403–404; Gage to Johnson, April 3, June 28, 1767, *Johnson Papers,* V, 535, 574; Penn to Johnson, Dec. 15, 1767, *ibid.,* VI, 4–5.

41. Gage to Johnson, May 16, 1764, *ibid.,* IV, 424.

42. Welbore Ellis to Halifax, June 16, 1764, *Calendar of Home Office Papers, George III,* I, 420.

43. Gage to Conway, Sept. 23, 1765, Alvord and Carter, *New Regime,* 87.

44. Gage to Barrington, March 29, 1766, *Gage Correspondence,* II, 345.

mind "will in many respects be very advantageous," particularly since it would mean a reduction in expenses. After all, the American colonists who "do not like to be taxed for our Ease," he noted wryly, constituted an expense to the mother country "it is scarce able to bear." [45]

In the spring of 1766, Gage modified the disposition of the frontier garrisons. He ordered the commanders in the Floridas to erect no new posts on the southern frontier,[46] but carried out a drastic reduction in the north. The British evacuated several of the smaller forts which had served as communication points between Albany, Detroit, and Fort Pitt. Those posts which remained on the line from Albany to the Lakes included Stanwix, Ontario, Niagara, Erie, Detroit, and Michillimackinac. Three forts—George, Ticonderoga, and Crown Point—secured the route from Albany to Canada. Forts Pitt and Ligonier linked the Ohio River to Pennsylvania. The Commander-in-Chief planned to reduce the garrisons at these posts "to such numbers as shall be merely necessary for their Defense . . . ." He presumed they would be sufficient to fulfill "every Purpose of Forts in the Indian Country" and that the mother country would be saved a great expense. The repeal of the Stamp Act had had its effect, but the Stamp Act riots had a more important consequence. Under the military arrangement set up by Amherst, the Commander-in-Chief had not been able to gather even two companies to meet an emergency; but now Gage expected that he could assemble a corps equal to three regiments.[47]

While the revolutionary East served to draw troops from the interior forts, to the west the Illinois country also constituted a drain on the limited forces available to the Commander-in-Chief. The Illinois and the lower Wabash valleys presented a unique problem. This area had not come under British occupation at the fall of New France, and the antipathy of the tribes

45. Conway to Gage, May 20, 1766, C. O. 5/84: 249.

46. Gage to Colonel Taylor, Aug. 11, 1766, Add. MSS 21663, ff. 114–115, PAC transcript. See also Douglas Stewart Brown, "The Iberville Canal Project: Its Relation to the Anglo-French Commercial Rivalry in the Mississippi Valley, 1763–1775," *Mississippi Valley Historical Review,* XXXII (1946), 491–516.

47. Gage to Conway, May 6, 1766, *Gage Correspondence,* I, 90.

frustrated subsequent attempts by way of the Mississippi to occupy the district after the Peace of Paris. To the British, the Illinois country was essential as a counterpoise to the French on the right bank of the Mississippi who were erecting fortifications which could be expected to attract the tribes. To nullify this potential threat, Gage considered constructing a British fort at the mouth of the Illinois River.[48] But first, in order to conciliate the Illinois tribes and to pave the way for occupation by the British army, in the summer of 1765, Gage sent George Croghan, deputy Indian agent, to the Mississippi. After a hazardous journey during which he almost lost his life at the hands of the belligerent natives, Croghan accomplished his mission. Detachments of regular troops from Fort Pitt and the Gulf Coast then took possession of the French forts remaining on the east bank of the Mississippi.[49] Although Croghan had stopped at "Post Vincent . . . A French Village of about 80 houses," [50] British troops did not occupy the Wabash Valley.

The occupation of the Illinois country brought additional problems which further depleted the resources available to Gage for controlling the interior. Unwilling at first to accept British rule, many of the inhabitants had moved west of the Mississippi to the new French centers at Ste. Genevieve and St. Louis; due to this migration, it was extremely difficult for the British garrisons in the Illinois country to obtain provisions from the immediate area. To transport supplies from the settled colonies some 1,400 miles away by the river system was almost impossible. In order to solve the problem, Gage devised a plan similar to the one he had suggested in 1764 for the posts at Niagara and Fort Pitt. In March, 1766, he recommended to Conway that the government establish semimilitary colonies in the Illinois country to alleviate the difficulty in supplying the garrisons. This plan would cost the government little, and, unless the ministers acted, the French

48. Gage to Halifax, Aug. 10, 1765, Alvord and Carter, *New Regime,* 70–71.

49. Gage to Conway, Nov. 9, 1765, *ibid.,* 115–116; Gage to Conway, Jan. 16, 1766, *Gage Correspondence,* I, 80.

50. See the entry in Croghan's journal dated June 15, 1765, *DRCHSNY,* VII, 780.

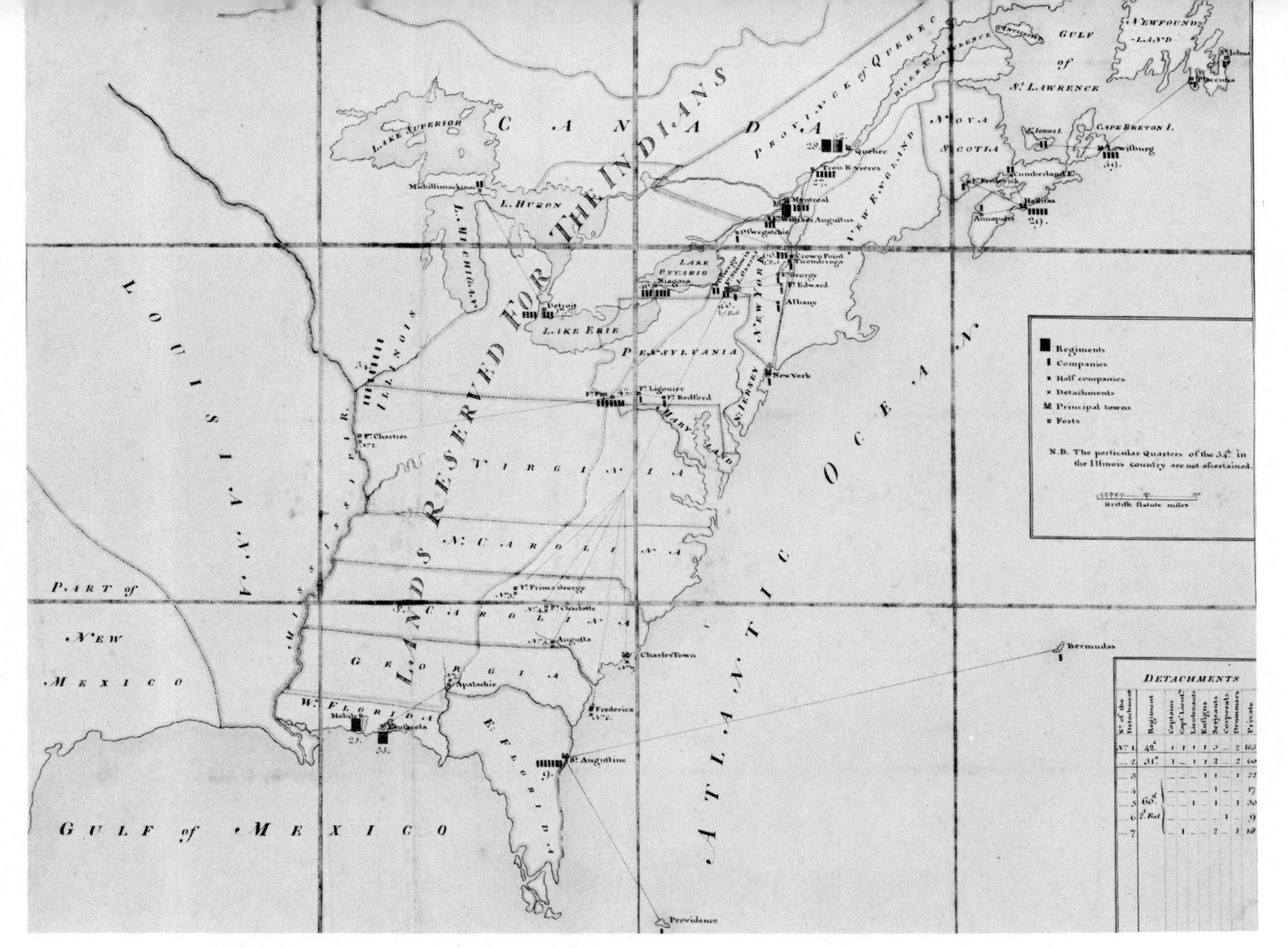

Cantonment of the Forces in North America, 1761. Courtesy William L. Clements Library, Ann Arbor, Michigan.

would always be able to exert the greater influence in the Illinois country, the Commander-in-Chief predicted.[51]

Henry Conway was pessimistic about the proposal. The probable destruction of Fort Chartres by the erosive waters of the Mississippi, the "immoderate" distance of the Illinois country, the hostility of the French, Spanish, and Indians, all militated against the success of a military colony. These factors would make such a settlement "a very troublesome and expensive one," he conjectured.[52] Nevertheless, in May, 1766, the Secretary of State referred the scheme to the Board of Trade,[53] perhaps with the tacit understanding that they would reject the proposal. Since the Rockingham ministry left office that summer, it was not until August, 1766 that a new board under the Earl of Hillsborough could come to any decision. In the interval, the Commander-in-Chief pressed the issue, stressing the illegal activities of the French fur traders in the Illinois country. Since French merchants at New Orleans paid higher prices for furs than did their rivals at the Atlantic ports, great quantities of peltry were going down the Mississippi River and never saw a British port. To disrupt this traffic, Gage proposed erecting forts at the mouths of the Ohio and Illinois rivers. He was unable to estimate the expense of such an undertaking, nor could he determine whether the commerce of the Illinois country could bear the charge. Yet the area was best situated to secure the whole of the interior for the British traders and to prevent the French from engrossing the trade of the entire region south of the Great Lakes.[54] With the fur trade went the Indian alliance.

On the formation of the Chatham ministry in the summer of 1766, the Commissioners of Trade under Hillsborough were able to consider the disposition of the Illinois country. But the board could only act at the request of the Privy Council or the Secretary of State, in this case, the Earl of Shelburne. Significantly, the

51. Gage to Conway, March 28, 1766, *Gage Correspondence,* I, 86–87.
52. Conway to Gage, May 20, 1766, *ibid.,* II, 38.
53. Conway to the Board of Trade, May 23, 1766, C. O. 323/18: 553.
54. Gage to Conway, July 15, 1766, *Gage Correspondence,* I, 99–100.

commissioners discussed the Illinois problem only once,[55] and then reported, on September 3, that they must defer making any recommendation since it was the opinion of Shelburne that "general regulations" placing the whole of the interior under "one uniform plan" were necessary in order to rectify existing disorders on the frontier.[56]

Apparently Shelburne was calling for a re-evaluation of western policy. In view of the developments on the frontier and the dilemma of financing the imperial program because of the controversy over taxing the Americans, it is not surprising that he did so. But Shelburne was not the first to realize that the government needed to review the situation.

Viscount Barrington—a close friend of Hillsborough—had served as Secretary-at-War in the Rockingham ministry and now held the same post under Chatham. Shortly after the Stamp Act riots in the fall of 1765 had revealed the inability of the imperial government to control the colonists, Barrington began corresponding privately with Gage in America on the disposition of the royal forces on the continent. Although their exchange centered on the specific problem of the interior posts and the garrisons in the Indian country, it had ramifications for western policy in general. Gage was instrumental in shaping Barrington's views on these problems. In turn, the Commander-in-Chief was influenced by the ideas of the chief military engineer in America, Captain Harry Gordon. In fact, Gordon and Gage worked closely on the question. The chief military engineer was perhaps the best qualified authority in the field, for he had inspected the interior forts during an intensive tour of the wilderness. Since he was intimately familiar with the immediate situation, Gordon tended to dismiss the self-styled experts who claimed to be highly informed on the fortifications in the West. He particularly resented General Jeffrey Amherst, who, although in England, "still continues to throw Squibs to this Distance." [57] In

55. *Journal of the Board of Trade, 1764–1767,* pp. 334–336.

56. C. O. 5/66: 367.

57. Gordon to Johnson, March 4, 1766, Alvord and Carter, *New Regime,* 161; to David Thoronton, May 20, 1766, printed in *Mississippi Valley Historical Review,* XV (1928), 93. For Gordon's detailed views on the North

1763, Amherst had insisted on complete military occupation of the West. In contrast, both Gage and Gordon recognized the need to curtail expenses and to consolidate troop positions. They had learned from the experience of the Stamp Act and Pontiac's rebellion.

The sentiments of Gage and Gordon assumed greater significance when Barrington wrote privately to the Commander-in-Chief in October, 1765, pointing out the necessity of altering the inefficient and expensive military disposition made by Amherst. It was apparent to the Secretary-at-War that, by evacuating the western posts and stationing the troops east of the Proclamation line, the ministry would alleviate the financial burden on Great Britain. In all justice to Amherst, Barrington recognized that the military disposition set by the former Commander-in-Chief had been correct for the situation in North America in 1763, but he was convinced that the interval of peace must have produced significant changes in the interior. One inconvenience of the system made by Amherst was immediately evident to Barrington. The troops were so widely dispersed that the Commander-in-Chief could not assemble a sizable force in case of emergency. But if the garrisons were relocated and conveniently stationed on the seacoast, the army could furnish immediate aid if required. Having discussed the problem in London with Lieutenant Colonel James Robertson, Deputy Barracks-master General in America, Barrington now desired Gage's opinion for the edification of the ministry.[58] In reply, General Gage sent the Secretary-at-War two reports on the fortifications in America. The first, dealing with the posts in the northern district, he dispatched on December 18, 1765.[59] The second, dated January 8, 1766, dealt with the installations in Georgia and the Floridas and had little bearing on the situation in the North. As Barrington had requested, the

American fortifications, see his "Memorial Concerning the Back Forts in North America," dated Dec. 17, 1765, Pargellis, *Military Affairs in North America,* 464–470.

58. Barrington to Gage (private), Oct. 10, 1765, Gage Papers, WLCL.

59. "Report of the Forts in North America, from their being first erected, to the present time, and Observations thereupon," *Gage Correspondence,* II, 319–322.

Commander-in-Chief took the liberty of expressing his opinions "with great freedom upon the whole of them." [60]

The northern posts were not sufficient, thought Gage, to deter Indian incursions, as the uprising of 1763 had demonstrated. But in time of peace they were of some use in protecting the Indians from fraud by the traders whose activities had won for the British a poor reputation among the tribes. But the forts were also of limited value as points of communication and as a check on the French traders operating from New Orleans and the Illinois country, who had infiltrated British territory up to the Ohio and Illinois rivers as far as Fort Pitt and Lake Michigan. Had it not been for the garrisons at the forts, the French would have been able to operate throughout the Indian country. As it was, they were inciting the tribes and hindering a peaceful adjustment between the British and the natives. Perhaps the occupation of the Illinois country by the British might curtail the French, but it was still too early to determine the consequences of this move. On the basis of these estimates, Gage deduced that the only advantages to be gained from the forts would lie in winning the fur trade, holding the allegiance of the tribes, and preventing the Indians, under the influence of the French, from raiding the white settlements. But even if these benefits were fully realized, would they be commensurate with the cost of maintaining the posts? To answer this difficult question would require a thorough knowledge of the value of the fur trade in the whole interior, from Canada to Virginia, and of the particular consequences to this traffic if the army abandoned specific forts. In view of the insolence and ingratitude of the colonists and their refusal to contribute their share to the exigencies of government, Gage preferred to leave the supervision of the trade to the provinces. But the merchants of the mother country who benefited from the traffic would then complain. Under the prewar arrangement, the provincials had managed the Indian trade without the use of forts, but they had cheated the natives and encroached on their lands so that the tribes had joined the French in the late war. To avoid a repetition of these mistakes in Indian relations, the imperial government had adopted the program of garrisoning the

60. Gage to Barrington (private), Jan. 8, 1766, Gage Papers, WLCL.

interior, maintaining an Indian boundary line, and regulating the trade with the natives. If the ministry should consider the advantages of the imperial system sufficient to justify keeping up the interior posts, how could they continue the program with the least expense?

Reductions in personnel and a modification of the system of provisioning the garrisons would lessen expenses. The northern forts between Canada and the older British colonies were of little value; except for Crown Point and Fort George, Gage would abandon them in the spring. As soon as he established a new supply system, he would also evacuate the communication posts between Montreal and Lake Ontario. While this retrenchment in the North would reduce expense, the construction of additional forts in the Illinois country to prevent the French from infiltrating British territory would wipe out any savings. Difficulties in provisioning posts in the Illinois country made such a plan expensive and hazardous, for the only eligible routes lay by way of the Ohio and Mississippi rivers from Fort Pitt and the Gulf of Mexico. These involved a hazardous journey of several months subject to interdiction at several points along the way by the Indians and the French. The French controlled New Orleans, and the Iberville River channel to the Mississippi had proved to be impractical for purposes of navigation.[61]

General Gage had presented two alternatives, as the Secretary-at-War quickly perceived. In the first, the colonists would manage Indian affairs, unassisted by royal troops or fortifications as had been the case before the French and Indian War. By the second, the imperial government would still be responsible for the interior but would abandon some forts and reduce the garrisons of those remaining. To Barrington, it seemed that the ministry could safely allow the Americans to resume control, for they should presumably have benefited from the experience of the late war and could manage Indian affairs much better than previously. Perhaps the desire to reduce the financial burden on Great Britain colored Barrington's judgment, but he seemed to postpone any final opinion until he could receive more data. In

61. "Report of the Forts in North America . . . ," *Gage Correspondence*, II, 319–322.

February, 1766, he asked Gage to submit further information on the alternative programs available to the government and as to the probable disposition of the troops should the ministry adopt either plan.[62]

Gage confirmed Barrington's analysis of his reports on the northern fortifications. Under the first plan, the Commander-in-Chief assumed that he would abandon the forts while the provincial governments would again regulate commercial and political relations with the tribes. This would relieve the mother country of the financial burden involved in administering the wilderness. But the attitude taken by the ministry in London toward the colonies and the tribes was decisive, in Gage's estimate. If the ministry felt that Great Britain could no longer bear the expense of the imperial program, and if the government would resist the outcries of the merchants and the colonists should the Indians become hostile, then it could adopt a program of provincial control. Gage assumed, and admitted openly, that war with the tribes would result, for the colonists would not be able successfully to manage Indian affairs. From prewar experience, he predicted that they would continue to defraud the Indians and deprive them of their lands. At present, it was all that the military could do to prevent such impositions. Gage presented an additional argument against colonial control. If the provinces did not properly manage the Indian trade, the tribes would turn to the French within easy reach on the west bank of the Mississippi River. Once they had become powerful by reestablishing their Indian alliances, the French could threaten the security of the new acquisitions. In the opinion of the Commander-in-Chief in America, the individual most qualified to judge, the ministry should not abandon the imperial program for regulating the wilderness. It could with safety evacuate some of the posts. In fact, Gage had already begun such a move.[63]

Gage's analysis offered the most rational exposition of the entire problem. Based on the concrete experience of men involved in actually administering the interior, it constituted the best

62. Barrington to Gage (private), Feb. 7, 1766, Gage Papers, WLCL.

63. Gage to Barrington (private), May 7, 1766, *Gage Correspondence,* II, 349–351.

answer to the arguments of those who challenged the imperial program. But Gage could not determine, he could only recommend, policy. The ministers had to make the decision.

Even before receiving confirmation from the Commander-in-Chief of his own interpretation of Gage's first report of December 18, 1765, Barrington began formulating his own plan to alter the dispositions of the troops in America. In March, 1766, he transmitted copies of his correspondence with Gage to Conway, stressing the danger in the riotous eastern colonies and the necessity of having forces available to use in an emergency. With the garrisons widely dispersed, it was impossible to collect a respectable force within a short time.[64] By May 7, the Secretary-at-War had drafted a plan based on the material supplied by Gage, Lieutenant Colonel Robertson, and others in London recommended by the Commander-in-Chief. Barrington circulated the document among the other ministers and then sent it to Gage for such emendations as Gage would deem necessary. By September, 1766, Barrington had received Gage's corrections. It was evident that the two men agreed on "the main points."[65] The Commander-in-Chief had limited his role to presenting alternative solutions to the minister and in pointing out the relative merits of each. Gage had not openly committed himself to a decision on policy which he properly considered the function of the ministers. But the tenor of his report and his subsequent observations on the Barrington plan clearly indicated that he favored continued imperial jurisdiction over the interior, although on a reduced level.

In his plan, Barrington employed many of the arguments Gage had advanced in depreciating the value of the fur trade and the forts, but he sharpened the position taken by the Commander-in-Chief. Except for one point, he did not differ markedly with Gage. Barrington argued against establishing colonies in the interior simply because inadequate transportation facilities made them of little value to the mother country. He objected to the continued maintenance of the forts in the Indian

64. Barrington to Conway, March 17, 1766, *Calendar of Home Office Papers, George III,* II, 26.

65. Barrington to Gage (private), May 7, Sept. 12, 1766, Gage Papers, WLCL.

country, since they were expensive to keep up, precariously situated, and so scattered that it was impossible to collect a respectable force in case of emergency. Citing the views of Sir William Johnson and General Gage that the forts did not serve to deter the Indians from raiding the frontier, Barrington argued that they need not be used in the Indian trade either. He was on weak ground on this point. Barrington assumed that, since the French were now located west of the Mississippi and the river itself offered a poor means of transportation, the Indians had no other alternative but to trade with the British. In these circumstances, they could just as well travel to the settled colonies to trade. Consequently, Barrington would return control of Indian affairs to the colonial governments. His reasoning was fallacious, and in the "Remarks" which became part of the Barrington plan, Gage emphasized the extent to which the French drained the fur trade by way of the Mississippi to New Orleans. On all of the other points, the two men were in agreement. Barrington proposed retaining some of the forts in the interior, those easily supplied by vessels on the Great Lakes—Oswego, Niagara, Detroit, and Michillimackinac. In order to exclude French traders from British territory, garrisons would occupy Fort Chartres in the Illinois country. These men would be supplied by way of the Ohio River. The heart of the Barrington plan lay in the provisions for reducing expenses and stationing a large corps of men in Quebec and Nova Scotia where they would be within easy sailing distance from the coasts of the seaboard colonies.[66] As they related to the interior, the main points of the Barrington plan did not differ greatly from Gage's recommendations. The only substantial point of disagreement had been on the evaluation of the French competition from New Orleans. Gage had corrected this in his "Remarks" which became part of the Barrington plan.

66. "Ld Barrington's Plan relative to the Out Posts, Indian Trade & c. with Remarks 10 May 1766," Shelburne Papers, 50: 45–64, WLCL; printed in Alvord and Carter, *New Regime*, 234–245. A copy was made for the King. See Fortescue, *Correspondence of George III*, I, 432–441, and Lewis B. Namier, *Additions and Corrections to Sir John Fortescue's Edition of the Correspondence of King George the Third (Vol. I)* (Manchester, England, 1937), 69.

Between the time the Secretary-at-War drew up his original proposal and the addition of Gage's corrections, a change in ministry occurred. Although Barrington had circulated his original plan among the Whig ministers, there is no indication of their reaction.[67] It was of little consequence, for they did not have to make any decision. Professional politician that he was, Barrington survived the fall of the Whig ministry in the summer of 1766 and retained his post of Secretary-at-War in the succeeding Chatham administration. Now he had an opportunity to present his proposals anew. In September, he informed Gage: "I have communicated my Paper to Lord Chatham & Lord Shelburne, who agree with me almost in every point . . . ." And he predicted, "Ere long you will hear from the ministry on the matter it contains." [68] Barrington's prognostication was correct, for very early in the Chatham administration, western policy became a material subject. As it turned out, Chatham himself did not play a prominent role in this discussion, indeed, in very few during his administration. Consequently, the Earl of Shelburne, as Secretary of State for the Southern Department, attempted to exert the dominant influence in forming colonial policy. His role was all the more important in view of the reduced status of the Board of Trade. It could only deal with matters the Secretary of State chose to refer to it. Under these circumstances,

67. Charles Ritcheson, *British Politics and the American Revolution* (Norman, Okla., 1954), 64, maintains that the Barrington plan "may be accepted" as a statement of the views "of the Rockingham ministry toward the west." Offering no evidence to support this view, he follows too closely the interpretation of Alvord. A comparison of the private correspondence exchanged between Barrington and Gage with the views expressed in Alvord and Carter, *New Regime,* 234–245, and Alvord, *Mississippi Valley,* I, 246–249, demonstrates how inaccurate Alvord's view was. He castigated Gage for political cowardice in not criticizing Barrington, apparently without knowing that most of the information that went into the Secretary-at-War's plan was originally supplied by Gage. *Ibid.,* I, 310. It must also be remembered that Gage's position was not to determine policy, which was a function of the ministry, but merely to offer information and the probable consequence of alternative programs. Contrary to the opinion of Alvord and Carter, it was Barrington, not Shelburne, who was responsible for the addition of Gage's "Remarks." They formed an integral part of the over-all plan.

68. Barrington to Gage (private), Sept. 12, 1766, Gage Papers, WLCL.

Shelburne's reaction to the various problems in the North American wilderness is important.

On assuming office, Shelburne had to face the challenge to the imperial system posed by the turbulent frontier. He seemed to react in much the same manner as Halifax and Conway, who had preceded him in office. In September, 1766, Shelburne informed Sir William Johnson, General Thomas Gage, and the colonial governors of the ministry's displeasure at the fraud and violence being perpetrated on the tribes who were under the King's protection and of the illegal settlements made in direct violation of the Proclamation of 1763. The situation was so critical that Shelburne was convinced that the government must institute a general plan to prevent a recurrence of these irregular and provocative assaults on the frontier. He now dispatched a circular letter to the colonial governors and the Commander-in-Chief, requiring them to cooperate in enforcing the Proclamation of 1763 "which if duly atented [*sic*] to might have been effectual for the Prevention of those Evils . . . ."[69] There was nothing startling about Shelburne's attitude at this time. He was reflecting sentiments held in administration circles since the French and Indian War. In no uncertain terms he had ordered colonial officials to uphold the policy evolved during that conflict and incorporated in the Proclamation of 1763.

But the replies from the officials in America indicated that this would be easier said than done. In spite of the difficulties involved, Gage pledged that nothing on his part would be left wanting to enforce the imperial policy. Sir William Johnson took this opportunity to forward a full exposition of his views to the minister, warning that the opposition encountered by the personnel of the Indian department almost prevented them from executing their duties under the program of the home government. The "thirst" for Indian lands among the colonists was now almost universal. Land speculators were unconcerned that their actions aroused the tribes and could lead to another bloody

69. Shelburne to Johnson, Sept. 13, 1766, *Johnson Papers,* V, 374–375; Shelburne to Gage, Sept. 13, 1766, *Gage Correspondence,* II, 45; his circular letter to the governors of the same date is printed in *Archives of Maryland,* XIV, 328–329 and *New Jersey Archives,* 1st ser., IX, 569–570.

Indian war. It was imperative that the home government immediately implement the plan of 1764 for managing Indian affairs to prevent the very abuses of which Shelburne complained.[70] The views of the Indian superintendent were in direct contrast to those of the recently appointed governor of Quebec. Guy Carleton informed the Secretary of State that since arriving in the colony he had not received "the least Intimation, either Publick or Private," that the inhabitants had mistreated the Indians residing within or adjacent to the colony.[71] Perhaps the French-Canadians were just in their dealings with the tribes, but the evaluation of the governor of Virginia on the behavior of the British colonists was less assuring. Francis Fauquier enumerated in detail the illegal activities of the frontiersmen and stressed the difficulty encountered by the colonial governments in trying to enforce the imperial policy. Since the lands between the mountains and the Ohio were said to be so extremely fertile, "people will run all risques whether from Governments or from Indians" to settle there "without the least plea of Right . . . ." [72]

Before receiving this letter, Shelburne informed the Virginia governor that "His Majesty expects daily" to hear that the provincial government had "brought to condign Punishment" those persons violating Indian treaties. Since the prosperity of the American colonists, especially the back settlers, depended so much on maintaining peace and friendship with the natives, "it is amazing," Shelburne wrote, "that such Enormities can remain any time undiscovered." The colonists could never expect a lasting peace with the Indians, he lectured, until "they convince them they would rather protect them than destroy them . . . ." But, he assumed, the traders, for selfish views, had inculcated "into the minds of these poor People, that nothing will satisfy the Colonies but their Extirpation . . . ." [73] The natives would naturally look upon the British as their guardians and de-

70. Gage to Shelburne, Nov. 11, 1766, *Gage Correspondence,* I, 112; Johnson to Shelburne, Dec. 16, 1766, *DRCHSNY,* VII, 880–883.

71. Carleton to Shelburne, Dec. 20, 1766, C. O. 42/27:12, PAC transcript.

72. Fauquier to Shelburne, Nov. 18, Dec. 18, 1766, C. O. 5/1345: 313–314; 338–340.

73. Shelburne to Fauquier, Feb. 19, 1767, C. O. 5/1345: 307–308.

fenders, "the only Refuge they will think of seeking in their Distress," if only they were convinced that the government would guarantee their lands and punish traders who cheated them.[74] It is clear that as late as February, 1767, Shelburne still supported the imperial system and that he blamed the whites on the frontier, not the Indians or the imperial system of regulation, for the disturbances which threatened the peace of the wilderness.

The reports of the colonial officials should have made Shelburne aware—indeed, as evidenced by his remarks to Fauquier, he was aware—of the difficulties involved in adjusting the program for the interior. But Shelburne exhibited a strange mentality and an ability to deceive himself and others as well. His thinking was confused and contradictory. On the one hand, he urged officials in America to uphold the Proclamation of 1763, and on the other, he attempted to alter completely the imperial program for the interior. For example, Shelburne rejected Sir William Johnson's plea that the government implement the plan of 1764 for the management of Indian affairs. It "requires nice Examination," he wrote, "being of a very dubious Nature in many of its most essential Points." [75] He was even more emphatic with Gage. The plan of 1764 had proved unsuccessful and had to be revised or totally scrapped. Shelburne was contradicting himself, for both the program for regulating Indian trade and the Proclamation of 1763 were part of the same integral policy. In his letter to Fauquier, he stated that the difficulty on the frontier stemmed from the fact that officials in America had not duly executed the Proclamation. In his correspondence with Gage, he claimed that the plan of 1764 was not working in practice. Whereas he criticized, in his letter to Fauquier, the colonial governments for not protecting the Indians, he wrote Gage that the most preferable system would be to leave the regulation of Indian trade to the colonies. Neither was the Secretary of State clear on what should be done with the western forts. The ministry was now considering Barrington's plan.

But of one point Shelburne was certain, that of revenue to

74. Shelburne to Johnson, Dec. 11, 1766, *Johnson Papers*, V, 447.
75. *Ibid.*

support the military establishment. The creation of an American fund "is so highly reasonable," he wrote to Gage, "that it must take place sooner or later." The most obvious method of raising revenue in America—or so it seemed to Shelburne—was to take "proper care of the quitrents, and by turning the grants of land to real benefit," in order to increase "rather than diminish the power of government in so distant a country . . . ." [76]

What influenced Shelburne to accept the impractical scheme of raising an American revenue by quitrents, a token sum paid annually to the royal government for land, usually two shillings per hundred acres? As early as October, 1766, the followers of Grenville were derisively circulating the rumor in London that the Chatham ministry planned to raise revenue by this technique.[77] Perhaps Shelburne was impressed when Gage had informed him earlier that the French inhabitants at Detroit paid such rents as a condition of land tenure under the French regime. The sum collected "must be trifling at present, tho' by an Increase of Inhabitants and Extention of the Settlement" it might become considerable, the Commander-in-Chief predicted. Gage had transmitted to the Secretary of State an account of the manner in which land grants were made at Detroit and a statement of the revenue accruing from them.[78] Evidently Shelburne valued this information, for he had a copy of the document made for his private papers.[79]

To collect rents from relatively submissive French inhabitants was one thing, but to do so from the highly individualistic British colonists was an almost impossible task. So Shelburne would learn when he received the replies of the colonial governors to an inquiry on the collection of the rents which he sent them in December, 1766.[80] If the government experienced so much diffi-

76. Shelburne to Gage, Dec. 11, 1766, *Gage Correspondence,* II, 48–50.

77. Whately to Grenville, Oct. 20, 1766, *Grenville Papers,* III, 334.

78. Gage to Shelburne, Oct. 10, 1766, *Gage Correspondence,* I, 110–111.

79. "State of the King['s] Rights and Revenues at the Detroit and Conditions on which Lots were granted in the Town and Lands in the Settlement & c in the time of the French," Shelburne Papers, 50: 287–290, WLCL.

80. Shelburne's circular letter, dated Dec. 11, 1766, printed in *New Jersey Archives,* 1st ser., IX, 573–574; *DRCHSNY,* VII, 880; and *Archives of Maryland,* XIV, 361. See volumes 55 and 56, Shelburne Papers, WLCL, for sum-

culty in collecting rents in the settled coastal colonies, what would be the chances of extracting revenue from the turbulent frontiersmen in the interior?

Shelburne did not derive his solution to the problem of revenue from any realistic evaluation of the situation in the colonies, but from his political commitments in England. As a follower of William Pitt, Earl of Chatham, Shelburne was committed to oppose the Declaratory Act passed by the Rockingham ministry by which Parliament affirmed its right to legislate for the colonies in all cases whatsoever. Chatham had denied the right of Parliament to tax the colonies. How could Shelburne raise revenue in America for the support of the western program without taxing the colonists? The solution seemed to be quitrents. But the reaction of the Americans to imperial supervision placed Shelburne in a dilemma. He expressed himself on this point in an interview with Dennys De Berdt, agent for the Massachusetts House of Representatives. The colonists might feel perfectly at ease about their just rights and privileges under the Chatham ministry, but the British must maintain the "dignity of government" and the Americans must pay "due regard to the administration here . . . ." [81] Here was the dilemma of the Chatham administration: to raise revenue in America for the support of its western program and maintain the authority of the British government, but at the same time not to infringe on the rights of the colonists. But the Americans had challenged the authority of the government by refusing to accept the Stamp Act, and they had flouted the imperial program for the wilderness by violating the Indian boundary line and ignoring the trade regulations. The repeal of the Stamp Act had momentarily quieted the controversy on taxation, but it had also undermined the program of military occupation of the West. For the moment, the army remained in the wilderness, but it constituted a severe drain on British finances. To some, the solution was obvious: either the Americans must contribute for the support of the army, or the

mary accounts of the colonial quitrents based on the responses of the governors in answer to this circular letter.

81. Dennys De Berdt to Thomas Cushing, Sept. 19, 1766, "De Berdt Letters," *Publications* of the Col. Soc. of Mass., XIII, 326.

British must evacuate the West. The violent reaction to the Stamp Act in America had inclined such men as Barrington and Gage to favor the latter alternative, if only because they saw the need for troops on the seaboard to enforce the authority of the mother country and to thwart what seemed to them to be impending revolution. In 1767, western policy brought the political dispute over taxation once more into the limelight. The connection was immediate and direct.

CHAPTER VI

Shelburne and the Lobbyists

WHATEVER factors caused the rupture between Great Britain and her colonies, the American Revolution was a political and constitutional struggle between two conflicting authorities: the British Parliament and the colonial legislatures. In the final analysis, the Americans justified their revolt by denying the right of the British Parliament to legislate for them. The conflict in authority was clear as early as 1764, when the colonists had sought to limit Parliamentary authority mainly on the question of taxation. But the claim of the Americans had motivated the Grenville ministry to assert the right with the passage of the Stamp Act. The colonial reaction to the revenue measure initiated the first step culminating in the American Revolution. Although the Rockingham ministry had repealed the offensive act and had shown the Americans some "leniency" by modifying the trade laws of the Grenville regime which the colonists had thought restrictive, it had declared the power of Parliament to legislate for the colonies in all cases whatsoever. The issue was clear to the British. Parliament was superior to any colonial legislature. But it was exactly this point which the assembly of New York disputed when it failed to comply with the terms of the British Mutiny Act which regulated the royal army in America. Passed in 1765, this law required colonial legislatures to provide certain services to royal troops in a manner specified by Parliament. Without directly rejecting the act, the assembly of New York evaded the measure, much to the displeasure of the Chatham ministry, which felt compelled to warn the New Yorkers. On August 5, 1766, the cabinet affirmed that "it is the duty" of the colonists "to obey acts of the legislature of Great Britain . . . ." The ministers could not doubt that after the "leniency" shown to the Americans by the repeal of the Stamp Act, the New Yorkers would not fail to comply with the Mutiny Bill.[1]

Although the New York legislature did pass a bill to implement the British act, it did not follow the procedures set by Parliament. The Board of Trade condemned the provincial law, since in one instance it did not conform to the Mutiny Act, and in another it was "repugnant" to the law of Parliament.[2] Shelburne, reportedly "very much disgusted," termed the conduct of the New York legislature "impudent and infatuated." The other ministers were equally incensed at this challenge to authority.[3] And they were all the more indignant when more than two hundred New York merchants challenged the traditional navigation system, a system which Chatham himself held dear. In November, 1766, the New York mercantile community petitioned that the commercial regulations enacted by the Rockingham ministry in 1766 "instead of remedying, have encreased, the heavy burthen" under which the colonial trade "already laboured." [4] The New York petition created a sensation in London. It "is likely the talk of the town," Shelburne reported. The colonists seemed to confirm what many had been saying. In the House of Commons, George Grenville would probably impute it as "rebellious." Chatham himself was furious at the "spirit of infatuation" which had possessed the New Yorkers. He termed their petition "highly improper," their pretentions "most excessive," and their reasoning "most grossly fallacious and offensive . . . ." They would draw upon themselves, he predicted, "a torrent of indignation"

1. Cabinet minute, Aug. 5, 1766, Chatham Papers, P. R. O. 30/8/97: 79.

2. Board of Trade report, March 26, 1767, C. O. 5/1130: 389–393.

3. William Samuel Johnson to William Pitkin, Feb. 12, 1767, Trumbull Papers, Massachusetts Historical Society *Collections,* 5th ser., IX, 216; Shelburne to Chatham [Feb. 16, 1767], Chatham to Shelburne and Grafton, Feb. 17, 1767, *Chatham Correspondence,* III, 206–210, 215.

4. Petition of the New York merchants, Nov. 28, 1766, Shelburne Papers, 49: 524–530, WLCL.

in Parliament and "resentment" from the nation at large "by their ingratitude . . . ." Ever sanguine, Shelburne hoped that the government would "distinguish between *New York* and *America,*" but Chatham was less discriminating. "New York has drunk the deepest of the baneful cup of infatuation," but none of the Americans "seem to be quite sober and in full possession of reason." They would deliver themselves into "the hands of their enemies." [5] Chatham was right, for when the ministry laid the New York petition before the House of Commons, Grenville and the other opposition politicians were confirmed in the warning they had given the previous year. ". . . nothing will give Satisfaction to the Colonists but an absolute Repeal of all Regulations and Restrictions and in the end Independence" from Great Britain.[6]

No faction in the House of Commons, administration supporters, independent country gentlemen, or the opposition groups, consequently, could be expected to have much sympathy for the colonists when the issue of American expenses further exacerbated the colonial question. The need for revenue to support the military establishment in America had led to the basic Grenville tax measures, but by the repeal of the Stamp Act, the Rockingham ministry had undermined the financial system established by the previous administration. Since the repeal of the Stamp Act and the reduction of import duties imposed by Grenville, American revenue had not yielded more than £80,000 annually.[7] The military expenditures remained as great a problem as ever.

On January 26, 1767, Barrington, the Secretary-at-War, brought into the House of Commons the estimated budget for the army in America for the coming year. The sum came to over £400,000, the equivalent of a shilling on the pound on the land tax in

5. Chatham to Shelburne, Feb. 3, 1767; Shelburne to Chatham, Feb. 6, 1767, *Chatham Correspondence,* III, 188, 191–193.

6. Charles Garth to the South Carolina Committee of Correspondence, March 12, 1767, *South Carolina Historical and Genealogical Magazine,* XXIX (1928), 217.

7. Edward Sedgwick to Edward Weston, Feb. 3, 1767, Historical Manuscripts Commission, *Tenth Report,* app., pt. I, 102.

England. At this point, George Grenville objected to Great Britain's paying such an amount to "support and defend countrys who deny'd we had a right to tax them." Instead the colonies for whose defense the burden was incurred should raise the money, he argued. It was "the greatest absurdity," Grenville maintained, for a nation under as great a financial strain as Great Britain to pay such heavy taxes to defend colonies who "in manner, deny our sovereignty over them." The debate reopened the old controversy on taxation and the merits of the Stamp Act. Charles Townshend, the Chancellor of the Exchequer, not Henry Conway, administration leader in the Commons, answered Grenville. Agreeing with the former minister that the colonists ought to contribute toward their own defense, Townshend "disclaimed in very strong terms" the distinction which Chatham had made the previous year between internal and external taxes. If the Parliament of Great Britain had the right to impose one, it had the authority to impose the other. While Conway said nothing in defense of the position Chatham had taken, Townshend pledged that in the current session he would propose a bill by which Parliament would tax the colonists "conformable to their abilities" and in a "manner that should be least burthensome and most efficacious." He would find a source of revenue, "if not adequate, yet nearly sufficient to answer the expense of America when properly reduced." [8] As it later developed, Townshend would reduce expenses in America by evacuating the army from the interior. The next night, in a cabinet meeting, he defended the commitment he had made by pointing out that it was the sense of the House that the colonies should contribute some

8. William Samuel Johnson to William Pitkin, Feb. 12, 1767, Massachusetts Historical Society *Collections*, 5th ser., IX, 215–216; Grenville to the Earl of Buckinghamshire, Jan. 27, 1767, Grenville Letterbook, Stowe Collection, St. 7, II, HEHL; Lord George Sackville to General John Irwin, Feb. 13, 1767, Historical Manuscripts Commission, *Report on the Manuscripts of Mrs. Stopford-Sackville, of Drayton House, Northamptonshire* (2 vols., London, 1904), I, 119; William Rouet to Baron Mure, Jan. 27, [1767], William Mure (ed.), *Caldwell Family Papers, Selections from the family papers preserved at Caldwell*, Maitland Club *Publications* (2 vols., in 3 pts., Glasgow, 1854), II, pt. ii, 100–101; and Shelburne to Chatham, Feb. 1, 1767, *Chatham Correspondence*, III, 184–185.

revenue. Conway admitted this to be the case, but Shelburne hoped to postpone any decision until he had gathered sufficient information from America on the collection of quitrents. If this traditional source of revenue proved sufficient, no new taxes would be necessary. Yet it would take at least a year to collect this information.[9] But would the temper of the House of Commons allow the ministers the year? As Barrington wrote Gage in America, "it was now absolutely necessary" that the government decide on the disposition of the troops. If the ministry adopted his own plan, "there will be an End of Indian Expences, and most of the contingent expences of the Army . . . ." [10] These were the exact points which caused another explosive debate in the Commons on February 18, when the Secretary-at-War brought in the extraordinary expenditures of the American army for the previous year. They came to over £300,000. Thus the annual cost of the American defense establishment to Great Britain was over £700,000. Only a relatively small portion of this sum, £20,000, went to the Indian departments. The difficulty in supplying the remote forts in the interior accounted for most of the added expense. When the ministerial benches advanced this explanation, Grenville moved that the government withdraw the troops from the wilderness to the settled colonies where it would be easier to provision them. Again he argued that Great Britain could not afford such exorbitant sums for a service intended solely for the protection of the colonies. There were two alternatives. Either reduce the expenses by abandoning the interior garrisons and returning control of Indian affairs to the provinces, or oblige the Americans to contribute some proportion of the expense of the defense establishment.[11] In effect, Grenville was

9. Sir William Anson (ed.), *The Autobiography and political correspondence of Augustus Henry, third Duke of Grafton* (London, 1898), 126–127; Shelburne to Chatham, Feb. 1, 1767, *Chatham Correspondence,* III, 185.

10. Barrington to Gage (private), Feb 10, 1767, Gage Papers, WLCL.

11. William Rouet to Baron Mure, Feb. 21 [1767], *Caldwell Family Papers,* II, ii, 106–108; Conway to the King [Feb. 18, 1767], Sir John Fortescue (ed.), *The Correspondence of King George the Third* (6 vols., London, 1927), I, 453; *Commons Journal,* XXXI, 171; William Samuel Johnson to Jared Ingersoll (private), Feb. 28, 1766 [1767], William Samuel Johnson Papers, Letters By 1767–1792 (2), Connecticut Historical Society; Lord Charlemont to Flood, Feb. 19, 1767, *Chatham Correspondence,* III, 210n.2.

proposing the Barrington plan of 1766. They were not alone in this view. The showdown in the cabinet came on the night of March 12, when Townshend adopted the position taken by Grenville. Under a threat of resignation, he insisted that the government transfer the forces to the seacoast, lay the charges of the Indian department on the colonies, and levy a tax on imports into America. He demanded that the cabinet consider the entire question and declare in the Commons its position on the interior forts, the disposition of the troops, and the Indian trade; "in short the whole arrangement considered with a view to a general reduction of expense, and a duty . . . to defray what remained . . . ." [12] Townshend was not the only minister who was dissatisfied with the indecision of the administration, for Barrington was particularly disturbed about the disposition of the troops and would not "suffer" his colleagues "to forget it." The reports of the Commander-in-Chief in America concerning the colonial challenge to the authority of the mother country made a "decision on this point peculiarly necessary," for there was no possibility of maintaining order "without considerable Corps of troops properly stationed." [13]

While Barrington and Townshend demanded prompt action, Shelburne, the Secretary of State, sought to delay any decision. In a paper probably presented to the cabinet on March 30, Shelburne argued against reducing American expenses for the present. The ministry had not yet had time to evaluate the plan of 1764 for the management of Indian affairs. Informed authorities had given conflicting opinions on reducing military and Indian expenditures and evacuating the interior posts. General Amherst and General Monckton had even urged the necessity of increasing the garrisons in the interior country. In his last dispatch,[14] Gen-

12. Grafton to Chatham; Shelburne to Chatham, March 13, 1767, *Chatham Correspondence,* III, 231, 232–233.

13. Barrington to Gage (private), March 13, Gage Papers, WLCL.

14. In a letter received on March 25, Gage had expressed the opinion that over half of the furs in America found their way to New Orleans due to the higher price for peltry paid at this port. He doubted if force in the form of blockading posts on the Ohio, Mississippi, and Illinois rivers could prevent this practice. He now realized the insufficiency of the system of restricting the trade at the specified forts, however, and recommended the French system of allocating districts for the traders. He still favored licensing and price

eral Gage had recommended erecting new posts at the mouths of the Ohio and Illinois rivers. Barrington had taken just the opposite view in recommending that the government evacuate most of the forts, abandon the fur trade, and station the bulk of the troops in Nova Scotia. While Shelburne at this point concluded that the ministers could abandon many of the posts, he saw the value of building additional forts to stop the drain in the fur trade down the Mississippi River to New Orleans. His solution to the revenue problem to defray the cost of the military and Indian services lay in properly regulating land grants and collecting quitrents. Since he had requested information on these points from the governors, it would be rash to decide on a new plan without waiting to receive their reports. Arguing that the situation in America could not deteriorate markedly within a year, he asked for time to work out an alternative solution to the drastic proposal favored by Townshend and Barrington.[15]

It was difficult for the cabinet to decide on a decisive program simply because there was no direction in the ministry. Chatham had not been taking part in the discussions for some time. Whether he was suffering from gout or simply using this as an excuse to avoid an embarrassing situation is difficult to determine, but he had abdicated responsibility. When pressed by members of his own administration to take the lead in solving the problems facing the ministry, he replied that his "fixed purpose has always been, and is, not to be a proposer of plans, but as far as a seat in one House enables, an unbiassed judge of them." [16] It was almost impossible to proceed with any settled program in the House of Commons, and Conway, the adminis-

control, however, hoping that proper attention by the governors and the personnel of the Indian Department might mitigate the conduct of the undisciplined traders. Should such a system be acceptable to the government, it would relieve the Crown of the burden of financing Indian affairs by selling the right of trade to the specified districts. Gage to Shelburne, Feb. 22, 1767, *Gage Correspondence,* I, 121–124.

15. "Reasons for not diminishing American Expence this year. 30 March 1767," Shelburne Papers, 85: 102 ff., printed in Alvord and Carter, *New Regime,* 536–541.

16. Chatham to Grafton, Feb. 23, 1767, *Chatham Correspondence,* III, 218–219.

tration spokesman, for one, complained of Chatham's unwillingness to lead.[17]

Faced with the immediate problem of presenting a budget, Townshend, as Chancellor of the Exchequer, could not wait. Chatham was absent from the scene, and Grafton, the First Lord of the Treasury, was incompetent. With no direction or unity in the cabinet, Townshend had a free hand. Recognized as the "principal manager" in the House of Commons, he pushed through his famous import duties that summer. But taxes on tea, paper, and paints were totally inadequate to meet the needs of the military establishment in America no matter how great the reduction of the forces. At best, the Townshend duties would yield £40,000 a year.[18] Even so, the imperial government intended to use this money first to pay the colonial civil establishment wherever necessary so that the royal governors and judges would be financially independent of the legislatures. The authority of government had to be upheld.

Finally Townshend had succeeded in establishing a separate fund for the colonial governors—a project he had developed as early as 1754 and had consistently pursued from that time.[19] Evidently the Chancellor of the Exchequer had been able to capitalize on the adverse sentiment in the House of Commons against the colonists for their challenge to British authority on the Mutiny and Trade Acts. The resentment over the exorbitant cost of the defense establishment for the interior had given him the opportunity of imposing additional taxes. His revenue measures would not solve the financial problem of the army.

The ministers still had to answer the question of the military establishment in the interior. That summer, Barrington wrote Gage: "I join sincerely with you" in wishing that the administration decide on the disposition of the forces. But only Shelburne, the Secretary of State for the Southern Department, could

17. For Conway's complaints see the statement of his cousin, Horace Walpole, *Memoirs of the Reign of King George the Third,* G. F. Russell Barker (ed.) (4 vols., London, 1894), II, 307.

18. *Ibid.,* III, 21.

19. See Sir Lewis B. Namier, *Charles Townshend. His Character and Career. The Leslie Stephen Lecture.* 1959 (Cambridge, England, 1959).

issue the necessary orders for relocating the garrisons, and Barrington had "for some time left off teasing the Minister" on a matter he found the cabinet "would not decide." He waited impatiently for the resurrection of Chatham, but when that would be "God only knows," and in the meantime, he complained bitterly, "we have no Government." [20]

Townshend probably would have supported Barrington, but he died on September 4. Just one week later, Shelburne presented to the cabinet his solution to the problem of the military establishment. The Secretary of State had virtually a free hand. The ministry was disintegrating, and he faced little opposition. By what process did Shelburne arrive at his solution? What factors shaped his program? In the first instance, because of his political ties with Chatham, Shelburne was susceptible to an arrangement which would provide revenue but would not raise the politically embarrassing question of Parliament's right to tax the Americans. Furthermore, from the time he entered office in the summer of 1766, Shelburne was the target of colonial lobbyists. They were primarily land speculators who sought to undermine the policy of 1763 and were canvassing support for the establishment of interior colonies in North America to further their own material aims. Ultimately they supplied the rationalizations for Shelburne's later program. But the key to this program was the reduction of military expenditures and the procurement of revenue by traditional means, not western expansion as historians have assumed. We should note that Shelburne's reaction to the expansionist proposals of the lobbyists was not uniformly favorable.

The Secretary of State, traditionally considered as a western expansionist by scholars, demonstrated little sympathy for one land-speculating organization, the Ohio Company of Virginia. Since Colonel Henry Bouquet and local officials in Virginia had prevented them from occupying the lands along the Monongahela provisionally granted to them in 1754, the members of the Ohio Company undertook to lobby with the home government. In 1763, they sent George Mercer as their agent to London. Confronted with the policy which prohibited settlement west of the mountains, Mercer took no conclusive action until the spring

20. Barrington to Gage (private), July 6, 1767, Gage Papers, WLCL.

of 1767, when he received word that the Virginia Burgesses had supported a petition of the frontiersmen of Augusta County to allow settlement west of the mountains along the Monongahela. Since this threatened the interests of his group, he reopened the question of the 1754 grant to the Ohio Company before the Board of Trade. The Commissioners of Trade, however, declined coming to a final decision on Mercer's petition until they knew more of the situation on the Virginia frontier. They merely advised Shelburne that the governor of the colony report on the matter. In the meantime, the ministry should discountenance the activities of the Virginia assembly in encouraging settlement.[21] While Mercer complained as much as he "dared to do" over the delay and especially the reference of the company's claim to the government of Virginia,[22] Shelburne further protracted the matter by more than three months. Finally, in October, 1767, he requested an account from Governor Fauquier of the claim of the Ohio Company and the circumstances of its grant.[23] But he did so almost a full month *after* he had persuaded the cabinet to accept a policy which scholars have thought advocated western expansion. Why did Shelburne not support the settlement of the Ohio Company? In view of the known opposition of the government of Virginia to the company, Shelburne's reference to Fauquier practically buried its claim. Perhaps he was sincere in his request for information, but it is certain that a complete file of documents relating to the company's grant since 1747 was available at the Board of Trade. Shelburne had ready access to it. Perhaps the Secretary of State did not respond enthusiastically to the Ohio Company because, under the terms of its prewar grant, it enjoyed an immunity from quitrents for ten years from

21. Mercer's instructions, dated July 4, 1763, are printed in Lois Mulkearn (ed.), *The George Mercer Papers Relating to the Ohio Company of Virginia* (Pittsburgh, 1954), 182. He did present a memorial in June, 1765 (C. O. 5/1331: 413–418), but did not carry the matter through at this time, for he left London for Virginia as a stamp distributor. *Journal of the Board of Trade, 1764–1767*, p. 395, 397. The board's report, dated June 26, 1767, in C. O. 5/1368: 327 and C. O. 5/24: 91.

22. Mercer to the committee of the Ohio Company, Nov. 21, 1767, Rowland, *Mason Correspondence*, I, 156.

23. Shelburne to Fauquier, Oct. 8, 1767, C. O. 5/1345: 386.

the time the lands were settled. In any case, no decisive action resulted from the reference to Virginia, and Mercer later had to employ other means in prosecuting his suit.

Shelburne also showed little interest in land speculators from Virginia and Maryland who had organized the Mississippi Company in 1763. Among its more influential members were the Washingtons, Lees, Fitzhughs, Adam Stephen and Thomas Bullitt. In September, 1763, the company had drawn up a memorial for a grant of land for two and a half million acres at the confluence of the Ohio and Mississippi rivers. Its London agent, Thomas Cumming, at that time had some influence with Shelburne, but ministerial opposition to western settlement blocked their plans. By March, 1767, on the basis of the report from Cumming on the political situation in London, the company decided that "the present is a more proper Crisis to renew our solicitation." [24]

A more direct approach for an internal settlement was that of Major Thomas Mant, one of the officers serving in Colonel John Bradstreet's expedition to Detroit in the fall of 1764. The following spring, Mant, on behalf of other officers, petitioned for the establishment of a British colony at Detroit. They proposed to settle six hundred families on tracts of one hundred and fifty acres. Each officer would receive a comparable amount of land for every family he sponsored. The Board of Trade in the Rockingham ministry postponed any decision on the proposal pending a resolution of western policy in general, but the accession of Shelburne as Secretary of State in August, 1766,[25] raised Mant's hopes. General Jeffrey Amherst endorsed the project, and Shelburne considered the former Commander-in-Chief to be an "expert" on American matters. The Secretary of State's con-

24. See the Articles of Agreement, dated June 3, 1763, printed in *Ohio Archaeological and Historical Society Publications,* XVII (1908), 436–439. The memorial, dated Sept. 9, 1763, is printed in Alvord and Carter, *Critical Period,* 23–29; Committee of the Mississippi Company to Thomas Cumming, March 1, 1767, C. E. Carter (ed.), "Documents Relating to the Mississippi Land Company, 1763–1769," *American Historical Review,* XVI (1911), 315.

25. The petition, dated May 8, 1765, is in C. O. 323/13: 393–394; *Acts of the Privy Council, Col.,* IV, 567–568; *Journal of the Board of Trade, 1764–1767,* pp. 221, 223–225.

fidence in Amherst was somewhat misplaced. Amherst had never really understood the culture of the North American Indians, nor did he appreciate the opposition of the tribes to settlements on their land. Resentful of the natives because of Pontiac's rebellion, he had advocated a war of extermination. By dispossessing the Indians "we secure to ourselves what seems Intended for us," he had written years before when still in America.[26] Even before Pontiac's uprising of 1763, Amherst had supported the proposals for settlements on Indian lands made by Major Philip Skene and General Phineas Lyman, only to have the imperial government reject these schemes as conflicting with the claims of the Six Nations in New York.

Following the war, Phineas Lyman of Connecticut had renewed his efforts to establish an interior colony—this time at the confluence of the Mississippi and Ohio rivers, the same area the Mississippi Company had selected. To prove that his proposal was practical, Lyman wrote Shelburne describing the navigation of the Mississippi—a stream extending for not "less than 1600 miles—" which would allow English merchants to supply "a Well Settled Country" from the Falls of St. Anthony "to the Gulf of Mexico with British Goods . . . ."[27] Lyman now described to Shelburne a grandiose scheme for five or six colonies along the Mississippi from the Falls of St. Anthony to West Florida. For the present, he would be content with only one colony. Promising to obtain the consent of the Indians for such a venture, Lyman pledged to bring in ten thousand settlers—mostly provincial soldiers—within a period of four years. Since these would serve as militia to defend the colony, the government could reduce the number of royal troops seated in the area. The settlers would supply provisions for the remaining troops. In time, the posts on the Great Lakes would also become unnecessary, for the frontier colony would act as a deterrent against Indian attacks. But the primary consideration for the mother country, Lyman argued, was that by an easy avenue of transportation, the Missis-

26. Amherst to Governor Boone of South Carolina, Aug. 17, 1763, Amherst Papers, 3: 63, WLCL.

27. Lyman to Shelburne, Oct. 28, 1766, Shelburne Papers, 48:113, 121–122, WLCL.

sippi River, the settlers could export staples in exchange for British manufactures. By the network of rivers and lakes they would wrestle the fur trade from the French and Spanish, and render useless the settlements of the Bourbon powers on the west bank of the Mississippi River.[28]

How much of this did Shelburne believe? He had a copy of Lyman's proposal made for his personal papers, and by April, 1767, the Connecticut speculator was of the "most fixed Opinion that he shall succeed in the affair . . . [of] the Ohio lands . . . ." William Samuel Johnson, special agent for Connecticut, learned that the prospect was "very favourable" for his fellow colonist, and by the end of July, Lyman himself reported to the agent that he had "great Encourage[men]t to expect a fav[orabl]e Issue of his affairs, as soon as any stable System shall take place at Court." [29] It would appear that Lyman had made an impression on Shelburne. Or did the minister want to be impressed?

A close associate of Phineas Lyman, the regular Connecticut agent, Richard Jackson, was involved in still another land company seeking a grant in the same area. This was the Illinois Company, which George Croghan had organized. As early as 1764 the Indian agent and trader had proposed to the Commissioners of Trade that the government establish a colony in the Illinois country. After his return from that area in March, 1766, he helped form a company in Philadelphia to exploit the Illinois country by purchasing whatever grants could be had from the French inhabitants.[30] The company's articles of agreement listed

28. "Plan Proposed by Genl. Lyman, for Settling Louisiana, and for erecting New Colonies between West Florida and the Falls of St. Anthony," Shelburne Papers, 48: 35–46, WLCL.

29. William Samuel Johnson to William Pitkin, April 10, 1767, W. S. Johnson Papers, box 309, CHS; William Samuel Johnson to Dr. Benjamin Gales, July 31, 1767, *ibid.*

30. Croghan to Sir William Johnson, Dec. 12, 1766, *Johnson Papers,* IV, 886–889. It is probable that this letter was intended to be shown in ministerial circles. A copy, C. O. 5/66: 227, bears an endorsement in Benjamin Franklin's hand; Croghan to Benjamin Franklin, Feb. 25, 1766, *Johnson Papers,* V, 37; C. O. 5/66: 231. Again it appears this letter was meant for ministerial eyes; Johnson to Croghan, March 28, 1766, *Johnson Papers,* V, 119; Croghan to Johnson, March 30, 1766, Alvord and Carter, *New Regime,* 205.

ten members. Two shares were outstanding. Among the prominent holders were Governor William Franklin of New Jersey, Croghan, Sir William Johnson, John Baynton, Samuel Wharton, George Morgan, and Joseph Galloway. The partners did not reveal the membership of the younger Franklin and the Indian superintendent in the venture, since they thought that the support of these royal officials would carry more weight with the home government if it appeared that they had no personal interest. Johnson had the opportunity of filling the vacant shares with influential persons in England, but if he had no preference, Benjamin Franklin would become a partner. Since he was "much attended to by the ministry" and could consequently be of service in securing permission to establish their colony, the company forwarded their proposal for a colony to the Pennsylvania agent in London. Sir William Johnson was also expected to use his influence with the ministry. In May, the Indian superintendent accepted a secret share in the venture and offered suggestions for a brochure or prospectus calculated to induce the ministry to accept the scheme.[31] That same month Benjamin Franklin in London approved the plan, and promised to "forward it to my utmost here." [32] The speculators had laid the groundwork.

Next, Samuel Wharton and Governor Franklin sent Johnson a propaganda tract enumerating the benefits of a British colony at the mouth of the Ohio. The piece was drawn up for the edification of the ministry, but William Franklin did not sign the covering letter, for, as he informed the Indian superintendent, Croghan thought their recommendations "of the Design" would have the "greater Weight" if it did not appear they "were interested in its Success." [33] The land speculators were not the most scrupulous of men.

In September, 1766, Benjamin Franklin acknowledged receipt

31. See the Articles of Agreement, dated March 29, 1766, in Alvord and Carter, *New Regime,* 203–204; Croghan to Johnson, March 20, 1766, *ibid.,* 205–206; Johnson to William Franklin, May 3, 1766, *ibid.,* 224–225.

32. Benjamin Franklin to William Franklin, May 10, 1766, Bigelow, *Franklin Works,* IV, 416.

33. William Franklin to Johnson, June 7, 1766, Ayer Collection, Newberry Library, Chicago.

of the tract,[34] which he delivered, not to Henry Conway, now Secretary of State for the Northern Department, but rather to his colleague, Shelburne. The Pennsylvania agent considered the latter "more favourably dispos'd towards such Undertakings" than Conway, who was opposed to "distant posts and settlements in America." The Board of Trade presented a problem, however, for Franklin thought that Hillsborough, the First Lord, was "terribly afraid of dispeopling Ireland." To further the project, Franklin contacted Phineas Lyman, then in London, and the Connecticut speculator "readily agreed" to join "the interest he had made" with the ministry with that of the Illinois Company. The lobbyists were thus in a stronger position, but a good deal would depend on the account of the Illinois country which Croghan as Indian agent would send the ministry. The speculators had made their plans well, and as Franklin pointed out, the approbation of Sir William Johnson "will go a great way in recommending it" to the ministers, "as he is much relied on in all matters that may have any relation to the Indians." [35]

With the stage now set, Franklin undertook a lobbying campaign with Shelburne. The Secretary of State reportedly considered the Illinois colony a "reasonable scheme," although he commented that it did not "match" with the sentiments of a few politicians in London. Franklin assumed that he meant Hillsborough, who was known not to favor new settlements. Some ministers had pointed out that the remoteness of the Illinois country made it almost useless to Great Britain. The area was difficult to defend and constituted a potential drain on the population of the mother country and the seaboard colonies in North America. The Pennsylvania agent reported Shelburne as saying that these arguments "did not appear of much weight" to him; consequently, Franklin "endeavoured by others to invalidate them entirely." While the Secretary of State would not commit himself at this stage, on being shown the area of the proposed

34. "Reasons for Establishing a British Colony at the Illinois with some Proposals for carrying the same into immediate Execution," Shelburne Papers, 48: 95–112; printed in Alvord and Carter, *New Regime,* 249–256.

35. Benjamin Franklin to William Franklin, Sept. 12, 1766, Smyth, *Franklin Writings,* IV, 461; Bigelow, *Franklin Works,* IV, 417.

colony on a map, he observed that it would coincide with Phineas Lyman's project and that "they might be united." Shortly afterwards Franklin conferred again with Lyman and learned that Shelburne's under-secretary of state, Maurice Morgann, was "much pleased" with the Illinois scheme. The two land speculators determined "to talk to him concerning it." [36] For years Morgann had served Shelburne in a public and private capacity. Historians frequently have taken his numerous memorials found among his patron's papers as "expressions of Shelburne's own opinions." [37] Morgann's support was important to the two lobbyists, for he played an important role in formulating the program for the West which Shelburne presented to the cabinet in September, 1767.

Yet Franklin had to face opposition to his plans. Although he reported that Shelburne "really approved" of the Illinois project, the Secretary of State had intimated in an interview in October, 1766, that every new expense for America would encounter great opposition. The Treasury was especially alarmed at the growing charges of the military and Indian services in the Illinois country.[38] This was a difficult point to refute, but several weeks later Franklin received some help in this campaign from his associate, Richard Jackson. The agent for Connecticut was "fortunate" in having a "particular friendship" with Shelburne.[39] When the Secretary of State referred the project of the Illinois Company to the Connecticut agent for his advice, Jackson, warmly supporting the plan, enforced the arguments of the land speculators with his own "strong reasons." Jackson's sentiments were not entirely unprejudiced, for he had worked them out previously with Franklin—a tactic which gave the Pennsylvania agent "great pleasure"—for Jackson thus confirmed to Shelburne what Frank-

36. Benjamin Franklin to William Franklin, Sept. 27, 1766, Bigelow, *Franklin Works,* IV, 418–419; Benjamin Franklin to William Franklin, Sept. 30, 1766, *ibid.,* IV, 419.

37. Humphreys, "Shelburne and the Proclamation," *English Historical Review,* XLIV (1934), 247.

38. Benjamin Franklin to William Franklin, Oct. 11, 1766, Bigelow, *Franklin Works,* IV, 419.

39. Jackson to William Pitkin (private), Nov. 8, 1766, "Pitkin Papers," Connecticut Historical Society *Collections,* XIX, 50.

lin had been advocating. Since this advice apparently came only from Jackson, it appeared "less to be suspected of some American bias." [40] Or so Shelburne was led to believe.

To reinforce still further the arguments in favor of the Illinois settlement and to undermine the objections of General Gage to the venture, early in 1767 Croghan wrote a letter to Franklin which the latter passed on to Shelburne. Croghan, the man who had organized the company, had "strong Reasons to suspect" that the Commander-in-Chief had "imbibed unfavourable & very unjust Sentiments" concerning the Illinois country. For the good of the King's service, Croghan now took the liberty of troubling Franklin (really Shelburne) with "some farther Animadversions thereon." Arguing against Gage's contention that the government should abandon the Illinois country because of the expense involved, Croghan contended that such a step would lead to a bloody war with the tribes, for it would be to the interest of the French to arouse the Indians against the British in order to engross the fur trade for themselves. The army could reduce the cost of provisioning the garrisons in the Illinois country by adopting the offer made by the Philadelphia merchant firm of Baynton, Wharton, and Morgan to raise supplies on the spot.[41]

In spite of the concerted efforts of the speculators—Lyman, Jackson, Franklin, and Croghan—to convince Shelburne, they still seemed far from achieving their goal. By June, 1767, Franklin complained that "The Illinois affair goes forward but slowly." Phineas Lyman, "almost out of patience," was threatening to carry out his settlers to the Mississippi "without leave" from the ministry. Although Shelburne reportedly approved of the project for an interior colony, others in the administration, particularly the Commissioners of Trade, were "not of his sentiments." [42]

The members of the Illinois Company had still another arrow

40. Benjamin Franklin to William Franklin, Nov. 8, 1766, Bigelow, *Franklin Works,* IV, 420.

41. Croghan to Benjamin Franklin (copy), Jan. 27, 1767, Shelburne Papers, 48: 135–143; printed in Alvord and Carter, *New Regime,* 500–503. To anyone familiar with Croghan's correspondence, it is obvious that this letter was doctored for Shelburne's benefit.

42. Benjamin Franklin to William Franklin, June 13, 1767, Bigelow, *Franklin Works,* IV, 420.

on the string to secure western lands, a project for territory in the upper Ohio Valley which paralleled, eventually merged with, and superseded the Illinois project. It had its inception among those Pennsylvania traders and merchants who had suffered losses inflicted by the French and their Indian allies in 1754 and again in 1763 during Pontiac's rebellion. Some had incurred financial setbacks simply by mismanagement or by overextending themselves in the Indian traffic. Most prominent among the Lancaster and Philadelphia merchants and traders were Croghan and his brother-in-law, William Trent, who was connected with merchants of Lancaster, including Joseph Simon, Levy Andrew Levy, and David Franks. The latter also belonged to the Philadelphia firm of Plumstead and Franks, while his brother, Moses Franks, was a prominent London merchant and army contractor. At one time David Franks had employed the German immigrant Bernard Gratz, until the latter established his own firm in partnership with his brother, Michael Gratz. The other major Philadelphia house engaged in the Indian trade was the Quaker firm of Baynton, Wharton, and Morgan.

The Pennsylvania merchants and traders sought to obtain compensation for their losses by having the Indians grant them lands. Although the "suffering traders" formally organized in December, 1763,[43] they were unable to make any progress until February, 1765,[44] when they presented their claims for compensation to Sir William Johnson. Involved in extensive land speculation himself, the Indian superintendent soon became implicated with the group. Johnson had brought up the subject of restitution for the Pennsylvanians at a conference with the Delaware and Six Nations in May, 1765. He argued that it was in the best interests of the tribes to grant the "suffering traders" lands so that the whites would continue trafficking with the natives. According to Johnson's report of this meeting, the Indians sup-

43. The merchants to Moses Franks and George Croghan, Dec. 12, 1763, *Johnson Papers,* IV, 269. The minutes of the meeting at the Indian Queen Tavern, Philadelphia are printed in *ibid.,* IV, 264–265.

44. Memorial dated Feb., 1765, HMC *Fourteenth Report,* app., pt. X, 14. For a list of the traders' losses see Charles A. Hanna, *The Wilderness Trail; or The Ventures and Adventures of the Pennsylvania Traders on the Allegheny Path* (2 vols., New York, 1911), II, 381–382.

posedly agreed to grant the "sufferers" lands about Fort Pitt.[45] Since this area was west of the current Indian boundary line, Johnson and the speculators could do nothing further until the superintendent received permission from the ministry to alter the line. They now undertook an intensive campaign to convince the Chatham administration that a new boundary line was essential and that the tribes would acquiesce in the grant. Both George Croghan, who had been given lands by the Indians earlier, and Governor Franklin, who underwrote the traders, now enlisted the aid of Benjamin Franklin in London. The matter was of great importance to the "sufferers," some of whom were their particular friends, William Franklin wrote. His father should lose no time in "presenting the Affair in its proper Light to the Ministry." [46]

Sir William Johnson was committed to obtain a grant of land for the "suffering traders" from the Six Nations whenever the government authorized the negotiation of a new boundary line.[47] Baynton, Wharton, and Morgan now sought to impress upon Benjamin Franklin the connection between the land grant and the revision of the boundary line. Unless the ministry authorized a new boundary, "The Indians cannot give us the Land," they emphasized. Franklin did not miss the point. His endorsement on their letter reads: "Very important about the Boundary—to be urged with the Min[istr]y." Leaving nothing to chance, the Philadelphia merchants also sought to enlist the services of Lauchlin MacLeane, a former resident of Philadelphia, whom Shelburne had appointed under-secretary of state in December, 1766. Baynton, Wharton, and Morgan always regarded MacLeane as a "fortune Hunter"; consequently, they were hopeful, for MacLeane was a "sensible Fellow & very sanguine, as to American schemes"—a man who might be "very useful, in Our Land Affairs." [48]

45. *DRCHSNY,* VII, 724, 729.

46. William Franklin to Benjamin Franklin, Dec. 17, 1765, *New Jersey Archives,* 1st ser., IX, 522; Croghan to Benjamin Franklin, Dec. 12, 1765, C. O. 5/66: 165.

47. Baynton, Wharton, and Morgan to Johnson, March 30, 1766, Alvord and Carter, *New Regime,* 207.

48. Baynton, Wharton, and Morgan to Benjamin Franklin, Aug. 28, 1766,

Expecting to find the Under-Secretary of State responsive to their blandishments, early in 1767 the Philadelphia merchants outlined to him a proposal by which they would provision the royal garrisons in the Illinois country. To sweeten the proposition, they offered him a seventh part of the profits in return for his influence with Shelburne in obtaining the contract.[49] They transmitted the offer through Benjamin Franklin. The day after he received their bid, MacLeane referred the proposal to Shelburne, commenting that the Philadelphia merchants should have known him better than to have offered him "a Bribe." MacLeane recognized the offer for what it was and resented the tactics the merchants had used, but since the proposals appeared very advantageous to the government and seemed to demonstrate the utility of a settlement in the Illinois country, he "was determined not to suppress their Letter . . . ." The Philadelphia firm expected to raise provisions for the troops on the spot. To MacLeane this demonstrated two things: first, that a settlement in the Illinois country was practical, and second, that it would not be expensive, since the merchants expected to make substantial profits.[50]

Samuel Wharton had meticulously laid his plans for both a colony in the Illinois country and the grant to the "suffering traders," so carefully, in fact, that he expected to be, "Ere long, a *Considerable* Proprietor of Terra Firma." [51] Land speculation was a powerful drive among colonial Americans, for real property brought not only material gain but also social prestige and eminence. In order to gain lands, Wharton and the other land specu-

---

Benjamin Franklin Papers, Misc., I, 54–55, LC; Baynton, Wharton, and Morgan to William Franklin, Aug. 28, 1766, Alvord and Carter, *New Regime*, 365; John Brooke, *The Chatham Administration, 1766–1768* (London, 1956), 251, describes MacLeane as "a rascally Irish adventurer . . . who trafficked with his patron's [Shelburne's] credit in East India stock." Samuel Wharton to William Franklin, Dec. 27, 1766, Franklin Papers, XLVIII, 129, APSL; Samuel Wharton to William Franklin, Dec. ?, 1766, *ibid.*, XLVIII, 130.

49. Baynton, Wharton, and Morgan to MacLeane (copy), Jan. 19, 1767, Shelburne Papers, 49: 579–591, WLCL.

50. MacLeane to Shelburne, n.d., *ibid.*, 49: 575.

51. Samuel Wharton to William Franklin, Dec. 27, 1766, Franklin Papers, XLVIII, 129, APSL.

lators, Croghan, Mant, and Lyman, had formed a powerful lobby, including Franklin, Sir William Johnson, and MacLeane, which tried to convince the Earl of Shelburne that the ministry must alter the program of 1763 for an Indian reservation. They made their appeal just when Shelburne was attempting to solve the dilemma of financing the imperial program through a traditional revenue from America and without resorting to new taxes. The resentment in the House of Commons over the heavy financial burden of the western program made it all the more imperative that he resolve the problem. The material interests of the colonial land speculators and the political solution Shelburne desired merged on this point.

The charges of Indian departments also inflated the cost of the existing imperial program for administering the West. While the merchants and traders of Philadelphia were seeking to alter the settlement of 1763 as it related to the Indian boundary line, to the north, others were endeavoring to alter imperial regulation of the Indian trade. The Canadian merchants and traders especially resented the requirement imposed by General Thomas Gage and Sir William Johnson that they traffic only at the posts in the interior where the officers and deputies could supervise the trade.

Governor Guy Carleton of Quebec staunchly supported the Canadians in a sharp controversy with the Indian Superintendent for the Northern District over alleged violations of trade regulations. Sir William Johnson insisted that traders from Canada, both French and British, disregarded the forts and trafficked without passes. When challenged by the military, they declared that they would trade wherever they pleased.[52] In Quebec, Carleton defended the Canadians, noting it was the "unanimous Opinion of all here" that the trade would suffer unless the government removed the restraints now imposed. The other colonies, not familiar with the interior nor so advantageously situated to engage in the Indian trade, "are the secret Causes," he charged, of the Canadians being "so severely fettered . . . ." [53] Carleton transmitted

52. Johnson to Carleton (copy), Jan. 27, 1767, C. O. 42/27: 77–78, 80, PAC transcript.

53. Carleton to Johnson (copy), March 27, 1767, C. O. 42/27: 82–83, PAC transcript.

to the Board of Trade a memorial containing the arguments of the Canadian merchants. The commissioners sent copies to Shelburne, in addition to a memorial of the London merchants interested in the commerce of Quebec, supporting the contentions of the Canadian traders.[54] Carleton himself wrote to the Secretary of State, enclosing his correspondence with Sir William Johnson which contained the repeated complaints of the merchants concerned in the trade of the upper country.[55] The Canadians were strongly opposed to the *ad hoc* program Gage and Johnson had imposed and which the Board of Trade had incorporated into the plan of 1764 for the management of Indian affairs.

For entirely different reasons, financial, some in London—Barrington, Grenville, and Townshend—also objected to the imperial program and would have liked to return control to the colonies. Shelburne's reaction to the problem of Indian affairs as revealed in his response to Carleton is significant in view of the attitude the Secretary of State took before the cabinet only three months later. In June, 1767, he wrote to the governor of Quebec that on "the best Consideration" he had been able to give the matter, the disorderly state of the back settlements and the Indian trade resulted primarily from the long prevailing practice of fraudulently granting and purchasing Indian lands. It was unfortunate, Shelburne noted, that the Indian trade was so "peculiarly circumstanced as to require any strict Regulations," for it was the "general Nature of Trade to regulate itself . . . ." Yet, he hoped, "it will in time do so in America" without the heavy expense which "at present attends it." At the same time, Shelburne informed Sir William Johnson that, as an exception to the general rule, he might allow the Canadian traders to visit the tribes north of the Ottawa River and Lakes Superior, Michigan, and Huron—those Indians who were too far from the forts. But Shelburne reiterated his analysis of the causes of the complaints

54. Carleton to the Board of Trade, March 28, 1767, C. O. 42/27: 138–139. The memorial of the Canadian merchants, dated Sept. 20, 1766, is in C. O. 42/27: 140–145; a copy will be found in the Shelburne Papers, 50: 261–272, WLCL. The memorial of the British merchants to Shelburne is in C. O. 42/26: 355, PAC transcript.

55. Carleton to Shelburne, March 28, 1767, C. O. 42/27: 73–74, PAC transcript.

by the natives on the frontier. The settlements made near the Ohio River by frontiersmen from Virginia and Maryland were so injurious to the Indians, so detrimental to the interests of the colonies, and such "an audacious Defiance" of royal authority as repeatedly expressed by the Proclamation of 1763 and subsequent instructions to the colonial governors, that they "can by no means be permitted . . . ." [56] The Secretary of State seemed to be emphatic in supporting the imperial system, but the attitude Shelburne expressed here differed markedly from that he had taken the previous autumn when he had held that the colonial governments could best manage Indian affairs. Was Shelburne really that confused?

A paper drawn up in 1767 either by Shelburne himself or by someone close to the minister sheds some light on his thinking. The document notes the several alternatives for western policy then under consideration. While Gage, the Commander-in-Chief in America, had contributed some corrections to the Barrington plan for a reduction of the garrisons in the interior, Jeffrey Amherst disapproved of the proposal. The replies of the colonial governors on the plan of 1764 for the management of Indian affairs were also available. Finally, Townshend had advocated a general project for the reduction of American expenses charged against Parliament.[57] How did Shelburne react to these alternatives? He had already declared himself in the cabinet against reducing expenditures and had indicated his preference for raising revenue by stricter control of quitrents and land grants. For an evaluation of the other two proposals, the Barrington plan and the project of 1764, he called for the opinions of three "experts," Benjamin Franklin, Amherst, and Richard Jackson—men he reportedly regarded as "the best authorities for any thing that related to America." [58] Shelburne's choice of these individuals was unfortunate. Amherst never did understand the Indians

56. Shelburne to Carleton, June 20, 1767, C. O. 42/27: 89–90, PAC transcript; Shelburne to Johnson, June 20, 1767, *Johnson Papers,* V, 566–567.

57. "Things to be considered of in North America," Shelburne Papers, 49: 17–18, WLCL.

58. Benjamin Franklin to William Franklin, Nov. 25, 1767, Bigelow, *Franklin Works,* IV, 423–424.

and had demonstrated a marked bias against them. In 1763 he had set the disposition of the troops—a disposition he advocated even now—with the intention of waging a war of extermination. He favored absorbing Indian lands in order to destroy the tribal culture. Franklin and Jackson were not particularly familiar with the interior and had their own special interests to further. They were land speculators. Such were the qualifications of the men to whom Shelburne referred Barrington's project and the plan of 1764 for the management of Indian affairs.

It is not surprising that Jackson attacked both programs claiming that the Secretary-at-War in particular was misinformed on the situation in the West. The Connecticut agent termed a "meer [*sic*] Bugbear" the proposition that the Indians were opposed to interior settlements. Nothing would more effectively prevent an Indian war, he claimed, than settling among the tribes and educating their offspring to the arts of civilized life. Jackson thought it dangerous to repeal the colonial laws regulating Indian affairs, for although these statutes had not prevented the whites from encroaching on Indian rights, there was no evidence that the plan of 1764 would remedy the situation any more effectively. As was to be expected, Jackson supported an interior colony in the Illinois country.[59] Franklin also objected to the repeal of the colonial laws on Indian affairs. They were the result of long experience of persons immediately familiar with the situation—men who were interested in orderly relations with the tribes. The ministry might do well to consider the matter thoroughly before repealing these statutes and imposing a new and untried scheme.[60]

While none of these contentions were valid—the experience of the French and Indian War and subsequent events demonstrated this as Shelburne was well aware—the minister employed the arguments of Franklin and Jackson. Maurice Morgann, Shel-

59. "Remarks on the Plan for the future Management of Indian Affairs by Mr. Jackson," Shelburne Papers, 57: 347–373; and "Remarks on Ld Barrington's Plan No. 2," *ibid.*, 50: 77–87, printed in Alvord and Carter, *New Regime*, 422–430.

60. "Remarks on a Plan for the future Management of Indian Affairs," Shelburne Papers, 57: 341–346; Bigelow, *Franklin Works*, IV, 243–247.

burne's secretary, incorporated the views of the agents in shaping the final document on western policy the minister presented to the cabinet.[61]

Late in August, 1767, Shelburne was ready to present his case on interior policy to the other ministers. Franklin dined privately with both Secretaries of State when they discussed the reduction of American expenses. According to the account of the Pennsylvania agent, Shelburne contemplated returning the management of Indian affairs to the individual colonies, for they could manage them more frugally than the imperial government did at present. Franklin then took the opportunity of urging a settlement in the Illinois country as one method of reducing expenses for the military outposts. He stressed the fact that Sir William Johnson had approved of the project. Furthermore, the members of the Illinois Company were willing to establish the colony at very little expense to the government in London. Seemingly convinced by these arguments, the ministers decided to appoint Johnson as governor of the new province if they abolished the office of superintendent when the colonies resumed control of Indian affairs. Only the Board of Trade remained to be won

61. Among Shelburne's papers is a copy of the plan of 1764 for the management of Indian affairs to which is added a parallel column headed "Remarks [and in Shelburne's hand] upon which are grounded the Minute submitted by me to the Cabinet in [the] Summer 1767," Shelburne Papers, 50: 356–383. There is a draft of these "Remarks" in Morgann's hand, headed "Observations upon a Plan for the future Management of Indian Affairs." Some time later the words "Ld Shelburne's" were added by a different hand to the heading. *Ibid.*, 60: 135–138. There are two other significant documents in Shelburne's papers. An undated and unsigned copy of Croghan's letter to the Board of Trade of June 8, 1764 (*DRCHSNY,* VII, 602), containing a proposal for a new boundary line and a colony in the Illinois country, is headed "Remarks relative to a Boundary being fixed with the Six Nation Indians," Shelburne Papers, 60: 123–125. Another document, "Remarks on Ld Barrington's Plan No. 1," *ibid.*, 50: 65–70, is probably by Amherst. It attacks the Barrington plan and the opinions of Gage and Johnson relative to Indian affairs, and presumes a knowledge for the motives in first establishing garrisons in the interior to contest the claims of the Indians. In the final analysis, the author would leave the disposition of the troops and the forts to the Commander-in-Chief. Alvord, *Mississippi Valley,* I, 310, ascribes authorship to Amherst and there seems to be little reason to contest this. The document exhibits many of Amherst's prejudices.

over. Shelburne and Conway agreed that the Commissioners of Trade were "to be brought over privately" before the matter should be referred to them officially.[62] Later Shelburne did just that, repeating the technique Mansfield had suggested in 1763. Egremont had probably used the same tactic on Shelburne himself when the latter presided over the Board of Trade.

The stage was now set for Shelburne to present his solution to the problem of American expenses and the West. Apparently he encountered little opposition. Since Chatham had not taken part in the government for some time, nominal leadership in the cabinet fell to Grafton, who was not up to it and recognized the fact. Conway vacillated between resigning or not. Dissatisfied with his office, he was "a Minister Malgre Lui . . . ." [63] Townshend, perhaps the only minister who could have effectively contested Shelburne, died on September 4. Only a week later the cabinet heard Shelburne's proposals. It was merely a token showing, for in addition to Shelburne, only Lord Chancellor Camden, Grafton, Conway, and the First Lord of the Admiralty (Sir Edward Hawke) attended.[64] The day after the meeting, the First Lord of the Treasury wrote to Barrington: "You will agree with me, that the King's servants have received a considerable blow by being deprived of Mr. Townshend's abilities." [65] Grafton had good cause for his sense of loss. Shelburne had presented an amazing document to the cabinet.

Shelburne had argued that, according to the information the ministers had received from officials in America, it was impossible to continue managing Indian affairs on the present basis. In addition, English and colonial merchants had complained of the grievances they had suffered under the current system. Continuing high expenses also demanded a change in the program either by a reduction in services or by providing for a positive

62. Benjamin Franklin to William Franklin, Aug. 28, 1767, Bigelow, *Franklin Works,* IV, 420–421.

63. William Knox to Grenville, Oct. 10, 1767, Knox MSS, 1: 22a, WLCL.

64. See Shelburne's minute of the meeting, "Genl. Conway's Office Sept. 11, 1767," Shelburne Papers, 161: unfoliated, WLCL.

65. Grafton to Barrington, Sept. 12, 1767, in *William Wildman, Viscount Barrington, Political Life, compiled from Original Papers, by his brother, Shute, Bishop of Durham* (London, 1814), 112.

source of revenue. Since the military establishment defrayed the cost of the Indian services, it was impossible to consider one without the other. Shelburne then reviewed the various measures previously employed to raise revenue. He found each wanting in some manner. The Secretary of State emphasized that the House of Commons had objected to the cost of the American establishment and that the ministry had been able to quiet these complaints only by promising that it would present some plan to reduce American expenses before the next session of Parliament.

Having thus established with his colleagues the need for some revision in the existing program, Shelburne then proceeded to analyze various alternatives. The plan of 1764 for the management of Indian affairs, as far as it had been applied by royal officials, was proving unsuccessful. Executed under the jurisdiction of the superintendents—imperial officers operating independently of the civil and military authorities in America—the plan sought by a variety of minute regulations to restrain the Indian traffic—a form of commerce "which can scarcely admit of any regulations which do not flow naturally from itself," Shelburne argued. In order to substitute a more tenable program, the ministers must examine the origins of the imperial system by which the separate colonial governments had lost control. Their relations with the tribes had been on the whole harmonious, and it was evident, so Shelburne maintained, that only the encroachment of the French in 1754 had first brought about the establishment of the imperial program under the superintendents. But if the ministers now appreciated the fact that they had removed the original source of difficulty—the French—then there was no longer any need for the imperial officers, and the administration could allow matters to "glide naturally into their former Channel" and allow the provinces once more to manage Indian affairs. They would willingly assume the financial burden. Close to the scene of events, the colonists would be the best judges of any measures thought necessary to regulate Indian relations. Since the peace of the frontier depended on the proper management of Indian affairs, there could be no reason to fear that provincial officers would be any less effective or zealous in preserving peace in the wilderness than Sir William Johnson and John Stuart, who were constantly complaining that they did not have sufficient power. Indeed, being independent of the civil and military authorities in America, the superintendents would never have sufficient authority. Shelburne presented another objection to the plan of 1764. To repeal the provincial laws regulating Indian affairs would be dangerous and, consequently, inadvisable. Many of these statutes were the result of long years of experience by persons on the frontier who were particularly interested in the consequences of this legislation. Some of the provincial laws were closely suited to conditions in specific colonies, and although they may not have been absolutely effective in eliminating disputes with the tribes, it did not follow that these evils were by their nature not subject to remedy or that officials far removed from the scene could resolve them any better than the colonists themselves. Instead of repealing these laws, would it not be better to restore to each colony the management of the trade, and—in order to give a certain degree of uniformity to the entire system—to recommend to the provinces such amendments to their statutes, or subject them to such regulations, as the Commissioners of Trade should think proper?

The strongest objection to a policy of provincial control—and with it evacuation of some of the interior forts—was that there would be no proper barrier between the Indians and the whites. If the colonists provoked the tribes into open hostilities, it would then prove difficult to supply the forts in the Illinois country and on the Mississippi River. But those who raised such objections based them on a misconception of the Proclamation of 1763, Shelburne claimed. If the line of demarcation set by the Proclamation was understood to bound not particular provinces, but the American settlements in general, it seemed founded on a contracted policy—little less than an attempt to set limits to increases in population and extensions of the British dominions. Such an attempt was impractical. It was impossible to prevent encroachments on Indian lands by any force whatever, much less by fifteen battalions of royal troops. On these grounds, Amherst, Johnson, and Gage (supposedly) recommended the establishment of several interior governments. Other individuals had also proposed various settlements. These governments would not be an expense to the mother country, for in a few years the quitrents would not only defray the original cost of colonization, but would, if properly administered, form a fund to defray the other expenses. Shelburne then cited the example of the French settlement at Detroit where the French regime had established a precedent for such revenue.

Thus the Secretary of State pictured a very simple system answering every purpose of government and eliminating every unnecessary expense. He would form two interior colonies, retain a few of the principal forts, and return control of Indian affairs to the provinces, subject to such general regulations as the Commissioners of Trade might impose. The inhabitants of the new colonies at Detroit and the Illinois country would raise provisions on the spot for the garrisons in the vicinity. Eventually they would secure the eastern provinces and render the present forts —now used only to convey supplies—almost useless. It was well known, Shelburne contended, that whenever the whites surrounded the Indians by settlements, the tribes became "enervated by their Intercourse with their new Neighbours" and then lost "their Turn for War." Consequently, the establishment of new settlements in the wilderness would in time either induce the tribes to migrate west, or become what the Americans termed "Domestick" and therefore dependent on the whites.

Under a system of interior colonies, the only posts the government need maintain to secure communications and the Indian trade were Crown Point, Frontenac, Michillimackinac, Fort Pitt, and three stations on the Mississippi River—at the mouths of the Ohio, Natchez, and the Iberville. For the immediate future, only four battalions, instead of the present fifteen, were necessary to garrison North America. The ministry could spare half of this force as soon as it had fairly well established the governments at Detroit and the Illinois country. Coupled with provincial management of Indian affairs, the new arrangement would mean a great saving to Great Britain. If the Indians were to object to the new colonies, the imperial government could alleviate their protests by calling a general congress and purchasing lands under the pretext of supplying the natives with the necessities they desired. Indeed, Shelburne argued, the Indians had never been adverse to selling their lands on reasonable terms whenever they had been properly approached and did not suspect any intent to defraud. Anyone who raised further objections to a policy of western settlement on the grounds of inadequate communication facilities with the mother country founded his criticism on erroneous information. The lakes and rivers afforded the best means of interior and foreign communication yet discovered in the New World.[66] In fact, the settlers in the West would have a choice of several routes by which to send their produce to market and receive British manufactures—by the St. Lawrence, the Mississippi, or the rivers flowing from and beyond the mountains into the Atlantic.

This was the seemingly plausible, yet wholly impractical, plan the skeleton cabinet accepted and referred to the Board of Trade.[67] In view of the chaotic state of the administration and their own lack of specific information on the West, there was little else they could do, for Shelburne was supposed to be the expert on the subject. But it is difficult to explain Shelburne's acceptance of this program. It was primarily the work of his secretary, Maurice Morgann, although in content and phrasing

66. Yet Shelburne wrote to the Governor of Quebec two months *later:* "As an accurate Knowledge of the Interior Parts of North America would contribute much towards enabling . . . Ministers to judge soundly of the true Interests of the different Provinces, I cannot too strongly recommend to you the encouraging such Adventurers as are willing to explore those Parts which have not hitherto been much frequented & consequently are scarcely, if at all known . . . ." Shelburne to Carleton, Nov. 14, 1767, C. O. 42/27: 210, PAC transcript. Shelburne's ignorance of the geography of North America, even as late as 1783, was common knowledge. See William Knox, *Extra Official State Papers* (Dublin and London, 1789), 29.

67. "Minutes submitted to the Cabinet the beginning [*sic*] of Summer 1767 relative to the System of Indian traffick, [and in Shelburne's hand] NB This business remained under consideration till Octr 1767 & then the Reference which goes before [Shelburne's letter of October 5, 1767 to the Board of Trade] was made to the Board of Trade, where the Business rested till the Change of the Department took Place," Shelburne Papers, 50: 185–217, printed in Alvord and Carter, *Trade and Politics,* 12–19. The heading was written in later, which probably accounts for the mistaken reference to the early summer of 1767. The paper was actually presented to the cabinet on Sept. 11, 1767. See Shelburne's minute of the cabinet meeting of that date. Shelburne Papers, vol. 161, unfoliated, WLCL.

it betrayed the strong influence of Jackson, Franklin, and Amherst, as well as the other lobbyists. Indeed, Shelburne later admitted to the Pennsylvania agent that he did not offer the concepts contained in his cabinet paper "merely as his own sentiments"; they represented the opinions of Amherst, Franklin, and Jackson, "three gentlemen that were allowed to be the best authorities for any thing related to America." [68] The program which Shelburne proposed and for which ultimately he had to bear responsibility was based on assumptions which were unrealistic and impractical to anyone acquainted with conditions on the frontier since 1754. By the evidence of his own correspondence with Gage, Johnson, and the colonial governors, Shelburne knew better, yet he maintained that the Indians would not resist new settlements, that the colonies were willing and able to assume control of Indian affairs, and would pay the cost of the service, that the traders and frontiersmen would show restraint in dealing with the tribes, and that the undisciplined frontiersmen would pay quitrents. When it took three to four months to row batteaux up the Mississippi to Fort Chartres in the Illinois country, it was also fallacious to assume that the *existing* means of water transportation made commercial exploitation of the interior country feasible. In accepting the views of the colonial lobbyists and misconstruing the advice of Gage and other imperial officials in the provinces, Shelburne was exercising poor judgment in irresponsibly advocating a program which would only serve to relieve him temporarily of the embarrassing problem of taxing the Americans for an imperial defense establishment.

The question of revenue is the central theme of the document Shelburne presented to the cabinet in September, 1767. It was not expansionist per se. Because of the controversy in the cabinet and House of Commons that year over the inordinately high expenses of the American establishment, Shelburne advocated a policy of interior settlement merely to raise revenue by quitrents

68. Benjamin Franklin to William Franklin, Nov. 25, 1767, Bigelow, *Franklin Works,* IV, 423–424. For Amherst's approval of the Shelburne program, see his letter to the Secretary of State, Sept. 22, 1767, C. O. 5/68: 303. Amherst favored another colony on the lower Mississippi as well as those intended for Detroit and the Illinois country.

and to reduce the expenses of the wilderness garrisons. This motive also explains his proposal to return the management of Indian affairs to the provinces. Although some have argued that Shelburne's basic assumption rested on the impossibility of preventing the Americans from expanding westward,[69] this contention does not obviate the fact that shortly before presenting this document to the cabinet, Shelburne had insisted that the colonial governments could have enforced the program promulgated in the Proclamation of 1763 if they had acted diligently. The most appropriate comment on the new policy was that of William Samuel Johnson, the special agent for Connecticut, who was close to the lobbyists, Phineas Lyman and Richard Jackson. The ministers had "in view to save the heavy expence they have been at in Indian affairs . . . ." As a result "G[eneral] L[yman]'s affairs now go on swimmingly." [70] Johnson's insight as to the motives for the new program and the influences which formed it was all too acute.

Shelburne did not refer the new program to the Board of Trade until October 5, when he sent the commissioners a long directive suggesting the course he wanted them to adopt.[71] In this respect it paralleled the letter Egremont had written to the Commissioners of Trade on May 5, 1763. To bolster his arguments, Shelburne also sent a set of enclosures consisting of letters, extracts of correspondence, and other documents from Gage, Amherst, the superintendents, the Canadian merchants, and the various colonial speculators. He had culled almost every bit of information that might support the program he now advocated. He continued to send additional information until late in December.[72]

69. Ritcheson, *British Politics and the American Revolution,* 110.

70. W. S. Johnson to Jared Ingersoll, Nov. 12, 1767, W. S. Johnson Papers, "Letters by, 1767–1792" (2) CHS. See also Johnson to William Pitkin, Sept. 15, 1767, "Trumbull Papers," Massachusetts Historical Society *Collections,* 5th ser., IX, 243.

71. Shelburne to the Board of Trade, Oct. 5, 1767, Shelburne Papers, 50: 173–184; *Calendar of Home Office Papers, George III,* II, 188–189; *DRCHSNY,* VII, 981–984.

72. For the documents sent to the Board of Trade see C. O. 323 vols. 25–26; and Shelburne Papers, vol. 52, WLCL; *Journal of the Board of Trade, 1764–1767,* pp. 420, 421, 423, 427, 429, 440, 441.

But the Board of Trade was not a rubber stamp. According to Benjamin Franklin's account of a conference he had with Lord Clare, the First Lord of Trade was not enthusiastic over Shelburne's program. He approved of the negotiation of a new boundary line, but since the mother country was "already so loaded" with expenses, he wondered who would reimburse the tribes for lands to be purchased. While Clare thought that a colony might be useful in securing the Illinois country, he did "not much approve" of a settlement at Detroit.[73]

Perhaps Shelburne was attempting to undermine this resistance when he conferred with Jeremiah Dyson, a long-time Commissioner of Trade. They agreed to one important alteration in the plan Shelburne had submitted. Should the Commissioners of Trade decide to retain the superintendents due to the longevity of their office and "because the Reason for their first appointment is not agreed upon," the ministry would divide control of Indian affairs. The superintendents would continue to govern political relations with the tribes, especially the purchase of lands by the Crown, while the provincial governments would manage trade and have jurisdiction over criminals in the Indian country. The Americans were to levy such duties as the Indian service might require and also cover any charges which might result from the use of royal troops if the colonists would require their aid against the tribes.[74] The significance of this alteration in the plan for managing Indian affairs should not be lost. Shelburne had based his entire argument before the cabinet in September on the assumption that the preceding administrations had initiated the superintendencies and, in fact, the entire imperial system solely because of the French threat in 1754. Since the danger no longer existed, he had argued, there was no longer any need for imperial officers. But he now allowed Dyson to question and even alter his interpretation of this crucial point. Having

73. Benjamin Franklin to William Franklin, Nov. 25, 1767, Bigelow, *Franklin Works,* IV, 424.

74. "The Substance of what passed between L[or]d Shelburne and Mr Dyson about the Superintendents, given afterwards to L[or]d Clare[,] Nov. 1767," Shelburne Papers, 50: 219–226, WLCL. The memorandum is in the hand of Maurice Morgann, while the endorsement is by Shelburne. A draft in Shelburne's hand is in *ibid.,* 50: 227–232.

achieved his desired goal—acceptance by the cabinet of his program—Shelburne no longer needed the rationalization by which he had justified his policy.

In order to gather support for the new program, the Commissioners of Trade called for the opinions of the London merchants trading with America. In view of their previous representations on the Indian trade and American taxation, it should not have been difficult to predict their answers. On October 29 the merchants met under the chairmanship of Barlow Trecothick. The disinterested "American experts," Jackson and Franklin, attended, as did Fowler Walker, agent for the Canadian traders and merchants, and Edward Montague, agent for Virginia. It is not surprising that they unanimously agreed to endorse the entire Shelburne program.[75] In addition, the Board of Trade called for the testimony of several officers supposedly knowledgeable in American affairs. Among them were Amherst, Monckton, Lyman, and Mant.[76] Since these men had previously supported interior settlements, there could have been little doubt as to their sentiments.

But speed was essential to the land speculators, especially to those who wanted a revision of the boundary line in order to exploit Indian lands. In difficult financial straits by having "stretched the Cord too tight," Baynton, Wharton, and Morgan had already called in their creditors and proposed to conduct their business under the supervision of trustees. Overextended in their trading ventures in the Illinois country and on the verge of bankruptcy, the Philadelphia merchants desired prompt action. George Croghan was also anxious. He had a stake in the Illinois Company and wanted a revision of the boundary line so as to confirm a grant of lands about Fort Pitt the Six Nations had made him. Croghan now engaged influential colonists to write the

75. Endorsed "Letter from Mr. Alderman Trecothick, dated Oct. 30, 1767, containing the Sentiments of the Merchants trading to N. America and of several Agents for the Colonies concerning the management of Indian Affairs, & the forming of new Governments in the Interior Country in North America," C. O. 323/24: 323; Shelburne Papers, 62: 205. See also Benjamin Franklin to William Franklin, Nov. 13, 1767, Bigelow, *Franklin Works,* IV, 421.

76. See the draft of a letter from John Pownall to the several officers, Nov. 5, 1767, C. O. 324/24: 467.

ministry urging the prompt adoption of a general boundary. The Indian agent, Samuel Wharton, and Joseph Galloway also wrote Franklin in London, emphasizing the need to negotiate a new line.[77] This correspondence was decisive.

As soon as Franklin received these letters he sent them to Shelburne, and the next day he dined with the Secretary of State. Clare, the First Lord of Trade, although invited, did not attend; Shelburne's under-secretary, MacLeane, did, however. When Franklin brought up the matter of the boundary, Shelburne claimed he knew nothing of a new line Sir William Johnson had previously negotiated with the tribes. He ordered MacLeane to search for the relevant documents concerning the negotiation. After some delay, the papers were located, and on December 19 Shelburne notified Johnson and Gage that a report on a new boundary would be forthcoming from the Commisioners of Trade shortly.[78] Four days later the Board of Trade issued the report to the Secretary of State.

The campaign conducted by the Pennsylvania lobbyists to revise the boundary had been successful, for the Commissioners of Trade cited their urgent letters which Shelburne had recently transmitted as justifying an adjustment of the line by the government before it considered the other questions of general policy which Shelburne had raised in his directive of October 5. The board now briefly discussed the history of the boundary. Complaints by the Indians of encroachments on their lands had resulted in the provisional arrangement in the Proclamation of 1763. Shortly afterwards, in its plan of 1764, the Board of Trade had proposed the establishment of a definitive line by solemn compacts with the tribes. Consequently the Indian superintend-

77. Joseph Galloway to William Franklin, Sept. 6, 1767, Franklin Papers, XLVIII, 134, APSL; Croghan to Sir William Johnson, March 1, 1768, Alvord and Carter, *Trade and Politics,* 180; Croghan to Benjamin Franklin, Oct. 2, 1767, Franklin Papers, II-1, 1, APSL; Shelburne Papers, 50: 97–100, WLCL; Samuel Wharton to Franklin, Sept. 30, 1767, *ibid.,* 50: 105–108.

78. Benjamin Franklin to William Franklin, Nov. 25, 1767, Bigelow, *Franklin Works,* IV, 422, 424. See also the extract from Franklin to [Galloway], Dec. 1, 1767, *Johnson Papers,* V, 855; Shelburne to Johnson, Dec. 19, 1767, *Johnson Papers,* VI, 22; Shelburne to Gage, Dec. 19, 1767, *Gage Correspondence,* II, 56.

ents had discussed this project with the natives, and John Stuart had actually negotiated portions of such a line in the southern district. When Sir William Johnson had broached the matter with the northern tribes in 1765, the Six Nations had described a line running from Owegy on the eastern branch of the Susquehanna to the source of the river by its west branch, then to Kittanning on the Ohio to the confluence of the Ohio and the Cherokee (Tennessee) River. But the line John Stuart had negotiated with the Cherokees had its northern terminus at the confluence of the Great Kanawha and the Ohio. Consequently it seemed inadvisable that the ministry allow the boundary settled with the Six Nations to extend any further than the mouth of the Great Kanawha. The extension might afford a pretense for settlements on lands which were, in fact, Cherokee hunting grounds, although the Six Nations also claimed them as part of their ancient dominions. The southern Indians might consider such settlements as an open violation of the prior agreements the imperial government had negotiated.[79]

Having issued this report on the boundary line but not as yet considered the general policy Shelburne had submitted, the Board of Trade adjourned until February 15.[80] On January 5, 1768, Shelburne authorized Johnson to complete the new boundary line with the Indians—a line "conformable" to that described in the report of the Board of Trade which he now enclosed to the superintendents.[81] At last the speculators who had found Shelburne so amenable had succeeded. Or so it appeared. This was the last significant order Shelburne issued. Due to one of the periodic alterations in the ministry which marked the early years of the reign of George III, Shelburne lost control of colonial affairs. He had been very useful to the land speculators and others in America who had sought to undermine and replace the program of imperial regulation of the American interior. Because of the domestic political scene, resentment in the House of Commons over the increasing cost of the American establishment and

79. Board of Trade to Shelburne, Dec. 23, 1767, *DRCHSNY,* VII, 1004–1005.

80. Clare to William Knox, Dec. 24, 1767, Knox MSS, 1: 24, WLCL.

81. Shelburne to Johnson, Jan. 5, 1768, C. O. 5/69: 5; *DRCHSNY,* VIII, 2.

the instability of the Chatham ministry, Shelburne had found it convenient to use the arguments of the lobbyists. It does not seem that he was legitimately convinced of the desirability of western expansion. He was merely trying to finance a program for the West. But by this time the wilderness was no longer uppermost in the minds of most British ministers. They viewed with alarm the increasing revolutionary tension on the seaboard and the challenge to the authority of the imperial government. Consequently, they were willing to come to some accommodation on western policy in order to concentrate the army in the established colonies. This attitude determined the next program for the West which the reconstituted ministry adopted in 1768.

CHAPTER VII

Adjustment and Accommodation

WITH little direction or unity the Chatham administration all but staggered through the Parliamentary session of 1767—a session in which the ministers had demonstrated their weakness in the face of an almost united opposition. The cabinet was torn by dissension, with Grafton, Camden, and Lord President Northington resenting Shelburne's "great coldness" and indifference.[1] When Chatham professed his unwillingness to take part in government, George III and Grafton devised a plan to maintain the administration by splitting the opposition and bringing one of the dissatisfied opposition factions into the ministry. The stratagem worked perfectly. George Grenville, Rockingham, and the Duke of Bedford could not agree on the spoils of office or on an American policy, and the ministry was able to reach an accommodation with the followers of Bedford at the end of the year. In the political realignment that followed, the Secretary of State for the Southern Department lost control of colonial affairs. A new post was created, the Secretary of State for the American Department. No longer would extraneous matters com-

1. The King to Chatham, May 30, 1767, *Chatham Correspondence,* III, 260–261.

plicate colonial administration.[2] After refusing the new position, Shelburne continued as Secretary of State for the Southern Department for a few months before resigning in October, 1768. The Earl of Hillsborough headed the new American department on January 21, 1768. Within a short time, he exerted almost complete control over colonial affairs by assuming the duties of First Lord of Trade and excluding colonial correspondence from the Board of Trade.[3]

Domestic politics shaped the alteration in the ministry. Yet the realignment had brought into office Hillsborough—a man who viewed the reaction of the colonists as a threat to British rule in America. Consequently, he sought to preserve British authority in the colonies by concentrating the army on the seacoast to enforce obedience to Parliamentary legislation. To him the territories acquired from the Bourbon powers at the Peace of Paris were no longer of primary importance. Thus he shared the views of Lord Barrington and Grenville. The government must make some accommodation in western policy in order to relieve Great Britain of the financial burden of protecting the wilderness and concentrate British strength in the East.

The ministry had to resolve the question of interior policy in the winter of 1767–1768. In spite of the alteration in the administration, the Commissioners of Trade had not yet issued a definite report on the general program Shelburne had submitted the previous October. They had declared in favor of a revision of the Indian boundary line in December, but Hillsborough would now determine what general policy they would recommend. Lord Barrington—a close friend of the new Secretary of State—gave some indication of what was to come when he confided to General Thomas Gage that "Hillsborough knows my Ideas & seems not to disapprove of them." The colonial secretary would soon bring the matter of western policy and the interior garrisons before the cabinet.[4] The expectations of the Secretary-at-War

2. George III to Grafton, Dec. 11, 1767, Fortescue, *Correspondence of George III,* I, 510.

3. See Hillsborough's circular letter to the colonial governors, July 4, 1768, C. O. 5/69: 391.

4. Barrington to Gage (private), Feb. 4, 1768, Gage Papers.

were well founded. He could not have asked for much more in the report the Commissioners of Trade issued on March 7, 1768.

Two themes dominated this report. The Board of Trade confirmed the decision to revise the Indian boundary line, and hoped to restrict the American colonists to an area which the army could control. Secondly, the commissioners sought to concentrate the army more effectively and to ease the financial burden of the military and Indian services on Great Britain. To achieve these ends, they were willing to make some adjustment in the policy for the West which had been in operation since the French and Indian War.

The Board of Trade would continue to restrict the Indian traffic in the southern district to the specified Indian towns. But this procedure seemed inappropriate for the northern district. Maintaining that the regulations should reflect local conditions, the commissioners recommended that the provinces once more manage Indian affairs. They hoped that the colonists would have learned by their past experiences that a well regulated trade was essential to their peace and security. The commissioners took a less sanguine attitude toward the capabilities of the colonists to defend the interior, recommending that armed vessels patrol the Great Lakes to secure communications with the posts at Niagara, Detroit, and Michillimackinac. The military should decide what additional forts would be required to maintain public safety and prevent incursions by the French and Spanish. But royal troops, not provincials, should garrison these posts.

Employing classic mercantilist arguments, the commissioners came out strongly against interior colonies. Located some 1,500 miles from the sea, these settlements would be inaccessible to shipping and would not constitute a ready market for British manufactures. They would injure, not secure, the fur trade as some had argued. Neither would they serve to protect the older colonies. On the contrary, they would require protection by the army. Interior colonies were not needed to help provision the garrisons in the West, for the French inhabitants already located in the wilderness could supply the troops. The Commissioners of Trade did recognize the need for an outlet to accommodate increasing population in the colonies, but they hoped that a revision of the boundary line would provide room for expansion.[5]

Except for their optimism concerning the ability of the colonists to manage the Indian trade and the French inhabitants to supply the interior forts, the Commissioners of Trade had adopted a realistic position on Shelburne's western program.

The cabinet considered their recommendations on March 11, but postponed a final decision until March 19.[6] In the interval, Barrington, Conway, and Hillsborough drew up a minute for the ministers incorporating the suggestions the Board of Trade had made. They recommended that the government not establish interior colonies and that it discontinue imperial supervision of the Indian trade under the royal officers. The garrisons would only occupy the forts at Detroit, Niagara, and Michillimackinac. But the cabinet did not adopt this minute, for two ministers objected to the almost complete evacuation of the West. A compromise was reached, on March 19. In addition to the three posts on the Great Lakes, for the present the army would retain Fort Pitt and Fort Chartres, or some other post in the Illinois country, as well as Ticonderoga or Crown Point to secure communications with Quebec. The ministers would defer to the judgment of General Thomas Gage, the Commander-in-Chief in America, as to the value of these fortifications. Gage could exercise his own judgment on the matter.[7] This arrangement allowed Barrington to subvert the compromise reached by the cabinet. He now assured the Commander-in-Chief that he could follow the original recommendations of Hillsborough, Barrington, and Conway and abandon the forts "without the least danger of displeasing any man on this side of the Water . . . ." If Gage agreed to the evacuation of Fort Chartres, Fort Pitt, and Crown Point, he could easily achieve this by informing the ministry that these installations were useless.[8] With the apparent support of Hillsborough,

5. The report of March 7, 1768, misdated March 17, is printed in *DRCHSNY*, VIII, 19–31.

6. Barrington to Gage (private), March 12, 1768, Gage Papers, WLCL.

7. Barrington to Gage (private), April 4, 1768, *ibid.* See the revised minute of the cabinet, dated March 18, 1768, C. O. 5/1008: 156. Barrington, who was not present, places the cabinet meeting on Saturday, which was the 19th of the month.

8. Barrington to Gage (private), April 4, 1768, Gage Papers, WLCL.

Barrington was thus able to undermine the compromise the cabinet had reached on the western garrisons.

To a great extent the Secretary-at-War and the deceased Charles Townshend had triumphed over Shelburne in the struggle over interior policy. As Hillsborough informed the Commander-in-Chief, by the new program the ministry hoped to reduce expenses, preserve the unity and discipline of the American forces so they might operate more effectively in any emergency, and secure the Indian alliances by offering the tribes a new boundary to alleviate their apprehensions over unauthorized attempts by the whites to occupy their lands, without fair payment.[9]

While the policy the government had finally adopted blocked the plans of most of the land speculators, the group promoting the grant by the Six Nations to the "suffering traders" was now in a position to attain its goal. The ministry had authorized a new boundary. Before relinquishing control over colonial affairs, Shelburne had issued instructions to complete the negotiations for the line. After the formation of the new American department, Franklin pressed the matter with Hillsborough, urging the "speedy execution" of the boundary and warning that the dissatisfaction of the Indians over white settlements on the lands might lead to open hostilities.[10] The new Secretary of State confirmed the decision made by Shelburne. On March 12, he sent to the superintendents duplicates of Shelburne's previous orders about the boundary, in addition to the report of the board of March 7 to which was annexed a map delineating the proposed line. It ran from the Susquehanna to the confluence of the Ohio and Great Kanawha, and then in a straight line to Chiswell's mines near the Virginia–North Carolina border.[11] The government expected that the new boundary would include the lands of those Virginia settlers west of the Proclamation line who had occupied their holdings under authorization given in 1754. The

9. Hillsborough to Gage, April 15, 1768, *Gage Correspondence,* II, 64.

10. Benjamin Franklin to William Franklin, March 13, 1768, Bigelow, *Franklin Works,* IV, 413.

11. Hillsborough to Johnson, March 12, 1768, *DRCHSNY,* VIII, 36. A facsimile of the map is reproduced in *ibid.,* VIII, between pp. 30–31.

Virginia Burgesses had supported these settlers in their claims.[12]

Consequent developments in the colonies threatened to undermine the negotiations for a new line, however. John Stuart, the Indian Superintendent for the Southern District, had an especially difficult time with the governor of Virginia, who had disputed with the superintendent on western policy. In February, 1766, Stuart informed Governor Fauquier that he had requested Governor William Tryon of North Carolina to cooperate with Stuart's deputy, Alexander Cameron, in negotiating a boundary between North Carolina and the tribes. Cameron was also to pay attention to any claims of Virginia that Fauquier might raise.[13] But when Tryon had completed preliminary negotiations with the Indians by the end of the year, Fauquier still had not answered Stuart about the request of the Cherokees for continuing the boundary behind Virginia.[14] Not until some months later did the Virginia governor deign to reply. Since the superintendent was in charge of Indian affairs, it was up to Stuart to demonstrate to the ministry the necessity of fixing a boundary. Besides, Fauquier complained, if the government had directed him to fix the line, he would have been "at a loss where to have begun . . . ." [15] In November, 1767, Shelburne, the American "expert," confused the issue even more by ordering Fauquier to complete the boundary line. But the Secretary of State was not clear which line he meant. Since the boundary between the Indians and the Carolinas had been completed, "as also between them and the Provinces of Pennsylvania and Maryland," Shelburne mistakenly noted, it was now necessary to continue it behind Virginia. It would begin at the terminal of the North Carolina boundary at Chiswell's mines and extend behind the Virginia settlements "till it falls in with that Point from whence the Northern Provinces set out." Such a line would alleviate friction between the natives and the white settlers and would also serve "to set determined and known Bounds to the several Colonies." [16]

12. See the report of the Board of Trade, dated June 10, 1768, C. O. 5/1346: 29–35.

13. Stuart to Fauquier, Feb. 10, 1766, C. O. 5/66: 783–785.

14. Stuart to the Board of Trade, Dec. 2, 1766, C. O. 5/67: 399.

15. Fauquier to Stuart, Sept. 17, 1767, C. O. 5/69: 265; C. O. 5/70: 281.

16. Shelburne to Fauquier, Nov. 14, 1767, C. O. 5/1345: 391–392; Shelburne Papers, 54: 73, WLCL.

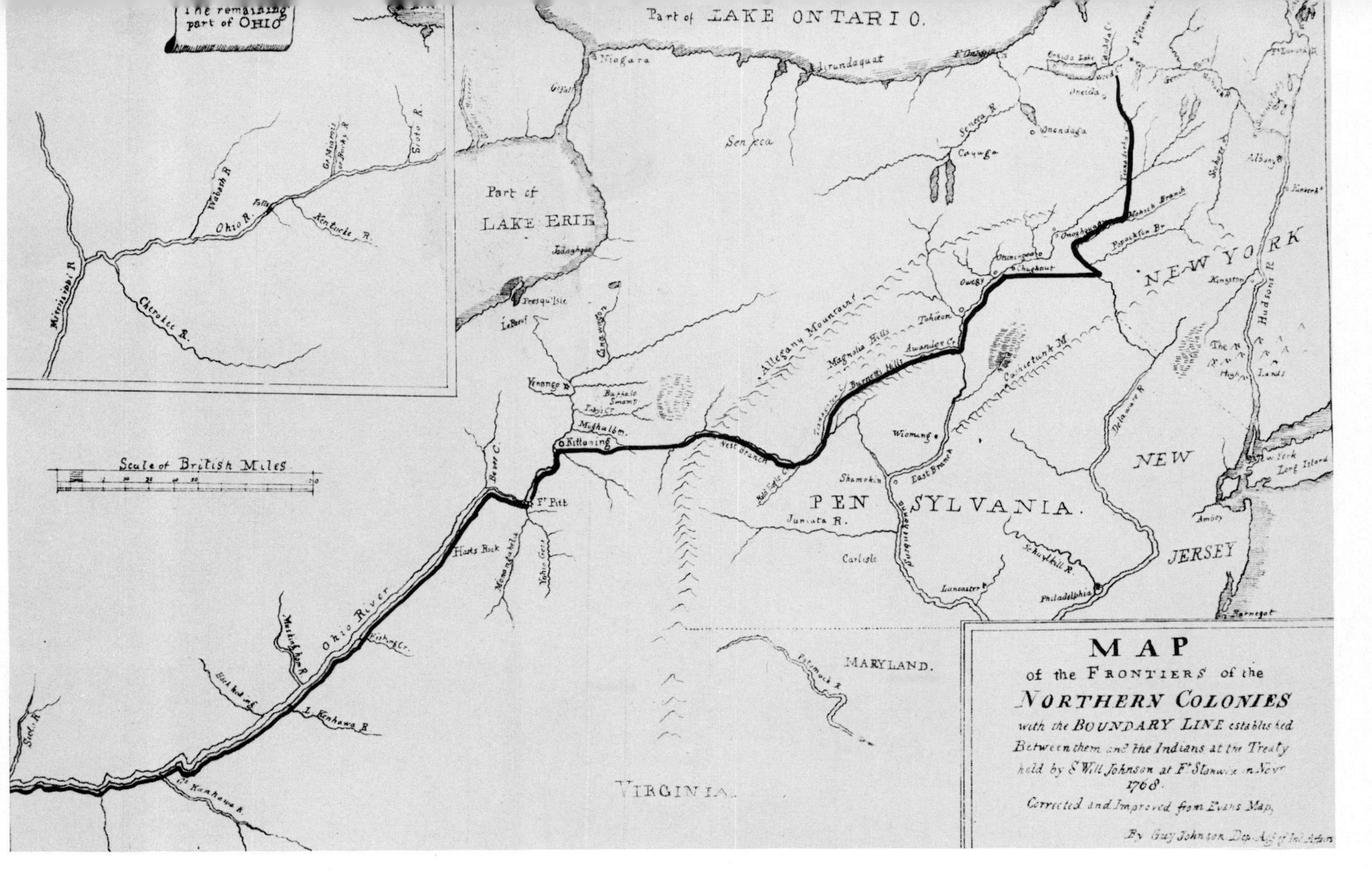

Indian boundary line as ordered by the Board of Trade, 1768. *Document Relative to the Colonial History of . . . New York,* vol. 8, 1857, between pages 30 and 31.

Shelburne's ignorance was appalling. Not only had he confused the Indian boundary with the Mason-Dixon line between Pennsylvania and Maryland,[17] but he had also mistaken the Indian boundary with the line marking the charter limits of the British provinces. It was little wonder that the receipt of Shelburne's order threw the Virginia government into a quandary. Governor Francis Fauquier had died recently. On the recommendation of the colonial council, John Blair, president of that body, wrote to the superintendents for advice. At the same time he expressed his fears to the Secretary of State that "we shall meet with great difficulties, the Line back of Pennsylvania not being run yet I find." [18] Until the imperial officers determined the course of the boundary line in the North, Blair informed Stuart, the Virginians by the terms of Shelburne's instructions had no directions on the course of the line from Chiswell's mines northward.[19] For his part, Stuart maintained that it was up to Sir William Johnson, Superintendent for the Northern District, to clear up any difficulties in that region arising from Shelburne's confused instructions.[20]

Finally in April, 1768, Johnson clarified the Secretary of State's error to Blair. The Secretary of State had "misunderstood" the line "between Maryland & Pennsylvania." This survey was "a private affair between those Colonies" and had no connection with the Indians. Johnson now informed Blair that he had received orders from the ministry to complete the boundary conformable to the report of the Board of Trade on December 23, 1767.[21] Thus the line between Virginia and the Indians would run in a straight course from Chiswell's mines to the confluence of the Ohio and Great Kanawha rivers.

While the intransigence of Governor Fauquier and the ignorance of the Earl of Shelburne had delayed the negotiation of the new Indian boundary, the imperial superintendents could now proceed with the matter.

After a brief exchange with the American secretary as to the

17. Alden, *Southern Colonial Frontier*, 269.
18. Blair to Shelburne, March 21, 1768, C. O. 5/1346: 15.
19. Blair to Stuart, March 12, 1768, C. O. 5/70: 289.
20. Stuart to Blair, April 4, 1768, C. O. 5/70: 293.
21. Johnson to Blair, April 23, 1768, Johnson MSS, IHS transcript.

advisability of altering the southern line so that it would run from Chiswell's mines to the mouth of the Catawba (Kentucky) River—a proposal Hillsborough rejected as unnecessarily expensive[22]—John Stuart proceeded to execute his original instructions. At a congress held at Hard Labor from October 13 to October 17, 1768, Stuart concluded a treaty which confirmed the boundary previously agreed to by the tribes and approved by the Board of Trade. The line ran from Tryon's mountain on a straight course to Chiswell's mines on a branch of the lower Kanawha and then northwest to the junction of that river with the Ohio. The Indians were asked to meet with commissioners from Virginia on May 10, 1769, to mark the boundary.[23]

Stuart's handling of the boundary in the southern district met with the approval of the ministry,[24] but the negotiations conducted by the Superintendent for the Northern District did not. While Stuart had followed the orders of the Commissioners of Trade, Sir William Johnson deviated from the line specified by the board in its reports of December 23, 1767, and March 7, 1768. Johnson's action upset the new plan proposed by the ministry and provided an opening for the land speculators which in time further exacerbated relations between the whites and the Indians.

In its reports the Board of Trade had approved the tentative line agreed to by Johnson and the Six Nations in 1765, but it had specifically rejected Johnson's proposal to extend the boundary down the Ohio from the mouth of the Great Kanawha to the Cherokee (Tennessee) River.[25] Although Johnson had clear

22. See Stuart to Hillsborough, July 14, Aug. 16, 1768, C. O. 5/69: 427–428, 555; and Hillsborough to Stuart, Sept. 15, 1768, C. O. 5/69: 448.

23. Stuart to Blair, Oct. 17, 1768, Henry R. MacIlwaine and John P. Kennedy (eds.), *Journals of the House of Burgesses of Virginia, 1766–1769,* xxvi–xxvii; *Virginia Magazine of History and Biography,* XIII (1905–1906), 20–21. See Stuart's journal of the proceedings at Hard Labor, C. O. 5/70: 151–172. Alden, *Southern Colonial Frontier,* 270, n31, corrects the error of T. P. Abernethy, *Western Lands and the American Revolution* (New York, 1937), 64–65, in confusing the survey by Cameron at Chiswell's mines and the Cherokee congress held by Stuart at Hard Labor.

24. Hillsborough to Stuart, March 24, 1769, C. O. 5/70: 355.

25. Hillsborough to Johnson, March 12, 1768, C. O. 5/69: 223–225; *DRCHSNY,* VIII, 36. A facsimile of the map is reproduced in *ibid.,* VIII, between pp. 30–31.

and specific instructions on the line he was to negotiate, he violated these orders on several key points. It is difficult to escape the conclusion that he deviated from these instructions in order to further the claims of the land speculators—in particular, the "suffering traders" of Pennsylvania and, to a lesser extent, the Virginians. Certain speculators and creditors, among them the firm of Baynton, Wharton, and Morgan; Joseph Galloway; William Trent; and Governor William Franklin of Pennsylvania had taken over the interests of the Pennsylvania traders.

These land speculators secretly sought to obtain a grant from the northern tribes as compensation for losses supposedly incurred at the hands of the Indians. Without revealing their true motive, they had successfully lobbied with the ministry for a rectification of the Indian boundary. They had intimidated the home government by warning of an Indian war unless it authorized a new line to compensate the Indians for the transgressions committed by squatters beyond the line set in the Proclamation of 1763.

Once the ministry authorized a new boundary, the land speculators were in a position to achieve their aims. The key figure in this lobby was Samuel Wharton of Philadelphia, who, as Joseph Galloway pointed out to the younger Franklin, was the only man astute and persuasive enough to negotiate the matter with the Superintendent for the Northern District and his deputy, George Croghan.[26] In order to obtain confirmation of a grant the Indians had made him some time before, Croghan was also interested in negotiating a new boundary line. In June, 1768, Croghan, Wharton, and William Trent (the attorney for the traders) visited the Indian superintendent at New London, Connecticut, where he was vacationing. From their correspondence it is clear that at least one day before Johnson received his dispatches from Hillsborough ordering him to negotiate a boundary settlement with the Indians, the superintendent had committed himself to obtaining a grant of land for the land speculators at the forthcoming congress with the northern tribes.[27]

26. Galloway to William Franklin, Sept. 6, 1767, Franklin Papers, XLVIII, 134, APSL.

27. Croghan to Thomas Wharton, June 22, 1768, Ayer Collection, Newberry Library (copy in Croghan Papers, Cadwallader Collection, box 34,

The speculators could now proceed with some assurance of success. By arrangement, Wharton met Trent later that summer. Until the month of September, they were engaged in using their "best Interest with the Indians, to obtain a Reimbursement of the Losses." [28] In spite of the anxiety of some of their associates that certain elements in Philadelphia headed by John Cox would dispute their right to act for the "suffering traders," Wharton and Trent were confident of success. Confident they were, for, from Fort Stanwix in the Mohawk country—the site of the proposed Indian congress—William Trent assured John Baynton that he should have had no cause for alarm if he had "attended to a letter Mr Wharton wrote you ab[ou]t the Virg[ini]a Commis[sione]rs" earlier in September.[29] Unfortunately, there is no record of what transpired between Wharton and the Virginia commissioners which made Trent so optimistic. But it is significant that the commissioners then in the Mohawk country were Thomas Walker, a member of the Loyal Company, and Andrew Lewis, one of the Virginia officers claiming lands on the Monongahela by the terms of Dinwiddie's proclamation of 1754.

The tardiness of some chieftains in arriving at Fort Stanwix caused a postponement of the Indian congress until October 12. Since this date was so close to the time set for the meeting with the Cherokees (October 25), the Virginians decided that Walker should return for the meeting with the southern tribe.[30] Late in September, Johnson informed the president of the Virginia council that he was "pretty certain" that the northern confederacy would persist in its claims to the territory beyond the Great Kanawha River. Consequently, if Johnson were to admit the allegations of the Six Nations, the whites could obtain a more favorable line than that ordered by the Commissioners of Trade

---

HSP); Samuel Wharton to Thomas Wharton, June 23, 1768, Wharton Papers, HSP; and William Trent to Thomas Wharton, June 30, 1768, *ibid.*

28. Samuel Wharton to Benjamin Franklin, Dec. 2, 1768, Franklin Papers, XLIX, 77, APSL.

29. Trent to Baynton, Sept. 30, 1768, Ohio Company Papers, I, 48, HSP.

30. Lewis and Walker to Johnson, July 29, 1768, *Johnson Papers,* VI, 297; Johnson to Blair, Sept. 25, 1768, *ibid.,* VI, 406. See also Walker's deposition printed in American Antiq. Soc., *Proceedings,* XLI (1931), 147.

in London.[31] Sir William finally opened the congress with the northern tribes at Fort Stanwix on October 24. What actually transpired at these meetings will perhaps never be known, for, as Croghan's biographer has noted: "Most of the real work was done in private conferences with the leading chiefs." [32] In view of the suspicious behavior of the superintendent and the conflicting story he later related to the ministry in London, his report of the congress at Fort Stanwix is open to question.[33] Ostensibly at the insistence of the Indians, Sir William extended the boundary line from the confluence of the Ohio and the Great Kanawha to the mouth of the Tennessee River.[34] He also allowed the Indians to grant lands to the "suffering traders" who had incurred damages in the uprising of 1763. The boundary of the grant to the traders began at the south side of Little Kanawha Creek and followed this stream to Laurel Hill and along this range to the Monongahela. It then followed the river to the southern boundary of Pennsylvania and along this line to the Ohio.[35] These lands—later called "Indiana"—were within the territory claimed by Virginia. Among the papers of William Trent there is a copy of the deed to this grant which bears the notation that the document belonged to George Morgan of the firm of Baynton, Wharton, and Morgan. A notation by Morgan indicated that he wanted the deed recorded at Williamsburg, the capital of Virginia.[36] Almost certainly there was a connection between the cession of lands along the Monongahela and the extension of the boundary past the Great Kanawha. According to the ac-

31. Johnson to Blair, Sept. 25, 1768, *Johnson Papers*, VI, 406–407.

32. Albert T. Volwiler, *George Croghan and the Westward Movement, 1741–1782* (Cleveland, 1926), 222.

33. Johnson's report is printed in *DRCHSNY*, VIII, 112–138.

34. The deed to the Fort Stanwix treaty, with the boundary stipulations, is printed in *Virginia Magazine of History and Biography*, XIII (1905–1906), 23–27; also in Edmund B. O'Callaghan (ed.), *The Documentary History of the State of New York* (4 vols., Albany, 1850–1851), I, 587–591. A sketch of the boundary line drawn by Guy Johnson on a corrected Evans map is reproduced in *ibid.*, I, between pp. 586–587.

35. A copy of the deed is printed in Kenneth P. Bailey (ed.), *The Ohio Company Papers, 1755–1817, Being Primarily Papers of the "Suffering Traders" of Pennsylvania* (Arcata, Calif., 1947), 192.

36. Ohio Company Papers, I, 51, HSP.

count of the congress at Fort Stanwix which Samuel Wharton sent to Benjamin Franklin, the Indians executed their deed to the "suffering traders" five days before they ceded the other lands to the royal government. The natives insisted on this, Wharton claimed, "as they said The one was an act of Justice and thc [other] was a condition of Sale." [37]

Sir William Johnson had violated his instructions in extending the boundary below the mouth of the Great Kanawha and in allowing the private claims of Croghan and the traders to be introduced into the Treaty of Fort Stanwix as a condition of the cession of lands by the tribes to the royal government. By these alterations the superintendent had opened Pandora's box. Was there any connection between these two acts? One historian has asserted that Johnson's extension of the Indian boundary line to the mouth of the Tennessee River was the *quid pro quo* for recognition by the Virginia commissioners of the grant to the "suffering traders." [38] Although the evidence is circumstantial, there is much to support this view. William Trent and Samuel Wharton made it a point to reassure John Baynton that their grant was secure because of the presence of the Virginia commissioners at Fort Stanwix. The attempt by George Morgan to register the deed at the Virginia capital also lends weight to this interpretation. In addition, Johnson had indicated to John Blair in September, *before* the opening of the congress, that it was possible and desirable to extend the boundary on the basis of the claims of the Six Nations. George Washington, one of the Virginia officers claiming lands along the Monongahela by the terms of Dinwiddie's proclamation, revealed another clue in a letter which he sent to the newly appointed governor of Virginia, Norbonne Berkeley, Baron Botetourt. According to a postscript to this letter, Thomas Walker, one of the Virginia commissioners at Fort Stanwix, had informed Washington that the area originally set aside for the provincial officers of Virginia by the Dinwiddie proclamation had been reserved for the traders of Pennsylvania.

37. Samuel Wharton to Benjamin Franklin, Dec. 2, 1768, Franklin Papers, XLIX, 77, APSL.

38. Ray A. Billington, "The Ft. Stanwix Treaty of 1768," *New York History*, XXV (1944), 192–193.

Boundary line negotiated at Fort Stanwix, 1768. *Documents Relative to the Colonial History of . . . New York,* vol. 8, 1857, between pages 136 and 137.

Washington now asked Botetourt to reserve another area for the Virginia veterans. In a notation to the draft of this letter, Washington wrote that if the Virginia government had to locate this alternative area immediately, it should follow the memorandum drawn up by Andrew Lewis, the other Virginia commissioner, provided it did not conflict with the territory reserved for the Pennsylvanians.[39]

While this evidence is not entirely conclusive, it strongly indicates that Johnson extended the boundary line to the Tennessee River so as to include lands coveted by the Virginians, in order to obtain their acquiescence to the grant for the traders in a district over which the southern colony claimed jurisdiction.

The superintendent sought to justify his actions to Hillsborough shortly after the Fort Stanwix cession. The Six Nations had insisted on their right to lands as far south as the Tennessee River. From what had transpired at several private meetings with the chiefs, Johnson had found that, in spite of his instructions from the Board of Trade, he could not deny the Six Nations their claim without endangering the entire boundary negotiation. He had inquired further but could not find that the Cherokees had ever claimed lands north of the Tennessee River—an area the Six Nations had insisted was always their territory. Consequently, he had judged it in the government's interest to acquiesce in the demands of the northern confederacy, for they were the "more formidable People" of the two Indian groups.[40]

Hillsborough was not convinced. He considered it unfortunate that Johnson had allowed the Six Nations to discover that the ministry doubted their right to the country beyond the Great Kanawha. From the superintendent's report it appeared that because of Johnson's indiscretion, and "this alone," he had to deviate from the instructions which the Board of Trade had issued. Johnson's commitment threatened to antagonize the Cherokees and thus undo the agreement Stuart had concluded in the southern district. To prevent such a rupture, the Secretary of State

39. Washington to Botetourt, Dec. 8, 1769, John C. Fitzpatrick (ed.), *The Writings of George Washington, 1745–1799* (39 vols., Washington, 1931–1944), II, 528–532 and 532 n16.

40. Johnson to Hillsborough, Nov. 18, 1768, *DRCHSNY,* VIII, 110.

ordered Sir William to convince the Six Nations that the ministry declined the additional cession, although it did not doubt the right of the northern tribes to sell these lands.[41] Thus Hillsborough sought to salve the pride of the Six Nations but not to antagonize the Cherokees by actually accepting lands used by the southern tribe.

The ministry also objected to the grants made by the Six Nations to Croghan and the "suffering traders." After some deliberation,[42] the Board of Trade issued a report in April, 1769, in which it condemned Johnson for exceeding his instructions. His commitment in favor of the Pennsylvanians adversely affected the entire boundary settlement, they charged. The Commissioners of Trade particularly objected to the claims and interests of private persons (not previously stated or approved by the royal government) being introduced, "not as Propositions submitted to the King's determination," but as rights derived from the Indians in which the acquiescence of the royal government was demanded as a condition of the treaty. Maintaining that the introduction of the claims of the traders and Croghan was due directly to the "indiscretion" of Sir William Johnson, the board recommended that the ministry reject the grants.[43] In consequence of this indictment, Hillsborough informed Johnson that the government would postpone consideration of the private grants. The ministry would not confirm them until the traders made direct application to the Crown and offered a full explanation of the affair. In addition, the superintendent was to reject the cession of lands beyond the Great Kanawha. If, however, the Six Nations should prove hostile to the idea, the ministry would confirm the treaty of Fort Stanwix rather than jeopardize the whole boundary negotiation. Even so, the Crown did not intend to allow settlement beyond the Great Kanawha.[44]

But it was impossible to go back to the arrangement for the original boundary line proposed by the Board of Trade. Nothing

41. Hillsborough to Johnson, Jan. 4, 1769, *ibid.*, VIII, 145.

42. *Journal of the Board of Trade, 1768–1774*, pp. 77–80, 84, 88.

43. The board's representation, dated April 25, 1769, in C. O. 5/70: 375–398.

44. Hillsborough to Johnson, May 13, 1769, *DRCHSNY*, VIII, 166.

demonstrated this more clearly than the reaction of the government of Virginia to Johnson's action at Fort Stanwix in purchasing the lands west of the line negotiated by John Stuart at the Hard Labor Congress.

The Superintendent for the Southern District had fully informed the Council of Virginia of the results of his negotiations with the Cherokees.[45] But the Virginians were in a stronger position to exert pressure on Stuart after the arrival in the colony of the new governor in the winter of 1768. Wholly unfamiliar with the previous transactions on the Indian boundary line, Lord Botetourt proved highly susceptible to the blandishments of the colonists. When the Virginia commissioners returned from the northern congress with a report of the action taken by Johnson, the Virginians had a lever by which they could alter the Hard Labor agreement and acquire additional Indian lands for settlement. Citing the steps taken by the Superintendent for the Northern District, in December, Botetourt wrote John Stuart about the area below the Great Kanawha. At the same time he instructed Walker and Lewis to confer with Stuart for a revision of the boundary line recently negotiated at Hard Labor.[46] After mutual recriminations and charges, the superintendent finally proposed a new Indian line to extend due west of the North Carolina–Virginia boundary to the Holston River and then, by a northeast course, to the mouth of the Great Kanawha. While this boundary would incorporate the Virginia settlements excluded by the old line, it would not antagonize the Cherokees, since they would retain their hunting grounds.[47] The ministry approved this proposal.[48]

Following a further exchange of letters lasting some months,[49] an adjustment of the southern boundary was now possible. By the terms of the treaty of Lochaber, signed on October 18, 1770,

45. Stuart to Blair, Oct. 17, 1768, C. O. 5/1332: 89–91.

46. Botetourt to Stuart, Dec. 20, 1768, C. O. 5/1332: 110.

47. Stuart to Hillsborough, Feb. 12, 1769, C. O. 5/70: 249–253.

48. Hillsborough to Stuart, May 13, 1769, C. O. 5/70: 407–408.

49. Stuart to Botetourt, Aug. 3, 1769, C. O. 5/70: 587; Botetourt to Stuart, Aug. 22, 1769, C. O. 5/70: 591; Botetourt to Stuart, Dec. 18, 1769, C. O. 5/71: 107; Stuart to Botetourt, Jan. 3, 1770, C. O. 5/71: 121–124; and Botetourt to Stuart, June 21, 1770, C. O. 5/71: 341.

the boundary line extended from the Virginia–North Carolina border to a point six miles east of Long Island in the Holston River. It then ran six miles above the island and, in a straight course, to the confluence of the Great Kanawha and the Ohio.[50]

With the signing of the Lochaber treaty, it appeared that the superintendents had finally completed the new boundary line. In July, 1770, at a congress with the Six Nations, Sir William had confirmed and ratified the Treaty of Fort Stanwix. There was one drawback, however, which frustrated the plans of the Pennsylvania land speculators. On orders from the ministry in London, Johnson did not include the grants from the Indians to George Croghan and the "suffering traders" in this negotiation of 1770.[51] In time the question of these grants led to a re-evaluation of the policy against interior settlements. It was to prove a highly controversial issue.

The program which the ministry instituted in 1768 was only partially implemented two years later. Basically, it constituted an accommodation of the original wartime policy to the challenge presented by the colonists to imperial authority. By returning control of the Indian trade to the provinces, and evacuating some of the interior garrisons, the administration had hoped to alleviate the financial burden on Great Britain, a burden which the colonists refused to share. By reducing the garrisons in the wilderness and prohibiting interior settlements, the government also hoped more effectively to control the colonists on the seaboard. But the extreme tactics used by the land speculators in forcing an extention of the boundary line indicated that they would not accept such restriction docilely. Colonial land speculation threatened to force a basic revision in British policy for the wilderness.

50. See Stuart's journal of the Lochaber congress, C. O. 5/72: 59.

51. See Johnson's report of the congress on July 21, 1770, *DRCHSNY,* VIII, 237.

CHAPTER VIII

Vandalia: an Interior Colony

THE reluctance of the British ministry to confirm the private grants of land made by the Indians to private individuals threatened to block the speculators who had cooperated so successfully with Sir William Johnson at the congress at Fort Stanwix. By the treaty negotiated in 1768, the Six Nations had granted lands west of the mountains which they themselves did not occupy as compensation to a Philadelphia syndicate for depredations committed by the Indians in Pontiac's uprising of 1763. But other traders had incurred losses at the outbreak of the French and Indian War at the hands of the natives and their French allies. The treaty of Fort Stanwix made no provision for these traders. A rival group in Philadelphia led by John Cox protested the right of the faction headed by Samuel Wharton and William Trent to act for the traders of 1763 and insisted that they share the lands with those merchants to whom the traders were indebted.[1] In the Quaker capital, rumor had it that Cox intended giving those whose names appeared on the Indian deed from the Six Nations "All the Opposition they can in England . . . ." He intended to peti-

1. Robert Callender to William Trent, Nov. 24, 1768, "Papers relating to Indian Losses 1766–1770," 16, Indian Records Collection, 1716–1856, HSP; Mathias Slough to Trent, Dec. 1, 1768, *ibid.*, 18.

tion the home government. If the ministry confirmed the grant, the lands should go to the Cox group for the losses of 1754 and as the creditors of the traders who had suffered in the uprising of 1763. Evidently the threat was serious, for William Trent and Samuel Wharton decided to leave for England as soon as possible in order to "have the final Stroke given to the Grant" and to offset the objections of Cox and his associates.[2]

Although William Trent was late in embarking, Samuel Wharton arrived in London early in the spring of 1769. He then drew up several petitions asking confirmation of the land grant by the Six Nations which he planned to have presented by a solicitor, Henry Dagge, as soon as Trent arrived. In the meantime, he was "making all the Interest" he could. Wharton achieved remarkable success in building up a lobby of almost unprecedented proportions. It included politicians both in and out of the administration. He soon established contacts with Lauchlin MacLeane,

2. Trent to [Callender], Dec. 1, 1768, Ohio Company Papers, II, 53, HSP. The case for the opposing faction is stated in a letter from Adam Hoops to General Robert Monckton, Feb. 22, 1769, "Aspinwall Papers," pt. 2, Mass. Hist. Soc. *Collections,* 4th ser., X, 64–66. To render the opposition ineffective, Trent, at the instigation of Wharton, collected statements from the various traders denying the authority of the Cox group and authorizing Trent to continue as their attorney. See Wharton's memoranda to Trent, Kenneth P. Bailey (ed.), *The Ohio Company Papers, 1753–1817, Being Primarily Papers of the "Suffering Traders" of Pennsylvania* (Arcata, Calif., 1947), 185, and Hugh Crawford to Trent, Dec. 10, 1768; James Silver to Trent, Jan. 2, 1769; Paul Pearce to Trent, Jan. 22, 1769; and John Gray to Trent, Jan. 23, 1769; Ohio Company Papers, I, 54, 60, 62, 63, HSP. Another lobby consisting of Edward Shippen, Jr., Joseph Morris, Benjamin Levy, David Franks, Thomas Lawrence, and Samuel Wharton was now formed to prosecute the claims of the traders of 1754. They now wrote to Moses Franks in London, appointing him sole agent for the traders of 1754 and requesting him to present a petition to the ministry for another grant within the Fort Stanwix cession. For full particulars, Franks was referred to Samuel Wharton and Trent, who were to convey the relevant documents to London. The chief aim of the two lobbyists, however, was to secure confirmation for the grant made at Fort Stanwix. To finance their voyage, they received the financial backing of William Franklin, Croghan, and Robert Callender. The articles of agreement, dated Dec. 30, 1768, are printed in Bailey, *Ohio Company Papers,* 205–210. See also the committee for the traders of 1754 to Moses Franks (copy), Jan. 4, 1769, Ohio Company Papers, I, 57, HSP.

Shelburne's secretary, and "Governor" Thomas Pownall, brother of John Pownall, secretary to the Earl of Hillsborough. The former executive of Massachusetts enjoyed a reputation as an expert on colonial administration. Wharton was soon able to report that he was "vastly fond" of the restitution for the traders and had promised to aid in securing confirmation of the grant. Benjamin Franklin had also pledged to "push it with all his Power and Influence . . . ." [3]

But the minister immediately responsible for colonial affairs remained obdurate. Wharton reported that Hillsborough and his secretary, John Pownall, had formed an "injurious Opinion" as to the negotiations for the boundary line at Fort Stanwix. They were displeased that Sir William Johnson had allowed the Six Nations to grant lands to Croghan and the other traders. In spite of the suspicions of the Secretary of State for the American Department, there was some hope for the speculators. Although he did not "dare commit names to Paper," Wharton confided to George Croghan in May, 1769, that there was "a powerful Body" in London who looked with misgivings on Hillsborough and his secretary and who were threatening that the two would answer for any "fatal Consequences" that would result if they failed to confirm the promises Sir William Johnson had made to the Six Nations. The Philadelphian may have been misrepresenting the situation, but he had another way of getting around Hillsborough. Wharton now recalled that Croghan had previously assured him of a letter Shelburne had written to Johnson, acknowledging the propriety of a compensatory grant to the traders. Wharton now suggested that if the superintendent were to quote from this letter to Hillsborough and support it by the correspondence of Hillsborough "himself in not objecting to it," this would "infallibly justify" the superintendent's action at Fort Stanwix and remove "all reasonable Objections" to the ministry's confirming the grant to the traders. Wharton's logic was fallacious, but his plight was des-

3. Samuel Wharton to George Croghan, April 3, 1769, Croghan Papers, Cadwallader Collection, box 37, HSP. Wharton's solicitor, Henry Dagge, did request the Board of Trade to make available copies of the negotiations between Johnson and the Delawares in 1765. The Board of Trade agreed to the request on April 18. *Journal of the Board of Trade, 1768–1775*, p. 87.

perate. "My *All* depends on the Confirmation of the Indian Grant," he implored Croghan.

Since it was essential to the speculators that Sir William defend his actions before the ministry, a few days later Wharton sent Croghan another letter—one which he intended the trader to show to the superintendent. The reliability of its contents is, consequently, questionable. Wharton contended that, at a meeting of the Board of Trade, Hillsborough strongly opposed confirming the grant to the traders, but fearing a rupture with the powerful Six Nations, the other commissioners had rejected his arguments. Wharton claimed that even the cabinet was determined to overrule Hillsborough on the issue. The Secretary of State had argued, however, that he must send Johnson an official letter as a minister of state expressing the royal government's disapproval of the superintendent's conduct. Nevertheless, Wharton claimed, it was the "fixed Determination" of the cabinet to ratify all of the transactions on the boundary line if the Six Nations *"will not recede from the Terms They fixed at Fort Stanwix."* Still writing for Johnson's benefit, Wharton alleged that Hillsborough had insinuated that the entire negotiation at Fort Stanwix "was a piece of Management" which clearly demonstrated that the superintendent desired to dominate Indian affairs. It was for this reason "That the Indians spoke in the manner They have in the Treaty." But the land speculators could force Hillsborough to back down, as Wharton perceived. If Sir William supported the terms of the treaty and the Six Nations adhered to the conditions they had stipulated at Fort Stanwix, the home government must confirm the entire negotiation. The ministers would have to overrule the Secretary of State, for they feared nothing more than to precipitate an Indian war.[4]

Samuel Wharton was attempting to counter the objections of the American secretary by inducing Croghan and Sir William Johnson to maintain a firm line with the natives. At the same time, Wharton sought to undermine Hillsborough by cultivating political support in London. Through the efforts of MacLeane and Richard Jackson, the Quaker merchant was travelling

4. [Wharton] to Croghan, May 18, 1769, Croghan Papers, Cadwallader Collection, box 37, HSP; [Wharton] to Croghan, May 27, 1769, *ibid.;* [Wharton] to Croghan, May 28, 1769, *ibid.*

in the best London circles. They introduced him "to the first People of the Nation . . . ." He dined frequently "with some of the Nobility, Members of Parliament," and others of the political world. People paid a "great deal of Attention" to Wharton "for his general knowledge of American Affairs," according to his colleague, William Trent.[5] Wharton's political contacts now proved of some benefit. On June 14, Thomas Walpole, an influential London banker, informed him that Lord Chancellor Camden had revealed the dissatisfaction of the ministry at Hillsborough's attitude. There "was not One Member" of the cabinet, so Wharton reported, who did not think Hillsborough "mad" for objecting to the Fort Stanwix treaty. As Walpole had related, it was the unanimous opinion of the cabinet to confirm the boundary negotiations *"in all its parts"* if the Six Nations insisted on the terms agreed to at the conference.

Since Hillsborough was apparently isolated in the cabinet, Wharton had an opportunity for further political maneuvering. He spent the summer of 1769 "spreading [his] interest . . . and making . . . Connexions every where . . . ." He claimed to be on "the best Terms" with the Earls of Hertford, Shelburne, Falmouth, and Camden, as well as with John and Thomas Pownall, and the Secretaries to the Treasury, Thomas Bradshaw and Grey Cooper. He was also cultivating Richard Stonehewer, private secretary to the Duke of Grafton, the First Lord of the Treasury. "In short," Wharton boasted, he had associated himself with "the first ruling characters" in the administration and Parliament. The Philadelphian now revealed to Croghan that there was "a Great Plan on foot" with the most influential people in London; a plan which would take place *"only"* if the Six Nations and the royal government would come to some agreement on the boundary. Croghan and Sir William Johnson were each to have a share in the venture. Wharton had solemnly pledged not to disclose this scheme until the administrative boards resumed business after the summer recess.[6]

5. William Trent to Croghan, June 10, 1769, *ibid.*

6. Wharton to Croghan, June 16, 1769, *ibid.* Wharton wrote substantially the same account to Johnson on June 14, 1769, *Johnson Papers,* VII, 18–19. Wharton to Croghan, Aug. 12, 1769, Croghan Papers, Cadwallader Collection, box 37, HSP.

With every reason to be confident, the Philadelphia merchant now went about looking "fresh and jolly," according to Benjamin Franklin. His affairs were "in a good train," but, since everything transacted in the great public offices took time, Wharton would not be able to return home until the following spring.[7] Franklin was overoptimistic, for Samuel Wharton was to spend several years in London lobbying for greater stakes than the mere traders' grant.

The "Great Plan" Wharton had mentioned was the Walpole Company, a syndicate he helped organize on July 24 to acquire some 2,400,000 acres of land ceded at Fort Stanwix by the Six Nations. The Crown had paid £10,460 for the lands acquired from the tribes. Since "several of the Nobility and other great personages" were disposed to have "estates in America," Wharton had suggested that they purchase from the Crown a large tract on the Ohio within the cession made by the Six Nations. After some negotiation during the summer, the Walpole Company presented a petition to the King. As Trent and Wharton explained the affair to Croghan, they had merged their interest with that of the Walpole group to avoid having to make a formal application to the Crown for the traders' grant. Their solicitor, Henry Dagge, had advised them not to appeal to the ministry until they learned what Hillsborough had written to Sir William Johnson concerning the negotiation at Fort Stanwix.[8] The Pennsylvania speculators now abandoned the traders' grant and devoted their efforts to securing the same lands on the frontier through the London syndicate they had helped form.

The Privy Council referred the petition of the Walpole Associates [9] to the Board of Trade. On December 20, a committee

7. Benjamin Franklin to Cadwalader Evans, Sept. 7, 1769, Bigelow, *Franklin Works,* V, 102.

8. Wharton to Croghan, Sept. 4, 1769, Croghan Papers, Cadwallader Collection, box 37, HSP; Trent to Croghan, April 11, 1770, *ibid.;* Wharton to Croghan, Dec. 6, 1769, *ibid.*

9. A copy of the petition by Thomas Walpole, Sir George Colebrooke, Thomas Pownall, Benjamin Franklin, Thomas Pitt, Lauchlin MacLeane, Moses Franks, Jacob Franks, Henry Dagge, Nepthali Franks, Anthony Todd, John Foxcroft, James Dagge, John Dagge, and Robert Trevor, on behalf of themselves and their associates in C. O. 5/1332: 285–287.

from the company attended the board to testify in support of their request for the territory on the left bank of the Ohio.[10] According to Wharton's account of this meeting, the Secretary of State for the American Department, Hillsborough, suggested that the syndicate purchase lands sufficient for a separate government. If the petitioners approved of "his Hint, He kindly offered to step down" to the Treasury—"whose province it was[,] and not the Board of Trade[,] to *sell*"—to see if they would treat with the Walpole group. The committee for the petitioners "thanked his Lordship for the Favor." Hillsborough then consulted with the Treasury Board and returned with the tidings that they had agreed to negotiate with the Associates.[11] The Commissioners of Trade then suggested that they would consider the political aspects of the grant after the petitioners presented their financial proposals to the Treasury.[12]

What motivated Hillsborough, who had consistently opposed similar proposals for transmontane settlements, to take this action? His under-secretary of state, William Knox, offered a probable explanation. Franklin had publicly stated that the approval of the Treasury of the proposal of the Walpole Associates to purchase the 2,400,000-acre tract for the price of the Fort Stanwix cession, £10,460, was "good for nought," since Hillsborough would "never let them have it." Aware of Franklin's declaration, Hillsborough, in order to "throw the odium off his own shoulders," had "artfully proposed" to the Walpole Associates that they petition for an increased grant of more than twenty million acres. He expected that the Treasury Board would raise the purchase price proportionally to £100,000, a sum Hillsborough thought the Walpole Associates could not meet.[13]

If this were really Hillsborough's plan to defeat the scheme for a transmontane settlement, it seemed at first to have succeeded. At a meeting at the Crown and Anchor Tavern on De-

10. *Acts of the Privy Council, Col.*, V, 202; *Journal of the Board of Trade, 1768–1775*, pp. 152, 155.

11. Wharton to Croghan, Sept. 4, 1770, Croghan Papers, Cadwallader Collection, box 37, HSP.

12. *Journal of the Board of Trade, 1768–1775*, p. 155.

13. William Knox MSS, 10: 19, WLCL.

cember 27, 1769, Samuel Wharton proposed to the Walpole Associates an enlarged land project in consequence of the "hint dropped" by Hillsborough that they purchase an area sufficient for a new colony. As outlined by Wharton, the boundary of the new government would begin on the Ohio opposite the mouth of the Scioto River, run south through Cumberland gap, and in a northeast direction extend along the Cumberland Mountains to the fork of the Great Kanawha formed by the junction of the Greenbriar and New rivers. It would then follow the Greenbriar to the source of its northeast branch and the Allegheny Mountains to Lord Fairfax's line. From this point it was to extend to the head of the north branch of the Potomac and along the western boundary of Maryland to the southern line of Pennsylvania. The line would run west to the Ohio, and then downstream to the point of origin opposite the mouth of the Scioto. Thus the proprietors of the newly proposed colony would annex western lands claimed by Virginia under its charter. Since the original grants by the Six Nations to the "suffering traders" of Pennsylvania and George Croghan also lay within this territory, Wharton proposed that the Walpole syndicate incorporate their claims as soon as it should obtain its grant from the Crown.[14]

With the new company now organized, the Associates empowered Thomas Walpole and Samuel Wharton to attend the Treasury Board in order to fix a time for a meeting with a committee of the company. Joined by Dr. Franklin and John Sargeant, on January 14, 1770, they presented their case to the Treasury Commissioners. Whether or not the connection between the speculators and the Secretaries of the Treasury was decisive we cannot know, but as Wharton put it: "We were so fortunate as to agree for the Consideration Money, being £10460. Sterling." [15] Thus Hillsborough's first attempt to thwart the scheme failed.

At this point, however, unexpected opposition delayed matters for the land speculators. The new colony they proposed to found

14. See the minutes of the meeting in Ohio Company Papers, I, 82, HSP.

15. Treasury Board Papers, Jan. 4, 1770, PRO, T 29/40: 164; and Samuel Wharton to Croghan, Sept. 4, 1770, Croghan Papers, Cadwallader Collection, box 37, HSP.

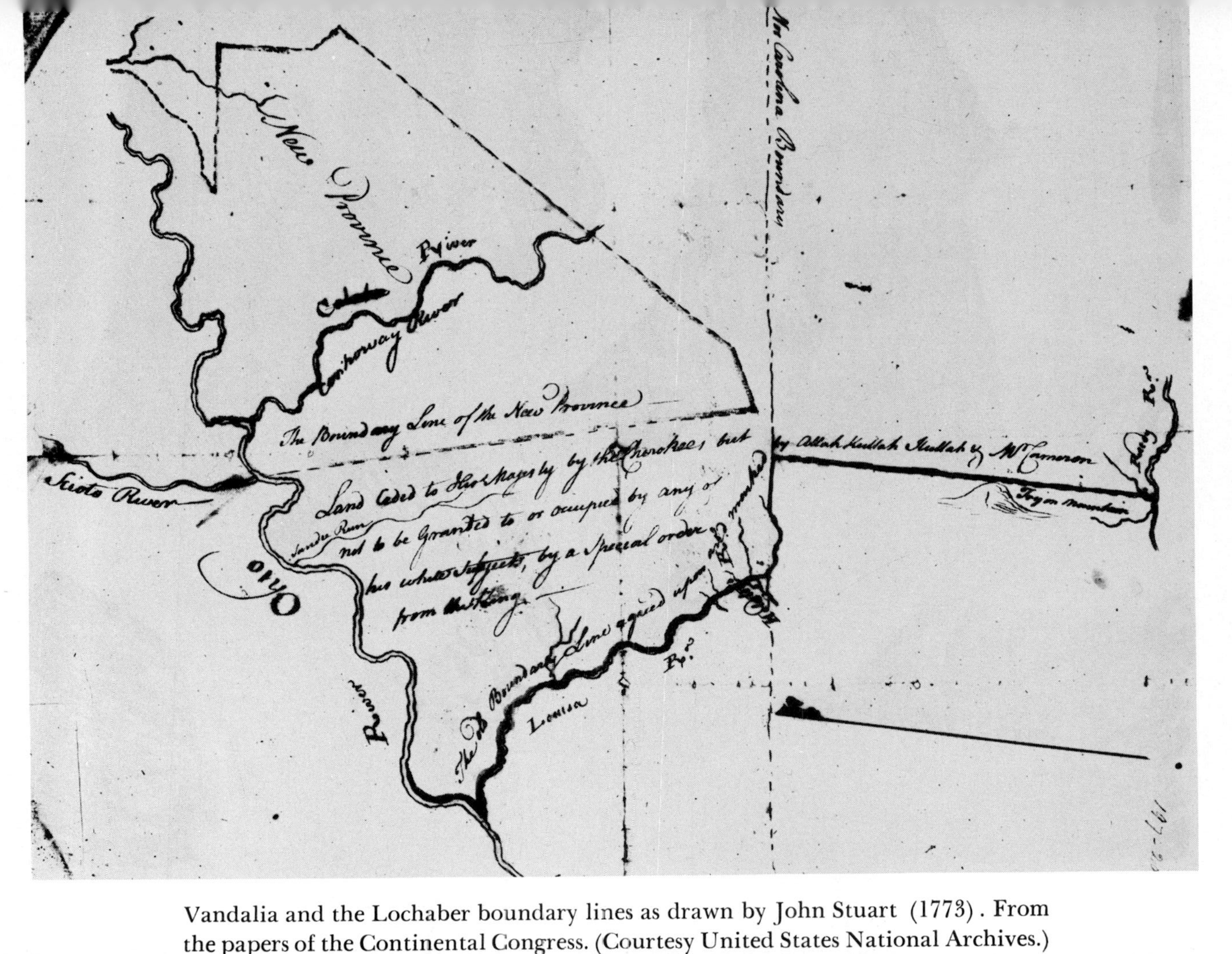

Vandalia and the Lochaber boundary lines as drawn by John Stuart (1773). From the papers of the Continental Congress. (Courtesy United States National Archives.)

would include the area west of the Great Kanawha and would thus cut off the Virginians' expansion. The plans of the Walpole Associates directly threatened the Virginia speculators. Evidently the Associates had attempted to conduct their negotiations with the government with as little publicity as possible, but one of the Treasury Commissioners had informed Edward Montague, agent for the Virginia House of Burgesses, of their activities.[16] The Virginia agent promptly filed a petition containing a caveat against the petition of the Walpole Company as encroaching on Virginia territory. On February 15, 1770, John Pownall referred Montague's protest to the Treasury.[17]

Others with land interests in the colonies—the proprietors of Pennsylvania,[18] William Lee, agent for the Mississippi Company, and George Mercer of the Ohio Company of Virginia [19]—were also concerned over the threat posed by the Walpole venture. But Mercer, for one, could do little to block the Associates. For some time he had received no instructions from Virginia. Fearing the strong political influence of the Walpole Associates,[20] Mercer merged his interests with the larger syndicate in the spring of 1770, accepting two of the seventy-two shares of the Walpole or Grand Ohio Company. He also made provision that the Virginia officers claiming 200,000 acres along the Monongahela under the terms of the Dinwiddie Proclamation of 1754 would receive their portion out of the share allotted to the "suffering traders" of Pennsylvania.[21] On May 10, 1770, Mercer

16. See Montague to the Virginia Committee of Correspondence, Jan. 15, 1770, *Virginia Magazine of History and Biography,* XII (1904–1905), 159.

17. Pownall to Grey Cooper, Feb. 15, 1770, PRO, T 1/475: 246.

18. *Journal of the Board of Trade, 1768–1775,* pp. 170–171.

19. *Ibid.,* 163. See the petition of William Lee, dated Jan. 24, 1770, C. O. 5/1332: 319. The Walpole Associates attempted to counter this move at the Treasury, but the latter board held that the dispute between the respective claimants fell within the sphere of the Board of Trade. Treasury minute, April 7, 1770, PRO, T 29/40: 218.

20. James Mercer to the committee of the Ohio Company, Jan. 9, 1772, Mulkearn, *Mercer Papers,* 312.

21. Mercer to Washington, Dec. 18, 1770, *Stanislaus Hamilton* (ed.), *Letters to Washington, and Accompanying Papers* (5 vols., Boston, 1902), IV, 40. The agreement between Mercer and the Walpole group in C. O. 5/1332: 365–366. The Virginia members of the Ohio Company had serious reservations as to

withdrew his petition against the Walpole Associates. By this time Samuel Wharton had also counteracted a petition of Arthur Lee in behalf of the Mississippi Company. Having apparently eliminated all opposition from the colonies, Walpole and Wharton then adjusted the final financial arrangements with the Treasury Board. In addition to the purchase price of the Fort Stanwix cession, £10,460, the speculators would pay a quitrent of two shillings per hundred acres of tillable land. The Treasury allowed an exemption of twenty years before quitrents were due. Most generous terms for an empire in the interior!

Completing the financial arrangements with the Treasury and eliminating the threat from the Ohio and Mississippi companies had taken five months, but at last the Walpole Associates were able to present another petition requesting an expanded grant sufficient for a new colony, as Hillsborough had suggested originally at the Board of Trade.[22]

Instead of acting on the new petition, Hillsborough and the Commissioners of Trade procrastinated for weeks.[23] In disgust, Walpole wrote to the Secretary of State for the American Department, protesting against the delay.[24] On July 18, 1770, Hillsborough brought his letter to the attention of the Commissioners of Trade. He also submitted to their consideration an unsigned note, dated July 9, 1770, which Walpole had enclosed, attacking the Council of Virginia for allegedly making illegal and extensive grants in the area the Associates sought. The government of Virginia had supposedly acted for land speculators who were members of the colonial council.[25] These anonymous charges—probably the work of Samuel Wharton—gave the Commissioners of Trade an excuse to postpone any decision until the Virginians had an opportunity to clear themselves. The Board of Trade

---

the advisability of the merger with the larger group. Thomas Ludwell Lee to James Mercer, Jan. 13, 1772, Mulkearn, *Mercer Papers,* 318. They never ratified Mercer's action.

22. Wharton to Croghan, Sept. 4, 1770, Croghan Papers, Cadwallader Collection, box 37, HSP: *Journal of the Board of Trade, 1768–1775,* p. 188.

23. *Journal of the Board of Trade, 1768–1775,* p. 194.

24. Thomas Walpole to Hillsborough, July 16, 1770, C. O. 5/1332: 403.

25. The anonymous letter, dated July 9, 1770, in C. O. 5/1332: 409–417.

voted unanimously to submit the allegations of Walpole to the colony.[26] If Hillsborough planned to block the Walpole Associates by referring their claims to Virginia, his stratagem was well calculated, for by this tactic he delayed action on the petition of the company for almost two years.

Since Governor Botetourt[27] had recently died, the president of the council, William Nelson, undertook to answer the allegations of the Walpole group. Terming the charges contained in the anonymous letter of July 9 as indecent and unwarranted, the indignant Nelson denied that the Virginia government had made large, unwarranted, or illegal grants west of the mountains. The royal government had sanctioned all of these settlements made before the war. Nelson now took the offensive and brought up the claims of the Virginia officers to lands along the Monongahela within the proposed colony—lands to which they were entitled by the terms of Dinwiddie's Proclamation of 1754. To support the contention of the provincial officers, the president of the council transmitted to Hillsborough a recent letter from George Washington to Governor Botetourt[28] in which the Virginia

26. *Journal of the Board of Trade, 1768–1775,* pp. 201–202.

27. His successor, appointed some time later, was John Murray, Earl of Dunmore, then governor of New York. For some reason, Dunmore, while governor of the northern province, made it his business to make inquiries on the proposed interior colony, and he wrote to Hillsborough in November, 1770, strongly representing against the proposal for the interior government. Dunmore to Hillsborough, Nov. 12, 1770, *DRCHSNY,* VIII, 253.

28. Washington to Botetourt, April 15, 1770, Fitzpatrick, *Washington Writings,* III, 9–12. Washington was playing a double game, however. He toured the west in the fall of 1770, making surveys for the officers with whom he met in August, and engaged periodically for the next two years in plotting these surveys. John C. Fitzpatrick (ed.), *George Washington Diaries, 1748–1799* (4 vols., Boston, 1925), I, 391; II, 9, 37, 84–87. In October, 1770, however, he contacted Colonel Michael Cresap of the Red Stone Creek settlement, who had just returned from England where he had been in touch with Wharton and Trent. *Ibid.,* I, 405. The following month Washington wrote to Croghan, offering to buy his share in the proposed new government provided that Croghan's name stood confirmed in the charter. Washington to Croghan, Nov. 24, 1770, Fitzpatrick, *Washington Writings,* III, 30. Cresap had given him to believe that some share in the government "might be bought very cheap from some of the present Members . . . ." Washington to George Mercer, Nov. 22, 1771, *ibid.,* III, 72. The following summer, Croghan promised that

officer objected to the proposed grant to the Walpole Associates.[29]

Hillsborough found the arguments of the Virginians convenient. Early in January, 1771, he assured Nelson that the ministry would pay due attention to bona fide settlers who claimed their lands on the basis of instructions from the prewar ministries to the government of Virginia. He reiterated the promise the following month. The Virginians could rest assured that the government would give proper attention to their rights when it considered the propositions of the English speculators.[30] This was a direct slap at the Walpole Associates who, in March, 1771, attempted to answer the Virginians in a statement of "Observations and Answers." [31] Probably drawn up by Samuel Wharton, the document had little effect.

The contest for lands west of the mountains between the Virginia government and the Walpole Associates became all the more complicated when, in the spring and summer of 1771, Colonel John Donelson marked the Indian boundary line negotiated at the Lochaber congress. He altered this line by running the boundary from the Holston River through the Cumberland Mountains to the Louisa (Kentucky) River and then to the Ohio.[32] Hillsborough first received news of this alteration in a

---

if the grant to the Walpole Associates was completed, and he were named a proprietor, he would make Washington a proposal. Croghan to Washington, Aug. 18, 1771, Hamilton, *Letters to Washington,* IV, 79.

29. Nelson to Hillsborough, Oct. 18, 1770, C. O. 5/1348: 321–330. Members of the Loyal Company of Virginia also objected to the Walpole grant. See Thomas Walker to Col. William Preston, May 27, 1771, Draper Collection, 2QQ126 (2), WHS.

30. Hillsborough to Nelson, Jan. 2, 1771, C. O. 5/1349: 1; Hillsborough to Nelson, Feb. 11, 1771, C. O. 5/1349: 88.

31. "Observations and Answers, humbly submitted To the Right Honorable Lords Commissioners of Trade and Plantations, by Mr. Walpole and his Associates, On the Extract of the Letter from Mr. Nelson . . . dated October 1770," C. O. 5/1333: 365–384.

32. There has been some dispute among writers over the identification of the "Louisa" River. Alden, *Southern Colonial Frontier,* 283–285, 344–350, establishes the fact that the boundary marked by Donelson and accurately described by Stuart followed the Catawba or Kentucky River. See also Stuart to Dartmouth, Feb. 25, 1773, C. O. 5/74: 123. Actually the line as finally marked fell in with that proposed by Stuart to Hillsborough in 1768, prior to the Hard Labor treaty.

letter which the newly appointed governor of the province, Lord Dunmore, sent him in March, 1772. Dunmore had quickly allied himself with the local land speculators—indeed, he soon became their most prominent member. Seeking to minimize the area which the Virginians had acquired by the recent survey, Dunmore wrote Hillsborough that the Donelson party had altered the course of the boundary but slightly. The new line ran from the intersection of the Virginia-Carolina boundary with the Holston River to a place where there was easier access to the source of the Kentucky. This alteration entailed only a slight additional cession to Virginia, he claimed, but had the advantage of setting up a natural boundary between the Virginians and the tribes. The Virginia governor was also quick to take advantage of the new cession and asked that the ministry now allow him to issue land patents. In the opinion of the colonial council, his current instructions prevented him from granting lands west of the Proclamation line.[33]

It was evident that land speculators in both the northern and southern districts had used the boundary-line negotiations to further their own interests. To Hillsborough their unauthorized proceedings confirmed his apprehension over the consequences of departing from the original boundary line set by the Proclamation of 1763.

For some time events in the North American interior had indicated that all was not well. As early as January, 1770, Sir William Johnson was forced to admit that the tribes on the upper Ohio were dissatisfied with the negotiations at Fort Stanwix. At a private conference with the Hurons, Ottawa, and Potawatami near Detroit, a party of Seneca, Shawnee, and Delaware had complained that the cession by the Six Nations had deprived them of their hunting grounds while the Iroquois had reserved to themselves the money and presents given in compensation. Furthermore, the large influx of settlers on the Susquehanna threatened to deprive them of vital territory. As a result of this dissatisfaction, a general Indian confederacy seemed imminent. Johnson admitted to Hillsborough that as far as he could

33. Dunmore to Hillsborough, March [20], 1772, C. O. 5/1350: 37–41, LC transcript.

ascertain, the Fort Stanwix cession "is the Cause of all the Commotions that have lately happened" among the Indians.[34] The next year, John Stuart, the southern superintendent, charged that the Stanwix treaty had induced the western tribes to unite.[35] Already the frontiersmen were exploring and marking lands from Red Stone Creek and the other tributaries of the Monongahela as far down the Ohio as Little Kanawha Creek. The tribes of the upper Ohio Valley were demanding compensation before they would allow the whites to settle.[36] In the summer of 1771, Croghan warned Samuel Wharton in London that a general Indian war was imminent, for the Shawnee, not having received compensation for the Stanwix cession, were belligerent.[37] At a congress on the Scioto the following spring, the Indians made a formal complaint to the superintendent. But Sir William Johnson still maintained to Hillsborough that the Six Nations exercised suzerainty over the western tribes who had no right to the lands in question.[38]

These developments confirmed for Hillsborough his previous apprehension over the recent boundary negotiations. After all the assurances he had received from Sir William that all of the tribes concerned in the Fort Stanwix negotiations had fully pledged their support of the treaty, it was disconcerting to find that the Shawnee were dissatisfied, if not disposed to disavow the cession of lands on the Ohio. Every passing day revealed more than ever, the colonial secretary complained to Johnson, the fatal consequences of abandoning the line prescribed in the Proclamation of 1763. Tribes as powerful, if not more numerous, than the Six Nations now denied the treaty. Instead of promoting the security of the colonies, the Fort Stanwix cession appeared to have had no other effect than extending distant settlements and, as evidenced by Johnson's own letters, provoking an Indian

34. Johnson to Hillsborough, Jan. 6, 1770, *Johnson Papers,* VII, 332; Croghan to Johnson, Dec. 22, 1769, *ibid.,* VII, 316.

35. Stuart to Hillsborough, April 27, 1771, C. O. 5/72: 421.

36. *Washington Diaries,* I, 441.

37. Croghan to Wharton, Nov. 2, 1771, Croghan Papers, Cadwallader Collection, box 37, HSP.

38. Johnson to Hillsborough, April 4, 1772, *DRCHSNY,* VIII, 292.

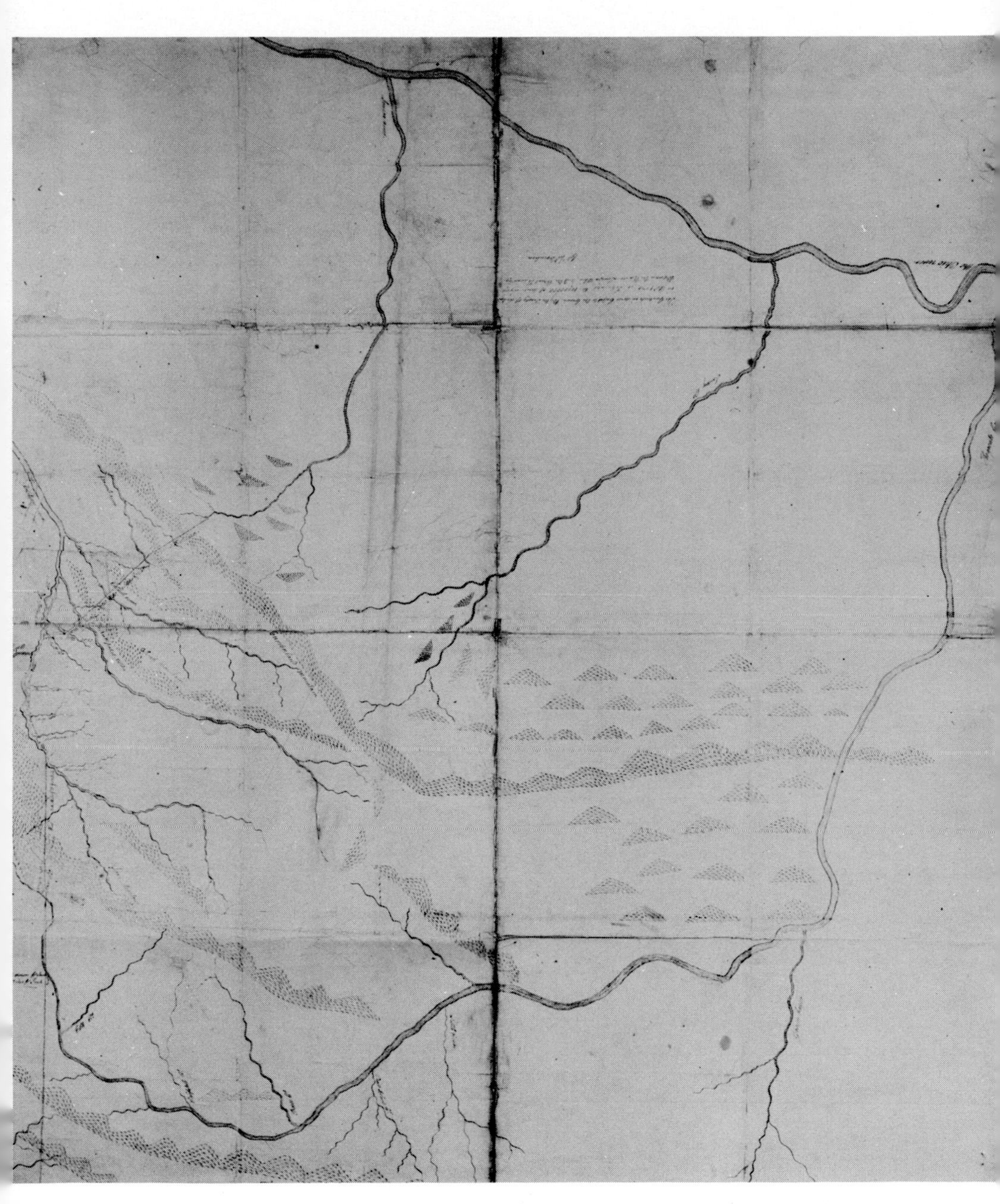

The Lochaber Boundary Line as surveyed and marked by the Donelson party. (Courtesy Public Record Office, London.)

war. The financial burden of such a conflict would fall on the mother country.[39]

Thus developments along the frontier provided Hillsborough with cogent reasons for opposing transmontane settlements even while the application of the Walpole Associates for an interior colony was before the Board of Trade.

Samuel Wharton had not been idle, however. In fact, he had been pursuing several alternatives to obtain title to western lands. Even if the Crown did not accept their proposals, Wharton assured a now skeptical George Croghan, the traders would still be on as good ground as ever with their titles from the Six Nations.[40] Perhaps it was the encouragements he received from Wharton as to the validity of the Indian titles, or simply the need for cash, which induced Croghan to set up a private land office in Pittsburgh in the winter of 1770–1771 without waiting for the ministry to confirm his Indian grant. Through the spring and summer of 1771 he continued to sell land while propagating the fiction that the district lay outside the jurisdiction of Pennsylvania. Disposing of his lots for ten pounds sterling per hundred acres, he even offered to guarantee title. His accomplice was Michael Cresap of the Red Stone Creek settlement, who circulated the story that the Pennsylvania boundary did not extend beyond the mountains and that the lands to the westward belonged to the Crown. These rumors induced doubts among the settlers as to the validity of their holdings. They also made it difficult to execute any laws in the district. One Pennsylvania official, Arthur St. Clair, feared that the situation might end in a "regulating scheme"—a frontier rebellion—such as had recently taken place in North Carolina.[41]

But in London, Samuel Wharton "rejoiced to find" that the

39. Hillsborough to Johnson, July 1, 1772, *ibid.*, VIII, 302.

40. Wharton to Croghan, June 13, 1770, Croghan Papers, Cadwallader Collection, box 37, HSP; Wharton to Croghan, Sept. 4, 1770, *ibid.*

41. Robert Lettis Hooper, Jr., to Sir William Johnson, Feb. 9, 1771, *Johnson Papers,* VII, 1132; William Crawford to Washington, Aug. 9, 1771; March 15, 1772, Butterfield, *Washington-Crawford Letters,* 22, 24; Arthur St. Clair to Joseph Shippen, Jr., Sept. 24, 1771, William H. Smith (ed.), *The Life and Public Services of Arthur St. Clair . . . with his Correspondence and other Papers* (2 vols., Cincinnati, 1882), I, 260–261.

settlers on the Ohio "are as Chearfully disposed" to buy lands under Croghan's Indian title as they were from the Crown or the Pennsylvania proprietors. It demonstrated their "good Sense," he wrote Croghan, and "That They reason naturally and justly upon the Subject . . . ." Wharton again assured Croghan that "from the lowest to the highest Counsellor and Personage" in the Kingdom "It is not pretended, The King can have, or has any Degree of Right to Lands, which He has not bought from the natural Original Proprietors." Wharton urged Croghan to "Go on therefore and sell for the best Price you can," promising to bring back with him "The ablest & most learned Counsellors['] Opinions in this Kingdom, in favor of your and our Rights." [42]

But Wharton was not a man to trust simply as to the legality or justice of his claim. That same day, July 21, 1771, he sent Croghan two other letters containing proposals which were staggering in their audacity and cunning. He transmitted all three letters of this date through his brother in Philadelphia, Thomas Wharton. In addition to the letter already cited, there was another, sealed but unsigned, which, as Samuel Wharton informed Croghan, "is intended to convey such very secret and important Ideas, That can and ought only with propriety to be known to Ourselves." In order "innocently to deceive [his] Brother," Samuel Wharton had informed Thomas that it was merely a personal communication to Croghan from a mutual friend.[43]

The third letter of this date, July 21, 1771, from Samuel Wharton and William Trent to Croghan and Michael Cresap, dealt with the difficulties Hillsborough had raised in objecting to transmontane settlements. In spite of the influence of Thomas Walpole, the Secretaries of the Treasury, and the peers connected with the Walpole Associates, it had been impossible to secure a cabinet meeting until July 5, when "the single question agitated, was—whether it was Policy to permit" the country west of the mountains to be settled. Under the "most solemn tie of inviolable Secrecy," Wharton and Trent now related that every

42. Wharton to Croghan, July 21, 1771, Croghan Papers, Cadwallader Collection, box 37, HSP.

43. [Samuel Wharton to George Croghan], July 21, 1771, Croghan Papers, Cadwallader Collection, box 36, HSP.

minister except Hillsborough approved the policy. They had determined to resolve the question by majority vote at their next meeting. In order to overrule Hillsborough, the ministers resolved that the "Minority should act as the Majority," and their decision reported to the King "as the *unanimous* Act" of the whole cabinet. With this scheme in mind, the Earl of Rochford had summoned the ministers to a meeting on July 12, but so few of them were in town that they could not transact business. Since Hillsborough had then secured the King's permission to remain in Ireland until October, it was "absolutely impossible to obtain the Decision" at this time. In spite of the fact that all of the ministers except Hillsborough favored a policy of transmontane settlement, there was "a Delicacy among Them, in overruling a Minister in his own Department . . . ." But persons whose names could not "be mentioned or trusted to Paper" had advised that a strongly worded petition from the settlers on the Ohio, signed by two or three hundred on behalf of all the whites in the district, would give "the L[or]ds who are our Friends and Partners, such public Grounds to go on, as must immediately destroy L[or]d H[illsboroug]h's foolish Ideas." At a "secret Meeting" held on the night of July 20 with some of the "most leading[,] important[,] and active of our Partners (who must be nameless)" a petition—six copies of which Wharton now transmitted to Croghan and Cresap—was drawn up "as calculated effectually" to serve this purpose. Croghan and Cresap were to have them signed without "Loss of Time" by frontiersmen who write "at least a legible Hand" taking care that no two signatures appeared "in One Mans" handwriting. Croghan and Cresap were not to let anyone take a copy, or to let any person read the petition who they did not think would sign. In particular, "beware all Penn's Surveyors and other Officers," the speculators warned. They were not even to let their most intimate friend or relation know that the petitions had originated in England.

In addition to these spurious documents, Wharton and Trent also sent a letter to be signed by thirty or forty of the principal settlers on the Ohio—men "who write a good hand . . . ." On behalf of all the settlers, they would request that Thomas Walpole serve as their agent in presenting the petitions. This letter,

Wharton and Trent advised, "is calculated to be made use of, by our friendly Lords at the Council, in support of the Petition." Consequently, Croghan and Cresap were not to disclose the contents of "this most confidential Letter," for should its secret leak out, "every lord would spurn us and instantly dissolve all Degrees of Connection with us and our Partners." The danger was so great that if there was any chance that Croghan and Cresap could not obtain sufficient signatures, or that the petitions would provoke a counter petition by those who opposed the scheme for a new colony, they were to drop the matter entirely.[44]

In the third letter of July 21, 1771—sealed and kept secret from Thomas Wharton—Samuel Wharton emphasized once more that the purpose behind the spurious petitions from the settlers on the Ohio was "to get some *strong publick* Grounds to support" their allies in the cabinet. Wharton had pledged to the Walpole Associates that Croghan would see to it that the petitions were *"instantly* compleated and sent hither . . . ." But at the same time the Philadelphian warned Croghan of the opposition of Dunmore and the Virginians to the new colony and that he should be on his guard and not let them obtain a copy of the petition.

Having conceived such an audacious scheme any other man would have been content—but not Samuel Wharton. He was engaged in still another land-speculating venture. Some of the rich and powerful in London with whom he was associated wanted to know if Croghan could purchase from the Six Nations a tract of land on the right bank of the Ohio. Would Croghan give his "real and unreserved Opinion" on this question? For everyone in London, except Hillsborough and his under-secretary of state, John Pownall, "laugh at the Idea of coming to England to get a Title to Lands" in the Indian country, when the "rightfull[,] independent & natural owners of those Lands" were willing to sell them. Croghan should consider the matter carefully, especially as the Americans would be acting "in Conjunction with Gentlemen of Weight, Dignity, and Fortune in this Country." The company would consist of eight or nine

44. [Samuel Wharton and William Trent] to [George Croghan and Michael Cresap], July 21, 1771, Croghan Papers, Cadwallader Collection, box 37, HSP.

members including Wharton, Trent, and Croghan. This was the last opportunity that "you and I shall have," Wharton counselled Croghan, "to do any Thing handsome for Ourselves . . . ." [45]

By speculating in Indian lands, Samuel Wharton could indeed profit materially, but only at the cost of antagonizing the natives who resided on the soil and possibly provoking an Indian war. At least Croghan recognized the danger when he answered the Philadelphian in the fall of 1771. He could purchase lands on the right bank of the Ohio from the Six Nations, but under the present circumstances he did not advise exploiting the lands. First the ministry should establish a government, settle the left bank of the river, and adopt uniform measures with the Indians whom the superintendent had been neglecting for some time. If the speculators in London would let the lands on the west bank lie unoccupied for some time, Croghan would join them in the venture. The sooner the better, for there were "Many Gentlemen of fortune" in the colonies who, being fully convinced of the sufficiency of titles from the Indians as independent peoples, were contemplating making purchases of the natives. Yet at the same time Croghan warned Wharton in a separate letter that the Shawnee west of the Ohio were restless.[46] This was probably the factor which caused a postponement of the additional purchase of lands from the Six Nations.

Samuel Wharton could still operate with the Walpole Associates to secure a grant from the Crown for a new interior colony. He had sent the spurious petitions to the frontier for this purpose. Unfortunately there is no evidence to indicate if Croghan ever returned them, or whether Wharton used them to undermine Hillsborough in the cabinet. But in any event, Wharton's political connections in London had virtually insured success. According to William Strahan, a Walpole Associate, Wharton had acquired "better *Connections* . . . than any American I know of, ever did." Benjamin Franklin had not been able to "stir in this Business," for not only was he on "bad Terms" with Hillsborough,

45. [Samuel Wharton to George Croghan], July 21, 1771, Croghan Papers, Cadwallader Collection, box 36, HSP.

46. Croghan to Wharton, Nov. 2, 1771, *ibid.;* Croghan to Wharton, Nov. 2, 1771, *ibid.,* box 37.

but with "the *Ministry* in General." The ubiquitous Franklin himself gave full credit to the "indefatigable" Wharton, for he knew of no one else who "would have been equal to the Task," so difficult was it to accomplish anything "in which some Party Purpose is not to be served . . . ."[47] Here is the key to Wharton's success in obtaining the support of the British politicians for the Walpole Associates. Factional politics merged with desire for material gain.

Among the papers of William Trent is a list of accounts received from various members of the Walpole Company. Included among the lesser political lights are Thomas Bradshaw, Grey Cooper, and John Robinson, all officials at the Treasury. Their motive in joining the company was the same perhaps as Lords Camden, Temple (George Grenville's brother), and Hertford, who each held a share for which they had paid £200.[48] They sought material gain by speculating in western lands. But the economic motive is hardly sufficient to account fully for Wharton's success in obtaining the support of influential British politicians. The account given by Hillsborough's under-secretary of state sheds further light on the motives of the politicians. According to William Knox, Wharton had approached the impecunious Earl of Rochford, the Secretary of State for the Southern Department, offering him a share in the proposed new gov-

47. William Strahan to William Franklin (extract), April 3, 1771, Franklin Papers, XLVIII, 139a, APSL; Benjamin Franklin to William Franklin, April 20, 1771, Smyth, *Franklin Works,* V, 314.

48. "List of Receipts signed by Mr. [Thomas] Walpole, July 10, 1773" marked "Re[ceive]d the above Receipts—Wm Trent," Ohio Company Papers, I, 104, HSP. Through one of the Associates, Thomas Pitt, Wharton offered a share in the venture to George Grenville. Although Grenville was then dangerously ill—he died within a few months—he, too, accepted a share in the speculating group. See Samuel Wharton to Thomas Pitt (copy), July 3, 1770, Stowe Americana, Misc. file, 1670–1813, Stowe Collection, HEHL; and Grenville to Thomas Pitt, July 29, 1770, Grenville-Murray Papers.

The interest of the Earl of Hertford in the Ohio colony was undoubtedly secured by Franklin's friend, William Strahan, who obtained a letter of introduction from David Hume. The latter had been secretary to the Paris embassy while Hertford was minister to France. See Hume to Strahan, Jan. 21, 1771, and Strahan to Hume, March 1, 1771, G. Birkbeck Hill (ed.), *Letters of David Hume to William Strahan* (Oxford, 1888), 160, 162 n3.

ernment. To gain further support for the venture, Rochford persuaded Earl Gower, the president of the council, also to accept a share. Since Hillsborough had shown himself hostile to the project, Rochford now engaged the King to intercede in favor of the Walpole grant. At his levee, George III reportedly asked Bamber Gascoine, Hillsborough's particular friend at the Board of Trade, if the commissioners had completed their report on the Ohio colony. As Knox later explained, this "hint" was sufficient for Hillsborough. He called a meeting of the Commissioners of Trade to deal with the Walpole petition.

There is no further evidence to corroborate Knox's story, but whatever the case, the journals of the Board of Trade show that on March 20, 1772, Hillsborough laid before the board the statements of the president of the Virginia Council defending the grants by that colony in the transmontane region, a paper by Walpole and his associates in answer to the Virginia claims, and extracts of the correspondence of General Thomas Gage and Governor Dunmore advising against the establishment of the new colony. The Commissioners of Trade now concluded that the matter was too important for them to decide without the advice of the ex officio members of the board. Consequently, they deferred consideration for one week. Walpole and his associates would then attend the board.

According to Knox, Hillsborough unsuccessfully attempted to consult other ministers before the board took action. Domestic political rivalries complicated the decision of the Ohio grant. Since they were resolved to overturn Lord North, who had replaced Grafton as First Lord of the Treasury, Gower and Rochford opposed Hillsborough. They regarded the colonial secretary as North's chief supporter in the cabinet. Rochford also sought to weaken the American Department so that he might reclaim colonial patronage for the Southern Department. By eliminating Hillsborough, Gower hoped to weaken North's position and eventually to replace him as chief minister. Gower and Rochford were joined in the attempt to defeat and oust Hillsborough by the Earl of Suffolk, Secretary of State for the Northern Department, who felt that the road for his own advancement lay in frequent changes of personnel. Such was the political situation described by Knox when Hillsborough proposed to call a meeting of the "grand Board of Trade." Refusing to attend, the ex officio members left it to the "ordinary Board" to report on the Walpole petition and reserved to themselves a decision when the matter came before a committee of the Privy Council.

As scheduled, the Commissioners of Trade met on March 27, 1772. But in spite of an invitation to testify on their petition, the Walpole Associates declined to attend. They had nothing further to offer on the subject, and merely requested a copy of whatever report the board saw fit to make. Either the Walpole Associates were extremely confident of eventual success, or they were convinced that nothing they could say would alter Hillsborough's decision. The board then proceeded to prepare their report, which they issued on April 29, 1772.

When the ministers had refused to attend the meeting of the board or to give their opinions on the Walpole grant, Hillsborough openly declared himself hostile to the interior settlement. As Knox related the story, the "cabal" tried to embroil the colonial secretary with Lord North by intimating that, since the two Secretaries of the Treasury, Thomas Bradshaw and Grey Cooper, were associated with the Walpole Company, Hillsborough's disapproval of the interior colony reflected unfavorably on the Treasury in arranging the agreement with the petitioners. To avoid falling into this "snare" Hillsborough based his opposition to the transmontane colony on the arguments the Board of Trade had used in their report of March 7, 1768, in rejecting Shelburne's proposal for interior settlements. The commissioners now transmitted their current report to the Privy Council. At this point, Gower, president of the council, declared that he was open to evidence against it. Before the Lords of the Committee for Plantation Affairs considered the report, the council allowed Samuel Wharton to have a copy and to prepare a statement in rebuttal.[49] The Walpole Associates then printed the report of the board with an appended "Observations and Remarks," attacking the position Hillsborough had taken.[50]

49. Knox MSS, 10: 19, WLCL; *Journal of the Board of Trade, 1768–1775*, pp. 293, 294, 297, 299.

50. [Benjamin Franklin and/or Samuel Wharton], *Report of the Lords*

On June 24, the committee of the council and the Associates put on a polished performance. Their lordships of the committee ruled that, although they could not hear the petitioners formally against the report of the Board of Trade, the Associates could submit evidence in support of their petition. Previously Walpole had informed the Commissioners of Trade that he had no further evidence to add. Now the Associates had an opportunity to present their prepared case against the report. When called before the committee of the council, they proceeded to read from this statement and offered additional evidence to reinforce the need for an interior colony. William Trent informed their lordships that between 1765 and 1767 no less than five thousand families had settled on the Monongahela. George Mercer corroborated this. Next Samuel Wharton testified that he had been present at the Red Stone Creek settlement when a detachment of royal troops had attempted unsuccessfully to evacuate the settlers. He offered to submit extracts from the orderly books to prove the claim, but the committee did not challenge the point. The petitioners then introduced extracts from the correspondence of such disinterested parties as Croghan, Robert Callender (one of the "suffering traders"), and Joseph Galloway, pointing out that the settlers were entering the area intended for the new colony and that they had made between four and five thousand improvements in 1769 alone. These families were not subject to any laws. To emphasize the need for some government

Commissioners for Trade and Plantations on the Petition . . . for a grant of lands on the River Ohio, in North America; for the purpose of erecting a new government With Observations and Remarks (London, 1772). John Almon, who printed the pamphlet, stated that it was intended for publication, i.e., sale, but when the Council decided in favor of the Walpole Associates, Benjamin Franklin—who wrote the tract, according to Almon—stopped sale on the very morning of publication "when not above five copies had been disposed of." John Almon, *Biographical, Literary, and Political Anecdotes of Several of the Most Eminent Persons of the Present Age. Never Before Printed. With An Appendix; Consisting of Original, Explanatory, and Scarce Papers.* (3 vols., London, 1797), II, 237–238. Almon apparently had some connection with the grant to the traders later referred to as "Indiana." Wharton wrote him some time later, "I shall take proper Care of your Son's Interest in Indiana." Wharton to Almon, March 20, 1777, Add. MSS 20733, f. 141.

in the territory, Mercer pointed out that Pittsburgh lay some 400 miles from Williamsburg and 320 miles from Philadelphia, the capitals of the nearest colonies. Various witnesses who claimed to have travelled recently in the provinces testified that not less than five thousand families from the middle colonies had settled on the Ohio in the past year. A total of thirty thousand families resided there under no effective regulations.

Having thus established the need for government, the petitioners now tried to demonstrate the commercial value of the settlements. The Commissioners of Trade had argued that facilities for large-scale transportation were inadequate for commerce. But Mercer contended that an acceptable wagon road led from Pittsburgh to Red Stone Creek and Fort Cumberland on the Potomac. The portage from the Potomac to the Youghiogheny River, a navigable tributary of the Ohio, was only some forty miles, while a mere seventy miles separated the Potomac from Red Stone Creek. Adequate wagon transport would serve to connect the water routes. The petitioners also produced several testimonials showing that the cost of waggonage in the interior was considerably less than that in Pennsylvania for a comparable distance. But the area was also valuable for exotic produce! The committee heard from a Mr. Patterson, "a Gentleman concerned in the Silk Manufacture." Called upon by the petitioners to give an account of a quantity of silk "imported from the Lands in Question," he testified that, on being processed, a batch of fiber given him by Benjamin Franklin had proved to be as fine as the best Italian product. One can imagine the frontiersmen raising silkworms!

The comedy, and it was that, was now at an end. A week later, on July 1, 1772, the committee approved the petition and sent it to the Privy Council.[51] It was all a set performance. Lord Barrington made the most valid comment when he wrote to General Thomas Gage about the affair. "It is amazing that so material a point of Government" should have been decided on a "cursory examination of Witnesses whose names had never been heard, & whose faces had never been seen before; brought by parties interested in the event, & examined *ex parte* only." It was equally

51. *Acts of the Privy Council, Col.,* V, 203–208.

astonishing, he noted, that the ministers should have settled this measure "without a reference" to the Commander-in-Chief in America.[52] Indeed, they had approved of the proposal contrary to Gage's advice.

In approving the petition of the Walpole Associates, the Committee for Plantation Affairs brought on a political showdown. Opposed by Gower and Rochford, Hillsborough threatened to resign if the council declared in favor of the petitioners. Attempting to play the role of mediator, Lord North sought to minimize their differences. Suffolk also wanted to avoid extremes. He hoped that he was not "ill with any of the parties concerned," since by accident he had not been present when the committee had acted and was thus "a good deal out of the scrape . . . ." North asked Gower to postpone the report on the "Ohio Business," but no compromise was possible since Hillsborough refused to accept the grant to the Walpole Associates. The ministry had to find a successor as colonial secretary before the council approved the grant. When Hillsborough resigned on August 13, the Earl of Dartmouth, Lord North's half brother, received the seals of office.[53] The path was now clear for the Walpole Associates.

The day after Hillsborough's resignation, the Privy Council passed the petition of the Walpole Company. The new colonial secretary would advise the tribes of the government's intention of establishing a colony on the Ohio, but it would also prohibit any settlement between the western boundary of the new province and the Hard Labor treaty line. The Virginians would receive some consideration, however, for the Board of Trade was to insert a clause in the instrument of government for the new colony reserving prior claims within the limits of the grant.[54]

One partisan, at least, expressed strong disapproval of the plan

52. Barrington to Gage (private), Dec. 2, 1772, Gage Papers, WLCL.

53. Knox MSS, 10: 19, WLCL; Suffolk to the King, July 21, 1772, Fortescue, *Correspondence of George III,* II, 369; the King to Suffolk, July 21, 1772, *ibid.,* II, 369–370; North to Earl Bathurst, Aug. ?, 1772, HMC *Report on the Manuscripts of Earl Bathurst* (London, 1923), 12–13; John Pownall to William Knox, Aug. 1, 1772, Knox MSS, 10: 51, WLCL.

54. *Acts of the Privy Council, Col.,* V, 208–209. The Order-in-Council, dated Aug. 14, 1772, in C. O. 5/27: 311 ff., IHS transcript.

to "settle the interior parts of America." Lord Barrington still hoped to block the grant. From America, General Thomas Gage had written to the Secretary-at-War expressing his apprehension over the establishment of a new colony on the frontier. His letter arrived too late to be of any service at the deliberations of the Privy Council. Perhaps no consideration would have altered the decision, but in the hope that Gage's sentiments would be of "weight and importance," Barrington had shown extracts of his correspondence to North, Gower, and Dartmouth.[55]

Yet it seemed that almost nothing could block the Walpole Associates. The Board of Trade was at work forming an instrument of government for the new colony, and Samuel Wharton was as indefatigable as ever. After receiving a letter of introduction to the new Secretary of State for the American Department, the Philadelphia speculator was able to assure George Croghan that "We are proceeding diligently & most favorably with the excellent Lord Dartmouth" in drawing up the charter for the new government. He hoped soon to set the date of his departure for America. Even at this early stage, he told Croghan of his plans to inform the Indians of the new colony and to distribute presents among them to pave the way for the settlements.[56]

There had been some disturbing developments on the Ohio, however—developments which called for prompt remedial action by the Walpole Associates. In November, 1772, Croghan had written of the uneasiness of the Shawnee and Delaware. Neglected by Sir William Johnson, they had not received the usual favors and presents from the superintendent. He warned that unless the whites relieved the apprehensions of the tribes, hostilities would break out in the summer. Early in February, Wharton sought to reassure Croghan that the Walpole Associates would pay as much attention to the Ohio tribes as to the *"Fa-*

55. Barrington to Gage (private), Sept. 2, 1772, Gage Papers, WLCL; Gage to Barrington (private), Aug. 5, 1772, *Gage Correspondence,* II, 615–616; Barrington to Gage (private), Sept. 18, 1772, Gage Papers, WLCL.

56. *Journal of the Board of Trade, 1768–1775,* p. 316; Sir Mathew Featherstonehaugh to Dartmouth, Aug. 26, 1772, Dartmouth MSS, IHS transcript. Wharton to Croghan, Dec. 24, 1772, Croghan Papers, Cadwallader Collection, box 37, HSP.

vorites . . . to the *Northwards.*" He now enclosed a letter to the Indians and a speech signed by the leading Associates. Croghan was to deliver them personally to the natives but not let Sir William Johnson, General Gage, or any other government official obtain a copy. Wharton promised that the speculators would take some measures with the ministry "before our Governor leaves this Kingdom," so that "something proper may be done" to secure the interest of the Indians and prevent further complaints. Croghan was to assure the natives that a shipment of presents, now being prepared under Wharton's supervision, would reach the Ohio in the spring.[57] The Philadelphian was so confident of success that he even sent Croghan instructions for erecting a house in Pittsburgh which he expected to occupy as governor of the new colony.

In London matters went slowly in the winter of 1772–1773. Wharton pressed Dartmouth about the representation the Board of Trade was drafting on the instrument of government for the new colony. The delay had been "very tedious," Wharton complained. The commissioners finally completed their work on May 6, 1773. They had first proposed to call the province "Pittsylvania," but, "in Compliment to the Queen," they named the colony "Vandalia; as her Majesty is descended from the Vandals." [58] Although the lands granted to the proprietors were those for which the Walpole Associates had petitioned in 1771, the jurisdiction of the new colony of Vandalia was extended to in-

57. Walpole to Croghan, Jan. 25, 1773, Feb. 3, 1773, *ibid.* By this time a rift had developed between Wharton and the Franklins, with Governor Franklin suspecting that Wharton was tampering with his correspondence with his father. William Franklin to Benjamin Franklin, Oct. 13, 1772, Franklin Papers, III-2, 126, APSL. For his part, Wharton accused William Franklin of ill conduct, and for this he wrote "I dispise [*sic*] Him," and "all my Sunshine, pretended Friends." Dr. Franklin, he maintained, had "no more Interest, Trouble or Concern in effecting" the negotiation of the Ohio colony, "than the smallest Farmer in Cumberland County." Neither father nor son "has the smallest Share of Interest" with the ministry, and all that "we were taught to believe, before I left America, was Bluff and Declamation." Wharton to Croghan, Feb. 3, 1773, Croghan Papers, Cadwallader Collection, box 37, HSP.

58. Wharton to Galloway and Thomas Wharton (copy), April 9, 1773, Franklin Papers, III-2, 145, APSL.

clude the additional area obtained by the alteration of the Lochaber treaty line as surveyed by John Donelson.[59] This arrangement prevented the Virginians from expanding into the territory west of the Great Kanawha for which they had so strongly contended in the negotiations on the boundary line.

On May 19, 1773, the Committee for Plantation Affairs approved the report of the Board of Trade, and on July 3, the Privy Council ordered the Attorney General and Solicitor General to prepare a draft of the grant on the terms proposed by the Commissioners of Trade.[60]

The report submitted on July 16 by the Crown Law Officers, Edward Thurlow and Alexander Wedderburn, proved another stumbling block—indeed the final one—to the Walpole Associates. The supposed benefits of the new colony, they pointed out, came from promoting rapid settlement and increasing the revenue from quitrents. But issuing grants of land under terms of joint tenancy as the Associates and the Commissioners of Trade desired would probably render it impossible to collect these quitrents. They posed a second objection to the grant. The description of the boundaries of the colony was "more loose and uncertain" than in any grant save those made to the earliest adventurers when the North American continent was "wholly unknown." Moreover, the dimensions of the colony, measured either in acres or square miles, were also unknown.[61]

The land speculators were not easily discouraged. They had

59. The boundary line of Vandalia followed the "Louisa" or Kentucky River to its source, then ran to the intersection of the Virginia–North Carolina boundary and the Holston River, and along the southern Virginia boundary to the forks of the Great Kanawha. It then followed the Greenbriar River by its northeast branch to the source, and by Fairfax's line to the north branch of the Potomac. By the western and southern boundaries of Maryland and Pennsylvania it came to the Ohio and then followed this stream to the Kentucky River. The Board of Trade report of May 6, 1773, with the names of the proprietors to be inserted in the grant in C. O. 5/1368: 326–355, 575. See also *Acts of the Privy Council, Col.*, VI, 541–543.

60. *Acts of the Privy Council, Col.*, V, 210.

61. Report of the Law Officers, dated July 18, 1773, Privy Council Office, Unbound Papers, 1773 (2), IHS transcript; Dartmouth Papers, M650: 351–353, PAC transcript; *Acts of the Privy Council, Col.*, VI, 543.

come too far to be frustrated at this point. In the absence of the Lord President of the Council, Rochford transmitted the report of the Law Officers to Dartmouth early in September. Walpole and his associates were "exceedingly uneasy at the Delay of their Grant," he reported. Attempting to dismiss the objections raised by Thurlow and Wedderburn, Rochford claimed that a map drawn at the Board of Trade, and now deposited at the Privy Council office, clearly delineated the boundaries of Vandalia. Besides, he remarked, the Law Officers seemed to have forgotten "the *modern* Case of Georgia as to the Bounds of that Colony." Since the Attorney General and Solicitor indicated that they would not be inflexible on the matter, Rochford offered to "send down the Business again" to Thurlow and Wedderburn. After all, he felt "very much for the American Gentlemen who have been so many Years detained here, at great Expence, from their Families." No doubt he felt his own financial embarrassment also.

Dartmouth agreed with Rochford in dismissing the objections of the Law Officers against granting the lands in joint tenancy. The Board of Trade had ascertained the boundaries of the new colony as clearly and distinctly as the present knowledge of the country would allow.[62] This appeared to be decisive. On October 28, 1773, a committee of the council—a token group consisting of Dartmouth, Rochford, the Archbishop of Canterbury, and Richard Rigby—ordered the Law Officers to prepare a draft of the grant conformable to the report the Board of Trade had issued on May 6. The grantees and the subtenants were to pay quitrents twenty years after they leased or settled the lands.[63]

But time was running out on the Vandalia proprietors. The drama of the American Revolution was about to open. Samuel Adams and his "Mohawks" had raised the curtain at the famous Boston Tea Party in December, 1773. Thomas Wharton in Philadelphia wrote to Walpole of the reception of the tea ships in the Quaker capital. He hoped that by this time the "business of

62. Rochford to Dartmouth, Sept. 7, 1773, Dartmouth Papers, M650: 345–347, PAC transcript; [Dartmouth] to Rochford, Sept. 9, 1773, Dartmouth MSS, IHS transcript.

63. Privy Council Office, Unbound Papers, 1773 (2), IHS transcript.

Vandalia is Compleated," for he feared that if it were not, "our Enemies will from the Scituation [*sic*] of Affairs on this Continent, have fresh Vigor & Oppose the Completion of it . . . ." [64]

The ministry had not passed the Vandalia grant, for in spite of the bitter protests of Samuel Wharton,[65] the Law Officers still procrastinated. The Walpole Associates presumed that Attorney General Thurlow's opposition was based on his dislike of Benjamin Franklin, who was a member of the syndicate. Thurlow presumably considered the Pennsylvania agent "unworthy of the Favours of the Crown." Acting on this assumption, the Associates concocted a scheme to make it appear that Franklin was no longer a partner in the company. At the request of Thomas Walpole, Franklin wrote a letter to the head of the syndicate—a letter intended to be shown—in which he supposedly resigned from the company. But with the full understanding of Walpole, the agent retained his two shares in the land-speculating venture. During the Revolution when he was the American minister to France, Franklin explained that he retained the shares in the English company in the hope that his "Posterity [might] reap the Benefits of them." [66]

If Wedderburn and Thurlow failed to approve the Vandalia grant because they disliked Benjamin Franklin, his bogus letter of resignation was of no use whatever, for the project of an interior colony faded into the background as tension between the mother country and her colonies reached a crisis. Something more was at stake. The colonists had failed to live up to the program of accommodation between imperial and provincial control over the wilderness adopted in 1768. Five years of provincial supervision of the frontier had proved the inadequacy of colonial control. By 1774, the ministry was on the verge of instituting a new policy.

64. Thomas Wharton to Thomas Walpole, Dec. 21, 1773, Wharton Letterbook, 1773–1784, HSP.

65. Samuel Wharton to Thomas Pitt, Jan. 25, 1774, Dartmouth MSS, IHS transcript.

66. Benjamin Franklin to Thomas Walpole, Jan. 13, 1774, New York Public Library. See also the attached memorandum explaining the circumstances behind the letter, written by Franklin at Passy, France, July 14, 1778.

CHAPTER IX

Disintegration, 1768-1774

THE hostile reaction of the American colonists to the British tax measures and their overt challenge to the policy set by the home government for the interior had brought about an accommodation in the ministerial program for the frontier. In March, 1768, the ministry had given the Commander-in-Chief in America permission to reduce the number of garrisons in the Indian country. The Indian superintendents were to negotiate a new boundary line with the tribes to provide for limited expansion, to cover legal settlements, and to prevent further encroachments on Indian lands. As another economy measure, the administration had returned control of commercial relations to the provinces in the hope that they would take concerted action to regulate the trade.

The government had adopted this program against the advice of the superintendents—the principal proponents of the imperial plan of 1764—who viewed provincial control of Indian affairs with little favor. In response to complaints from Sir William Johnson, the Earl of Hillsborough emphasized the motives for the new arrangement. The implementation of the plan of 1764 had been dependent upon garrisons in the interior, the concurrence of the colonists as to the commercial advantages of the Indian trade, and the establishment of a fund in the colonies to defray the cost of the system. The decision of the government to withdraw many of the troops and to abandon some of the forts compromised the earlier program. The colonists themselves considered a general regulatory scheme inconsistent with their interests. Furthermore, it had become difficult—and this was an understatement—"in the present State of the Colonies to create a general fund to defray the expence" of the plan of 1764. While Hillsborough himself preferred this plan, he hoped that on the advice of the superintendents the colonies would adopt such aspects of the imperial scheme "as would improve the Trade, and fix the Affection" of the Indians.[1]

The inertia of the colonial assemblies and the competition between the older colonies and Quebec impaired effective cooperation among the provinces. Because of their long-standing association with the Indians, the traders and merchants of the former French colony possessed an advantage in the contest, while the itinerant French-Canadians operating in the Indian villages prevented the British from participating in the traffic. So divergent were the views of those engaged in the Indian commerce that General Thomas Gage thought it would be impossible to implement necessary regulations and at the same time to satisfy the "Humor or views of every Trader . . . ." Subsequent events justified his pessimism. By the end of the year, the colonies had taken no action to regulate the trade so that the Commander-in-Chief and Sir William Johnson had to continue employing the personnel of the imperial Indian department. To anyone familiar with the past record of the provincial assemblies, Johnson noted sarcastically, it should not appear strange that they would not see the necessity of contracting any expense for managing the traffic with the natives. By undoubted authorities he could prove, the superintendent vowed, "their extreme parsimony and backwardness" even when "their very all was at stake . . . ." The past performance of the assemblies made him apprehensive that they would not assume responsibility for Indian affairs.[2]

1. See Hillsborough's circular letter to the governors, April 18, 1768, C. O. 5/69: 229–233; Hillsborough to Johnson, Oct. 12, 1768, C. O. 5/241: 112–114.

2. Gage to Hillsborough, May 15, 1768, *Gage Correspondence,* I, 174; Johnson to Gage, April 8, 1768, *Johnson Papers,* VI, 185–186; Gage to Johnson, April 18, 1768, *ibid.,* VI, 198; Johnson to Frederick Haldimand, Nov. 24, Dec. 19, 1768, Add. MSS 21678, ff. 112, 114, PAC transcript; Johnson to Hillsborough, Feb. 13, 1769, *DRCHSNY,* VIII, 151.

Nevertheless, royal authorities had to make some attempt to resolve the problem. Gage wrote to several of the colonial governors, suggesting a cooperative venture in which the various provinces would assume jurisdiction for specific areas in the interior.[3] But the implementation of this system depended on the ability of the colonies either to accept regulations suggested by the superintendents or to propose and enforce suitable alternatives. Hillsborough emphasized the need for some action when he pointed out to Gage that it was useless for the provinces to expect that Great Britain would "again take upon itself the enormous expence attending Indian affairs upon the former plan . . . ."[4]

A distressing situation prevailed in the South. In the summer of 1769, John Stuart reported that the provincial assemblies in his district had not yet agreed to regulations for managing the Indian trade or preventing disorders on the frontier. As a result, the Indians were constantly complaining. The tribes in the North made similar protests over the removal of the smiths, interpreters, and commissaries appointed by the imperial government. It was apparent that the claim of some of the colonial agents in London —Franklin, Jackson, Montague, and Fowler Walker—that the colonists would gladly regulate the Indian trade, had little basis in fact. The situation required prompt action, as Johnson pointed out to Governor Henry Moore of New York, for the "Licentiousness" of the frontiersmen in conjunction with the "artifices" of the French on the Mississippi threatened to bring on an open rupture with the tribes.[5]

By the end of the year, the colonial assemblies still had not acted. Sir William Johnson, among others, felt that there was little possibility that they would.[6] Finally, in January, 1770, the legislature of New York passed an act appointing commissioners

3. Gage to John Penn, March 24, 1769, *Minutes, Provincial Council of Pennsylvania,* IX, 581; Gage to Penn, April 16, 1769, *Pennsylvania Archives,* 1st ser., IV, 337; and Gage to Hillsborough, April 1, 1769, *Gage Correspondence,* I, 222.

4. Hillsborough to Gage, March 24, 1769, *Gage Correspondence,* II, 86–87.

5. Stuart to Hillsborough, July 25, 1769, C. O. 5/70: 493; Gage to Hillsborough, Sept. 9, 1769, *Gage Correspondence,* I, 235; Johnson to Moore, Sept. 1, 1769, *Johnson Papers,* VII, 153–154.

6. Johnson to Thomas Penn, Jan. 30, 1770, *ibid.,* VII, 363.

to meet with any delegates the other colonies might name to concert a general plan for regulating the Indian trade.[7] The governors of New York, Pennsylvania, Quebec, Virginia, and Maryland in principle agreed to such a measure.[8] But Hillsborough, the colonial secretary, did not view the prospect of an intercolonial meeting with favor. He remembered the Stamp Act Congress and the attempt of the Massachusetts Assembly to organize intercolonial action in opposition to the Townshend duty acts. In April, 1770, he wrote to Cadwallader Colden that "the dangerous use that has been made" of the other "meetings of the Commissioners from the several colonies" had induced "great doubts" of the propriety of encouraging a congress to regulate the Indian traffic. He reprimanded Colden for having consented to any law appointing commissioners for such a congress without having received prior permission from the home government. But before Hillsborough's injunction arrived at New York, the provincial council, having received Governor Guy Carleton's letter accepting the principle of a congress, had set the meeting of the commissioners at New York City for July 10, 1770. In June, the Virginia legislature passed an act appointing delegates for the congress,[9] but before the government of the Quaker colony learned of this development, the Pennsylvania commissioners on June 28 resolved that a full congress would not materialize since Virginia, Maryland, and New Jersey had not appointed any commissioners. Consequently, their own deliberations would be useless, the Pennsylvanians concluded.[10] Only a week before the opening of the meeting, Colden received notice from Carleton that the commissioners from Quebec could not meet during the

7. The act is printed in *Pennsylvania Archives,* 1st ser., IV, 361–362.

8. Colden to John Penn, Feb. 6, 1770, *Minutes, Provincial Council of Pennsylvania,* IX, 656; John Penn to Botetourt, March 5, 1770, C. O. 5/1349: 115; Botetourt to Penn, March 24, 1770, C. O. 5/1349: 115; Carleton to Colden, March 13, 1770, C. O. 5/1349: 112–113; Eden to Colden, May 9, 1770, *Pennsylvania Archives,* 1st ser., IV, 369.

9. Hillsborough to Colden, April 14, 1770, *DRCHSNY,* VIII, 210; Colden to Botetourt, April 16, 1770, C. O. 5/1349: 117; Botetourt to John Penn, June 17, 1770, *Pennsylvania Archives,* 1st ser., IV, 371.

10. For the report of the Pennsylvania commissioners see *ibid.,* 1st ser., IV, 372; also Penn to Colden, June 28, 1770, C. O. 5/1349: 155.

summer. They would only be able to attend during the winter months. Communications among the colonial governments now proved faulty, for the two Virginia commissioners, Patrick Henry and Richard Bland, arrived in New York not knowing that Colden had cancelled the Indian trade congress. It was not until the day after the conference was to have opened that Colden informed the Virginians of the development.[11] In any case, Colden doubted—as did Sir William Johnson—that the commissioners—"by reason of the different interests of the several Colonies"—would have been able to come to any agreement had the congress been held.

The superintendent was especially apprehensive over the situation now, particularly since the northern tribes had complained at the congress at German Flatts of the chaotic state of the Indian trade. Furthermore, the non-importation agreements entered into by the colonial merchants to force the British ministry to repeal the Townshend Acts had resulted in a shortage of trade goods.[12]

Distressed at the delay of the colonial governments in assuming control over the trade, Hillsborough sent a circular letter to the governors in November, 1770, ordering the executives of New York, New Jersey, Virginia, North Carolina, Quebec, and Pennsylvania to bring the matter to the attention of their assemblies.[13] The replies of the provincial executives were not forthcoming until early the next year. They revealed the difficulties entailed in colonial control of the frontier and the attitudes of the legislatures. Nelson of Virginia, Franklin of New Jersey, and Dunmore of New York doubted that the different legislatures acting separately could devise a uniform system. Franklin held that each colony would consider only "its own immediate interest." Dunmore concurred. A general plan "must spring from and have the authority of Parliament." Apparently John Penn was the

11. Carleton to Colden, May 30, 1770, C. O. 5/1349: 153; Colden to Bland and Henry, July 11, 1770, C. O. 5/1349: 149.

12. Colden to Hillsborough, July 7, 1770, *DRCHSNY*, VIII, 216; Johnson to Hillsborough, Aug. 14, 1770, *ibid.*, VIII, 225.

13. Hillsborough's circular letter, Nov. 11, 1770, C. O. 5/71: 441–444. An exception was made in the reference for Quebec, which had no assembly. As governor, Carleton could take action with the council.

only governor who felt that commissioners from the colonies should make another attempt to concert a general plan—a program which the legislatures of the separate provinces would later confirm.[14] But when Dunmore of New York began corresponding with Hector Cramahé, the lieutenant governor of Quebec, about another intercolonial conference, Hillsborough effectively squashed the proposal. He was not unaware of the difficulties entailed in drawing up a general regulatory system while depending on the concurrence of various colonies with divergent interests and views. This was not the only instance, he felt, which demonstrated the need of "a general superintending Power over all the British Dominion in America . . . ." Consequently, he could but lament over "the Obstacles which have been unhappily thrown in the way of the just exercise of such a Power," by the imperial government. But some common action was necessary. Hillsborough now urged the superintendents to frame a general law and recommend it to the respective governors.[15]

At the same time, the ministry took action to prevent the colonies from holding a congress on Indian affairs. While the colonial secretary ordered Cramahé to take no further action in the matter, the Privy Council disallowed the act of the Virginia Assembly appointing commissioners for such a meeting. With the publication of the disallowance and the failure of Maryland to appoint delegates to the congress, the Pennsylvania commissioners realized the futility of their acting alone. In view of these developments, Governor William Tryon of New York signified to the colonial secretary the collapse of the movement for an intercolonial conference on Indian affairs. But he also expressed doubt whether the colonies could have formulated a general plan

14. Franklin to Hillsborough, *New Jersey Archives,* 1st ser., X, 222–223; Dunmore to Hillsborough, Jan. 18, 1771, *DRCHSNY,* VIII, 261; Nelson to Hillsborough, Feb. 5, 1771, C. O. 5/1349: 111; Nelson to Johnson, Feb. 5, 1771, *Johnson Papers,* VII, 1130; John Penn to Hillsborough, Feb. 28, 1771, C. O. 5/1284: 4.

15. Cramahé to Hillsborough, April 29, 1771, C. O. 42/31: 36–37, PAC transcript; Hillsborough to Gov. Eden of Maryland, June 5, 1771, C. O. 5/1284: 191–192; Hillsborough to Franklin, May 4, 1771, *New Jersey Archives,* 1st ser., X, 275; Hillsborough to Stuart, July 3, 1771, C. O. 5/72: 482–483.

for managing the traffic with the tribes.[16] Hillsborough still regarded regulation of Indian affairs by an act of Parliament the only sensible solution. For the time being, he agreed with the Commander-in-Chief that the deputies of the Indian department should continue to reside among the western tribes. But even this proved inadequate, for in the summer of 1772, Gage transmitted to the home government the complaints of the officers in the interior forts who were unable to restrain the traders in their irregular practices. By now Hillsborough had resigned over the Vandalia affair, but the Under-Secretary of State acquainted the new colonial secretary, Dartmouth, with the urgency of the situation in the North American interior.

Sir William Johnson continually protested the absence of a consistent plan for the tribes and the negligence of the colonies. In February, 1773, Dartmouth wrote the superintendent that, while he fully appreciated the advantages of a regular system, he feared the Crown did not have "sufficient authority" to establish such a program. Since the provinces did "not seem disposed" to concur in any general regulatory scheme, the Secretary of State for the American Department was "at a Loss to suggest any Mode" for maintaining the Indian service other than by the "interposition of the Authority of the supreme Legislature." Yet it would be inadvisable for the home government to exercise control until "Truth and Conviction have removed the unhappy prejudices which have so long prevailed in the Colonies on this Subject." [17]

In time the chaotic condition on the frontier made Dartmouth

16. Dunmore to Hillsborough, Oct. 30, 1771, C. O. 5/1349: 348. Dunmore, in the meanwhile, had been transferred to Virginia, and William Tryon, formerly chief executive of North Carolina, became governor of New York. Hillsborough to Cramahé, July 19, 1771, C. O. 42/31: 40, PAC transcript; Penn to Tryon, Nov. 30, 1771, *Pennsylvania Archives,* 1st ser., IV, 447; Pennsylvania commissioners to Penn, Nov. 30, 1771, *ibid.,* 1st ser., IV, 448; Tryon to Hillsborough, Jan. 9, 1772, *DRCHSNY,* VIII, 288.

17. Hillsborough to Gage, April 18, 1772, *Gage Correspondence,* II, 143; Gage to Hillsborough, Sept. 2, 1772, *ibid.,* I, 333; John Pownall to Dartmouth, Sept. 19, 1772, Dartmouth MSS, IHS transcript; HMC *Fourteenth Report,* app., pt. X, 96; Dartmouth to Johnson, Feb. 3, 1773, C. O. 5/74: 29 ff.

less squeamish about exercising imperial authority. Throughout the spring of 1773 the temper of the western tribes mounted, and the irregular methods by which the colonists conducted the trade was one of their principal complaints. The inability of the commanders at the posts to prevent the traders from going among the tribes and cheating the Indians made the situation all the more dangerous. Describing the traders in general as "the outcasts of all Nations, and the refuse of Mankind," Major Henry Bassett at Detroit would have liked sufficient police power so as "to make these Vagabonds tremble . . . ." The military could take no action to punish offenders without the traders raising a cry of "English Liberty" and threatening to sue the officers in the courts of the settled colonies. It was impossible, Bassett maintained, for the commanders to prevent the traders from defrauding the Indians without risking prosecution in the civil courts. He needed additional authority to confine the traders and send them either to New York or Quebec for adjudication.[18]

The situation was deteriorating rapidly by the end of 1773; the attempt at provincial control of the Indian trade had proved entirely unsatisfactory. Dartmouth was now forced to come to a decision as to the right of Parliament to exercise jurisdiction. By this time, increased tension between the colonies and Great Britain outweighed any doubts over the propriety of imposing imperial control. Mounting revolutionary disturbances on the eastern seaboard also necessitated a new disposition of the troops and forts in the interior which had been settled by the program of 1768. The home government also had to view the dispersal of the royal troops against the background of the failure of the British government to tax the colonists for the maintenance of the army.

In spite of the meager revenue expected from the Townshend Acts, the opposition of the Americans to these "external taxes" had been as marked as their resistance to George Grenville's stamp measure. Just as Benjamin Franklin and Dennys De Berdt had denied in 1765 and 1766 that there was any necessity for

18. Johnson to Gen. Frederick Haldimand, June 30, 1773, Add. MSS 21670, f. 105, PAC transcript; Bassett to Haldimand, April 29, 1773, *Michigan Pioneer and Historical Collections,* XIX (1891), 298–299.

taxing the colonists to support a royal army in the interior, so colonial spokesmen in 1768 also denied that British troops were necessary in the Indian country or that there was any legitimate colonial interest served in the West. In a petition which Alderman William Beckford presented to the House of Commons, the Council of Massachusetts remonstrated that, while the acquisition of a large portion of the North American continent was "a great national good" and greatly benefited the colonists by relieving them of the French menace, it had in several respects operated to the detriment of the colonies, particularly in diminishing the value of real estate and draining off population to settle the newly acquired territories. Moreover, there was no justice in taxing the Americans for the cost of the late war, or to pay for the defense of the recent acquisitions, for the new territories had occasioned an increased demand for British manufactures. This was sufficient to compensate the mother country for the expense she had incurred in securing the continent.[19]

In his *Letters from a Farmer in Pennsylvania,* the most famous colonial exposition against the Townshend Acts, John Dickinson also held that it was unfair to require the Americans to pay for the defense and protection of the new acquisitions. However advantageous to Great Britain, they injured the colonies, for they depreciated land values in the settled colonies, the principal source of property in the provinces. The natural increase of "our own people" within the settled provinces, Dickinson maintained, would have raised the value of real estate still higher. Furthermore, in compact settlements the Americans would have been better able to resist their enemies. Now the inhabitants would be thinly dispersed over an immense tract, for those desiring lands would choose to make new settlements "rather than pay great prices for old ones." Such were the adverse consequences to the Americans, Dickinson maintained, "of the hearty assistance they gave" to Great Britain in the French and Indian War—a war undertaken "solely for her own benefit." Employing the same arguments Benjamin Franklin and Dennys De Berdt had used against the Stamp Act, Dickinson charged that the provincials had

19. The petition, dated July 7, 1768, is printed in Mass. Hist. Soc. *Collections,* 6th ser., IX, 96; and in *Parliamentary History,* XVI, 482.

been able to defend themselves before the late war, even when they had been in a relatively weaker position. They could now do so again "against any that might properly be called *their* Enemies." Should France and Spain attack, then, as members of the British Empire, "perhaps they might be in distress," but it would be a "British quarrel." [20]

Thus the colonists would not accept responsibility for the interior, and at the same time many Americans refused to acknowledge the necessity of the measures the home government had adopted to protect the area. Since the ministers were acutely aware of the need for a reduction of the financial burden on Great Britain, they carried out a gradual withdrawal of the forces from the interior in the years from 1768 to 1774. Indeed, the mounting tensions which increased the need for troops on the turbulent seacoast accelerated the process.

In March, 1768, the cabinet had decided to maintain Detroit, Michillimackinac, and Niagara on the Great Lakes, and either Ticonderoga or Crown Point to secure communications with Quebec. For the present, the army would retain Fort Pitt and Fort Chartres or some other post in the Illinois country. The ministers would defer to the Commander-in-Chief's judgment on these posts. Gage was also to have full discretion on the disposition of the other fortifications.[21] As a consequence of this decision by the administration, the Commander-in-Chief ordered the evacuation of the forts on the lower Mississippi. He was concerned about those further up the river also, for Fort Chartres in the Illinois country and its supply post, Fort Pitt, accounted for more than half the expenses for the entire Indian department in the northern district. On the whole, Gage did not believe that any post in the Illinois country was worth the expense of maintaining it. Consequently, he proposed that the government collect the French inhabitants at one station, and form them into a military colony headed by a governor and an appointed council, with priests to be named by the bishop of Quebec. After the establishment of such a government, the British forces could withdraw.

20. P. L. Ford (ed.), *The Writings of John Dickinson* (Philadelphia, 1895), I, 360–361.

21. Minute of the cabinet, dated March 18, 1768, C. O. 5/1088: 156.

The other posts presented a different problem. Niagara was vital for communication with the interior, while Michillimackinac served to secure a considerable volume of furs about the region of Lake Superior and to the north. The only justification for maintaining a garrison at Detroit was to check the French inhabitants. "Those cursed French Settlements," Gage complained. Together with "the Strolling French and Canadians" who inhabited every Indian village, they were constantly fomenting trouble.[22]

Lord Barrington, the Secretary-of-War, could offer Gage little comfort other than to assure him that the colonial secretary shared their views. But the rest of the cabinet procrastinated in coming to any decision on the garrisons. By 1770, Hillsborough had come to agree with Gage that the cost of the establishment in the Illinois country exceeded any possible benefit which the government might derive from that district. But since the administration took no action on his proposals, the Commander-in-Chief suspected that the ministers might fear "Clamours from the Traders." He erred in this judgment, but Gage was so perplexed over the problem of controlling the interior that he wrote privately to Barrington: "I wish most sincerely that there was neither Settler nor Soldier in any part of the Indian country" and that Great Britain was free of both the trouble and expense of Indian affairs. Barrington assured Gage that on this point the sentiments of the ministers "are not different, tho' hitherto they [had] not acted with the decision which their Stations require." [23] But circumstances forced the ministry to act when Gage, in the summer of 1771, indicated that he would have to abandon Fort Chartres. The post was decaying rapidly. On December 1, 1771, the cabinet finally agreed that Gage could evacuate the fort, as well as its supply post, Fort Pitt, and submit

22. Gage to Haldimand, June 27, 1768, Add. MSS 21663, f. 297, PAC transcript; Gage to Johnson, April 4, Aug. 7, 1768, *Johnson Papers,* VII, 177, 313; Gage to Hillsborough, June 16, 1768, *Gage Correspondence,* I, 175–179; Gage to Barrington (private), March 4, 1769, *ibid.,* II, 502.

23. Barrington to Gage (private), June 4, June 27, 1769, Gage Papers, WLCL; Hillsborough to Gage, Feb. 17, 1770, *Gage Correspondence,* II, 98; Gage to Barrington, Sept. 8, 1770, *ibid.,* II, 557; Barrington to Gage (private), Nov. 1, 1770, Gage Papers, WLCL.

his plan for a civil establishment in the Illinois country "on the lowest plan of Expence" for the consideration of the ministers. He could maintain a temporary garrison at Kaskaskia, however. For the present the cabinet agreed unanimously to retain the other fortifications in the interior.[24]

The decision to abandon Chartres and Pitt—"two such expensive and troublesome Posts"—afforded Gage "great Pleasure." If in the future the colonists forced the tribes into war "by using them ill, let them feel the Consequences, we shall be out of the Scrape," he wrote Barrington.[25] By September, the army had razed Fort Chartres, left a detachment of only fifty men at Kaskaskia, and had evacuated the garrisons at Fort Pitt to Philadelphia.[26] The abandonment of Fort Pitt distressed Governor John Penn, who was caught between the clamors of the frontiersmen for protection and the refusal of the Pennsylvania Assembly to authorize a provincial garrison for the forks of the Ohio.[27] The Quaker legislature was no more responsible in its actions now than it had been at the onset of the French and Indian War. Furthermore, the evacuation of Fort Pitt by the royal army now opened the way for a three-cornered struggle for control of the upper Ohio among the Vandalia proprietors, Penn, and Governor Dunmore of Virginia. Busily engaged in land speculation, Dunmore was to prove an especially persistent and unprincipled protagonist.

The alteration of the Lochaber treaty line by which the Virginians acquired a larger district than that stipulated in the treaty John Stuart had negotiated with the Cherokees raised an immediate problem along the Ohio. When Colonel John Donelson had marked and altered the line, he had provided the Vir-

24. Minute of the cabinet, Dec. 1, 1771, Dartmouth MSS, IHS transcript; M650: 269, PAC transcript; Hillsborough to Gage, Dec. 4, 1771, *Gage Correspondence,* II, 137.

25. Gage to Barrington, March 4, 1772, *ibid.,* II, 601.

26. Gage to Johnson, Sept. 7, 1772, *Johnson Papers,* VIII, 593; Gage to Barrington (private), Sept. 2, 1772, *Gage Correspondence,* II, 619.

27. See Gage to Penn, Nov. 2, 1772, *Pennsylvania Archives,* 1st ser., IV, 457–458; Penn to the Assembly, Jan. 9, Feb. 6, 1773, *Minutes, Provincial Council of Pennsylvania,* X, 68–69, 71; and Galloway to Penn, Feb. 3, Feb. 19, 1773, *ibid.,* X, 70, 74.

ginia land speculators with an opportunity to disrupt the boundary settlement with the tribes. Without authorization from the home government—indeed, contrary to its express orders—the Virginia governor made a "very obliging offer" to George Washington, who represented the provincial officers claiming lands under the Dinwiddie Proclamation of 1754. Although he could not invest them with an "absolute and bona fide" title, yet Dunmore did agree to take such steps as others were pursuing to secure their grants. Prompt action was necessary, of course, since the Walpole Associates were attempting to obtain the lands ceded by the Six Nations at Fort Stanwix and the Cherokees at Lochaber. At the same time, officers of the Virginia regiments petitioned the Virginia Council for grants on the Great Kanawha on the basis of the Proclamation of 1763 which promised lands to soldiers serving in the French and Indian War. It was questionable whether the provincials qualified under the Proclamation, but they now entered surveys made by Washington's friend William Crawford of Pennsylvania, which the Virginia Council registered later in 1772.[28]

This action by Virginia led to a direct conflict with the prospective Vandalia proprietors whose claim in the North was also contested by the government of Pennsylvania. The status of this area west of the Alleghenies was particularly confused. Rumor had it that Michael Cresap's settlers at Red Stone Creek on the Monongahela had resolved to oppose the jurisdiction of the Pennsylvania courts, for Croghan and Cresap were actively spreading the report that the western boundary of Pennsylvania did not extend past the mountains. Attempting to support his contentions, Croghan pointed out to Arthur St. Clair, an official of Westmoreland County, Pennsylvania, that the Quaker assembly during the war had refused to bear the expense of a garrison at the forks of the Ohio, claiming that it was beyond the limits of the Penn grant. Many of the settlers, he held, came from Virginia

28. Washington to Dunmore, June 15, 1772, Fitzpatrick, *Washington Writings*, III, 85–87; W. P. Palmer *et al.* (eds.), *Calendar of Virginia State Papers* (11 vols., Richmond, 1875–1893), I, 265; some of these surveys, bearing notations as to the action of the Virginia Council, are in Huntington Miscellaneous, HM 5547, HM 5012, HEHL.

and Maryland, colonies with as good a claim to the area as Pennsylvania. The extension of the Mason-Dixon line beyond the limits of Maryland signified nothing, Croghan maintained, for it was not done by royal authority. Even after Pennsylvania officials circulated a published map by their provincial surveyor delineating the western boundary of the colony, Croghan claimed that it was a fraud, published in order to deceive the settlers at Pittsburgh. He had personally ordered a survey of the Monongahela and Youghiogheny rivers and could assure Thomas Wharton that they fell within the limits of Vandalia.[29]

In the three-sided struggle ensuing in 1773 for control over lands along the Ohio and Monongahela, some men did not wait for an official resolution of the problem of jurisdiction or confirmation of their titles. In the summer of 1773, after the Virginia Council had passed his grants, Washington, advertising in the press, offered to sell his surveys on the Ohio and Great Kanawha. He even guaranteed to prospective purchasers the validity of the grants "notwithstanding the unsettled counsels respecting a new colony on the Ohio," i.e., Vandalia. He was also engaged in land speculation with William Crawford, the Pennsylvania surveyor for whom Dunmore had offered to patent lands on the Little Kanawha if the ministry did not confirm the area to the Walpole Associates. Crawford had attempted to sell Washington's surveys along the Monongahela to squatters now occupying the lands, but the settlers had refused, for Croghan had informed them that the Virginia officer had no right to the property and Crawford no authorization to make the surveys.[30] Contrary to express orders from the ministry, Thomas Bullitt, a Virginia officer, began surveying the left bank of the Ohio opposite the Scioto River in the summer of 1773 on authority from Dunmore. The Walpole Associates were attempting to obtain this region also as

29. Robert Lettis Hooper, Jr., to Arthur St. Clair, July 10, 1772, Smith, *St. Clair Papers,* I, 264; Croghan to St. Clair, June 4, 1772, *ibid.,* I, 262–263; Croghan to Thomas Wharton, Nov. 11, 1772, "Croghan-Wharton Letters," *PMHB,* XV (1891), 431–432.

30. Fitzpatrick, *Washington Writings,* III, 144–146; Crawford to Washington, Nov. 12, 1773, Butterfield, *Washington-Crawford Letters,* 35–36; Hamilton, *Letters to Washington,* IV, 275.

part of the new colony, Vandalia. When Bullitt had been at Pittsburgh earlier that year, Croghan had reported to Thomas Wharton that he had carried instructions from Dunmore to secure lands on the Ohio which the Virginia governor would patent. A number of Pennsylvania officers who claimed lands under the Proclamation of 1763 now sent a delegate to Bullitt in order to obtain surveys in the Kentucky basin.[31] Other reports confirmed Bullitt's activities. In spite of all efforts to adjust the claims of the Indians and the whites by negotiating a new boundary, chaos reigned on the frontier as land speculators disregarded the program of the home government. On orders from the ministry, John Stuart had pledged to the Indians that there would be no settlements west of the Hard Labor line. He had hoped that the assurances given the southern tribes would quiet the fears the natives entertained over the frequent demands of the Virginians for an extension of the boundary. The whites in many cases simply ignored the line and continued to transgress on Indian lands. Due to these unauthorized encroachments, the tribes of the northwest headed by the Shawnee and Delaware sought to unite with the southern Indians in a general confederacy to resist further settlements.[32]

The failure of many of the northwestern tribes to give positive approval of the Fort Stanwix cession of 1768 was as disconcerting to the Earl of Dartmouth as it had been to Hillsborough, his predecessor. Early in 1773, Dartmouth pointed out to Sir William Johnson that, unless the tribes who actually resided within the limits of the Vandalia colony would accept the new government, it would be impractical to implement the proprietary venture.[33] Throughout that year reports were current that the tribes, especially the Shawnee, were apprehensive over the settlements and particularly the activities of the Virginians. Royal officials in America suspected that the Indians had formed a

31. Croghan to Thomas Wharton, May 11, 1773, "Croghan-Wharton Letters," *PMHB,* XV (1891), 434; Crawford to Washington, Aug. 17, 1773, Hamilton, *Letters to Washington,* IV, 248–249.

32. Johnson to Dartmouth, Sept. 22, 1773, *DRCHSNY,* VIII, 395; *Johnson Papers,* VIII, 889; Stuart to Dartmouth, June 16, 1773, C. O. 5/74: 287; Stuart to Dartmouth, Jan. 4, 1773, C. O. 5/74: 43–44.

33. Dartmouth to Johnson, Feb. 3, 1773, C. O. 5/74: 29 ff.

general confederacy and only awaited an opportunity to strike.[34]

In view of the rising temper of the tribes and the disorderly system of disposing of lands in the colonies, the imperial government sought to impose more stringent control by issuing additional instructions to the colonial executives. The Privy Council directed the Board of Trade to consider what alterations were necessary in the orders to the royal governors; in the meantime, the provincial executives would refrain from making any grants, pending the receipt of further instructions. The only exceptions to the proposed new regulation for granting lands were to be in cases of officers and soldiers entitled to grants under the provisions of the Proclamation of 1763. On April 7, 1773, at a meeting attended by the King, Gower, Suffolk, the Earl of Sandwich, Rochford, Dartmouth, and Lord Mansfield, the Privy Council ordered the Board of Trade to draft a report on the new regulations. Pending further instructions, the governors were to suspend all land grants and licenses held by private individuals to purchase lands from the Indians. The council upheld, however, the exception for soldiers claiming grants under the Proclamation of 1763.[35] The commissioners worked out the details of the new program in the course of 1773; they incorporated the new restrictions in instructions to the respective governors.[36] On February 5, 1774, Dartmouth sent a circular letter to the executives of Nova Scotia, New Hampshire, New York, Virginia, the Carolinas, Georgia, and the Floridas, describing the new program. He made it clear that the royal government did not intend the new plan

34. Johnson to Haldimand, June 30, 1773, Add. MSS 21670, f. 105, PAC transcript; Haldimand to Dartmouth, Aug. 31, 1773, Add. MSS 21695, ff. 33–34, PAC transcript; Johnson to Dartmouth, Sept. 22, 1773, *DRCHSNY,* VIII, 395; *Johnson Papers,* VIII, 889.

35. *Journal of the Board of Trade, 1768–1775,* p. 325; Dartmouth to the Lord President (Gower), April 2, 1773, C. O. 5/133: 27; *Acts of the Privy Council, Col.,* V, 360; *New Jersey Archives,* 1st ser., X, 402–403; *DRCHSNY,* VIII, 357–358.

36. *Journal of the Board of Trade, 1768–1775,* p. 357; draft of the additional instructions, dated June 3, 1773, C. O. 324/18: 450–462; order of the Committee of Council, dated October 28, 1773, in Board of Trade Papers, Plantations General, 31: 1–2, HSP transcript.

to preclude persons from executing grants who had obtained Orders-in-Council for lands and had not as yet located them. Neither did the ministry intend to exclude any claims founded on previous authorization that could "in Equity give a title to such a Grant." But for the future, surveys of the lands designated on maps must precede the actual grants; the colonial governments were to sell lands in small lots to the highest bidder at a publicly designated time and place. Four months prior, they must publish notification of the auction in the neighboring provinces.[37]

The new policy proved of little value in checking the activities of the Virginia land speculators. Dunmore expressed his intention of granting patents for lands in the Kentucky basin to the officers and soldiers claiming titles under the Proclamation of 1763. When the Virginians received the news that the Privy Council had exempted soldiers under the Proclamation from the new restrictions on granting lands, Washington pressed Dunmore on behalf of the provincial officers. They conceived this exemption to be "so strong an implication" of the governor's right to grant them lands that they now petitioned for the region opposite the Scioto River. Dunmore had a right to grant patents, for these lands belonged to Virginia; the Six Nations had sold them at Fort Stanwix in 1768. The "nominal line, commonly called the Ministerial Line," did not impair title of the Virginia government, Washington claimed, since that transaction "seems to have been considered" by the ministry "as a temporary expedient," instigated by John Stuart to satisfy the Cherokees. The ministers themselves had regarded it in no other way.[38] Such was Washington's interpretation of the boundary set by the Hard Labor Treaty.

Dunmore adopted this line of reasoning when he transmitted

37. Dartmouth's circular letter, Feb. 5, 1774, in C. O. 5/75: 53–54; Order-in-Council of April 7, 1773, *DRCHSNY,* VIII, 357–358.

38. Washington to Dunmore, Sept. 12, 1773, printed in *William and Mary Quarterly,* 2nd ser., XX (1940), 164; see also Washington to Crawford, Sept. 25, 1773, Fitzpatrick, *Washington Writings,* III, 149–150; Washington to Dunmore, Nov. 2, 1773, *ibid.,* III, 157.

to the ministry a petition from the settlers in the back country of Virginia protesting the establishment of the Vandalia colony. He had been too brash, however. In the spring of 1774, Dartmouth replied that, regardless of the decision of the ministry to assign the lands in question to the new province, it seemed to him "at least very doubtful" whether the Proclamation of 1763 included the provincial troops as eligible for lands. Pending further word from England, consequently, Dunmore was neither to sanction additional grants to the Virginia officers nor to issue patents. While Dunmore resorted to the fiction that the ministry had never officially notified him of the claim of the Walpole Associates,[39] he sought to undermine the jurisdiction of both Vandalia and Pennsylvania over the lands on the upper Ohio.

Taking advantage of the withdrawal of royal troops from Fort Pitt and the failure of the Pennsylvania Assembly to garrison the post, Dunmore sent Dr. John Connally to Pittsburgh with a commission empowering him to establish county government under the jurisdiction of Virginia. Connally took possession of the post and renamed it Fort Dunmore. George Croghan now made a realistic adjustment to the situation. Apparently he realized the futility of Samuel Wharton's lobbying in London and sought to make his peace with the Virginians by applying at Williamsburg for confirmation of his Indian grant. In April, 1774, he wrote Dunmore: "I am ready to comply with the Terms of the Colony . . . ." In Pittsburgh, Connally correctly interpreted Croghan's motive. The trader had sought to secure his Indian title now that Vandalia, "the great Government Scheme, is blown over . . . ." Like the "mountain in Labor," he exulted, it has "bro't forth a Mouse." Dunmore's bold gamble seemed to have succeeded when Dartmouth sanctioned temporarily the Virginia county government at the forks of the Ohio. Presumably Dartmouth saw the need for some law enforcement in the disputed area. Perhaps he also wanted to prevent an extension of the proprietary government of Pennsylvania which would have prej-

39. William Knox to the clerk of the Privy Council, June 9, 1774, C. O. 5/250: 158; Dartmouth to Dunmore, April 6, 1774, C. O. 5/1352: 1–2; see Dartmouth's rebuttal to Dunmore, Oct. 5, 1774, *Pennsylvania Archives,* 1st ser., IV, 579.

udiced the rights of the Crown to the revenue from these lands. In any case, Dunmore would govern the disputed territory only until the ministry passed the Vandalia grant.[40]

The coup Dunmore and his agent Connally had carried out, in addition to their provoking the tribes into an open conflict—Dunmore's War—placed the governor in control of the upper Ohio. In September, 1774, Patrick Henry in a conversation with Thomas Wharton in the Quaker capital explained the motives of the Virginia executive. After dwelling on the prospects for the Vandalia colony and the consequences of Dunmore's War, Henry claimed to be familiar with the origins of the conflict. He had been with Dunmore at Williamsburg when Connally had first approached the governor and had described to him the extremely fertile lands on both sides of the Ohio. According to Henry, the orders from the ministry prohibiting land grants in the region had led the governor to press the war on the natives to force them to cede territory on the right bank of the river. Dunmore had confided to Henry that "from Every Authority that the Law knew" a purchase from the natives was "as Full & Ample a title as could be obtained . . . ." The Virginians had "L[or]d Campden [*sic*] & Mr Yorke's opinions on that Head . . . ."[41]

The Yorke-Camden opinion has since become famous, but its origin had nothing to do with the lands of the North American aborigines. The two lawyers in question were Charles Pratt (later Lord Camden) and Charles Yorke (later Baron Morden). In 1757, as the English Attorney General and Solicitor General respectively, they had delivered a commentary on the rights of the East India Company for the guidance of the Privy Council in reply to a petition of the corporation. As one scholar has pointed out, from the circumstances in which the law officers delivered the

40. Thomas Wharton to Thomas Walpole, Jan. 31, May 2, 1774, *PMHB*, XXXIII (1909), 327, 331–332; Croghan to Dunmore, April 9, 1774, Croghan Papers, Cadwallader Collection, box 34, HSP; Connally to Washington, June 7, 1774, Hamilton, *Letters to Washington*, V, 8; Dartmouth to Dunmore, June 1, July 6, 1774, C. O. 5/1352: 93–94, 178.

41. Thomas Wharton to Samuel Wharton, Sept. 23, 1774, "Wharton Letter-book, 1773–1784," HSP.

opinion at that time, it represented a specific answer to a question respecting India which the petitioners had raised. Their opinion of 1757 reads as follows:

As to the latter part of the prayer of the petition relative to the holding or retaining Fortresses or Districts already acquired or to be acquired by Treaty, Grant or Conquest, We beg leave to point out some distinctions upon it. In respect to such Places as have been or shall be acquired by treaty or Grant from the Mogul or any of the Indian Princes or Governments[,] Your Majestys Letters Patent are not necessary, the property of the soil vesting in the Company by the Indian Grants subject only to your Majestys Right of Sovereignty over the Settlements as English Settlements & over the Inhabitants as English Subjects who carry with them your Majestys Laws wherever they form Colonies & receive your Majestys protection by virtue of your Royal Charters, In respect to such places as have lately been acquired or shall hereafter be acquired by Conquest the property as well as the Dominion vests in your Majesty by Virtue of your known Prerogative & consequently the Company can only derive a right to them through your Majestys Grant.[42]

This opinion of 1757 drew a distinction between those areas in India conquered by the Crown and those regulated by the company as a corporation under its charter rights. In the latter case, the company had obtained title from the sovereign and independent Indian princes by treaty or grant.

Under what circumstances American land speculators obtained this opinion is an open question.[43] What is known is that as early as the spring of 1773 a garbled version of the opinion was in the

42. The opinion as quoted above was discovered in the records of the East India Company in London by Professor Wayne E. Stevens and is printed in Shaw Livermore, *Early American Land Companies; Their Influence on Corporate Development* (New York, 1939), 106 n69.

43. The explanations given by Alvord, *Mississippi Valley,* II, 210 n; *Memorial of The United Illinois and Wabash Land Companies* (Baltimore, 1816 ed.), 23–24; Archibald Henderson, *Conquest of the Old Southwest* (New York, 1920), 201, and Abernethy, *Western Lands and the American Revolution,* 116–120, cannot be reconciled with relevant, extant evidence. Compare the accounts in the above works with George Croghan to William Trent, July 13, 1775; Ohio Company Papers, II, 6, HSP; James Hogg to Richard Henderson, n.d., Peter Force (ed.), *American Archives,* 4th ser., IV, 543–545; and the letters of George Croghan, William Trent, and Samuel Wharton in the Croghan Papers, Cadwallader Collection, boxes 36, 37, HSP.

possession of William Murray, an agent for Michael and Bernard Gratz, the Philadelphia merchants. The statement in Murray's possession carried a heading denoting that it was the opinion of the late Lord Chancellor Camden and Lord Chancellor Yorke (actually Morden) on "Titles derived by the King's Subjects from the Indians or Natives," and bore the further notation that the document was "a true Copy compared in London the 1st April 1772." This opinion reads as follows:

In respect to such places as have been or shall be acquired by Treaty or Grant from any of the Indian Princes or Governments; Your Majesty's Letters Patents are not necessary, the *property of the soil vesting in the Grantees by the Indian Grants;* Subject Only to your Majesty's Right of Sovereignty over the Settlements and over the Inhabitants as English Subjects *who carry with them your Majesty's Laws wherever they form Colonys* and receive your Majesty's Protection by Virtue of your Royal Charters.[44]

Someone had so edited and altered the original opinion of 1757 so as to eliminate the references to India and the East India Company. The opinion now failed to note the distinction between lands foreign powers had ceded to the British King and those the King reserved for the use of the North American aborigines. Nor did it include the vital reference to the King's charter by which the company exercised quasi-governmental powers in India. For reasons of expediency the British government had to acknowledge native ownership in the soil to the North American Indians, but vis-à-vis British subjects and foreign powers, the British King, of course, had the dominion as well as the ownership of the lands by virtue of the Peace of Paris. To acknowledge the implication of the edited "Yorke-Camden opinion," one would have to deny that by the Treaty of Paris the British monarch had obtained even a first option to purchase lands of the sovereign American Indian tribes. The British government could not accept such a proposition. By the Proclamation of 1763, the ministry had reserved the lands in the interior under the King's dominion for the use of the Indians.

Nevertheless, on the basis of this questionable opinion, the

44. C. O. 5/1352: 155, LC transcript. This copy was given by William Murray to Dunmore and transmitted to Dartmouth on May 16, 1774.

land speculators began forming a syndicate, the Illinois Company. Its members included Murray, a trader in the Illinois country; his employers, Michael and Bernard Gratz, merchants of Philadelphia; David and Moses Franks; and several Pennsylvania traders, among them Joseph Simons, Levy Andrew Levy, and Robert Callender.[45] There was some duplication in personnel with the "suffering traders" whom Samuel Wharton and William Trent then represented in London. With the Illinois Company partially organized in the spring of 1773, Murray set out for the Illinois country. En route he stopped at Pittsburgh, where he saw George Croghan. Murray wrote his employers that Croghan "assures me, That Lords Camden & Yorke Personally Confirmed to him the Opinion respecting Indian Titles, when C[rogha]n was last in England . . . ." [46] From the particular phrasing he used, it would seem that up to this time Murray was not certain of the validity or source of the opinion in his possession. Yet by June 11 he was in the Illinois country, where he presented the document to Captain Hugh Lord, commanding at Fort Gage at Kaskaskia. In his report, Lord described the document as "The opinion of my Lord Camden & the late Lord Morden, that His Majesty's subjects were at liberty to purchase whatever quantity of lands they chose of Indians . . . ." Murray then entered into negotiations with different tribes for territory between the Wabash and the Illinois rivers, although Lord had warned him that he would not allow him to settle any of the lands, for this was expressly contrary to royal orders. The commandant promptly wrote to the Commander-in-Chief in New York for instructions.[47] In July, Murray contracted a deed [48] with the tribes for lands; Lord's

45. For a list of the original proprietors of the Illinois Company see "Illinois and Wabash Land Company Minutes, 1778–1812," f. 1, HSP.

46. William Murray to Michael and Bernard Gratz, May 15, 1773, Ohio Company Papers, I, 102, HSP. At the time Croghan was in England in 1764, Camden (then Charles Pratt) was Lord Chief Justice of the Court of Common Pleas. In what connection Croghan might have consulted him on titles for Indian grants is not known. The whole story is suspect, for if Croghan was convinced of the sufficiency of his Indian title, why should he merge his grant with the "suffering traders" to obtain confirmation by the ministry?

47. Lord Gage, July 3, 1773, Add. MSS 21730, f. 132, PAC transcript; copy in Gage Papers, WLCL, sent as enclosure in Haldimand to Gage, Oct. 6, 1773.

48. A copy of the deed sent by Murray to Dunmore and transmitted to

letter to army headquarters did not reach New York until September 10. By this time General Thomas Gage was in England for a conference with the home government and his temporary replacement, General Frederick Haldimand, did not forward Lord's report until October 6. In the meantime, from the Illinois country Lord wrote to Haldimand with more disquieting news. Following the example Murray had set, two of the local French inhabitants had also purchased lands from one of the minor tribes. The Frenchmen had applied to Lord to register their deeds, but the commandant had refused, for he regarded those lands to be the property of the British monarch, "ceded to him on the peace by the French King."

These land purchases evoked a sharp response in London. The Secretary of State for the American Department himself wrote Haldimand about Murray's activities in the Illinois country. They were "proof," he charged, "of the Unwarrantable Attempts to acquire Title to possessions of lands in a part of the Country where all Settlement has been forbidden by the King's Proclamation . . . ." Dartmouth instructed Haldimand to give Captain Hugh Lord at Kaskaskia all possible assistance to enable him to prevent the speculators from establishing any settlements in consequence of "those pretended Titles" and to authorize the local commander in the Illinois country to declare the "King's disallowance of such unwarrantable proceedings" which could have no other effect than to bring the authority of the Crown "into Contempt" and disrupt the peace of the frontier by antagonizing the Indians.[49] Acting on these orders, Haldimand issued a proclamation on March 10, 1774, prohibiting the private purchase of land from the natives. He also instructed Lord at Kaskaskia to delete from the public notary's register any of the proceedings relating to purchases already made and to declare publicly that they were invalid.[50]

William Murray and the other members of the Illinois Com-

Dartmouth on May 16, 1774, C. O. 5/1352: 157–160; printed in *Memorial of the United Illinois-Wabash Land Companies to the Senate and House of Representatives of the United States* (Baltimore, 1816), 33–39.

49. Lord to Haldimand, Sept. 3, 1773, Add. MSS 21731, f. 7; Dartmouth to Haldimand, Dec. 1, 1773, Add. MSS 21695, f. 53, PAC transcripts.

50. A copy of the proclamation, enclosure in Haldimand to Gage, June 10,

pany had not been idle, however. In order further to promote their title to the lands in the western district, they had contacted Lord Dunmore, claiming that the Illinois country fell within the jurisdiction of Virginia. They sent the governor copies of their deed and the Yorke-Camden opinion. Dunmore supported the speculators with the ministry. As he wrote to Dartmouth, the later Yorke-Camden opinion "held, as it appears, that purchases made by His Majesty's Subjects of Indians are good, and his Majesty's Letters Patent not Necessary . . . ." But whatever might be the law respecting their title, the Virginia governor suggested, for several reasons the ministry should comply with the petition of the speculators and assign their acquisition, if not to the jurisdiction of Virginia, then to some other colony. It was impossible, he held, to set bounds to settlements in America. Consequently, to preserve order in the back country, the King "should indulge the views of adventurers," such as the Illinois Company, who would accept the authority of Virginia. The support of the land speculators north and south of the Ohio by Lord Dunmore and his blatant disregard of instructions finally exasperated Dartmouth. In a letter unusually severe for the mild-mannered Methodist, he chastised the governor for countenancing the Illinois speculators and ordered him to disavow the purchase Murray had made. The Secretary of State further criticized the governor's favoring the speculators who had violated the Indian boundary line. Dunmore could not have been ignorant, he charged, of the measures the government had previously adopted. Nor could he have been unaware that the ministry's "invariable Policy" had been to prevent, by every means possible, any settlements where the whites would antagonize the Indians and where they would be out of the control and protection of the imperial government. The various ministries had based the Proclamation of 1763 and the successive conferences on the boundary line on these considerations. During the negotiations for the boundary

---

1774, Gage Papers, WLCL; printed in *Johnson Papers,* VIII, 1074–1075. See also Haldimand to Johnson, April 7, 1774, *ibid.,* VIII, 1118; Haldimand to Lord, March 9, 1774, enclosure in Haldimand to Gage, June 10, 1774, Gage Papers, WLCL.

line and the Vandalia grant, the King had pledged to the tribes that the government would not allow settlements on tribal lands. Dartmouth now warned Dunmore that the ministry would consider any attempt to encroach on the Indian reservation as a gross violation of the dignity and honor of the Crown.[51]

While Dartmouth was struggling with the problem created by colonial violations of the Indian reservation, he also sought some solution to the status of the French inhabitants in the interior. The purchase of lands by Murray in the Illinois country had only made acute a problem which had perplexed the ministry for some time, especially after General Thomas Gage had withdrawn the garrisons from Fort Chartres in 1772. Gage had left for England in June, 1773, for talks with the ministry on, among other things, the Illinois country.

For some time the Commander-in-Chief had experienced difficulty with the French inhabitants in the interior, especially in the Illinois country and at Vincennes, or Post St. Vincent, a village on the Wabash where many vagabonds or stragglers had congregated. There was no military detachment at the post, and consequently no legal authority existed under the military regime at the Wabash village. In the belief that many of the inhabitants residing there had settled illegally, General Gage, with the approval of Hillsborough, had ordered the evacuation of the Wabash settlement.[52] But the inhabitants claimed to hold their possessions by legal title. In March, 1773, the new colonial secretary, Dartmouth, acknowledged that they no longer appeared to be "lawless vagabond Banditti," as previously described, but rather subjects of the King, claiming his protection and countenance for their lands. Yet when Gage left for England in June, 1773, royal officials still did not know on what specific basis the Vincennes inhabitants claimed their settlements.

In any case, by September both Lord North, the chief minister, and Dartmouth, the colonial secretary, were "equally embarrassed

51. Dunmore to Dartmouth, May 16, 1774, C. O. 5/1352: 141; Dartmouth to Dunmore, Sept. 8, 1774, C. O. 5/1352: 231–238.

52. On the background for this move see J. M. Sosin, "The French Settlements in British Policy for the North American Interior, 1760–1774," *Canadian Historical Review,* XXXIX (1958), 200–203.

what to do" with both the Vincennes and Illinois settlements. Whether the inhabitants occupied their possessions "by good or bad Titles," the ministers were not at all inclined to oblige the French to evacuate.[53] By the end of the year, however, the ministers came to a decision. They would grant the inhabitants in the area north and west of the Ohio River civil government. The French in the Illinois country as well as British merchants located at Detroit had exerted strong pressure on the ministry to establish civil government for the inhabitants in the Indian country.[54] In fact, before departing for England, Gage had received two French delegates from the Illinois country, Daniel Blouin and William Clajon, who had presented suggestions for such a government.

The Secretary of State for the American Department had expressed interest in the views of the two Frenchmen and had indi-

53. Dartmouth to Gage, March 3, 1773, *Gage Correspondence,* II, 157; Gage to Haldimand, June 3, 1773, Add. MSS, 21664, f. 143, PAC transcript; Gage to Haldimand, Sept. 14, 1773, Add. MSS 21665, ff. 189–190, PAC transcript. The French were able to present some documents to support their claims, however, for that same month, Lord, commanding at Kaskaskia, transmitted to Haldimand a certificate from Louis St. Ange de Bellerive, formerly commandant at Vincennes and later at Fort Chartres, in favor of the inhabitants on the Wabash. The current notary public now claimed that his predecessor had destroyed more than half of the documents entrusted to his care. Because of this "unfortunate accident" the inhabitants were prevented from sending copies of their grants. Lord had attempted to make further inquiry, but could not obtain any authenticated information as to the original settlement. Should the certificates by St. Ange be considered insufficient, he doubted if the inhabitants could produce better support for their claims. St. Ange had testified that he had been authorized by the various governors of Louisiana to grant lands, but that many of the deeds had been lost, and some of the inhabitants had no other title to prove possession. Lord to Haldimand, Sept. 3, 1773, Add. MSS 21731, f. 708; Haldimand to Gage, Jan. 5, 1774, Add. MSS 21665, f. 189; Haldimand to Dartmouth, Jan. 5, 1774, Add. MSS 21695, f. 62, PAC transcripts. The statement of the French claims is in Add. MSS 21688, f. 288, PAC transcript.

54. See the letter from Major Henry Bassett, commanding at Detroit, to Lord Scarsdale, Dec. 24, 1772, C. O. 5/124: 193, transmitting a request for civil government from a leading merchant at Detroit, James Sterling. Sterling's letter to Bassett, dated Dec. 22, 1772, is in C. O. 5/154: 65. Scarsdale referred the matter to the colonial secretary. Scarsdale to Dartmouth, May 27, 1773, C. O. 5/154: 63.

cated that the ministers would not consider them as inadmissable. But the Commander-in-Chief charged that Blouin and Clajon had merely presented him with a sketch of the government proposal—a system in which the local French populace would choose their own governor and magistrates. They had patterned their ideas, Gage informed Dartmouth, on "some Republican Model; a good deal similar to that of the Colony of Connecticut." He expressed his apprehension to the local commander at Kaskaskia that Blouin and Clajon had deceived the inhabitants by instilling in them "Ideas of an English Government quite incompatible with out Constitution . . . ." [55] Blouin pressed the matter, however, and wrote directly to Dartmouth, imploring the intercession of the colonial secretary for the "Establishment of a Civil Government . . . on British Principles . . . ." On December 1, 1773, Dartmouth answered the Frenchman in a letter which revealed the outlines of future British policy. None of the propositions for a civil government which had come to his attention were suited to the circumstances of the populace of the Illinois country. But some form of government was necessary, and although he did not think the ministers could provide any arrangement for the inhabitants which would place them outside the jurisdiction of any of the King's other colonies, yet he assured Blouin that the administration would not neglect the interests of the French in the interior.[56]

On the same day that Dartmouth informed Blouin that the ministry would probably extend the jurisdiction of some established colony over the inhabitants in the Indian country, he notified Hector Cramahé, lieutenant governor of Quebec, that the affairs of Canada were then "actually under the immediate Consideration of His Majesty's Servants," and would probably be settled in a very short time. The "Limits of the Colony," Dartmouth wrote, would constitute "a necessary part of this extensive Consideration." There was no longer any hope of perfecting the

55. Dartmouth to Gage, Nov. 4, 1773, *Gage Correspondence*, II, 151; Gage to Dartmouth, Jan. 6, 1773, *ibid.*, I, 342–343; Gage to Lord, Feb. 20, 1773, *ibid.*, II, 151.

56. Daniel Blouin to Dartmouth, Oct. 6, 1773, C. O. 5/74: 349–352; Dartmouth to Blouin, Dec. 1, 1773, C. O. 5/74: 361–362.

policy respecting the upper country which the Grenville ministry had contemplated when it had issued the Proclamation of 1763. At that time, the administration had not fully known the circumstances of the French inhabitants. But now there were other considerations, at least in Dartmouth's judgment, which induced him to doubt the "justice and Propriety of restraining the Colony to the narrow Limits" prescribed in the Proclamation of 1763.[57]

Dartmouth's correspondence indicates that by the end of 1773, the ministry had decided to scrap the program of accommodation which the government had adopted in 1768 to reconcile the objections of the colonists to imperial regulation and to reduce the financial burden on the mother country. The failure of the colonies to legislate for the Indian trade, the withdrawal of the interior garrisons, and the increased tension with the tribes in the face of continuous encroachments on their lands had forced the North ministry to try a new approach for the northern wilderness. Having been forced to abandon the policy of military occupation of the interior in the face of mounting revolutionary tendencies on the seaboard and having witnessed the inadequacy of provincial regulation, the imperial government was about to institute a new program. It would exercise jurisdiction through the province of Quebec, the only colony which had demonstrated an ability to get along with the native tribes.

57. Dartmouth to Cramahé, Dec. 1, 1773, C. O. 42/32: 93–94, PAC transcript.

CHAPTER X

The Quebec Act: the Final Decision

FOUR days after the Secretary of State for the American Department had revealed the principal aspects of the revised ministerial program for the West, Abigail Adams informed a friend: "The Tea[,] that bainful weed[,] is arrived." She referred, of course, to the appearance at Boston of the tea ships of the East India Company. The news of the subsequent destruction of the tea at Boston, as well as the spirit of resistance to the royal government, spread quickly down the Atlantic seaboard. Early the following month, Thomas Wharton wrote to his brother in London that he most ardently wished that the ministry would complete the Vandalia grant before it received a full account of the conduct of the colonists. If not, he feared, the news would strengthen the position of their enemies who opposed the grant for the interior colony.[1]

There was much more at stake, however. With this dramatic expression of open defiance against the authority of the British

1. Abigail Adams to Mercy Warren, Dec. 5, 1773, *Warren-Adams Letters, being chiefly a correspondence among John Adams, Samuel Adams, and James Warren,* Mass. Hist. Soc. *Collections,* LXXII, 18; Thomas Wharton to Samuel Wharton, Jan. 11, 1773 [should be 1774], Wharton Letterbook, 1773–1784, HSP.

legislature, the tension between the colonies and the mother country, mounting for almost a decade, reached a peak. The ministers summoned Parliament to consider the disturbances in America and, speaking through the King, requested the legislature to "enable him effectually to take such measures as might be most likely to put an immediate stop to the present disorders in North America . . . ." Parliament was to take into its "most serious consideration" the measures the ministers deemed necessary for "better securing the just dependence of the colonies upon the Crown and Parliament of Great Britain." [2] The resulting legislation directed against Massachusetts and known as the "Intolerable" or "Coercive" Acts precipitated at last the break between the colonies and Great Britain. Later that session the ministers introduced another measure for America, the Quebec bill. But we cannot properly include it among the Coercive Acts, for they conceived of this bill before news of the colonial reaction to the tea ships reached England. Nor on the other hand can we divorce the program for the French in both Quebec and in the interior from the mounting revolutionary crisis. As the need for British troops on the seaboard increased and the capacity for maintaining direct control and supervision of the French subjects proportionally diminished, the administration needed some policy to secure the alliance of the French inhabitants to the British Crown. They achieved this object by the provisions of the Quebec Act of 1774.

By the summer of 1773, after a decade of discussion and false starts, the ministry had resolved to institute a final arrangement for the province of Quebec.[3] The provisions of the Proclamation of 1763 had unsatisfactorily and only temporarily determined the governmental and religious establishment of this colony. The task of devising an equitable settlement fell, in the main, to the two under-secretaries of the American Department, John Pownall and William Knox.[4] Alexander Wedderburn, the Solicitor General, was primarily responsible for drafting the Quebec bill

2. *Parliamentary History,* XVII, 1159.

3. Francis Maseres to Dartmouth, Aug. 26, 1773, *DRCHC,* 375. See also Lord Chancellor (Bathurst) to Dartmouth, Aug. 4, 1773, *ibid.,* 374 n3.

4. John Pownall to William Knox, Dec. 3, 1773, Knox MSS, 2: 4, WLCL.

which Dartmouth brought into the House of Lords on May 1, 1774. The bill extended the boundaries of the province, restricted by the Proclamation of 1763, to include the territory north and west of the Ohio and Allegheny rivers. It provided for a military governor and a council, nominated by the Crown and possessing full legislative powers. The act also combined English criminal law with traditional French civil law and allowed Roman Catholics complete toleration and full legal rights.

The British ministers had arrived at this solution for the northern district of the American interior by a process of elimination after other measures had proved unsuccessful. In a sense they took a calculated risk. But they had attempted every other expedient to insure the lands reserved to the Indians and to conduct the traffic with the natives under proper regulations. The successive ministries had deemed this measure necessary to insure the stability of the frontier and to provide for the security of the continent. Direct imperial control had proved impractical because of the difficulty in maintaining and financing the royal garrisons and an imperial Indian system. In the face of mounting disturbances, the demand for troops in the East had further precluded effective military occupation of the interior. The British colonists had refused to acknowledge the necessity for imperial control of the wilderness and the taxes required to finance such a program. When given an opportunity to exercise control over Indian relations and the frontier, they had failed to assume their responsibility. Only the Canadians—and in this Governor Guy Carleton fully supported them—had demonstrated an ability and willingness to deal satisfactorily with the tribes. In addition, with the withdrawal of the bulk of the troops from the interior, the problem of the French had become acute. Some concession was necessary to hold their allegiance to the British Crown. The extension of the government of Quebec over the interior, under a form of government following the traditions and circumstances of the French inhabitants, was the logical solution after a decade of experimentation.

Wedderburn did not insert the clause annexing the hinterland until the third draft of the bill in April, 1774. By this procedure, the British government annexed to the colony of Quebec, for and during the pleasure of the Crown, all of the territory extending south to the Ohio, west to the Mississippi, and north to the southern limits of the area granted to the Hudson's Bay Company. A notation on the third draft of the bill explained that the ministry had introduced the first preamble and enacting clause at this stage in order to encompass those territories at present without the protection or control of "any Government whatever." The Crown might have remedied this deficiency on its own authority, but legislation by Parliament would remove all doubts which might arise if the government used executive action.[5]

Among the papers of the Earl of Dartmouth, then the colonial secretary, is one document, probably by William Knox, which sheds some light on the determining factors behind the decision to extend the jurisdiction of the northern province. At the time the Grenville administration had restricted the limits of Canada by the Proclamation of 1763, the ministers were "induced" to confine the colony "from an apprehension" that there were no settlements of Canadian subjects or lawful possessions in the interior. The Grenville ministry had also hoped to place the wilderness "under one general control & Regulation by Act of Parliament." But this plan had proved "abortive"; consequently, "an immense tract of very valuable Land" containing, in fact, "many Possessions and actual Colonies" founded during the French regime and protected by the terms of the Treaty of Paris, was without government. As long as these French settlements remained outside the protection and control of civil government, an unstable situation would prevail, a situation which would disrupt the peace of the interior and weaken the authority of Great Britain. By extending the boundaries of Quebec, the government would correct the defective state of the hinterland.[6]

Following the addition of the clauses extending the boundary, William Knox, on orders from Dartmouth, sent a copy of the bill to the Earl of Hillsborough. Two days before the colonial secretary introduced the measure into the House of Lords, Hills-

5. The third draft of the bill, in *DRCHC,* 382–383.

6. "Paper relative to the extension of the Limits of Quebec," Dartmouth Papers, 2358, PAC transcript; calendared in HMC *Fourteenth Report,* app., pt. X, 568.

borough submitted his sentiments on the bill. On the basis of objections which he raised, and, to some extent, on those of Governor Guy Carleton, then in London, Knox suggested certain alterations in the wording of the bill.

The former Secretary of State objected strenuously to the boundary provisions, for if the extension was merely for the sake of placing the French inhabitants in the Indian country under the jurisdiction of some government, it was within the power of the Crown to "give such Jurisdiction if it thought fit." By the terms of the bill extending the boundary to the Ohio and Mississippi, Hillsborough assumed that it was the intention of the ministers to have Parliament "*declare* that it is right and proper to *settle* the Territories annexed," for the bill placed this area and the inhabitants in the interior in the same status as those within the current limits of Quebec. By granting them French laws, the customs of Canada, and the free exercise of their religion, the measure was an inducement to the Roman Catholic subjects of Quebec as well as the other colonies to migrate into the interior. If this were the case, Hillsborough declared, he would offer the same objections he had used against the Vandalia grant, but "with Tenfold Strength." Governor Guy Carleton had made similar observations on the wording of the bill, Knox reported.

Within twenty-four hours Dartmouth notified Hillsborough of his intention of presenting the Quebec bill to the House of Lords the following day. He had transmitted Hillsborough's objections to the cabinet, who were unanimous in the opinion that the extension of the boundaries of the province to the Ohio and Mississippi rivers was "an essential & very useful part of the Bill . . . ." While it would establish a civil government for the French inhabitants in the interior, the bill by no means implied any intention to settle further the lands annexed to Quebec.[7]

Attention now centered on Parliament. As the *Annual Register* observed, the session was drawing to a close when the ministry introduced the Quebec bill; many members, "fatigued with long

7. Knox to Dartmouth, April 30, 1774, Dartmouth Papers, 2341; Memorandum by Knox, "Lord Hillsborough's objections to the Quebec Bill in its present form," Dartmouth Papers, 2360; Dartmouth to Hillsborough, May 1, 1774, *ibid.*, 2343, PAC transcripts.

attendance on the [other] American bills," had already withdrawn to the country. The measure encountered little opposition in the Lords; [8] but serious debate in the Commons began on May 26 with the second reading.

The opposition did not exhibit a profound knowledge of the North American wilderness during the course of the bill's progress. Thomas Townshend opened the attack on the administration measure. He observed that the bill bestowed the French law and the French religion on the interior country, a great part of which—"as far as it can be called settled at all"—Townshend held, was populated by "people who are natives of the British colonies," for the area was really part of Virginia. Was the Quebec bill to be the foundation of a future program whereby the British ministry would apply French laws to all the colonies? he asked.

Such was not the case, as Lord North explained in taking up the argument for the administration. The extension of the boundary of Quebec did not include an area "regularly planted by British settlers," but only one occupied by military detachments—a territory without any government except that of the respective commanding officers. Both the Canadians and the merchants and traders who trafficked in the region desired the solution now proposed by the ministry. They felt that they could not conduct the Indian trade with safety as long as the interior remained outside the jurisdiction of some civil authority. But Townshend continued to contest the point. He claimed that "Near the Illinois and Fort du Cane [*sic*]" there were at this time "upwards of five and twenty thousand British settlers." A formidable number! In supporting Townshend, John Dunning also attacked the boundary provisions of the bill as violating the charters of the British colonies. The Ohio River originated in Pennsylvania and ran through the province of Virginia; all the territory on the right bank of the river "has been lopped off . . . and becomes instead a part of Canada," he asserted. What objections were there, he asked, to making additional settlements in the wilderness? Whatever they were, he ventured, they were

8. *Annual Register,* XVII (1774), 74; Peter Force (ed.), *American Archives,* 4th ser., (Washington, 1837–1846), I, 170–171.

trivial compared to placing the whole region under the form of government proposed by the ministry in the present bill.

Speaking for the administration, Edward Thurlow, the Attorney General, denied that the boundaries described in the bill encompassed any British settlements. The floor now went to Isaac Barré, Shelburne's violent "bulldog," who voiced his suspicion that, in the extension of the boundaries of Quebec, "there was some secret purpose . . . ." No one speaking for the measure, Barré continued, had thought fit to answer why the administration should have run the "frontier at the back of almost all our capital settlements . . . ." He suspected something behind this move, a motive which "has not yet come out."

The point was crucial. Alexander Wedderburn, the Solicitor General, rose to answer. The one great advantage accruing from the extension of Quebec was that the colonists of the British provinces would have "little temptation to stretch themselves" into the interior. Wedderburn, for one, would not say to the Americans " 'Cross the Ohio, you will find the Utopia of some great and mighty empire.' " Rather he would tell them, " 'This is the border, beyond which, for the advantage of the whole empire, you shall not extend yourselves.' " Such a prohibition would control the colonists, Wedderburn felt, better than any restrictions on their governments. In granting lands in America, Great Britain ought to confine the colonists, to keep them "according to the ancient policy of the country," along the line of the sea and rivers. Wedderburn had touched on the most significant point of the boundary question; he spoke for those who sought to control the colonies by direct force, if necessary.[9]

A full discussion of the boundary provisions of the bill did not come again until June 2 and 3, when the House heard the testimony of several witnesses. While Francis Maseres, former Attorney General of Quebec and a vigorous opponent of the bill,

9. John Wright (ed.), *Debates of the House of Commons in the Year 1774, on the Bill for Making more effectual provision for the government of the Province of Quebec Drawn up from the Notes of the Right Honourable Sir Henry Cavendish* (London, 1839), 2–3, 7–10, 14–17, 24–26, 41–42, 50–58; Force, *American Archives,* 4th ser., I, 180–183; and *Parliamentary History,* XVII, 1357–1361.

declared that he was "ignorant of the bounds of what was called ancient Canada," he had heard that the province "is joined to Louisiana." But where one began and the other ended, unfortunately, he could not say. Governor Guy Carleton gave a much fuller exposition. Defending the bill, he testified that the extension of the boundary would enable officials to operate in the area so that "there may not be an asylum for all the vagabonds to take shelter there." In addition, some 1,400 French inhabitants, excluded from government by the Proclamation of 1763, would be under civil jurisdiction. The governor denied that the extension of the boundary would give the exclusive privilege of the Indian trade to the Canadians at the expense of the other colonies. But it was necessary that some legal authority enforce order so as to conduct the Indian trade.[10]

On June 6, the House of Commons considered the enacting clause of the bill. By its provisions the government proposed to extend Quebec south to the Ohio, west to the Mississippi, and north to the boundary of the Hudson's Bay Company grant. Territories not within the limits of some other British colony as allowed and confirmed by the Crown would be part of the northern province. George Johnston, former governor of West Florida, objected on the grounds that, by the extension, Quebec gained almost eleven and a half million acres—land which had not been part of French Canada.[11] At this point, Edmund Burke, agent for New York, proposed to give Quebec a precisely determined, rather than a "constructive," boundary, for the line described in the present bill was expressed in terms referring to the boundaries of the other colonies, some not having been actually surveyed or determined.[12] Consequently, Burke moved to amend the bill so that a line along the forty-fifth parallel to the St. Lawrence River would then run to Lake Ontario, across to the Niagara River to Lake Erie, and then to the northwest point of the boundary of Pennsylvania and on to the Ohio River. After some debate, Lord North agreed to the amendment. The House then resolved to

10. Cavendish, *Debates on the Quebec Bill,* 134–148.

11. Force, *American Archives,* 4th ser., I, 203–204.

12. See Burke's letter to the committee of correspondence of the New York Assembly, July 5, 1774, Hoffman, *Burke–O'Hara Correspondence,* 254–259.

continue the boundary along the Ohio and north to the Mississippi to the territory of the Hudson's Bay Company.[13] On June 10, a committee of the House consisting of Burke, Sir William Baker, and Richard Jackson made one final revision to the amendment to cover the contingency that the northern boundary of Pennsylvania might not intersect the southern shore of Lake Erie. But these were only minor alterations which did not materially change the administration's proposal. On June 13, the Quebec bill passed the House of Commons by a vote of fifty-six to twenty.[14]

There was only cursory debate in the upper house, where the Lords assented to the amendments added by the Commons by a margin of twenty-six to seven.[15]

The Quebec Act received a hearing in the political pamphlets.[16] Probably the most authoritative statement—one which closely corresponded with the thinking of the ministers—was that by William Knox, Under-Secretary of State for the American Department. After reviewing the measures the government had taken after the promulgation of the Proclamation of 1763, Knox emphasized that the events of the past few years rendered it impractical for the government to tax the colonists for the support of the previous western policy. He stressed another factor: during the period of English dominion, unlawful settlers had penetrated the wilderness. In order to stabilize a chaotic frontier and to prevent the establishment of distant settlements, the ministry had placed the interior under the jurisdiction of Quebec "with the avowed purpose of excluding all further settlements therein," and for the establishment of uniform regulations for the Indian trade.

13. Cavendish, *Debates on the Quebec Bill,* 184–187; *Parliamentary History,* XVII, 1391; Force, *American Archives,* 4th ser., I, 204.

14. North to the King, June 13, 1774, Fortescue, *Correspondence of George III,* II, 112. For a comparison of the texts of the enacting clause containing the amendment on the boundary, before and after the action of the Commons, see John Robinson to Dartmouth, June 13, 1774, *DRCHC,* 390 n3.

15. *Parliamentary History,* XVII, 1402–1407.

16. *An address to the Right Honourable L[or]d M[an]sf[iel]d; in which the measures of government, respecting America, are considered in a new light: with a view to His Lordship's interposition therein* (London, 1775), 28, opposed the bill, while *Thoughts on the Act for making more effectual provision for the government of the Province of Quebec* (London, 1774), 28–29, favored the measure.

The government had chosen Quebec because of the easy access by water from that province to the interior. It could not have "parcelled" out the territory among the several colonies bordering on the region, for experience fully testified that the Americans would not have been able to evolve a general plan for regulating trade and for limiting settlements.[17]

The new policy constituted a major setback for the land speculators in London. Although the Walpole Associates petitioned the Privy Council in August for the execution of their grant,[18] it was clear to Samuel Wharton at least that there was little hope in London of confirming the titles to the Indian lands. As early as May, 1774, he reopened his negotiations with George Croghan in America for a secret purchase of lands west of the Ohio before the government placed this area under the jurisdiction of Quebec. In the spring of 1775, Wharton and William Trent transferred their lobbying activities to the Continental Congress in Philadelphia in the hope of ratifying the original grant from the Six Nations to the "suffering traders" of Pennsylvania.[19]

The speculators had timed their move well, for even while the Quebec bill was before Parliament, the colonial office began considering measures to prevent unlawful settlement in the interior, to administer justice more effectively in the subordinate districts annexed to Quebec, and to regulate the Indian trade.[20] The ministry finally resolved these questions in the additional instructions issued to the governor of Quebec in January, 1775. He was

17. [William Knox], *The Justice and policy of the late act of Parliament for making more effectual Provision for the government of the Province of Quebec, asserted and proved; and the conduct of the administration respecting that province stated and vindicated* (London, 1774), 39–40. For authorship see Knox, *Extra Official State Papers* (London edn., 1789), pt. ii, p. 6.

18. See *Acts of the Privy Council, Col.*, V, 210; VI, 555 and also Thomas Pitt to Dartmouth, June 15, 1774, HMC *Eleventh Report*, app., pt. V, 354; Thomas Walpole to Dartmouth, Oct. 27, 1774, *ibid.*, 360.

19. Samuel Wharton to Croghan (secret), May 2, 1774, Croghan Papers, Cadwallader Collection, box 36, HSP; Wharton to Croghan, April 17, 1775, *ibid.*, box 37; and Wharton to Benjamin Franklin, April 17, 1775, Franklin Papers, IV-1, 50, APSL.

20. "Queries relative to the Government of Quebec for Consideration in case the Bill passes in its present Shape," Dartmouth Papers, 2355, PAC transcript.

to institute inferior governments with limited jurisdiction in criminal and civil matters in the Illinois country, Vincennes, Detroit, and Michillimackinac. A responsible official would administer each of these districts and fix definite boundaries beyond which he would allow no settlements. Thus the whites would not antagonize the tribes and impair the trade. Pursuant to the Proclamation of 1763, the traffic with the natives would be open to subjects from all the colonies who would obtain licenses from the governors and observe any regulations the council of Quebec would impose. To provide a guide, the ministry annexed to Carleton's instructions a copy of the plan of 1764 for the management of Indian affairs.[21]

II

The circle of British policy for the northern wilderness was thus complete. The experiment of colonial control had failed; no other alternative seemed feasible but to impose imperial regulation through the government of Quebec. Although the Quebec Act was sound policy in that it granted a religious and governmental establishment conformable to the desires and circum-

21. See articles 31 and 32 of the additional instructions to Carleton, dated Jan. 3, 1775, *DRCHC,* 428. The ministry would not back down on the provisions of the Quebec Act. During the winter of 1774–1775 Benjamin Franklin was negotiating with emissaries of the Earl of Dartmouth—Dr. John Fothergill and David Barclay—for an accommodation between Great Britain and her colonies. On December 6, 1774, Franklin submitted a list of seventeen proposals, one demanding the repeal of the Quebec Act. In his account of these negotiations Franklin related that Fothergill and Barclay told him that the ministry was willing to amend the Quebec Act so as to reduce the boundaries of the colony to its ancient limits. Albert Henry Smyth (ed.), *The Writings of Benjamin Franklin, Collected with a Life and Introduction* (10 vols., New York, 1905–1907), VI, 373. But by the available evidence it is clear that Barclay, Fothergill, or Franklin himself was misrepresenting what happened. There is a copy of Franklin's proposals among the papers of the Earl of Dartmouth ("Hints for a Conversation upon the Subject of Terms that may probably produce a *Durable* Union between Great Britain and her colonies," Dartmouth Papers, II, 1007). Among the same papers there are two copies of the Secretary of State's reply; the draft copy is in Dartmouth's hand ("Hints & c," *ibid.,* II, 1124). Dartmouth's answer reads: "As to the Quebec act, this article rejected." That is, no concession would be made on this law. The ministry would not amend the boundary provisions of the Quebec Act as is implied in Franklin's account.

stances of the French Catholic subjects, in another sense it was a calculated risk by the British ministers: a gamble they had to take to win the allegiance of the French inhabitants. The measure was all the more necessary since the ministry had to withdraw the royal garrisons from the interior in the attempt to control the revolutionary seacoast. Justice and the exigencies of administration demanded that they grant the French inhabitants civil government. The most expedient and effective method of accomplishing this goal was to annex the Northwest to the province of Quebec. At the same time, this solution provided the means for promoting stable and harmonious relations with the tribes and preventing encroachments by the aggressive British colonists which threatened to embroil the government in a general Indian war.

In the years preceding the Revolution, one can discern a constant element in British policy: the desire to secure the frontier. To achieve this goal, the ministers had to satisfy the tribes; prevent encroachments on their lands; and accord them an equitable trade program. Having fought the French and Indian War primarily for the security of the British colonies and retained the interior country for this objective, it was obvious to the ministers that they could only preserve the victory by reconciling the Indians. The war illustrated the deficiency of the traditional defense system by which the provinces had been responsible for the defense of the continent and relations with the natives. Royal officials in America had benefited by their experiences during the conflict and had implemented an *ad hoc* system to correct these errors. The Grenville ministry adopted this imperial system and then attempted to tax the Americans for the support of a standing army which would protect the newly acquired territories. At this point open resistance leading to the American Revolution began. It is impossible, after this crisis, to divorce any British western program from the development of the Revolution.

III

Were the British ministers justified in attempting to institute imperial control over the wilderness? We cannot resolve the question of colonial contributions to the French and Indian War in absolute terms. Certainly the colonists—especially the New Englanders—contributed to the war effort under the requisition system, but responsible officials in the colonies viewed the system as cumbersome and inadequate. Developments in the years preceding the outbreak of the Revolution confirmed for the ministers their conviction that the colonists had evaded the responsibility for their own defense and that imperial control was needed. Even in 1768 when the ministry returned the conduct of the Indian trade to the provincials, they still avoided their duty. The basic question seems to center on the refusal of the colonists to recognize and accept their responsibilities, not only as members of a greater community, the Empire, but more specifically for the more direct and immediate task of their own defense. Historians sometimes suggest that by the middle of the eighteenth century the colonists were too mature to remain within the framework of the British empire. Constitutional and political arguments as to the right of taxation, sovereignty, and representative government complicate the question, but certainly one manifestation of political maturity lies in the ability to recognize and accept responsibility and obligations. The concept of no taxation without representation is a worthy one, but was it relevant? Americans were hardly more willing later to pay taxes for the support of a Continental Congress, but they were certainly represented in that governing body. Perhaps they feared the dangers of any central government, no matter how representative. Can we say that the early American states fully accepted responsibility for their own defense or their obligations to the larger political community, the United States? Did Washington, as Commander-in-Chief of the American Revolutionary Army, or the Continental Congress receive more support from the new revolutionary state governments than the British commanders and ministers had during and after the French and Indian War? Did Georgia and the other states comply more fully with the general Indian program of the Federal government than the colonies had with the British policy regulating Indian affairs? Certainly Madison could not have been impressed with the political maturity and responsibility of the New England Federalists during the War of 1812.

Perhaps provincialism better explains eighteenth-century American behavior. How can we account for an attitude which refused to recognize not only a legitimate interest in the Empire as a whole, but even in the restricted setting of North America? New Englanders traded with the enemy during the French and Indian War, the Revolution, and the War of 1812. The northern colonies refused to raise troops for service against the French except in those areas adjacent to their own borders. The Pennsylvanians were even worse. In 1754 the legislature of Maryland was extremely reluctant to come to the aid of a colony as close as Virginia and would not defend its own western borders. All too often—witness the case of Pennsylvania in 1772—the assemblies of the colonies, representing the eastern sections of the provinces, failed to provide for the needs of the frontier.

We may also note the irresponsibility of individuals who sought to influence British policy for the wilderness. Samuel Wharton, later a member of the Continental Congress, certainly thought more of doing "something handsome" for himself than of the legitimate requirements of the Empire in America. Benjamin Franklin paid less attention to this problem than of benefiting his posterity by speculating in western lands. Both men were not above misrepresenting issues and overstating the facts, and in some cases they were not adverse to falsification in order to further their material ends. What of Washington, who violated governmental policy in his search for western lands, with the full knowledge that the consequences of his actions might endanger the peace of the frontier? Neither can such royal officials as Lord Dunmore, Sir William Johnson, and Governor William Franklin escape criticism on this score.

Any evaluation of the provincial attitude of the Americans must take into account the previous administration of the colonies by Great Britain—a regime which had meant little or no actual control or exercise of governmental powers. Whatever the benefits of the policy of "salutary neglect"—to use Burke's words—it had not prepared the provinces for the exigencies of government. Rather it had conditioned them to the unrealistic attitude of little or no government. With the advantage of hindsight, we at times assume that some form of commonwealth or dominion status for the colonists would have offered a solution to the imperial crisis. But would this have solved the problem? Regardless of the fact that few in Great Britain conceived of such a solution—fewer still would have supported such an arrangement—what would this have achieved? There is some evidence—witness the Stamp Act Congress and the Non-Importation Agreements—to indicate that the colonies could unite for negative action. But at the time was there any concrete experience to show that, even with dominion status, they would have been able to cooperate in devising a positive, constructive program? They did not support the plan of the Albany Congress and were unable to act in concert for the management of the Indian trade. Consequently there was little to indicate to the British ministers, who were faced with practical problems of administration, that such a solution was advisable.

What of British policy in the pre-Revolutionary War years? The attempt to guarantee the Indians their rights in order to preserve the peace of the frontier led to the imposition of the imperial regulations during the Anglo-French war. The Grenville ministry later incorporated these into the Proclamation of 1763. This program did not restrict further white expansion, but merely regulated and channeled it so as not to antagonize the tribes. There is no indication that in the years prior to the Stamp Act disturbances of 1765 the successive ministries were considering absolute restriction. They made provision for settlement on the Gulf Coast and in the interior as they gradually freed the lands of Indian title.

It was only with the tension of the first revolutionary disturbances between the colonists and the mother country over the Stamp Act that sentiment gradually developed to restrict the Americans to an area which would be under the immediate and direct control of the royal government. The violent reaction to the Stamp Act also marked the point when American policy became a divisive force in British politics. The political and constitutional struggle in England over the role of the monarch impaired an early resolution of this issue. The question of the dismissal and appointment of ministers made for a rapid turnover in administrations during this crucial period and prevented the imperial government from adopting a decisive, specific policy for the colonies. In the final years before the outbreak of the Revolution some degree of stability was achieved, but the balance in the ministry fell to those who favored a policy of rigidly controlling the colonists and prohibiting them from penetrating into the interior. Perhaps the first exponent of this view was Lord Barrington. But by 1772 the Earl of Hillsborough shared his attitude. Edward Thurlow, as well as Alexander Wedderburn and William Knox—significantly, members of the moribund Grenville faction—agreed with them.

Developments on the frontier and in the wilderness reinforced the attitude of this group. The failure of the revenue measures designed to support the garrisons in the interior and an imperial system for Indian affairs, coupled with repeated violations of the Indian reservation by land speculators and frontiersmen alike, made it difficult, if not impossible, to enforce the program of the home government. The development of the revolutionary movement in the East further complicated the issue; it necessitated a basic decision as to the deployment of the troops. It was impossible with the limited forces available to garrison the interior and maintain control over the turbulent seacoast at the same time.

The partial evacuation of the western garrisons did not mean the abandonment of the interior; after 1774, the imperial government would exercise control through Quebec. We cannot consider the Quebec Act aside from the development of the Revolution or previous imperial policy for the wilderness. Once the home government had decided to devote maximum force in an effort to control the colonies—the backbone of the first British Empire—then it needed some measure to hold the allegiance of the French in the interior and to the North. The North ministry achieved this through the Quebec Act by allowing Catholicism, French civil law, and a governmental system suited to the inhabitants. The annexation of the interior to Quebec would strengthen the economic position of the colony; an economic means thus served a political end. But an equitable Indian trade would also help reconcile the natives.

The extension of the boundary of Quebec seemed the only logical alternative after the failure of previous measures. Possibly the home government could have opened the interior to full-scale commercial exploitation, but the practicality of such an attempt is open to question. A general Indian war would have resulted. Moreover, such exploitation would have been impossible without a technological revolution in transportation. With the Bourbon powers controlling the mouth of the Mississippi and in the current state of water transportation, such a project was not possible on a scale large enough to warrant unrestricted settlement. This limitation applied to the early national period as well as during the British regime. It is difficult to justify attacks on British ministers for failing to envision technological development, for at this time transportation in bulk was conducted by coastal or overseas shipping. This remained the case for some years to come.

The final program of the ministry seems a responsible decision in the face of a difficult and complex task. If we designate as statesmen politicians who successfully foresee and provide for future contingencies, it is nonetheless true that as responsible ministers they must also resolve the immediate problems of administration. Under the circumstances, if the North ministry had continued the policy of military occupation of the interior, it would have jeopardized any attempt to retain the old empire—an impossible task as was *later* proved. To have left a vacuum in the interior would have been irresponsible. The Quebec Act was an honest attempt at an alternative policy of imperial control.

REFERENCE MATTER

Appendix: The Yorke-Camden Opinion

CONTEMPORARIES and later historians have presented conflicting views as to the circumstances by which colonial land speculators obtained the edited and abbreviated Yorke-Camden opinion. Professor Clarence Alvord conjectured that about 1770–1771 the opinion became common property among the speculators in America, although William Murray did not use it in the Illinois country until 1773.[1] This does not seem to have been the case. There is no evidence that the speculators circulated the opinion before Murray used it or that, before the spring of 1773, it was in the possession of anyone in America other than Murray and Colonel James Robertson, Quarter Master General of the Forces in New York. The Gratz-Murray group passed the opinion on to Lord Dunmore of Virginia *after* July, 1773; the Virginia governor then showed it to Patrick Henry. In the fall of 1774, Henry told Thomas Wharton in Philadelphia of the document. The Quaker merchant then mentioned the opinion

1. Alvord, *Mississippi Valley in British Politics,* II, 210n.

in a letter to his brother, Samuel Wharton, in London.[2] There is no indication —nor has anyone demonstrated—that Samuel Wharton was aware of the existence of the Yorke-Camden opinion *before* this time.

There is a copy of the abbreviated opinion written on the first flyleaf of George Washington's diary for 1773, which would seem to indicate that he obtained the document during or after that year, probably from the governor of Virginia, Lord Dunmore.[3] Richard Henderson, the North Carolina land speculator, also knew of the opinion in Dunmore's possession and obtained a copy,[4] from James Hogg, his agent. Hogg learned from the Gratz-Murray group in Philadelphia that the "suffering traders" of Pennsylvania had petitioned the Crown for confirmation of the land grant made them by the Six Nations at the Congress of Fort Stanwix in 1768. The King had then laid their petition before Lord Chancellor Camden and Charles Yorke, the Attorney General. In turn they issued the Yorke-Camden opinion.[5] This explanation does not conform to certain ascertainable facts. Camden served as Lord Chancellor from July 30, 1766, to January 17, 1770. During this period Charles Yorke was Attorney General only to August 1, 1766. There was no grant to the traders at this time. Furthermore, Samuel Wharton and William Trent, agents for the "suffering traders," did not arrive in England until 1769, and they never petitioned for confirmation of the grant the Six Nations had made at Fort Stanwix.[6]

The successors to the Murray-Gratz syndicate, the United Illinois and Wabash Land Company, gave another variation of this same explanation. In a memorial presented to the Congress of the United States in 1816, they stated

2. Dunmore to Dartmouth, May 16, 1774, P.R.O., C. O. 5/1352: 141; Thomas Wharton to Samuel Wharton, Sept. 23, 1774, "Wharton Letterbook, 1773–1784," Historical Society of Pennsylvania.

3. John C. Fitzpatrick (ed.), *George Washington's Diaries, 1748–1799* (4 vols., Boston, 1925), II, 96. On the connection between Washington and Dunmore on western lands see Washington to Dunmore, June 15, 1772; Nov. 2, 1773, John C. Fitzpatrick (ed.), *The Writings of George Washington from the Original Manuscript Sources, 1745–1799* (39 vols., Washington, 1931–1944), III, 85–87, 157.

4. Kentucky Manuscript, Henderson Papers, Draper Collection, 1-36CC1-1, Wisconsin Historical Society, Madison, Wisconsin.

5. Hogg to [Henderson], n.d., Peter Force (ed.), *American Archives* (9 vols., Washington, 1837–1853), 4th series, IV, 545. St. George Sioussatt, "The Breakdown of the Royal Management of Lands in the Southern Provinces, 1773–1775," *Agricultural History,* III (1929), 88 n40, points out the unconvincing nature of the argument of Archibald Henderson, *The Conquest of the Old Southwest* (New York, 1920), 201, that Richard Henderson applied to the highest judicial authorities in England for his source for the Yorke-Camden opinion. Archibald Henderson's grossly inaccurate treatment is more directly controverted by Hogg's letter cited above.

6. Samuel Wharton to Croghan, Sept. 4, 1770, Croghan Papers, Cadwallader Collection, box 37, HSP.

that Camden, Yorke, and John Dunning, "who were then the Crown Lawyers," officially gave the opinion to the King in council. Being consulted by the council in 1772 as to the legal status of the Indian grants and royal patents, that year they issued the abridged Yorke-Camden opinion.[7] This story is completely unsatisfactory, for these men were not the Crown lawyers at that time; rather Lord Bathurst, Edward Thurlow, and Alexander Wedderburn were Lord Chancellor, Attorney General, and Solicitor General respectively. If the Privy Council had desired an opinion, it would have consulted Bathurst, Thurlow, and Wedderburn, rather than Camden and Dunning, who were in opposition, and Yorke, who had died by this time. Of all the contemporaries known to have had some knowledge of the opinion, only Samuel Wharton acknowledged that Yorke and Camden had delivered the statement in 1757 respecting the East India Company. But he did so in a pamphlet[8] written *after* Murray had used the edited opinion in the Illinois country and *after* Thomas Wharton had informed him that such an opinion was in Dunmore's possession. Since Samuel Wharton was then in London and associated with Camden in the Vandalia project, it is possible that Camden informed him of the original 1757 opinion regarding lands in India.

Historians have fared little better in explaining the circumstances by which the opinion came into the possession of colonial land speculators. Shaw Livermore in his study on American land companies has printed the initial statement of 1757 which Professor Wayne E. Stevens uncovered among the records of the East India Company in London. Livermore noted the discrepancies between the opinion of 1757 and that which Murray used in 1773, but he made no attempt to explain the circumstances behind the editing of the original document.[9]

Professor Alvord did not differentiate between the opinion of 1757 and that employed by the colonial land speculators later. He assumed that in 1769 before the death of Yorke in January, 1770, he and Camden gave a private opinion to William Trent and Samuel Wharton after the two speculators arrived in London. To support this explanation, Alvord referred to a story which Trent gave the "suffering traders" at a meeting in Pittsburgh in 1775, after his return from England. In explaining his failure to obtain confirmation for the traders' grant from the Six Nations, Trent told the group that he had not submitted the grant to the Crown since such confirmation was unnecessary in Camden's

7. *Memorial of the United Illinois and Wabash Land Companies to the Senate and House of Representatives of the United States* (Baltimore, 1816), 23–24.

8. [Samuel Wharton], *Plain Facts: Being an examination into the Rights of the Indian Nations of America, to their respective countries: and a Vindication of the Grant, from the Six Nations of Indians: to the Proprietors of Indiana, against the Decision of the Legislature of Virginia, together with Authentic Documents proving that the Territory Westward of the Allegheny Mountains never belonged to Virginia* (Philadelphia, 1781), 9.

9. Livermore, *American Land Companies,* 106 n69.

opinion. It should be noted that, although Samuel Wharton, in his correspondence with George Croghan in 1775, claimed that Camden held Indian titles to be valid,[10] there is no reason to assume, as Alvord did, that Camden gave either *the* original or *the* abridged opinion to the land speculators. Moreover, Trent's story to the traders at Pittsburgh was not entirely truthful, for he and Wharton did not seek confirmation from the Crown because they had Camden's opinion, as Trent told the traders, but because they feared that if they did apply they would meet with a flat refusal.[11] On the advice of a lawyer, Henry Dagge, they did not solicit the Crown, since they did not have verbatim copies of the correspondence between the Earl of Hillsborough and Sir William Johnson. Hillsborough, the Secretary of State for the American Department, considered the congress negotiated at Fort Stanwix as a "piece of Management."[12] Indeed it was. Because of the opposition of Hillsborough, Wharton had set about organizing the Walpole Company,[13] which eventually petitioned for all the lands ceded at the Stanwix congress.

By the spring of 1775 even this venture collapsed, and Trent left for America to lobby before the Continental Congress. He carried with him a letter to Croghan from Wharton. The latter had drawn up a "*Case*" relating to Indian grants. In addition, he had received the opinions of two English solicitors, John Glynn and Henry Dagge, on the subject. As Wharton reported to Croghan, Lord Camden "entirely agrees" with Glynn and Dagge as to the validity of Indian titles.[14] To support the argument, Wharton engaged with Dr. Edward Bancroft—Franklin's friend and later a double agent during the Revolution—to write a pamphlet entitled "View of the Title to Indiana."[15] The tract does not mention the Yorke-Camden opinion. Trent left England in April, 1775, carrying with him the statements by Glynn and Dagge as to the sufficiency of land titles based on Indian grants. Evidently he did not bring back the Yorke-Camden opinion, for it is not among those collected by him and entered in a volume of his papers in the Historical Society of Pennsylvania which supported

---

10. Wharton to Croghan, April 17, 1775, Croghan Papers, Cadwallader Collection, box 37, HSP.

11. Wharton to Croghan, Sept. 4, 1770, *ibid.*

12. Wharton to Croghan, May 27, 1769, *ibid.*

13. Wharton to Croghan, Sept. 4, 1770, and Trent to Croghan, Dec. 6, 1769, *ibid.*

14. Wharton to Croghan, April 17, 1775, *ibid.*

15. See Bancroft to Benjamin Franklin, August 7, 1775, *Pennsylvania Magazine of History and Biography,* XXVII (1903), 158; and [Samuel Wharton and Edward Bancroft], *View to the Title of Indiana, a Tract of Country on the River Ohio: Containing Indian Conferences at Johnson Hall in May, 1765 . . . the Deed of the Indians, settling the boundary line between the English and Indian lands—and the Opinion of the Council on the Title of the Proprietors of Indiana* (Philadelphia, 1776). "Indiana" was the original traders' grant on the left bank of the Ohio. It had no relation to the present state by that name.

the contention that Indian titles were valid. All that Trent had with him on his return to America was a statement based on the doctrine of natural law which Dagge had given in London on March 20, 1775. The Indians held the land from "preoccupancy" and, as the "natural owners," had the right to alienate their property. There was a concurring opinion by Glynn, dated April 13, 1775. The "supreme power" over the interior country resided with the Six Nations. These tribes had an "absolute power" to alienate their holdings; there was no law restraining British subjects from purchasing lands in "Foreign dominions." On arriving in America, Trent solicited two brief concurring statements from Benjamin Franklin and Patrick Henry.[16]

If the doctrines contained in these statements were valid, then the Treaty of Paris of 1763 was worthless; it signified nothing. To admit these contentions, one would have to deny that by the treaty the British Crown had even a first option to purchase lands from the sovereign tribes. Such a view was hardly tenable in England. In addition, the omission of any statement from Camden is damaging to the contention that he agreed to the theory justifying Indian grants. If the speculators sought to build up as impressive a legal case as possible, certainly a positive statement by as eminent an authority on jurisprudence as Camden, a former Lord Chancellor, would have been worth more than the statements of Dagge and Glynn.

In spite of the complexity of the factors involved, perhaps the most ambitious explanation given by historians as to the Yorke-Camden opinion of 1773 is that of Professor Thomas Abernethy. Unfortunately, he did not use all of the sources now available and drew an unjustifiable conclusion from the material he did consult. He presented the following evidence. (1) The date of April 1, 1772, on the abbreviated Yorke-Camden opinion; (2) the letter from William Murray to Bernard and Michael Gratz of May, 1773,[17] in which Murray related that Croghan had assured him in Pittsburgh that Camden had verified the opinion respecting Indian titles when Croghan was last in London; (3) a letter from Croghan to Bernard Gratz[18] at about the same time which indicated that Samuel Wharton was to arrive from London shortly to hold a congress with the tribes of the upper Ohio and would give them a cargo of Indian goods from the Vandalia proprietors to placate the tribes for the proposed new colony; (4) a letter from Thomas Wharton to Samuel Wharton of November,

---

16. "Opinions Regarding the Grant to Wm Trent 1775," MS volume, Historical Society of Pennsylvania. These opinions are printed in *Memorial of the United Illinois and Wabash Land Companies to the Senate and House of Representatives of the United States* (Baltimore, 1816), 45–48, and also in [Samuel Wharton and/or Edward Bancroft], *View to the Title to Indiana, A Tract of Country on the Ohio River,* 40–44, 44–46.

17. Murray to Bernard and Michael Gratz, May 15, 1773, Ohio Company Papers, II, 102, Historical Society of Pennsylvania.

18. Croghan to Bernard Gratz, May 11, 1773, Draper Collection, 7J136-8, Wisconsin Historical Society.

1773,[19] noting that Croghan had held a meeting with the Indians on authorization contained in a letter signed by Samuel Wharton, Lord Camden, and others; (5) a letter from Samuel Wharton to Thomas Wharton, of January, 1775,[20] in which Wharton informed his brother that a cargo of goods on the Potomac was to be used to purchase lands west of the Ohio—a purchase which Croghan had secretly prepared three years before; (6) and finally, a letter of July, 1775, from Croghan to William Trent,[21] in which Croghan denied having heard anything further about the trans-Ohio purchase since Samuel Wharton had originally proposed the project. He had made one for himself, however, and now offered, for a price, to share the land with Wharton and Trent. What Professor Abernethy does not mention is that, in the letter from Samuel Wharton to Thomas Wharton of January, 1775, it is clear that Croghan had not yet made the purchase, and also that, in his letter to Trent of July, 1775, Croghan specifically asked for compensation for the cost of calling the Indians to Pittsburgh for their projected conference with Samuel Wharton, the prospective governor of Vandalia.

On the basis of this evidence, Professor Abernethy offered the following interpretation as to how the American land speculators obtained the Yorke-Camden opinion. It must have been Camden who suggested to Trent that he copy the opinion of 1757 which the jurists had delivered with regard to India. Trent did so on April 1, 1772; at the same time, he edited the document. The speculators then sent the abridged version to America with a letter signed by Samuel Wharton, Camden, and others, instructing Croghan to use the opinion in purchasing a tract west of the Ohio River. The speculators had to maintain secrecy and provide goods to pay the natives for their land. Consequently, they devised a rather complicated scheme. Trent was to return to America with a cargo of Indian goods which he was to land on the Potomac and forward to Croghan, telling him that the governor of Vandalia (Samuel Wharton) and his entourage would arrive in Pittsburgh the following summer. Thus the speculators would create the impression that they intended the shipment of goods as a present to the Indians for the meeting of the Vandalia governor with the tribes. But the real motive behind the shipment of Indian goods—payment for a trans-Ohio tract—was masked. As Abernethy further relates the story, the Yorke-Camden opinion and the accompanying letters eventually reached Thomas Wharton in Philadelphia. He naively entrusted them to William Murray for delivery to Croghan. "One cannot escape the conclusion," Abernethy went on, that Murray then read the letters and copied the Yorke-Camden opinion. He then engaged with the Gratz brothers, the Franks' firm, and others to organize the Illinois Company before proceeding to Pittsburgh. There Croghan confirmed for him that in 1764 Camden had vouched for the validity of Indian grants. If

---

19. Thomas Wharton to Samuel Wharton, Nov. 30, 1773, Wharton Letterbook, 1773–1874, Historical Society of Pennsylvania.

20. Samuel Wharton to Thomas Wharton, Jan. 31, 1775, *ibid.*

21. Croghan to Trent, July 13, 1775, Ohio Company Papers, II, 6, Historical Society of Pennsylvania.

Abernethy's argument is valid, then one cannot help but admire Murray's effrontery, for having pilfered Croghan's secret mail, he then proceeded to discuss the contents with the owner. But Abernethy speculates that Murray then proceeded to the Illinois country where, using the Yorke-Camden opinion, he purchased lands from the Indians. When Trent returned to the colonies in 1775, he contacted Croghan about the purchase west of the Ohio which Croghan was supposed to have made. According to Abernethy's interpretation, or his reading of the letter Croghan sent in reply, Croghan did remember such a proposal from Samuel Wharton over three years ago—Abernethy says, "it was actually two years"—but he had heard nothing more about it since that time. He had assumed that the speculators in London had dropped the matter. But Croghan now offered to let Wharton and Trent share in a private purchase he had made for two-thirds of the purchase price.[22]

This whole interpretation breaks down at a number of points. In the first place, the Croghan-Wharton correspondence in the Cadwallader Collection at the Historical Society of Pennsylvania (not available at the time Abernethy wrote) shows that Wharton made the proposal to Croghan for a purchase of a tract west of the Ohio in a letter of July 21, 1771 [23]—not in 1773, as Abernethy claimed. Furthermore, the letter was sealed and kept secret from Thomas Wharton. This same correspondence also demonstrates that Croghan was right in his contention to Trent that he had taken no action on this matter. Wharton's letter to Croghan of May 2, 1774,[24] shows that Wharton did not reopen the affair until that time, and then only to complete the purchase before the government of Quebec took over jurisdiction in the area. The ministry had introduced the Quebec bill into the House of Lords the day before—May 1, 1774. The letters in the same collection from Wharton to Croghan prove that the goods sent to America were originally intended to compensate the Ohio tribes [25] for the Vandalia lands, *not* to purchase a tract west of the river,[26] as Abernethy contended. Abernethy himself ignored the statement in Croghan's letter to Trent of July 13, 1775,[27] in which he complained that the Walpole

22. Thomas P. Abernethy, *Western Lands and the American Revolution* (New York, 1937), 116–120.

23. Croghan Papers, Cadwallader Collection, box 36, Historical Society of Pennsylvania.

24. *Ibid.*, box 36.

25. The Ohio tribes resented the fact that the Six Nations had received the compensation from the Crown for the Fort Stanwix cession, while they, the actual residents, had received little or nothing.

26. Wharton to Croghan, Feb. 3, 1773, *ibid.*, box 37, and Thomas Walpole to Croghan, Jan. 25, 1773, *ibid.*

27. Professor Abernethy was right, however, in that Croghan was misrepresenting the issue by denying that he had ever heard anything of a trans-Ohio tract after it was originally proposed. But the important point is that the proposition was originally made in July, 1771, and only reopened as late as May, 1774.

Associates had not compensated him for the expense of calling the Ohio tribes for the congress which Wharton and Trent had ordered. It was not until January, 1775, that Wharton misrepresented the case to his brother (and confused Professor Abernethy) by erroneously informing him that Croghan had already taken the preliminary steps for the secret land speculating group in London. It was only in 1775 that Wharton diverted the goods intended to compensate the Ohio tribes for the Vandalia tract to effect a purchase of land west of the Ohio. Furthermore, in 1771, Wharton had proposed that Croghan purchase the trans-Ohio lands from the Six Nations, not the Ohio tribes.

These documents destroy the timetable and the rationale used by Abernethy. On the basis of the evidence he presented, there is no justification for introducing the Yorke-Camden opinion into the scheme by Wharton and Trent in 1771 and 1774 to obtain lands west of the Ohio. The fact that Croghan and Murray discussed the opinion at Pittsburgh in May, 1773, does not prove that Murray obtained the document in the manner which Professor Abernethy suggested. There was no need for Croghan to have had such an opinion to have made a secret purchase from the Indians. It is doubtful if the Six Nations or the tribes of the upper Ohio would have appreciated the subtle reasoning involved in such a document. It was designed to be shown to some responsible official in order to obviate any objections to a purchase of Indian lands in an area closed to whites by the Proclamation of 1763. In effect, Murray used the opinion this way. Unfortunately, neither Captain Hugh Lord at Kaskaskia nor the ministers in London would have any part of it. The Secretary of State for the American Department ordered Murray's purchase disallowed.

Is there any evidence that Camden himself thought the opinion of 1757 was applicable to the lands of the North American aborigines? He *may* have given the original or abridged opinion to the speculators, but it is doubtful if he admitted this after 1773 when the ministers in London learned of Murray's activities. The Earl of Dartmouth was anxious to see the opinion at that time, but he had to obtain a copy from Lieutenant Colonel James Robertson in New York. Since Camden was purportedly one of the authors of the opinion, it would have been much simpler for Dartmouth to have secured the opinion from him. General Thomas Gage, then in London, wrote that no one in England could believe that Camden could have given such an opinion. On the other hand, he also conjectured that, if Camden had rendered the document, he could not have been fully informed as to conditions in America.[28] This seems to indicate that the ministers had not consulted Camden on the document used by Murray.

What has been overlooked is that Robertson had a copy of the opinion of 1773 which he showed to the Commander-in-Chief sometime before Gage left the colonies in June, 1773. Consequently, Robertson had the opinion before, or about the same time, that Murray used it in the Illinois country when from all indications it was a well-kept secret. Several additional questions remain un-

---

28. Gage to Haldimand, Feb. 2, 1774, Add. MSS 21665, f. 215; Gage to Haldimand, Nov. 28, 1773, *ibid.*, f. 198, PAC transcripts.

answered. How did Robertson obtain the document? Did he bring the opinion from England? What connection, if any, did he have with Murray and how did the latter obtain the opinion? Evidence which does not appear at present to be extant may provide a more satisfactory solution than those writers have hitherto advanced. Perhaps the analysis presented here may help future scholars to solve the problem.

Bibliography

Manuscripts

Archives des Affaires Etrangères, Paris, Correspondance Politique, Angleterre; Espagne; Mémoirs et Documents, Amerique; Angleterre.

Almon, John, Papers, British Museum, London.

Amherst, Jeffrey, Papers, William L. Clements Library, Ann Arbor, Michigan.

Amherst, Jeffrey, Papers, Public Archives of Canada, Ottawa, transcripts.

Ayers, Edward, Collection, The Newberry Library, Chicago.

Board of Trade Papers, Plantations General, Historical Society of Pennsylvania, Philadelphia, transcripts.

Bouquet, Henry, Papers, British Museum, transcripts Public Archives of Canada, Ottawa.

Chatham Papers, Public Record Office, London.

Colonial Office, Public Record Office, London, Class 5; Class 323; Class 324.

Croghan, George, Papers, Historical Society of Pennsylvania, Philadelphia, Cadwallader Collection.

Dartmouth, William Legge, Earl of, Papers, William Salt Library, Stafford; transcripts, Illinois Historical Survey, Urbana, Illinois; transcripts M650, Public Archives of Canada, Ottawa.

Dowdeswell, William, Papers, William L. Clements Library, Ann Arbor.
Draper, Lyman C., Collection, Wisconsin Historical Society, Madison.
Egremont, Charles Wyndham, Earl of, Papers, Public Record Office, London. G. D. 47.
Franklin, Benjamin, Papers, American Philosophical Society Library, Philadelphia.
Franklin, Benjamin, Papers, Library of Congress, Washington.
Franklin, Benjamin, and Galloway, Joseph, Letters, William L. Clements Library, Ann Arbor.
Gage, General Thomas, Papers, William L. Clements Library, Ann Arbor.
Grenville, George, Papers, in the possession of Sir John Murray, London.
Haldimand, Frederick, Papers, British Museum, transcripts, Public Archives of Canada, Ottawa.
Hardwicke, Philip Yorke, Earl of, Papers, British Museum.
Huntington Miscellaneous Collection, Henry E. Huntington Library, San Marino, California.
Jenkinson, Charles, Papers, British Museum, London.
Johnson, Sir William, Papers, transcripts, Illinois Historical Survey, Urbana.
Johnson, William Samuel, Papers, Connecticut Historical Society, Hartford, Connecticut.
Knox, William, Papers, William L. Clements Library, Ann Arbor.
Loudoun, James Campbell, Earl of, Papers, Henry E. Huntington Library, San Marino, California.
Morgan, George, Letter Book, 1767–1768, Historical Society of Pennsylvania, Philadelphia.
Newcastle, Thomas Pelham-Holles, Duke of, Papers, British Museum.
Ohio Company Papers (William Trent Papers), Historical Society of Pennsylvania, Philadelphia.
"Papers relating to Indian Losses, 1766–1770," Historical Society of Pennsylvania, Indian Records Collection, 1716–1856.
Privy Council Office, Unbound Papers, transcripts, Illinois Historical Survey, Urbana, Illinois.
Public Archives of Canada, Ottawa, Colonial Office Transcripts, Class 42, Public Record Office, London.
Shelburne, William Petty, Earl of, Papers, William L. Clements Library, Ann Arbor.
State Papers, France, 78, Public Record Office, London.
Stowe Collection, Stowe Americana, Henry E. Huntington Library, San Marino, California. Miscellaneous file; George Grenville Letter Books; boxes 101, 103-abc.
Treasury Board Papers, Public Record Office, London, Class 1; Class 28; Class 29.
War Office, Public Record Office, London, Class 34.
Wharton Manuscript, transcripts, Illinois Historical Survey, Urbana.

Wharton Letterbook, 1773–1784, Historical Society of Pennsylvania, Philadelphia.
Wharton Papers, Historical Society of Pennsylvania, Philadelphia.

PRINTED SOURCE MATERIALS, BRITISH AND CONTINENTAL

A great deal of material on political events is to be found in the *Reports* of the Royal Historical Manuscripts Commission. The papers of Edward Weston, under-secretary to Bute, Grenville, and Halifax are in the Weston-Underwood papers, HMC *Tenth Report,* app., pt. VI (London, 1885). HMC *Report on Various Collections,* VI (London, 1909) has the manuscripts of William Knox. The papers of North's Lord Chancellor are contained in the HMC *Report on the Manuscripts of Earl Bathurst* (London, 1923), 4–25. The HMC *Report on the Manuscripts of the Marquess of Lothian preserved at Blicking Hall, Norfolk* (London, 1905), has some correspondence of political interest between George Grenville and the Earl of Buckinghamshire.

PRINTED DOCUMENTS, STATE PAPERS, AND RECORDS OF PUBLIC OFFICIALS

For the legislation of this period see *Statutes at Large* (Charles Eyre and Andrew Straham, 10 vols., London, 1786). The standard, but totally inadequate, source for the Parliamentary debates is William Cobbett (ed.), *The Parliamentary History of England from the Earliest Period to the Year 1803* (36 vols., London, 1813). [John Almon], *The Debates and proceedings of the British House of Commons . . . 1743–1774* (11 vols., London, 1766–1775) must be used with caution. This is also true of his *The Parliamentary Register; or History of the Proceedings and Debates of the House of Commons* (17 vols., London, 1777). [John Debrett], *The History, debates and proceedings of both houses of Parliament . . . 1743 to 1774* (2 vols., London, 1792) follows Almon for the House of Commons debates. Historians have been blessed with the publication of John Wright (ed.), *Sir Henry Cavendish's debates of the House of Commons, during the thirteenth Parliament . . . commonly called the unreported Parliament . . . 1768–1774* (2 vols., London, 1841–1843). Of special interest is John Wright (ed.), *Debates of the House of Commons in the Year 1774, on the Bill for Making more effectual provision for the government of the Province of Quebec Drawn up from the Notes of the Right Honourable Sir Henry Cavendish* (London, 1839).

The Journals of the House of Commons, Volumes XXVIII–XXXIX, covering the period 1760 to 1774, are based on existing minutes and contain the same information, but in a more convenient arrangement than the official contemporary account, *Votes of the House of Commons,* published by the House. A convenient reference aid is Edward Moore, *A General Index to, or digest of . . . the Journals of the honourable House of Commons* (London, 1778). See also *Reports from Committees of the House of Commons . . . not inserted in the Journals, 1715–1801* (16 vols., London, 1803–1806). Volume 16 is a general index. Unlike the *Votes of the House of Commons,* the *Journals of the House of Lords,* although based on manuscript minutes, were not printed in the eighteenth century. Volumes XXX to XXXIV, dealing with the years 1760 to 1774, may be supplemented by James E. Thorold Rogers, *Complete Collection of the protests of the Lords* (3 vols., Oxford, 1873). A convenient reference aid is Thomas Brodie (comp.), *A General Index to the Journals . . . 1714–1779* (London, 1817).

Various printed collections of material of an official nature are valuable. Benjamin J. Poore (ed.), *Federal and State Constitutions, Colonial Charters . . . of the United States,* rev. ed. (2 vols., Washington, 1878), offers sources for the boundary limits of the colonies and the principal English patents. The volumes of the *Journal of the Lords Commissioners for Trade and Plantations* (London, 1920–1938), arranged by dates, offer merely an outline for the work of the Board of Trade, showing the days on which particular matters were handled, witnesses and documents available to the board. Of the same nature is James Munroe (ed.), *Acts of the Privy Council, Colonial Series* (6 vols., Edinburgh, 1908–1912). Some interdepartmental and ministerial correspondence is printed in Joseph Redington and Richard A. Roberts (eds.), *Calendar of Home Office Papers of the reign of George III, 1760–1775* (4 vols., London, 1878–1899). A valuable printed source for documents of an official nature, but not restricted to this alone, are volumes X, XI, XVI, and XVII of the *Illinois Historical Collections;* Clarence W. Alvord and Clarence E. Carter edited *The Critical Period, 1763–1765* (Springfield, Ill., 1905); *The New Regime, 1765–1767* (Springfield, Ill., 1916); *Trade and Politics, 1767–1769* (Springfield, Ill., 1921); and Theodore C. Pease edited *Anglo-French Boundary Disputes in the West, 1749–1763* (Springfield, Ill., 1936). The last item also contains materials dealing with the peace negotiations drawn from French and Spanish archives. Also valuable for the peace negotiations is L. G. Wickham Legg (ed.), *British Diplomatic Instructions, 1689–1789* (4 vols., London, 1927), vols. XXXV, XXXVIII, XLIII, and XLIX, Royal Historical Society *Publications,* new series.

The correspondence between various departments in London and the Commander-in-Chief in America will be found in Clarence E. Carter (ed.), *The Correspondence of General Thomas Gage* (2 vols., New Haven, 1931–1933). Further Gage material, letters to the commandants in the Illinois country, are printed in Charles Ambler (ed.), "Some Letters and Papers of General Thomas Gage," *The John P. Branch Historical Papers of Randolph-Macon College,* IV (1914), 86–111. For the correspondence of the imperial Indian superintendent for the northern district see James Sullivan *et al.* (eds.), *The Papers of Sir William Johnson* (12 vols., Albany and New York, 1921–1957). See also "Illustrative Letters from the Sir William Johnson Manuscripts," American Antiquarian Society *Proceedings,* XVIII (1906–1907), 404–410; and "Letters of Sir William Johnson to William Franklin," American Antiquarian Society, *Transactions,* XXVII (1934), 1–27.

Valuable for the war period is Gertrude S. Kimball (ed.), *Correspondence of William Pitt, when Secretary of State, with Colonial Governors, and*

Military and Naval Commanders in America (2 vols., New York, 1906). Francis Thackeray's *A History of the Right Honourable William Pitt, Earl of Chatham* (2 vols., London, 1827) is worthless as a biography, but is valuable for the correspondence dealing with the peace negotiations of 1761. For some revealing correspondence of a long-time Secretary-at-War, see Edward Channing and A. C. Coolidge (eds.), *Barrington-Bernard Correspondence, 1760–1770* (Cambridge, Mass., 1912). For materials on British military officials and others during the war see Charles H. Lincoln (ed.), *Correspondence of William Shirley Governor of Massachusetts and Military Commander in America, 1731–1760* (2 vols., New York, 1912); Robert A. Brock (ed.), *The Official Records of Robert Dinwiddie, Lieutenant-Governor of the Colony of Virginia, 1715–1758* (2 vols., Richmond, Va., 1883–1884), and William H. Brown (ed.), *Correspondence of Governor Horatio Sharpe* (3 vols., Baltimore, Md., 1888–1895), vols. VI, IX, and XIV in *Archives of Maryland* (60 vols., Baltimore, Md., 1883—).

Of special interest for the reports of the military are *The Northcliffe Collection* (Ottawa, 1926), containing summaries of the papers of General Robert Monckton and General George Townshend dealing with the fall of New France; Alfred P. James (ed.), *Writings of General John Forbes Relating to His Service in North America* (Pittsburgh, 1938), for the middle years of the war and the campaign against Fort Duquesne; and John C. Webster (ed.), *The Journal of Jeffrey Amherst* (Toronto and Chicago, 1931). For material bearing on the war and shortly thereafter in Pennsylvania see Sylvester K. Stevens and Donald H. Kent (eds.), *The Papers of Colonel Henry Bouquet* (12 vols., Harrisburg, Pa., 1940–1942), a mimeographed edition of the originals in the British Museum; and S. K. Stevens and D. H. Kent (eds.), *Wilderness Chronicles of North Western Pennsylvania* (Harrisburg, Pa., 1941), a collection of documents and papers mainly from the Bouquet Papers and French archives. Some items from the Bouquet Papers have been printed in Helen Jordan (ed.), "Selections from the Military Correspondence of Colonel Henry Bouquet, 1757–1764," *Pennsylvania Magazine of History and Biography,* XXXII (1908), 433–458, XXXIII (1909), 102–107, 216–227. "The Aspinwall Papers," Massachusetts Historical Society *Collections,* 4th series, vols. IX—X (1871), contain military correspondence, principally of Bouquet and Monckton. Further material of this nature from the Bouquet and Haldimand papers will be found in *Michigan Pioneer and Historical Collections,* XIX (1891), 27–28, 295–676. Letters from officers commanding the western posts are printed in the "Gladwin Manuscripts," *ibid.,* XXVII (1896), 605–680, while papers concerning Indian affairs are to be found in *ibid.,* XX (1892), 300–704. Stanley M. Pargellis (ed.), *Military Affairs in North America, 1748–1765: Selected Documents from the Cumberland Papers in Windsor Castle* (New York, 1936), is extremely valuable for the views of officers and Indian officials on the interior.

Various documents by British officials concerning American policy for the interior have been printed. Clarence E. Carter edited "Observations of Superintendent John Stuart and Governor James Grant of East Florida on the

Proposed Plan of 1764 for the Future Management of Indian Affairs," *American Historical Review,* XX (1915), 815–831, while R. A. Humphreys edited "Governor [James] Murray's Views on the Plan of 1764 for the Management of Indian Affairs," *Canadian Historical Review,* XVI (1935), 162–169. Some material on British army administration of the interior will be found in Florence G. Watts, "Some Vincennes Documents of 1772," *Indiana Magazine of History,* XXXIV (1938), 199–212; Clarence E. Carter, "Documents relating to the occupation of the Illinois Country by the British Army," Illinois State Historical Society, *Transactions for 1907* (Springfield, 1908); Reuben G. Thwaites (ed.), *The British Regime in Wisconsin, Collections* of the State Historical Society of Wisconsin, XVIII (1908), 223–468. In editing the "Hints relative to the Division and Government of the Conquered and Newly Acquired Countries in America," *Mississippi Valley Historical Review,* VIII (1922), 367–373, Verner W. Crane ascribed authorship to Henry Ellis.

Several documents have been published bearing on the interior fortifications. See "Captain [Harry] Gordon's Views of the British Military Establishment in America," *Mississippi Valley Historical Review,* XV (1928), 92–95; William R. Riddell (ed.), "Last Official Report on the French Posts in Northern Parts of North America," Ontario Historical Society *Papers and Records,* XXVIII (1932), 132–139; and W. R. Riddell (ed.), "Last Official Report on the French Posts in the Northern Part of America. Translation of the Portion of Special Interest in Pennsylvania," *Pennsylvania Magazine of History and Biography,* LVI (1932), 56–67.

Materials on the colonial agents in London are pertinent on a number of points. Lewis B. Namier, "Charles Garth, Agent for South Carolina," *English Historical Review,* LIV (1939), 632–652, is valuable for the correspondence reporting the conference between Grenville and the agents on the Stamp Act. In this connection, see also the correspondence between Thomas Whately and John Temple printed in "Bowdoin and Temple Papers," Massachusetts Historical Society *Collections,* 6th series, vol. IX. For material in the correspondence of other agents on colonial policy see "Trumbull Papers," *ibid.,* 5th ser., vols. IX–X; Albert Mathews (ed.), "Letters of Dennys De Berdt, 1757–1770," *Publications* of the Colonial Society of Massachusetts, XIII (1910), 293–461; *Jasper Mauduit, agent in London for the province of Massachusetts-Bay, 1762–1765,* Massachusetts Historical Society *Collections,* LXXIV (Boston, 1918); Franklin B. Dexter (ed.), "A selection from the correspondence and miscellaneous papers of Jared Ingersoll," New Haven Colony Historical Society, *Papers,* IX (New Haven, 1918), 201–472; and vols. XVII–XIX of the Connecticut Historical Society *Collections* edited by Albert Bates, *The Pitkin Papers . . . 1766–1769* (Hartford, Conn., 1921), and *The Fitch Papers* (2 vols., Hartford, 1918–1920).

PRINTED SOURCES, PRIVATE, GREAT BRITAIN

There are several editions of the correspondence of George III. W. E. Donne (ed.), *The Correspondence of George III with Lord North, 1768–1783*

(2 vols., London, 1867), has been superseded. Bonomy Dobrée (ed.), *The Correspondence of King George III* (London, 1935) is still valuable for the editorial comments. Sir John Fortescue (ed.), *The Correspondence of King George the Third, from 1760 to December 1783, Printed from the Original Papers in the Royal Archives at Windsor Castle* (6 vols., London, 1927), is poorly edited and replete with errors. In this connection see Lewis B. Namier, *Additions and Corrections to Sir John Fortescue's Edition of the Correspondence of King George The Third (Vol. I)* (Manchester, England, 1937). Brilliantly edited by Romney Sedgwick, the *Letters from George III to Lord Bute, 1756–1766* (London, 1939), illustrates the almost pathological early relationship between the immature prince and his "dearest Friend."

For the elder Pitt, see W. S. Taylor and J. H. Pringle (eds.), *Correspondence of William Pitt, Earl of Chatham* (4 vols., London, 1838–1840), the standard collection. Of value also is Romney Sedgwick (ed.), "Letters from William Pitt to Lord Bute, 1755–1758," in Richard Pares and A. J. P. Taylor (eds.), *Essays Presented to Sir Lewis Namier* (London, 1956), which reveal the relationship between Pitt and the Leicester House faction before Pitt "arrived." William J. Smith (ed.), *The Grenville Papers, being the Correspondence of Richard Grenville Earl Temple, K.G., and the Right Hon. George Grenville, their Friends and Contemporaries* (4 vols., London, 1852–1853), and Ninetta Jucker (ed.), *The Jenkinson Papers, 1760–1766* (London, 1949) are extremely valuable for the politics of the period, but have little information on the colonial policies of George Grenville.

Several works contain material on the Whigs. Sir Richard Bourke and Charles William Earl Fitzwilliam (eds.), *Correspondence of the right honourable Edmund Burke* (4 vols., London, 1844), is disappointing. Very revealing, on the other hand, are the letters printed in Ross J. S. Hoffman (ed.), *Edmund Burke, New York Agent, with . . . Intimate Correspondence with Charles O'Hara* (Philadelphia, 1956). These contain Burke's almost spontaneous comments on politics and the workings of the Rockingham faction. See also the two volumes of Burke material, T. W. Copeland and L. S. Sutherland (eds.), *The Correspondence of Edmund Burke* (2 vols., Chicago, 1958–1960). In this connection see also Mary Bateson (ed.), *A Narrative of the changes in the ministry, 1765–1768, told by the Duke of Newcastle in a series of letters to John White, M. P.,* Camden Society *Publications,* new ser., LIX (London and New York, 1898); and George Thomas Keppel, Sixth Earl of Albemarle, *Memoirs of the Marquis of Rockingham and his contemporaries. With original Letters and Documents now first published* (2 vols., London, 1852). Another source for the Whig group is Philip Chesney Yorke, *The Life and Correspondence of Philip Yorke, Earl of Hardwicke, Lord High Chancellor of Great Britain* (3 vols., Cambridge, England, 1913). For some additional materials, see George Harris, *The Life of Lord Chancellor Hardwicke with Selections from his Correspondence, Diaries, Speeches, and Judgments* (3 vols., London, 1847); Sir William Anson (ed.), *The Autobiography and political correspondence of Augustus Henry, third Duke of Grafton, K.G. from hitherto unpublished documents in the possession of his family*

(London, 1898); and *Correspondence of John, 4th Duke of Bedford* (intro. by Lord John Russell, 3 vols., London, 1842–1846).

For material of the political figures at one time or another connected with Bute, see William Mure (ed.), *Caldwell Family Papers, Selections from the family papers preserved at Caldwell,* Maitland Club *Publications* (2 vols., in 3 pts., Glasgow, 1854); James Oswald, *Memorials of the public life and character of the Right Honourable James Oswald of Dunnikier contained in a correspondence with some of the most distinguished men of the last century* (Edinburgh, 1825); Lord Edmund Fitzmaurice, *Life of William, Earl of Shelburne, afterwards first Marquess of Lansdowne, With Extracts from his papers and correspondence* (3 vols., London, 1875); and Henry Fox's "Memoir on the Events Attending the Death of George II And The Accession of George III," in Countess of Ilchester and Lord Stavordale (eds.), *Life and Letters of Lady Sarah Lennox, 1745–1826* (2 vols., London, 1902). For other materials on the elder Fox see the correspondence printed in Giles Steven Holland Fox-Strangways, 6th Earl of Ilchester, *Henry Fox, First Lord Holland, His Family and Relations* (2 vols., New York, 1920), and *Letters to Henry Fox Lord Holland with a Few Addressed to His Brother Stephen, Earl of Ilchester* (London, 1915), which is extremely revealing on the reformation of the ministry in September, 1763.

The best edition of the correspondence of Chesterfield, an acute political observer, is Bonomy Dobrée (ed.), *Letters of William Stanhope, Earl of Chesterfield* (6 vols., London, 1932). For devastating commentaries on English politics from north of the Tweed see G. Birkbeck Hill (ed.), *Letters of David Hume to William Strahan* (Oxford, 1888); Joseph Y. T. Grieg (ed.), *The Letters of David Hume* (2 vols., Oxford, 1932); and Raymond Kilbansky and Ernest C. Mosser (eds.), *New Letters of David Hume* (Oxford, 1954).

Robert Henley, *Memoir of the life of Robert Henley, Earl of Northington, lord high chancellor of Great Britain* (London, 1831), and Claud Nugent, *Memoirs of Robert, Earl Nugent* (London, 1898) are of limited use for the political scene. James Waldegrave, second Earl of Waldergrave, *Memoirs from 1754–1758* (London, 1821), has some valuable material on the youth of George III and the men associated with the Leicester House faction. On the whole, *William Wildman Viscount Barrington, Political Life, compiled from Original Papers by his brother, Shute, Bishop of Durham* (London, 1814) is disappointing. Oscar Browning (ed.), *The Political memoranda of Francis, fifth duke of Leeds, now first printed from the originals in the British Museum,* Royal Historical Society *Publications,* new ser., XXXV (London, 1884), barely touches on the period under consideration.

Often inaccurate but at times valuable are the works of Horace Walpole. His *Journal of the reign of King George the third, from the years 1771 to 1783,* ed. by Dr. Doran (2 vols., London, 1859), and re-edited by Archibald Francis Steuart, as *The Last Journals of Horace Walpole during the reign of George III* (2 vols., London, 1910), must be used with caution. A critical examination will be found in Carl L. Becker, "Horace Walpole's Memoirs of the Reign of George the Third," *American Historical Review,* XVI (1911),

255, 496. For Walpole's views of the period from 1760 to 1771 see George Fisher Russell Barker (ed.), *Memoirs of the Reign of King George the Third* (4 vols., London, 1894). For Walpole's more spontaneous observations, see W. S. Lewis, *et al.* (eds.), *Yale Edition of the Horace Walpole Correspondence* (14 vols., New Haven, 1940—). A more convenient chronological arrangement will be found in Mrs. Paget Toynbee (ed.), *Letters of Horace Walpole* (16 vols., Oxford, 1903).

BRITISH PAMPHLETS

The Quebec Act was the subject of some pamphlet literature. See, for example, *An address to the Right Honourable L[or]d M[an]sf[iel]d; in which the measures of government, respecting America, are considered in a new light with a view to His Lordship's interposition therein* (London, J. Almon, 1775); *A Letter to the Earl of Chatham, on the Quebec bill* (London, T. Cadell, 1774), attributed to Sir William Meredith and to Thomas, Baron Lyttelton; and *Thoughts on the act for making more effectual provision for the government of the province of Quebec, asserted and proved; and the conduct of the administration respecting that province stated and vindicated* (London, J. Wilkie, 1774).

The Vandalia issue and matters relating to Indian titles and interior settlements saw some pamphlets issued. They represented, for the most part, propaganda efforts on the part of the Walpole group.

[Samuel Wharton?], "Statement for the Petitioners in the case of the Walpole Company," [London, 1772], transcript in the Illinois Historical Survey of a pamphlet with no title page in the John Carter Brown Library.

[Samuel Wharton, and/or Benjamin Franklin], *Report of the Lords Commissioners for trade and plantations on the petition of the Honourable Thomas Walpole, Benjamin Franklin, John Sargeant, and Samuel Wharton, esquires, and their associates: for a grant of lands on the river Ohio in North America; for the purpose of erecting a new government. With observations and remarks* (London, 1772); the rebuttal drawn up to be used before the committee of the Privy Council against the Board of Trade report.

[Samuel Wharton], *Considerations on the Agreement of the Lords Commissioners of his Majesty's Treasury with the Honourable Thomas Walpole and Associates, for lands upon the Ohio, in North America* (London, 1774), the arguments of the Walpole group against the objections of the Crown Law Officers.

[Samuel Wharton and Edward Bancroft], *View of the Title to Indiana, a tract of Country on the River Ohio: Containing Indian conferences at Johnson Hall in May, 1765 . . . the Deed of the Six Nations to the Proprietors of Indiana—the minutes of the Congress at Fort Stanwix in October and November, 1768—the Deed of the Indians, settling the boundary line be-*

tween the English and Indian lands—and the Opinion of the Council on the Title of the Proprietors of Indiana (London, 1775, Philadelphia, 1776). Wharton's appeal to the Continental Congress after the failure of the lobby in London.

[Thomas Walpole], *The Memorial of the Honourable Thomas Walpole, in Behalf of himself and the Earl of Hertford, Earl Temple, the Right Honourable Charles Lord Camden, the Honourable Richard Walpole, the Honourable Robert Walpole, Sir Harry Featherstonehaugh, Baronet, Sir George Colebrooke, Baronet, Thomas Pitt, Esq. Richard Jackson, Esq. John Sargeant, Esq. and Samuel Wharton, Esq. and their Associates* (London, 1774), the last petition of the Vandalia group for confirmation of the grant.

SOURCES, COLONIAL

State Collections of Documents and Papers of Public Officials.

Reference should be made to previously mentioned works in British sources for material of colonial origin. A valuable collection is Peter Force (ed.), *American Archives: Consisting of a Collection of Authentick Records, State Papers, Debates, and Letters and Other Notices of Public Affairs, the Whole Forming A Documentary History of the Origin and Progress of the North American Colonies: of the Causes and Accomplishments of the American Revolution; and of the Constitution of the Government of the United States, to the Final Ratification Thereof* (9 vols., Washington, 1837–1853). This set was to consist of six series, but the first three never appeared, the fifth was left unfinished, and the sixth was never undertaken. The fourth series (6 vols., Washington, 1837–1846) covers the period from March 7, 1774, to July 4, 1776. The fifth series (3 vols., Washington, 1848–1853) was left unfinished and ends with the year 1776.

The first of the great state collections was Edmund B. O'Callaghan and Berthold Fernow (eds.), *Documents relative to the colonial history of the state of New York* (15 vols., Albany and New York, 1856–1887), which includes correspondence and papers of the New York governors, the Indian superintendent, the Board of Trade, Secretaries of State, Orders-in-Council and Board of Trade reports. Edmund B. O'Callaghan also edited *The Documentary history of the State of New York* (4 vols., Albany, 1850–1851), which contains some material of interest in this study. See also *Letters and Papers of Cadwalader Colden . . . between 1760 and 1776* published at large in the New York Historical Society *Collections* (11 vols., New York, 1877–1936); *Letter book of John Watts, Merchant and Councillor of New York,* vol. LXI of New York Historical Society *Collections* (New York, 1928); and *The Lee Papers, 1754 [–1811]*, vols. IV–VII of New York Historical Society *Collections* (4 vols., New York, 1872–1875).

Arthur S. Doughty and Adam Shortt (eds.), *Documents relating to the constitutional history of Canada, 1759–1791* (Ottawa, 1907), prints papers of the Board of Trade, correspondence of the governors of Canada and the

Secretaries of State in addition to holdings from the Dartmouth Papers. Some additional material is to be found in W. P. Kennedy (ed.), *Documents of the Canadian Constitution* (Toronto, 1918).

A well edited and extensive collection is William Brown *et al.* (eds.), *Archives of Maryland,* Maryland Historical Society (60 vols., Baltimore, 1883—). Various volumes contain the correspondence of Governor Horatio Sharpe. See also "Correspondence of Governor Robert Eden, with the American Secretaries," *Maryland Historical Magazine,* II (1902), 1–13, 97–110, 227–244, and 293–309.

Circular letters to the colonial governors, Board of Trade reports, and Orders-in-Council will be found in Frederick W. Ricord and William Nelson (eds.), *Archives of the State of New Jersey* (36 vols., Newark, 1881–1941). See especially the first series *Documents relating to the Colonial History of the State of New Jersey,* vols. IX (Newark, 1885), and X (Newark, 1886), dealing with the administrations of President John Reading and Governor William Franklin, 1757–1776.

Henry R. McIlwaine and John P. Kennedy have edited *Journals of the House of Burgesses of Virginia [1619–1776]* (13 vols., Richmond, Va., 1905–1913), which contain some correspondence between the Virginia governors and the Secretaries of State. A major source for printed materials is *Pennsylvania Archives,* 9 series (Philadelphia and Harrisburg, 1852—). The materials for this study, in the form of miscellaneous letters and papers of the governors, military commanders, Secretaries of State, and Indian agents, are found in volumes I–IV of the first series, and in volumes VI–VIII of the second series. For additional material see also *Minutes of the Provincial Council of Pennsylvania, 1693–1776,* 10 vols. in *Colonial Records of Pennsylvania* (16 vols., Harrisburg, 1851–1853). See especially vols. IX–X for messages of the governors, military commanders, and Secretaries of State to the assembly of the province.

Dunbar Rowland (ed.), *Mississippi Provincial Archives, 1763–1766* (Nashville, Tenn., 1911), was the first volume of a projected series, never extended, of documents in the Public Record Office. It contains correspondence of the governors and military commanders in West Florida of interest for the area of the lower Mississippi River. In this connection, see also the correspondence printed in Mrs. Dunbar Rowland, "Peter Chester Third Governor of the Province of British West Florida under British Dominion, 1770–1781," *Publications* of the Mississippi Historical Society, V (1925).

PUBLISHED COLONIAL SOURCES, PRIVATE

Several important collections have been printed containing materials on the activities of colonial land speculators. Kenneth P. Bailey (ed.), *The Ohio Company Papers, 1753–1817, Being Primarily Papers of the "Suffering Traders" of Pennsylvania* (Arcata, Calif., 1947), contains letters from the Historical Society of Pennsylvania collections of William Trent, George Croghan, and the Gratz family. The editing leaves something to be desired. James C.

Ballagh (ed.), *The Letters of Richard Henry Lee* (2 vols., New York, 1911–1914), has information on the Mississippi Company. See also Clarence E. Carter (ed.), "Documents Relating to the Mississippi Land Company, 1763–1774," *American Historical Review,* XVI (1911), 311–319; and Richard Henry Lee, *Life of Arthur Lee . . . with his political and literary correspondence and his papers* (2 vols., Boston, 1829). Archibald Henderson's "Dr. Thomas Walker and the Loyal Land Company of Virginia," American Antiquarian Society *Proceedings,* new ser., XLI (1931), 77–178, is an uncritical and sympathetic account of value for the documents printed from the Draper Collection.

Some of the correspondence of George Croghan is printed in "Letters of Colonel George Croghan [to Thomas Wharton]," *Pennsylvania Magazine of History and Biography,* XV (1891), 429–439; and William E. Lingelbach, "William Trent calls on Benjamin Franklin," *ibid.,* LXIV (1950), 43–50. Material on land speculation and especially on the Vandalia project will be found in "Some Letters of Franklin's Correspondents," *ibid.,* XXVII (1903), 150–175; Charles Henry Hart (ed.), "Letters from William Franklin to William Strahan," *ibid.,* XXXV (1911), 415–462; "Correspondence between William Strahan and David Hall, 1763–1777," *ibid.,* XII (1888), 116–122, 240–251; X (1886), 86–99, 217–232, 322–333, 461–463; XI (1887), 98–111, 223–243, 346–357, 482–489; J. E. Pomfret (ed.), "Some further letters of William Strahan Printer," *ibid.,* LX (1936), 455–489; and "Selections from the Letter-book of Thomas Wharton of Philadelphia, 1773–1783," *ibid.,* XXXIII (1909), 319–339; XXXIV (1910), 41–61.

For documents on the Connecticut land speculators, see Julian P. Boyd *et al.* (eds.), *The Susquehanna Company Papers,* Sheldon Reynolds *Memorial Publications of the Wyoming Historical and Genealogical Society* (4 vols., Wilkes-Barre, Pa., 1930–1933). For various other land speculating ventures see Lois Mulkearn (ed.), *George Mercer Papers relating to the Ohio Company of Virginia* (Pittsburgh, 1954); and Kate M. Rowland, *The life of George Mason, 1725–1792, including his speeches, public papers, and correspondence* (2 vols., New York, 1892). The best sources for Franklin's interests are Albert H. Smyth (ed.), *The Writings of Benjamin Franklin* (10 vols., New York, 1907); John Bigelow (ed.), *Works of Franklin* (12 vols., New York, 1904); and Carl Van Doren (ed.), *Letters and Papers of Benjamin Franklin and Richard Jackson, 1753–1785* (Philadelphia, 1947).

On Washington see John C. Fitzpatrick (ed.), *George Washington's Diaries, 1748–1799* (4 vols., Boston, 1925). Fitzpatrick also edited *The Writings of George Washington from the original manuscript sources 1745–1799* (39 vols., Washington, 1931–1944). Of special interest for this study is Consul W. Butterfield (ed.), *Washington-Crawford Letters. Being the correspondence Between George Washington and William Crawford, from 1767 to 1781 concerning western lands* (Cincinnati, O., 1877). For other letters see Stanislaus Hamilton (ed.), *Letters to Washington and Accompanying Papers* (5 vols., Boston, 1898–1902).

Peter O. Hutchinson (ed.), *Diary and Letters of Thomas Hutchinson* (2 vols., London, 1883–1886), is valuable for the items in the diary reflecting the reaction of British officials to the American crisis in 1774. Wilbur R. Jacobs (ed.), *Indians of the Southern Colonial Frontier: The Edmund Atkin Report and Plan of 1755* (Columbia, S. C., 1954), the description given British officials of the relationship of the tribes and the various colonies. For the proposals dealing with the interior and presented by Henry McCulloch to Bute in 1761 see "Miscellaneous Representations Relative to our Concerns in America," in William Boyd (ed.), *Some Eighteenth Century Tracts Concerning North Carolina* (Raleigh, N. C., 1927), 149–156. Material for the activities of the agents for the Canadian merchants and traders will be found in William S. Wallace (ed.), *Maseres Letters, 1766–1768* (Toronto, 1919). Some valuable correspondence of Arthur St. Clair, agent for the Penns in the controversy with Dunmore and Croghan for jurisdiction over the left bank of the upper Ohio, will be found in William H. Smith (ed.), *The Life and Public Services of Arthur St. Clair, Soldier of the Revolutionary War: President of the Continental Congress: and Governor of the North-western Territory, with his Correspondence and other Papers* (2 vols., Cincinnati, O., 1882).

COLONIAL PAMPHLETS

For the publications of land speculators during the colonial and early national period see:

[Samuel Wharton], *Plain Facts: Being an Examination into the Rights of the Indian Nations of America, to their respective countries: and a Vindication of the Grant, from the Six Nations of Indians; to the Proprietors of Indiana, against the Decision of the Legislature of Virginia, together with Authentic Documents proving that the Territory Westward of the Allegheny Mountains, never belonged to Virginia, etc.* (Philadelphia, 1781).

An account of the proceedings of the Illinois and Wabash land companies, in pursuance of their purchase made of the independent natives, July 5th, 1773, and 18th October, 1775 (Philadelphia, 1786).

Memorial of the United Illinois and Wabash Land Companies, to the Senate and House of Representatives of the United States (Baltimore, 1816).

TRAVEL ACCOUNTS AND JOURNALS

The standard collection of travel accounts for western America is Reuben G. Thwaites (ed.), *Early Western Travels* (32 vols., Cleveland, O., 1904–1907). But indispensable is Thomas O. Clark (ed.), *Travels in the Old South: A Bibliography* (2 vols., Norman, Okla., 1956). For specific items of interest and the reactions of the acute Swedish observer and sometimes French agent, see Peter Kalm, *Travels into North America,* translated by John R. Forster, 2nd ed. (2 vols., London, 1772). The account of Gage's chief military engineer will be found in "Journal of Captain Harry Gordon, 1766," in Newton D. Mereness (ed.), *Travels in the American Colonies* (New York, 1916), 464–489.

The various descriptions given by Major Robert Rogers, partisan leader and one-time commandant at Michillimackinac, must be used with discretion. See Robert Rogers, *A concise account of North America: Containing a description of the several British colonies on that continent . . . also of the interior or westernly parts . . .* (Dublin, J. Miliken, 1769), and Franklin B. Hough (ed.), *Journals of Major Robert Rogers* (Albany, 1883). The latter is valuable for the British occupation of the western forts in the winter of 1760. For other accounts see Jonathan Carver, *Travels through the Interior Parts of North America in the Years, 1766, 1767, and 1768* (London, T. Payne, 1775), and "The Narrative of Peter Pond," in Charles M. Gates (ed.), *Five Fur Traders of the Northwest* (London and Toronto, 1933), 11–59. Alexander Henry, *Travels and adventures in Canada and the Indian Territories between the years 1760 and 1776* (2 pts. New York, 1809), new ed. by James Bain (Toronto, 1911), is often inaccurate and must be used with discrimination.

Several reliable accounts of travelers in the interior are of note. See William M. Darlington (ed.), *Christopher Gist's Journal with historical, geographical and ethnological notes and biographies of his contemporaries* (Pittsburgh, 1893); Howard H. Peckham (ed.), *George Croghan's Journal of His Trip to Detroit in 1767 With His Correspondence Relating Thereto: Now Published for the First Time from the Papers of General Thomas Gage in the William L. Clements Library* (Ann Arbor and London, 1939); Nicholas B. Wainwright (ed.), "George Croghan's Journal 1759–1763 from the original in the Cadwallader Collection of the Historical Society of Pennsylvania," *Pennsylvania Magazine of History and Biography,* LXXXI (1947), 305–444; [John Jennings], "Journal from Fort Pitt to Fort Chartres in the Illinois Country, March–April, 1766," *ibid.,* XXXI (1907), 145–156; and "John Jennings' Journal at Fort Chartres and Trip to New Orleans, 1768," *ibid.,* XXXI (1907), 304–310; and Albert T. Volwiler (ed.), "William Trent's Journal at Fort Pitt, 1763," *Mississippi Valley Historical Review,* XI (1924), 390–413.

SECONDARY WORKS

British Political History in the Reign of George III

Modern historiography of the eighteenth-century politics may be divided into two phases, the first having its tradition extending into the nineteenth century. Basil Williams, *The Whig Supremacy, 1716–1760* (Oxford, 1939), probably the best introduction to the period, carries the narrative to the conclusion of the Peace of Paris. The student may consult two works by Dennys A. Winstanley, *Personal and Party Government, A Chapter in the Political History of the Early Years of the Reign of George III, 1760–1766* (Cambridge, England, 1910), and *Lord Chatham and the Whig Opposition* (Cambridge, 1912). Winstanley is generally friendly to the opposition groups. C. Grant Robertson, *England under the Hanoverians,* 16th ed. (London, 1949), is the best one-volume work of the period from the traditional viewpoint.

Bibliography

From the time of its publication, Lewis B. Namier's *The Structure of Politics at the Accession of George III* (2 vols., London, 1929), has revolutionized the historiography of not only the political history of the reign of George III, but of the eighteenth century as a whole. A one-volume revised edition was published in 1957. See also "Monarchy and the Party System," "King George III: a Study of Personality," and "Country Gentlemen in Parliament," in L. B. Namier, *Personalities and Powers* (New York, 1955). Namier has also authored "The Circular Letter; an eighteenth century whip to members of Parliament," *English Historical Review,* XLIV (1929), 588–611; and "Charles Garth and His Connections," *ibid.,* LIV (1939), 443–470. Namier's detailed study of politics from 1760 to 1763, based on the Newcastle papers and the Bute manuscripts, *England in the Age of the American Revolution* (London, 1930), should be read with his *Structure of Politics.*

Richard Pares has written a series of brilliant essays, *George III and the Politicians* (Oxford, 1953). Interpretive and functional, they are the best introduction to the study of politics in the second half of the eighteenth century. An intelligent and incisive view is given in Keith Feiling, *The Second Tory Party, 1760–1832* (London, 1938), a Tory interpretation. Two of the most striking examples of the Namierian school are represented by very recent works. J. Brooke, *The Chatham Administration, 1766–1768* (London, 1956), is more of a history of the political maneuvering of the opposition during this period than anything else. While sound on research, it is open to question on interpretation. Brooke acknowledges the importance of the American issue in the ministry, but he makes little attempt to deal with the problem. The student may refer to Winstanley for this period. Although properly speaking Eric Robson's *The American Revolution in Its Political and Military Aspects, 1763–1783* (New York, 1955), does not belong in a discussion of political works, it is so included because it represents one aspect of the Namierian school in the extreme. Blatantly royalist in viewpoint, it is of little use in its interpretations of the American Revolution. It confuses the polemics of the colonial patriots with the position of the English Whigs of 1782–1784. It is basically a defense of the political system of George III against the "aristocratic" doctrines of government as set forth by Burke and Charles James Fox.

BRITISH GOVERNMENTAL INSTITUTIONS

Edward and Ann G. Porritt, *The Unreformed House of Commons* (2 vols., Cambridge, 1903), and Arthur S. Turberville, *The House of Lords in the XVIII Century* (Oxford, 1927), are the standard works on the subject of Parliament. At times inaccurate, they should be checked with the volumes by Namier. No modern study using the Namierian approach has appeared on the institutions of the cabinet and the Privy Council. The student may use Edward R. Turner, *The Privy Council of England in the Seventeenth and Eighteenth Centuries* (2 vols., Baltimore, 1927–1928); and *The Cabinet Council in England in the Seventeenth and Eighteenth Centuries, 1622–1784* (2 vols., Baltimore, 1930–1932). See also E. R. Turner's "The Cabinet in the Eighteenth Century," *English Historical Review,* XXXII (1917), 192–203; William R. Anson, "The Cabinet in the Seventeenth and Eighteenth Centuries," *ibid.,* XXIX (1914), 56–78; and H. W. V. Temperly, "Inner and Outer Cabinet and Privy Council, 1679–1783," *ibid.,* XXVII (1912), 682–699. A scholarly study of an important office is Mark A. Thompson, *The Secretaries of State, 1681–1782* (Oxford, 1932).

IMPERIAL ADMINISTRATION

An excellent study is to be found in Arthur S. Basye, *The Lords Commissioners of Trade and Plantations Commonly Known as the Board of Trade, 1748–1782* (New Haven, 1925). Margaret M. Spector, *The American Department of British Government, 1768–1782* (New York, 1940), is the best work on the Colonial Office, but see also A. S. Basye, "The Secretary of State for the Colonies," *American Historical Review,* XXVIII (1922), 12–23; and Mary Patterson Clark, "The Board of Trade at Work," *ibid.,* XVII (1911), 17–43. Dora Mae Clark's "The British Treasury and the Administration of Military Affairs in America, 1754–1774," *Pennsylvania History,* II (1935), 197–204, is too cursory a treatment for so complex a subject.

Clarence E. Carter, "The Significance of the Military Office in America, 1763–1775," *American Historical Review,* XXVII (1923), 475–488, argues that the commander-in-chief was intended to exercise the functions of a viceroy. The view is ably contested in John R. Alden, *John Stuart and the Southern Colonial Frontier, A study of Indian Relations, War, Trade, and Land Problems in the Southern Wilderness, 1754–1775* (Ann Arbor, 1944), 144–155. See also Alden's "The Albany Congress and the Creation of the Indian Superintendencies," *Mississippi Valley Historical Review,* XXVII (1940), 193–210.

George L. Beer, *British Colonial Policy, 1754–1765* (New York, 1907), a pioneer study in the field, is dated, as is Oliver Morton Dickerson, *American Colonial Government, 1696–1765: a study of the British Board of Trade in its relation to the American Colonies, political, industrial, administrative* (Cleveland, 1912). A good survey of a controversial topic for this study is given in Beverly W. Bond, Jr., *The Quitrent System in the American Colonies* (New Haven, 1919). Eugene K. Klauss, *British Colonial Theories, 1570–1859* (Toronto, 1944), treats of both mercantilism and opposition to it.

THE FIRST BRITISH EMPIRE

The best introduction to the subject, containing a critical analysis of the literature to date, will be found in Vincent T. Harlow, *The Founding of the Second British Empire, 1763–1793* (London and New York, 1952). J. Holland Rose, A. P. Newton, and E. A. Benians (eds.), *The Cambridge History of the British Empire* (8 vols., New York and Cambridge, 1929–1940), the standard multivolume work, is dated. Lawrence H. Gipson, *The British Empire before the American Revolution* (9 vols., Caldwell, Idaho, and New York, 1936—), in progress, is the most extensive work on the subject, but while authoritative at points, it is uneven in a few places.

Certain regional studies are significant. A. L. Burt's *Old Province of Quebec* (Minneapolis, Minn., 1937), is a good one-volume treatment of Canada during the first era of British rule. Also useful are the volumes in Adam Shortt and Arthur J. Doughty, *Canada and Its Provinces* (22 vols., Toronto, 1914–1917), and William Kingsford, *The History of Canada, 1608–1841* (10 vols., 1887–1898). For the relationship of Canada to the upper country, see John B. Brebner, *North Atlantic Triangle* (New Haven, 1945), and D. C. Creighton, *The Commercial Empire of the St. Lawrence, 1760–1850* (New Haven, 1937).

Several excellent studies are available for the coast of the Gulf of Mexico and the lower Mississippi River regions: C. N. Howard, *The British Development of West Florida, 1763–1769* (Berkeley and Los Angeles, 1947); Cecil Johnson, *British West Florida, 1763–1783* (New Haven, 1947), and Charles Lock Mowat, *East Florida as a British Province, 1763–1774* (Berkeley, 1943).

The leading writer in the field of the interior country under British rule has been Clarence W. Alvord. Unfortunately, his *Mississippi Valley in British Politics* (2 vols., Cleveland, Ohio, 1917), is at many points unsound. For a fuller discussion, see J. M. Sosin, "The North American Interior in British Colonial Policy, 1760–1775," dissertation, Department of History, Indiana University, 1958. Alvord's other efforts in this field exhibit the same faults. His "British Ministry and the Treaty of Fort Stanwix," Wisconsin State Historical Society *Proceedings,* LVI (1909), 163–183, is corrected in part by Ray A. Billington, "The Ft. Stanwix Treaty of 1768," *New York History,* XXV (1944), 182–194. For correctives to Alvord's "Genesis of the Proclamation of 1763," *Michigan Pioneer and Historical Collections,* XXXVI (1908), 2–52; his "Lord Shelburne and the Founding of British American Goodwill," *Proceedings of the British Academy,* XI (1924–1925), 369–396; as well as Charles H. Metzger's "An Appraisal of Shelburne's Western Policy," *Mid-America,* IX (1937), 169–181, which follows Alvord closely, see a series of articles by R. A. Humphreys, "Lord Shelburne and a projected Recall of Colonial Governors in 1767," *American Historical Review,* XXXVII (1932), 269–272; "Lord Shelburne and British Colonial Policy, 1766–1768," *English Historical Review,* L (1935), 257–277; and "Lord Shelburne and the Proclamation of 1763," *ibid.,* XLIX (1934), 241–264. Even Humphreys does not state as strong a case against Alvord as could be made. Many of the accounts of British rule in the interior which follow Alvord must be used with caution; Nelson V. Russell, *The British Regime in Michigan and the Old Northwest, 1760–1796* (Northfield, Minn., 1939); W. R. Riddle, *Michigan under British Rule: Law and Law Courts, 1760–1796* (Lansing, Mich., 1926); and Louise P. Kellogg, *The British Regime in Wisconsin and the Northwest* (Madison, Wisc., 1935).

Duncan McArthur, "The British Board of Trade and Canada, 1760–1774: The Proclamation of 1773 [*sic*]," Canadian Historical Association *Annual Report for 1932,* pp. 97–113, offers little evidence for the view that Shelburne was significant in a policy role. Max Farrand, "The Indian Boundary Line," *American Historical Review,* X (1905), 782–791, is a general sketch. A good treatment of British administration and policy for Canada may be found in R. A. Humphreys and Morley S. Scott, "Lord Northington and the Laws of Canada," *Canadian Historical Review,* XIV (1933), *ibid.,* I (1930), 166–186; and William S. Wallace, "The Beginning of British Rule in Canada," *ibid.,* VI (1925), 208–221.

For an important consideration bearing on British policy, see George R. Mellor, "Emigration from the British Isles to the New World, 1765–1775," *History,* new ser., XL (1955), 68–83; and Frank Spencer, "An Eighteenth Century Account of German Emigration to the American Colonies," *Journal of Modern History,* XXVIII (1956), 55–59.

Douglas S. Brown, "The Iberville Canal Project: Its Relation to the Anglo-French Commercial Rivalry in the Mississippi Valley, 1763–1775," *Mississippi Valley Historical Review,* XXXII (1946), 491–516, deals with the difficulty faced in the navigation of the interior water routes. Brief summaries of British land policy will be found in Burke A. Hinsdale, "The Western Land Policy of the British Government from 1763–1775," *Ohio Archaeological and Historical Quarterly,* I (1887), 207–229, and Herbert C. Laub, "British Regulation of Crown Lands in the West: the Last Phase, 1773–1775," *William and Mary Quarterly,* 2nd ser., X (1930), 52–55.

THE REVOLUTIONARY BACKGROUND

The literature on this subject is voluminous and no attempt will be made at an extensive discussion. Charles Ritcheson, *British Politics and the American Revolution* (Norman, Okla., 1954), is at times too facile and hasty in generalization. Of questionable validity is Dora Mae Clark, *British Opinion and the American Revolution* (New Haven, 1930), which is based on newspaper, magazine, and pamphlet literature. The representative and responsible qualities of such sources are open to question. Fred J. Ericson, *The British Colonial System and the Question of Change of Policy on the Eve of the American Revolution* (Chicago, 1943), is a brief treatment based mainly on pamphlet literature and Parliamentary speeches. The validity of this material is questionable, for no attempt is made to correlate the opinions there expressed with the views of responsible politicians and administrators. G. H. Guttridge, *English Whiggism and the American Revolution* (Berkeley, 1942), and Fred J. Hinkhouse, *The Preliminaries of the American Revolution as seen in the Press, 1763–1775* (New York, 1926) are scholarly and reliable. Robert E. Brown would have benefited from more research and thought on British policy before publishing his *Middle-Class Democracy and the Revolution in Massachusetts, 1691–1780* (Ithaca, 1955).

Certain works dealing with the Stamp Act are worthy of mention. Edmund S. Morgan and Helen M. Morgan, *The Stamp Act Crisis: Prologue to Revolution* (Chapel Hill, N. C., 1953), and Edmund S. Morgan, "George Grenville and the Postponement of the Stamp Act," *William and Mary Quarterly,*

3rd ser., VII (1950), 543–592, suffer from inadequate investigation of English sources and a misunderstanding of George Grenville. Charles R. Ritcheson, "The Preparation of the Stamp Act," *ibid.*, 3rd ser., X (1953), 543–559, also has many inaccuracies. The problem of the Stamp Act in British politics is discussed in William T. Laprade, "Stamp Act in British Politics," *American Historical Review,* XXXV (1930), 735–757. Victor L. Johnson, "Internal Financial Reform or External Taxation: Britain's Fiscal Choice, 1763," American Philosophical Society, *Proceedings,* XCVIII (1954), 31–37, argues that internal financial reform would have met the need for imperial revenue. This ignores the fact that the prevailing attitude in English political circles was that America should help pay for its own defense. Fred J. Ericson, "Contemporary British Opposition to the Stamp Act, 1764–1765," *Papers of the Michigan Academy of Science, Arts, and Letters,* XXIX (1943), 489–505, attempts to show that some Whig politicians opposed the stamp measure in the House of Commons, and for this reason Grenville postponed the bill for one year. Ericson confuses opposition to Grenville for reasons of domestic politics, principally on the issues of general warrants and dismissal of officers, with opposition to his stamp measure. He is wrong in saying that opposition in England forced Grenville to postpone the Stamp Act.

One aspect of British policy, the Quebec Act, is of special interest to this study. Victor Coffin's "The Quebec Act and the American Revolution," American Historical Association, *Report for 1894,* 273–280, and Justin Winsor, "Virginia and the Quebec Bill," *American Historical Review,* I (1896), 436–443, are of little value. Louise P. Kellogg, "A Footnote to the Quebec Act," *Canadian Historical Review,* XIII (1932), 147–156, points out the importance of the measure for the inhabitants of the interior country, but underestimates the influence of the Earl of Hillsborough in determining policy. For the best treatment of the act, see Burt, *The Old Province of Quebec,* and Reginald Coupland, *The Quebec Act: A Study in Statesmanship* (Oxford, 1925). See also J. M. Sosin, "The French Settlements in British Policy for the North American Interior 1760–1774," *Canadian Historical Review,* XXXIX (1958), 185–208.

THE SEVEN YEARS' WAR AND THE PEACE OF PARIS

There are several excellent studies of the Treaty of Paris as it dealt with the North American settlement. Richard Pares, *War and Trade in the West Indies, 1739–1763* (Oxford, 1936), is sound and scholarly. Zenab Esmat Rashed, *The Peace of Paris, 1763* (Liverpool, England, 1951), is the best over-all treatment of the subject, based on research in the leading European archives. On the question of the American interior in the peace negotiations, see the excellent treatment in Max Savelle, *The Diplomatic History of the Canadian Boundary, 1749–1763* (New Haven, 1940), and the introduction to Theodore C. Pease (ed.), *Anglo-French Boundary Disputes in the West.* See also T. C. Pease, "The Mississippi Boundary of 1763: A Reappraisal of Responsibility," *American Historical Review,* XL (1935), 278–286, a definitive analysis based on the secret Viry-Solar correspondence. Richard Waddington, *La Guerre de sept ans: historie diplomatie et militarie* (4 vols., Paris, 1899–1907), the standard French work, is now outdated. Arthur Aiton, "The Diplomacy of the Louisiana Cession," *American Historical Review,* XXXVI (1931), 701–720, is based on original sources in the foreign archives and deals with the Franco-Spanish negotiations of 1762–1763. His "A Neglected Intrigue of the Family Compact," *Hispanic American Review,* XI (1931), 387–393, reveals the duplicity resorted to by the Bourbon powers to mask the aggressive aspects of the Family Compact.

In addition to the analysis given in Alvord, *Mississippi Valley in British Politics,* see William L. Grant, "Canada *versus* Guadeloupe," *American Historical Review,* XVII (1912), 735–743, for a review of the pamphlet literature on the controversy. It merely shows commercial thought and makes no attempt to reflect these considerations on political action or to demonstrate that they had any relation to the peace negotiations. The same may be said of C. E. Fryer, "Further Pamphlets for the Canada-Guadeloupe Controversy," *Mississippi Valley Historical Review,* IV (1917), 227–230. Fred J. Ericson, "British Motives for Expansion in 1763; Territory, Commerce, or Security," *Papers of the Michigan Academy of Science, Arts, and Letters,* XXVII (1941), 581–594, re-evaluates the pamphlet literature and points out that the pamphleteers also stressed the issue of security. He does not deal with the attitude of the diplomats or politicians, and shows no correlation between this group and the pamphleteers. Elijah W. Lyon, *Louisiana in French Diplomacy, 1759–1804* (Norman, Okla., 1934), also places credence in the pamphlet literature and offers little of value in this field.

The standard work on the Seven Years' War is Julian S. Corbett, *England and the Seven Years' War* (2 vols., London, 1907). Somewhat critical of Pitt's war leadership is Stanley M. Pargellis, *Lord Loudoun in America* (New Haven, 1933), who sees the issue in terms of logistics and not in strategy. For the vital issue of strategy, see Richard Pares, "American *versus* Continental Warfare, 1739–1763," *English Historical Review,* LI (1936), 429–465. See also in this connection Thad W. Riker, "The Politics behind Braddock's Expedition," *American Historical Review,* XIII (1908), 742–752.

THE INDIAN AND FUR TRADE

There are two excellent studies in this field: Harold Innis, *The Fur Trade in Canada: An Introduction to Canadian Economic History* (New York and London, 1930), and Murray G. Lawson, *Fur: A Study in English Mercantilism, 1700–1775* (Toronto, 1945). A general narrative treatment is Paul C. Phillips, "The Fur Trade in the Maumee-Wabash Country," in *Studies in American History Inscribed to James Albert Woodburn, Professor Emeritus of American History in Indiana University by His Former Students* (Bloomington, Ind., 1926). Still useful are Wayne E. Stevens, *The Northwest Fur Trade, 1763–1800* (Urbana, Ill., 1928); W. E. Stevens, "The Organization of the British Fur Trade, 1760–1800," *Mississippi Valley Historical Review,* III (1916), 172–

202; and Ida A. Johnson, *The Michigan Fur Trade* (Lansing, Mich., 1919). For the Illinois country, see Charles M. Thomas, "Successful and Unsuccessful Merchants in the Illinois Country," *Journal of the Illinois State Historical Society,* XXX (1938), 429–440. Charles A. Hanna, *The Wilderness Trail; or the Ventures and Adventures of the Pennsylvania Traders on the Allegheny Path* (2 vols., New York, 1911), an account of the penetration of the upper Ohio valley by British traders, contains much information of value. Another regional study is M. G. Jackson, "The Beginning of British Trade at Michillimackinac," *Minnesota History,* XI (1930), 231–270. Arthur H. Buffinton, "The Policy of Albany and English Western Expansion," *Mississippi Valley Historical Review,* VIII (1922), 327–366, offers a good introduction to fur trade rivalry in the first half of the eighteenth century. This may be followed with W. Neil Franklin, "Pennsylvania-Virginia Rivalry for the Indian Trade of the Ohio Valley," *ibid.,* XX (1934), 463–480. For the northern area, see Ernest Cruikshank, "Early Traders and Trade Routes in Ontario and the West, 1760–1783," Royal Canadian Institute, *Transactions,* III (1891–1892), 253–274.

LAND SPECULATION

Thomas P. Abernethy's *Western Lands and the American Revolution* (New York, 1937) is ambitious in its scope but is sometimes careless in research and judgment. It must be used with discrimination. Short sketches of the various land companies and brief descriptions of their projects will be found in Shaw Livermore, *Early American Land Companies: Their Influence on Corporate Development* (New York, 1939). Clarence W. Alvord, *The Illinois-Wabash Company* (Chicago, 1915), is an uncritical sketch. Edith A. Bailey, *Influence toward Radicalism in Connecticut, 1754–1775,* in *Smith College Studies in History,* vol. IV, no. 4 (Northampton, Mass., 1920), contains a good treatment of the Susquehanna Company. The best work is Julian P. Boyd, *The Susquehanna Company* (New Haven, 1935). Kenneth P. Bailey, *The Ohio Company of Virginia and the Westward Movement, 1748–1792* (Glendale, Calif., 1939), and George E. Lewis, *The Indiana Company, 1763–1798: A Study in Eighteenth Century Frontier Land Speculation and Business Venture* (Glendale, Calif., 1941), are much too brief for so complex subjects. Archibald Henderson, *The Conquest of the Old Southwest* (New York, 1925), is a sympathetic and uncritical account of southern speculators. On Washington's activities, see Hugh Cleland, *George Washington in the Ohio Valley* (Pittsburgh, 1955); and Charles H. Ambler, *George Washington and the West* (Chapel Hill, N. C., 1936).

INDIAN RELATIONS

Two excellent accounts have been published on the Indian uprising of 1763. Francis Parkman's *The Conspiracy of Pontiac and the Indian War after the Conquest of Canada* (2 vols., Boston, 1851), while a literary masterpiece, is open to question as to interpretation. In this respect, see Howard H. Peckham, *Pontiac and the Indian Uprising* (Princeton, N. J., 1947); Wilbur R. Jacobs, "Was the Pontiac Uprising a Conspiracy?," *Ohio Archaeological and Historical Quarterly,* LIX (1950), 26–37; and W. R. Jacobs, "Presents to the Indians as a Factor in the Conspiracy of Pontiac," *Michigan History,* XXXIII (1949), 314–322. For an examination of the policy of subsidizing the tribes, see W. R. Jacobs, *Indian Diplomacy and Indian Gifts: Anglo-French Rivalry along the Ohio and Northwest Frontier, 1748–1763* (Stanford, 1950).

Bernhard Knollenburg, "General Amherst and Germ Warfare," *Mississippi Valley Historical Review,* XLI (1954), 489–494, analyzes the charge that Amherst used infected blankets to spread smallpox among the tribes during the uprising of 1763 and concludes that, while he would have liked to have done so, there is no evidence that he actually did. A detailed analysis of the revolt as seen from Amherst's headquarters is Charles S. Grant, "Pontiac's Rebellion and the British Troop Moves of 1763," *ibid.,* L (1953), 75–88. A fuller coverage of sources might have led the author to different conclusions. For a penetrating analysis of the second Indian war of this period, see Randolph G. Downes, "Dunmore's War: An Interpretation," *ibid.,* XX (1934), 311–330, which places the conflict within the perspective of Virginia land speculation and the treaty of Fort Stanwix of 1768.

Clarence E. Carter, "British Policy towards the American Indians in the South, 1763–8," *English Historical Review,* XXXIII (1918), 37–56; and Helen Louise Shaw, *British Administration of the Southern Indians, 1756–1783* (Lancaster, Penn., 1931), have been largely superseded by Alden's *Southern Colonial Frontier.* For the preceding period, see the excellent study by Verner W. Crane, *The Southern Frontier, 1670–1732* (Durham, N. C., 1929). For a general treatment of the northern tribes under British administration, see Randolph G. Downes, *Council Fires on the Upper Ohio: A Narrative of Indian Affairs in the Upper Ohio Valley until 1795* (Pittsburgh, 1940), and the introduction by Charles H. McIlwain (ed.), *An abridgment of the Indian affairs [by Peter Wraxall] Transacted in the Colony of New York, from the Year 1678 to the Year 1751* (Cambridge, Mass., 1915). Also useful are Anthony F. C. Wallace, *King of the Delawares: Teedyuscung, 1700–1763* (Philadelphia, 1949); Joseph S. Walton, *Conrad Weiser and the Indian Policy of Colonial Pennsylvania* (Philadelphia, 1900); Paul A. Wallace, *Conrad Weiser, 1696–1760* (Philadelphia, 1945), and Arthur D. Greaff, *Conrad Weiser, Pennsylvania Peace Maker* (Fogelsville, Penn., 1946). Basic is Arthur Pound, *Johnson of the Mohawks* (New York, 1930).

THE FRONTIER AND THE NORTH AMERICAN INTERIOR

Several early works in this field are of value; Justin Winsor, *The Mississippi Basin, The Struggle between England and France 1697–1793* (Boston, 1895), and *The Westward Movement of the Colonies and the Republic West of the Alleghenies, 1763–1798* (Boston, 1897). See also Louis K. Koontz, *The*

Virginia Frontier, 1754–1763 (Baltimore, 1925). A brief treatment is afforded in Charles Moore, *The Northwest under Three Flags, 1635–1796* (London and New York, 1900). Charles E. Kemper, "Early Westward Movement of Virginia," *Virginia Magazine of History and Biography,* XII (1905), 337–352, is of value. George H. Alden's *New Governments West of the Alleghenies before 1780* (Madison, Wisc., 1897) is dated. A good summary is presented in Solon J. and Elizabeth Buck, *The Planting of Civilization in Western Pennsylvania* (Pittsburgh, 1939). The best introduction to the subject will be found in Ray A. Billington, *Westward Expansion: A History of the American Frontier,* 2nd ed. (New York, 1960).

BIOGRAPHIES

For additional materials, the student should consult the section on memoirs and correspondence. Only the better biographies or those of figures, nominally of lesser rank, but of great importance for this study, will be considered here.

There are two works dealing with the Earl of Bute; unfortunately, both are poor: J. A. Lovat-Frasier, *John Stuart, Earl of Bute* (Cambridge, 1912), and Mrs. E. Stuart Wortley, *A Prime Minister and His Son* (London, 1925). The student would do well to consult the introduction to Sedgwick's correspondence of George III to Bute. The best biography published to date on Burke is Sir Philip Magnus, *Edmund Burke* (London, 1939). Henry S. Eeles, *Lord Chancellor Camden and His Family* (London, 1934), offers very little. Two useful studies of the elder Fox have been published: Thad W. Riker, *Henry Fox, First Lord Holland: A Study of the Career of an Eighteenth Century Politician* (2 vols., Oxford, 1911), and Giles Stephen Fox-Strangways, Sixth Earl of Ilchester, *Henry Fox, First Lord Holland: His Family and Relations* (2 vols., New York, 1920). A devastating analysis of how Fox made his fortune is given in Lucy S. Sutherland and J. Bennsey, "Henry Fox as Paymaster General of the Forces," *English Historical Review,* LXX (1955), 229–257. A quadruple biography and an excellent study of the politics of the eighteenth century will be found in Erick Eyck, *Pitt versus Fox, Father and Son: 1735–1806* (London, 1950).

There is a great amount of literature on the elder Pitt. Albert von Ruville, *William Pitt, Earl of Chatham,* trans. by H. J. Chaytor (3 vols., London and New York), although an extensive treatment, leaves something to be desired. Basil Williams, *William Pitt, Earl of Chatham* (2 vols., London, 1913), is a sympathetic and scholarly treatment. The best one-volume work is by Brian Tunstall, *William Pitt, Earl of Chatham* (London, 1938). O. A. Sherrad has published three volumes of *Lord Chatham* (London, 1953–1958).

George III has been the subject of two biographies, both, on the whole, unsatisfactory; Colwyn Edward Vulliamy, *Royal George: a Study of King George III, His Experiment in Monarchy, His Decline and Retirement, with a View of Society, Politics, and Historical Events during His Reign* (New York and London, 1937); and Manfred S. Guttmacher, *America's Last King:*

An Interpretation of the Madness of George III (New York, 1911), the work of a psychiatrist.

An uncritical but flavorful treatment of the Duke of Grafton is provided in Bernard Falk, *The Royal Fitz Roys Dukes of Grafton through Four Centuries* (London and New York, 1950). Cecil H. S. Foot, *Lord Mansfield* (Oxford, 1936) does not offer a satisfactory account; neither has Lord North received adequate treatment in W. Pemberton Baring, *Lord North* (London and New York, 1937), which is a slight improvement over Reginald J. Lucas, *Lord North, Second Earl of Guilford, K.G., 1732–1792* (London, 1913). Percy H. Fitzgerald, *Charles Townshend, Wit and Statesman* (London, 1866) is of little use. A delightful, though uncritical, study of Edward Thurlow may be found in Robert Gore-Browne, *Chancellor Thurlow: The Life and Times of an XVIIIth Century Lawyer* (London, 1953).

Several items have appeared on leading land speculators which are too general in scope to be of great value in this study. See C. A. W. Pownall, *Thomas Pownall, Governor of the Colony of Massachusetts Bay* (London, 1908); Percy B. Caley, "The Life-Adventures of Lieutenant-Colonel John Connolly," *Western Pennsylvania Historical Magazine,* XI (1928), *passim;* Max Savelle, *George Morgan, Colony Builder* (New York, 1932); Sewall E. Slick, *William Trent and the West* (Harrisburg, Penn., 1947); Albert T. Volwiler, *George Croghan and the Westward Movement, 1741–1782* (Cleveland, 1926); Nicholas B. Wainwright, *George Croghan Wilderness Diplomat* (Chapel Hill, 1959).

INDEX

Index

A NOTE ABOUT THE AUTHOR

JACK M. SOSIN was born in Hartford, Connecticut, in 1928, and was educated at the University of Connecticut (B.A., 1950; M.A., 1951) and Indiana University (Ph.D., 1958). Since 1958 he has been a member of the faculty of the University of Nebraska, where at present he is an Assistant Professor of History.

During the course of his research for WHITEHALL AND THE WILDERNESS Professor Sosin examined documents and other source materials in British, Canadian, and American archives. His previous publications include articles in the *American Historical Review,* the *Canadian Historical Review,* and the *William and Mary Quarterly*. Currently he is at work on a study of the influence of American colonial agents and English merchants on British colonial policy leading to the American Revolution.